NAVIGATING SOCIAL JOURNALISM

Public trust in the once powerful institutions of the News Establishment is declining. Sharing, curating and producing news via social media channels may offer an alternative, if the difficult process of verification can be mastered by social journalists operating outside of the newsroom. *Navigating Social Journalism* examines the importance of digital media literacy and how we should all be students of the media. Author Martin Hirst emphasizes the responsibility that individuals should take when consuming the massive amounts of media we encounter on a daily basis. This includes information we gather from online media, streaming, podcasts, social media and other formats. The tools found here will help students critically evaluate any incoming media and, in turn, produce their own media with their own message. This book aims both to help readers understand the current state of news media through theory and provide practical techniques and skills to partake in constructive social journalism.

Dr Martin Hirst is a freelance scholar, author, journalist and artist working in Melbourne, Australia. He has worked as a journalist and editor since 1975 and taught journalism in Australia, New Zealand and the UK between 1993 and 2016. Dr Hirst is a founding editor of the open access journal *The Political Economy of Communication*, published by the Political Economy section of the International Association of Mass Communication Research. He is also the author of seven books about journalism.

NAVIGATING SOCIAL JOURNALISM

A Handbook for Media Literacy and Citizen Journalism

Martin Hirst

Routledge
Taylor & Francis Group

NEW YORK AND LONDON

First published 2019
by Routledge
711 Third Avenue, New York, NY 10017

and by Routledge
2 Park Square, Milton Park, Abingdon, Oxon, OX14 4RN

Routledge is an imprint of the Taylor & Francis Group, an informa business

Library of Congress Cataloging in Publication Data
Names: Hirst, Martin, author.
Title: Navigating social journalism : friends, enemies, followers and
likes / Martin Hirst.
Description: New York : Routledge, 2019.
Identifiers: LCCN 2018025111| ISBN 9781138224988 (hardback) |
ISBN 9781138225008 (pbk.) | ISBN 9781315401263 (ebk.)
Subjects: LCSH: Citizen journalism--Social aspects. | Online
journalism--Social aspects. | Online social networks--social aspects.
Classification: LCC PN4784.C615 H57 2019 | DDC 070.4/33--dc23
LC record available at https://lccn.loc.gov/2018025111

ISBN: 978-1-138-22498-8 (hbk)
ISBN: 978-1-138-22500-8 (pbk)
ISBN: 978-1-315-40126-3 (ebk)

Typeset in Bembo
by Integra Software Services Pvt. Ltd.

For my girls: Calliope Cutlass, Hibou and The Bird Lady

CONTENTS

ACKNOWLEDGEMENTS

This book would not have been possible without the love and support of my wife, Tiffany White. She is the main reason I was able to sit at this desk for days on end to complete the manuscript. I must also thank my colleague and friend, Dr Roger Patching. His spiritual guidance, good humor and no-nonsense attitude have sustained me through 25 years. There's also a bunch of people who I can't thank by name, but my regular conversations with them have been extremely useful in helping me re-balance my life over the past two years. Without the inner peace these people helped me to find, *Navigating Social Journalism* would not have survived the crash.

PROLOGUE

Media Literacy in the Digital World

This is a book that discusses media literacy, but you won't find these words used together like this too often outside of this prologue. So, perhaps I should rather frame it as: "This is a book *for* media literacy." It is a handbook, rather than a textbook; and by this I simply mean that it is meant to be useful for everyone and anyone. It is not an academic text, only for limited use in the classroom; or worse to be bought as a required course reading, and then left unread gathering dust. This is a book for students of the media, and that should be all of us.

The basic premise of this book is that the media—particularly the news media—is too important to be left to the experts. Media literacy means taking responsibility, individually and collectively, for ensuring that the news is accurate, fair, and balanced—where that's reasonable—and that it serves the public interest. We are the public, and we are no longer content to just sit back passively waiting for the news to come to us. And that's where literacy comes in.

Literacy is literally the ability to read and to write. So, already we are obliged to see it as both an act of consumption and an act of production. Literacy is about more than just absorbing information, it is about creating it too. This has never been more important than it is today in the world of digital communication, mobile devices that bring us news constantly, and social media that encourages us to create our own forms of news. Digital media literacy is the basis on which we engage with online media, video streaming, podcasts and social media. All of us need to up our game—to drastically improve our digital media literacy—if we are going to survive the current crisis in the news media.

The first half of this book is all about the crisis in the news media, and I'll say a bit more about it in this Prologue, but first I want to explain what digital media literacy means to me and what it should mean to you. Media literacy in the digital age—let's just call it digital media literacy (DML) for now—is a refinement of basic reading and writing skills adapted to the world of computing, online news and information, and social media. DML is a basic competency in the following areas: the ability to access digital media resources, the acuity and facility to analyze digital media resources, the skills to evaluate what you find, and the capacity to create media of your own. There is a formal definition, developed by the Center for Media Literacy, and it is serviceable for our purposes:

> Media Literacy is a 21st century approach to education. It provides a framework to access, analyze, evaluate, create and participate with messages in a variety of forms — from print to video to the Internet. Media literacy builds an understanding of the role of media in society as well as essential skills of inquiry and self-expression necessary for citizens of a democracy.
> *(Center for Media Literacy 2017)*

The references to "inquiry," "self-expression" and citizenship in this definition are important in the context of social journalism and the news crisis. In the context of this book, this does not mean that we should all expect to be Pulitzer Prize-winning journalists (though having that as a career goal might be a good motivator for some); improving your DML means that you will be better able to critically evaluate any incoming media you consume and, if you feel like it and want to do it, you will be able to craft a meaningful and original message via your various social media channels. Again, without rehearsing all of my arguments in this Prologue, this is what, for all practical purposes, I mean by amateur social journalism. Of course, if you want to take your production skills further, either on your own or with others collectively, this book is a good place to start that journey too. This is a book for media literacy in the sense that it is not designed to teach you about media literacy, it assumes that you already know that media literacy is important. This book is designed to help you be more media literate by explaining basic concepts in media and communication theory and placing these theoretical perspectives into an historical context. The purpose of this exercise is to help you to access, analyze, and evaluate incoming media. The second objective of the book is to alert you to the tools and skills you will need to be an effective creator of news-like digital information. This is not a book about media literacy, it is a book for media literacy that is both a theoretical reading of the state of the news media and a practical guide to developing your own media literacy through a guided introduction to the tools, techniques and technologies of social journalism.

The News Media in Crisis

If you pay even passing attention to the news media today you can't help but notice it is in crisis. Newspapers are getting smaller and/or closing down their print edition entirely. Television and radio news bulletins are getting lighter and appear to be less interested in covering difficult stories. Newsrooms are shrinking, fewer important stories are being covered in-depth, instead we seem to be getting more low-value news about trivia. This nexus is damaging to the public sphere and to the public interest. Consequently our ability to participate as active citizens is being compromised. It is examined in the context of concerns about a "democracy deficit" in chapter one.

Alongside the crisis in journalism, our news consumption habits are changing rapidly. Today the majority of us get at least some of our news from social media feeds (Shearer and Gottfried 2017), and we're less likely to turn up for appointment television, like the evening news bulletin. YouTube, Facebook, Snapchat and Twitter are now our go-to news destinations. But this has brought with it a new set of problems—the rise of fake news and our declining trust in mainstream news sources. According to credible recent research, the deluge of fake news has the potential to confuse us, to literally "break our brains" (Panko 2017). We want to challenge the credibility of news organizations more, but many of us lack the intellectual means—the media literacy—to do so effectively. Thus, we find it difficult to hold the media to account, or to standards of truth. Increasing your media literacy—whether or not you become a news producer yourself—is a great way to protect your brain; or even to unbreak it. It is never too late.

Is Social Journalism the Answer?

I am not sure if we can successfully navigate our way out of the news crisis any time soon, but I am more certain that the news industry cannot save itself. The reasons for this are laid out in the first five chapters. In chapters six and seven I attempt to put forward a theory of social journalism as a way of helping us overcome the democracy deficit caused (in part) by the news crisis. I have tried to avoid the problem of merely inventing a new term for something that has been adequately described in the past; so I have situated my discussion of alternative and critical news media in an historical context, and I've tried to cover as much of the industry-related and academic literature as I can, without bogging down in it. You can be the judge of how well I have managed this task.

What is social journalism? Well, read the book to find out, but to start, here is an attempt at a brief definition that I hope will hold your attention and spark your curiosity:

> Social journalism is the act of curating, commenting on and creating a news feed through social media channels that enables and increases the critical understanding of both media and social issues for those who consume and/or produce it.

In my view, social journalism is both an individual act of media literacy and "democratic learning" as well as an act of "social change" achieved by "disseminating information … and by urging dialogue and activism" (Caton-Rosser and McGinley 2006: 5). Social journalism is something we can all do. It's also perhaps something we all *should* do, given the parlous state of the News Establishment media. Social journalism happens outside of the newsroom—though it can be a collaboration with newsrooms—and it should remain beyond the control of the News Establishment.

Reading this Book

This book is a blend of four things that I think are useful for the exercise of increasing our media literacy and making sense of the social media tools that enable social journalism to happen:

- a review of the state-of-play in journalism and the news media taken from recent headlines—a commentary on how journalists perhaps see themselves and their future;
- a critical review of the scholarly research into what has been variously defined as "citizen" or "participatory" journalism in the past few years (Wall 2017);
- a deliberate mix of theory and practice; and
- a handbook for both professionals and amateurs seeking advice and tips on how to use social media to do journalism either inside or outside the traditional newsroom structure.

Theory is important to provide context, historical background and a baseline of knowledge about the news media. Practice encompasses both my own history as a working journalist for more than 40 years and also your own practice, whether professional, or amateur. I have tried to find the right blend of theory and practice to make this book useful to readers, whether you are a student, a journalist, an interested news consumer, or someone planning to make the transition from audience to producer (the "social journalist"). I have attempted to balance the use of references with the need to make sure the text flows easily and is readable. I have tried to ensure that my use of jargon is minimalist and where a term is introduced, you will find it explained and defined in plain English.

   This is important in a book designed as much for general consumption as for use in an academic or classroom setting. This is also why I have attempted to translate some of the more esoteric language of journalism scholarship into easily understood concepts. I have found it necessary to do this, almost in spite of my own academic background, because when I've been reviewing the literature in preparation for writing this book I have sometimes found myself wondering "What does that mean?" I also discovered again, because I've really always thought this way, that when scholars write for an audience of scholars they tend to prefer their own definitions and descriptions of something over having a common language and common terms for pretty much the same thing. When it comes to the subject of this book—the theory and practice of social journalism—the number of competing definitions for what is essentially non-professional news production by the people we used to think of as passive consumers is almost overwhelming. In just one edition of the academic journal *Journalism Practice*, non-professional journalism is described as "citizen" journalism, "participatory" journalism, "collaborative journalism," "non-journalists self-organizing," "connective journalism," "folk communication," "reciprocal journalism," "networked journalism," "citizen contributors," "amateur news content distributors" and "ambient journalism." It sounds confusing, but it needn't be. What is essentially being described and theorized in these discussions is just two things, which are different, but which share connections. The connection is collaboration between journalists and non-journalists. The first type of collaboration occurs under the control of professional journalists; the second type is amateur, non-professional journalism that is autonomous from mainstream newsrooms—the production of "news-like" content by the people who used to be the audience. This connection runs throughout the book, which is conveniently divided into two halves; the first is analytical, the second is more practical. Chapters 1–7 set the scene for our navigation of social journalism. These form a discussion of the "who" "what," "why," "where," "when" and "how" of the crisis in journalism and the origins of social journalism. Chapter 8–12 are about the "doing" of social journalism, both inside and outside of newsroom setting.

In the first set of chapters we establish a way of reading the route that journalism is taking from being a once solid, reputable and stable institution to the troubled profession and industry it is today, to what it might become. There is no way of knowing the future with any certainty, the best chance we have is to establish, with as much clarity as possible, where we are today and how we got here. We begin our journey from where we are, not where we're trying to get to. To understand where we are, a short diversion into theory is necessary. This section concludes with a discussion of the ways in which non-journalists are being incorporated into the professional/commercial news production process through so-called "engagement" strategies and collaboration with reporters (Chapter 6). In chapter seven the focus is on non-professionals organizing to do a form of journalism that is independent of commercial newsrooms. Both forms are valid and both warrant attention in this book. However, as I argue in chapters two and three, the motivations for professional and commercial collaboration, and the more social forms of independent news gathering and reporting, are counterposed and perhaps even in competition with each other. The dichotomy is clear and well-established as one of the important fault lines in contemporary journalism. One side of this dialectical contradiction is that, despite more than a decade of experimentation, the value of participation may be illusory. There is some doubt thrown up about collaboration and audience engagement with the news actually working to increase the democratic valency of journalism. One corollary is that perhaps outside of the news industry, non-journalists are finding ways to cooperate with each other using social media, thus building a real foundation for social journalism, and bypassing the mainstream (Wall 2017: 134).

The second section is focused on practical advice about how social media can be used effectively, both inside and outside the newsroom, to create forms of social journalism. This is not meant to be comprehensive, it is an introduction to tools and techniques across the key areas of research and verification, writing, publishing and distribution. It fulfils the aim of increasing digital media literacy, it is not a substitute for your own study of the nuts and bolts of digital journalism. Chapters 8 and 9 are a guide to ethical methods and to the difficult task of verification, which is so essential in an age of "fake news." Chapter 10 introduces news writing in both short and long-form, with an emphasis on writing for digital media. Chapter 11 is an overview of the key publishing platforms and applications (apps) that link social media and social journalism together. Your knowledge and abilities in this area will only improve if you adopt good habits from the beginning and work consistently to maintain your skill levels with each of your favored platforms and apps. The final chapter is a brief excursion into the "future" of journalism. I argue that it is a future that, for all intents and purposes, is already here.

I hope you find this book both useful and enjoyable and that when you put it down you feel confident that your media literacy has improved along with your knowledge of the news media, past, present and future. If you are inspired to build your own social journalism practice, or even to just be more savvy about your own social media use, then I will be satisfied.

References

Caton-Rosser, Mary, and Jennifer A. McGinley. 2006. "Alternative Media and the Learning Culture of Civil Society: Outreach and Teach Strategies." *InterActions: UCLA Journal of Education and Information Studies* 2(1): 1–19.

Center for Media Literacy. 2017. "Media Literacy: A Definition and More." Accessed January 24, 2018. www.medialit.org/media-literacy-definition-and-more.

Panko, Ben. 2017. "How Fake News Breaks Your Brain." Smithsonian. June 30. Accessed June 21, 2018. www.smithsonianmag.com/science-nature/how-fake-news-breaks-your-brain-180963894/

Shearer, Elisa, and Jeffrey Gottfried. 2017. *News Use Across Social Media Platforms 2017.* Washington, DC: Pew Research Center.

Wall, Melissa. 2017. "Mapping Citizen and Participatory Journalism." *Journalism Practice* 11 (2–3): 134–141.

1

THE DEMOCRATIC DEFICIT

The News Establishment and Social Journalism

The "Democratic Deficit" and "Alternative Journalism"

The purpose of this book is to encourage a greater level of public involvement in the practice of journalism, broadly defined as the production, distribution and consumption of news and news-like information. I believe greater public participation—the foundation of what I am calling "social journalism"—is necessary to rebuild democracies that are in danger of collapsing into authoritarian populism. Part of the process of encouragement is an attempt to fill what I believe is a gap in the literature about various forms of what, broadly speaking, we might call "alternative journalism." This term was coined by two communication researchers in a book called *Alternative Journalism* (Atton and Hamilton 2008) to describe, in broad terms, various experiments in combining professional and non-professional journalists in the news production process, both inside and outside the traditional newsroom. As a concept and a set of practices, alternative journalism is even more relevant today because of a second issue, the perceived failure of mainstream journalism—and the news industry—to overcome what has become known as the "democracy deficit," or what journalism academic Lucas Graves (2017) calls the "democracy *recession*." This is the notion that institutions, governments and politicians are failing us by coming up short in their promises to defend and extend democracy; it also hints at a rise in authoritarian and anti-democratic regimes and politics in many parts of the world. The election of Donald Trump in the United States, with a decidedly authoritarian bent and a hatred for what he calls the "fake news" media, is one alarming example that features heavily in the following pages.

In an interview with *The Atlantic* magazine in January 2018, Harvard professor Steven Levitsky, one of the authors of the book *How democracies die*, said that the

United States had not yet become a failed democracy, but "alarm bells" were ringing. "In our book, we develop a litmus test for [authoritarian politicians] and Trump tests positive. He has exhibited the kind of behavior and the kind of language characteristic of other authoritarians," Levitsky said (Friedman 2018). Trump's praise for demagogues like Russian president Vladimir Putin, whose regime has murdered dozens of journalists, and Rodrigo Duerte, the Philippines leader who boasts about shooting drug peddlers, is also a signal that we may indeed be moving away from democracy, rather than towards it. In fact, Duerte may well surpass other emerging authoritarians—even Turkey's Erdogan—in the anti-democratic stakes. In January 2018 the Philippines government launched an all-out assault on media freedom when it began actions to shutter the nation's pre-eminent public advocacy news site, *Rappler*. The site, which describes itself as a "social news" provider and home to "citizen journalism" had—until January 2018—been a beacon of democratic journalism and a thorn in the side of the Duerte regime since it was launched in 2012, and CEO Maria Ressa bravely continues to publish despite many death threats and legal challenges. The Philippines government tried to shut *Rappler* down on spurious grounds, but as of August 2018 it was still publishing. The news site's senior political reporter, Pia Ranada, was also banned from Presidential press briefings, a move that drew condemnation from Reporters Without Borders and other human rights groups (Rappler 2018). The ongoing harassment of *Rappler* is a serious blow to media freedom in the Philippines and has drawn the attention and protests of international press freedom organization, the Committee to Protect Journalists (CPJ), among others. Journalists and press freedom are under attack all over the world today, even in ostensibly liberal nations like Australia, which has enacted legislation allowing spy agencies to target citizens and criminalizing media whistleblowers, that media organizations say will have a "chilling effect" on public interest journalism. Such repressive moves are not limited to authoritarian regimes, they are (unfortunately) becoming typical in many so-called liberal democracies. The CPJ says that techniques to censor news media are becoming more sophisticated each year and range from the subtle—like laws against whistleblowers—to the extreme "Repression 2.0":

> Repression 2.0 is an update on the worst old-style tactics, from state censorship to the imprisonment of critics, with new information technologies including smartphones and social media producing a softening around the edges. Masked political control means a systematic effort to hide repressive actions by dressing them in the cloak of democratic norms. Governments might justify an internet crackdown by saying it is necessary to suppress hate speech and incitement to violence. They might cast the jailing of dozens of critical journalists as an essential element in the global fight against terror.

Finally, technology capture means using the same technologies that have spawned the global information explosion to stifle dissent, by monitoring and surveilling critics, blocking websites and using trolling to shout down critical voices. Most insidious of all is sowing confusion through propaganda and false news.

These strategies have contributed to an upsurge in killings and imprisonment of journalists around the world.

(Simon 2017)

From Trump's America, across much of Eastern Europe, in Asia, the Pacific region, and parts of Africa, the suppression of information goes hand in hand with anti-democratic political action by state actors and the local, national and transnational elites they protect and serve. It is no wonder that experts are worried about where so-called democratic nations are headed. The literature on the question of the "democracy deficit" is extensive; some has a focus on the Middle East and various Arab states, some also questions the future of democracy in an increasingly divided Europe, and more still are focused on North America, including Canada. As Stanford Law School professor Nathaniel Persily wrote in an article with the disturbing title, "Can Democracy Survive the Internet?", Donald Trump's success in the 2016 US Presidential election was only possible because "established institutions—especially the mainstream media and political-party organizations—had already lost most of their power, both in the United States and around the world" (Persily 2017: 64).There is no doubt that rising authoritarian figures and regimes are a global problem, one perhaps exacerbated, rather than ameliorated, by the Internet, despite the early nostrums of the digital evangelists that the World Wide Web would bring more freedom and more democracy to the world. After 20 years of the World Wide Web we are finally awake to the contradiction—the *digital dialectic*—at the heart of twenty-first century communications technologies; they are as much a tool of repression and propaganda as they are a technology of liberation (Tucker et al. 2017). The democratic void left by the failure of mainstream institutions, writes Nathaniel Persily, has been "filled by an unmediated populist nationalism tailor-made for the Internet age," and such populist, nationalist—and ultimately racist—politics have also emerged in European nations, in Asia, and in Australia. We cannot ignore the failure of the traditional news media in this scenario. Hardly any serious American news organizations were able to foresee Donald Trump's victory. In fact, it is potentially worse than this. A detailed study, published in the respected *Columbia Journalism Review*, found that as much—if not more—blame for the rise of Trumpian populism should be laid at the feet of mainstream news outlets, including the *New York Times*, the *Wall Street Journal*, the *Washington Post*, CNN and MSNBC, which are, ironically, Donald Trump's favorite targets for accusations of "fake news." The authors, both senior researchers at the Microsoft corporation, wrote:

> To the extent that voters mistrusted Hillary Clinton, or considered her conduct as secretary of state to have been negligent or even potentially criminal, or were generally unaware of what her policies contained or how they may have differed from Donald Trump's, these numbers suggest their views were influenced more by mainstream news sources than by fake news.
>
> *(Watts and Rothschild 2017)*

Of course, they would say that wouldn't they? After all, Microsoft is a giant tech company and other giant tech companies, notably Google, Twitter and Facebook, came under sustained criticism post the 2016 US elections for allowing so-called "fake news"—much of it allegedly generated by Russian-financed robot (bot) accounts—to rise through their secret sauce algorithms to dominate social media feeds (Leong 2017).

Much has been made of the ways in which both Google and Facebook—by their sheer size and economic weight—are distorting the so-called "marketplace of ideas" and helping to undermine the commercial viability of journalism (Bell and Owen 2017). Certainly, this is a problem, but I do not think we can lay all of the blame at the foot of these platform giants. In 2011 I wrote a book about how journalism was facing two crises, largely of its own making, my title was *News 2.0: Can Journalism Survive the Internet?*. The twin crises I outlined were the ongoing turmoil around declining profits and advertising revenues, and rising levels of public mistrust of mainstream news. Today we are still confronted by my fundamental question; it remains unclear if journalism will survive the era of digital disruption. All we've done is add to it Nathaniel Persily's equally perplexing query, substituting "democracy" for "journalism." This is an interesting, and not unnatural juxtaposition, because for two centuries common sense has told us that good journalism (public interest journalism) is vital to the democratic purpose. Without the "Fourth Estate" playing a watchdog role and holding those in power to public account, we were led to believe, democracy would not survive. This belief might have been common sense, but was it accurate? Journalism and the news industry have always had a troubled and contradictory relationship with the public interest. Often public interest is defined in terms that benefit elites in business, finance, politics and culture; it reflects a status quo of market forces that are never fundamentally challenged. Ultimately, journalism is bounded by an ideology that upholds fundamental class divisions between those who work and those who benefit from the labor of others. As a profession—and despite its noble ethical ideals—journalism is dominated by the economic rules of capitalism "characterized principally by intense competition and speed" (Champagne 2005: 52), and "the constant search for new niches in which profitability can be generated" (Faraone 2011: 202).

Today we are confronted by the fact that democracy is failing and journalism is failing too. Surely this cannot be a coincidence? Perhaps not. I don't think so anyway. For me, the two are intrinsically linked. As the for-profit capitalist model of the news industry appears to be irredeemably broken, so too is public trust in the institutions of the Fourth Estate. In the following pages I hope to offer the outlines of a potential solution to this problem. If the traditional—legacy, if you like—models of journalism and the news industry are broken, then what are we (citizens) going to do about it?

I would argue that the democracy deficit means we cannot wait around for the legacy news media to fix itself, or find a way out of its current economic woes. I'd even take this a step further, the news industry cannot fix itself because its fate is tied into the fortunes of an economic system—global capitalism—that is, itself, fundamentally broken (Frase 2016). As I elucidate in the early chapters of this book, for a century or more, journalism has taken the form of a commodity, reliant on both sales and also on the commodification of audiences—the sale of eyeballs to advertisers. This is no longer generating enough profit to sustain the news industry as it has been organized for roughly the last century. The Internet has broken the old duopoly of print and broadcasting, and it has lowered the price of advertising to a fraction of what it cost to advertise in newspapers and on television. The legacy publishers and broadcasters are still struggling to adjust, despite having now had more than 20 years to try and figure out a solution. They hadn't been able to fix it when I wrote *News 2.0* and, as my extensive review of the literature shows, they haven't fixed it yet. In fact, I don't think the news industry, or professional journalists can fix the problems on their own. Both are part of the problem—the News Establishment—not part of the solution.

Establishment News is Broken

I have dedicated several chapters to discussing the crisis in journalism and the news industry because this is the starting point for any discussion of alternatives that allow us to begin addressing the democracy deficit by taking positive action, based on increasing our digital media literacy. Understanding the origins of, the extent and possible solutions to this crisis is a key aspect of expanding digital media literacy. In this chapter, I want to elucidate my key thesis: that there is an "establishment" in the news industry that serves as a controlling elite, and that has a vested interest in maintaining the system of commodity journalism, despite its obvious and many flaws. Acknowledging this should not be controversial, because for any establishment, or social elite, maintaining its powerful position is of paramount importance. The news media is an important weapon in the arsenal of the ruling class (Forgacs 2000). This "News Establishment," as I have decided to name it, is so invested in the current economic and political configuration of journalism and news that it cannot escape the downward spiral of the crises of trust and profitability at the core of the problem. Further, the ideological blinkers worn by many in the Establishment—coupled with the material economic interest they have in the system—make them incapable of developing alternatives that might actually help turn the situation around. So, who are the News Establishment?

There are four main groupings who make up the News Establishment: "News Capitalists" are members of the ruling class and this grouping is made up of the owners of news industry capital and the senior managers who look after their interests—company CEOs and their senior lieutenants who manage media capital. Reporters and editors with a conscious or unconscious ideological investment in the news industry as currently constituted are the Systemic Journalists. Alongside the invested Systemic Journalists sits another group of reporters and editors who are more committed to the principles of Fourth Estate journalism. I call this cohort the "Fourth Estate Idealists" and argue that it has a conflicted view of journalism and of itself—a belief in public interest journalism is combined with a supportive view of the news industry. It is a serious contradiction and it also affects the fourth group in the News Establishment, the "Normative Scholars" of journalism. The scholars' role is to provide arguments and justifications for maintaining the system as it is—and devising ways to save it. The Fourth Estate group and the Normative Scholars want to save and to improve mainstream journalism, but they also want to find ways to help the news industry to survive. In my view—and as I establish in this chapter—these two aims are incompatible and almost impossible to reconcile within the framework of capitalism. The News Establishment has its own belief system "that defines the appropriate practices and values of news professionals, news media, and news systems" (Nerone 2012: 447). It is a belief system worth describing and analyzing if we are to learn how to deal with this powerful elite.

News Capitalists

The News Capitalists are the easiest group to deal with. They are not necessarily the most important when it comes to exercising influence over public opinion; but they are the most powerful group when it comes to making investment or dis-investment decisions that affect the overall economic structuring of the industry. Saying this is to state no more than a basic principle of the political economy of the news media business (see Chapter 2). Journalism and news must inevitably take the form of a generic commodity when produced under dominant capitalist relations of production. In true dialectical fashion, form and content are defined by political economy, "what is considered popular and sellable" (Fuchs 2010: 179), but the news is also ideological—it has a role in legitimating the system. This functionality is structurally represented by the commodity form, which is endemic to capitalism and the news industry. Thus, the news industry follows the same basic crisis-prone dynamics that beset the system as a whole (Berberoglu 2016). These dynamics manifest as an over-reliance on unstable finance capital; wage stagnation and falling demand as a result of neo-liberal austerity measures; falling productivity and a global fracturing resulting in systemic failures at national and regional levels (the 2008–2009 recession and "Brexit," for example) and the climate crisis (Moore 2014). Therefore, journalism cannot be immune to these dialectical pressures and fault lines. Hence, the economic crisis in the news industry—while certainly a partial product of digital disruption—is symptomatic of the generalized crisis of profitability that afflicts capitalism.

Capitalists (and their senior captains of industry) will always try to save the sinking ship, even if it results in mass drownings. In the News Establishment this translates into the News Capitalists fighting to defend their investments—through cost-cutting measures, putting up prices, etc.—even though they know the business model is broken. News company executives are also usually able to structure their pay packets in such a way that they get a bonus each year, no matter how poorly the business is performing. They have well-remunerated life rafts available to them when the ship finally succumbs to the waves. This is why any belief that potential benefactors like Geoff Bezos or Warren Buffet can save the news industry are magical thinking. While this group is highly influential in terms of the economics of the news industry, with only one or two exceptions (think Rupert Murdoch) they do not have a great deal of day-to-day influence over editorial projects. This ideological stewardship is left to the largest and highly diverse cohort of the News Establishment, the Systemic Journalists.

The Systemic Journalists

Systemic journalists are split into two distinct subsets, the "Conscious Believers" and the Fourth Estate Idealists previously mentioned. This distinction is important because it is a material expression of what, in my PhD thesis, I called the "dialectic of the front page" and the "duality of the news commodity." I have developed this idea subsequently, particularly in relation to journalism ethics, but the terms have a simple meaning. The "duality" of news in its commodity form expresses the tension between journalism's liberal-democratic function of informing the public and the necessary dynamic imposed on the news by the profit motive embedded in its political economy. The "dialectic of the front page" refers to the ideologically contradictory messages that the news media disseminates on a daily basis. This dialectic is why, on any given day, the news will be filled with anti-worker and anti-union propaganda, while at the same time appealing to a working-class audience. This dialectic serves to normalize capitalism and present a narrative of dominance that undermines working class solidarity and promotes the interests of the ruling class as a homogeneous and "natural" public interest (Beharrel and Philo 1977). However, being a dialectic, there is a contradiction which means that, on occasion, the news media reacts against type and actually promotes news that does not serve a ruling class interest. This dialectic is why the Fourth Estate Idealists can continue to function in the face of serious opposition from the Conscious Believers. This latter group is more influential, so it is appropriate to describe them first.

Consciously pro-system journalists—the Conscious Believers—know that capitalism and the capitalist news industry promote inequality, but they are happy to engage in the essentially propagandistic exercise of supporting it, because they are committed to preserving a system of class rule and they benefit from it. They benefit in the form of very good salaries and even stock options. They are able to leverage their notoriety across more than one outlet—for example conservative newspaper journalists who are regular talking heads on conservative television networks. They are well rewarded for their ideological loyalty to the News Establishment and to the system as a whole. Globally, the Murdoch empire—Fox News in the United States, Sky TV in the UK and Australia, and a stable of right-wing newspapers in several nations—is at the core of the News Establishment and it employs the most Conscious Believers. It is unlikely that a Fourth Estate Idealist would last long in the News Corp empire and any Conscious Believer who loses faith and jumps ship is treated like a pariah. There is a Murdoch-type figure in many capitalist nations everywhere on the political spectrum from liberal democracies to the more authoritarian regimes. For example, in Turkey, Russia, China and the Philippines, pro-government oligarchs control most of the media and ensure it props up the regime in return for favorable treatment. Rupert Murdoch operates in the USA, the UK and Australia, Even in seemingly liberal and diverse nations like Canada, there is a virtual duopoly—most of the influential media is owned by only two giant, vertically integrated corporations (Fontaine 2013).

While Murdoch is not everywhere, similar institutions exist in other nations right across the cadre of western journalism. As we've previously discussed, in an age of a growing democracy deficit, pro-government, conservative and pro-business news organizations are going to benefit from state patronage, while more critical, liberal media—populated by Fourth Estate Idealists—are going to be persecuted, or even shut down. Conscious Believers are openly and unapologetically conservative and partisan. They may represent a numerically small group, but it tends to be an influential one that can set a news agenda that other media have to follow. Conscious Believers also tend to be in leadership positions—they constitute a cadre of professional intellectuals who articulate a ruling class agenda that permeates the news markets in which they operate. For this reason, the pro-market, conservative world view is imposed on the news industry as a whole—subject of course to the dialectic outlined above.

The ideological power exerted by the Conscious Believers operates to mentally discipline a secondary layer of Establishment journalists: the "Unconsciously Systemic." This is a cadre of reporters who do not necessarily have a political commitment to the ruling class and capitalism, but who end up unwittingly promoting systemic values because they simply don't care and can't be bothered with intellectual curiosity about their chosen profession. The Unconsciously Systemic journalist is a committed anti-intellectual who thrives on the artificial glamour and excitement of being a D-list celebrity. This group is largely devoted to lifestyle reporting of one type or another—sport, food, fashion, entertainment—and is largely apolitical. By this I only mean that as a cohort this group takes little or no active interest in politics. The attention of this cadre is devoted to what's cool in their individual chosen specialism. The Unconsciously Systemic reporter or editor spends little, if any, time thinking about journalism from an intellectual perspective and has little interest in following, or participating in debates about journalism's problems or its future. Alongside this group is another section of cadre who do spend time thinking about the news industry and its many issues, but they do so from a position inside the Establishment; these are the Fourth Estate Idealists.

The Fourth Estate Idealists

The Fourth Estate Idealists (the Idealists) are the product of journalism's dialectic—the contradiction between the news business and the news as a public service. They have a conscious world view which is grounded in the philosophy of the Fourth Estate tradition *as they understand it*. This is a very important caveat because, I will argue, their understanding of the Fourth Estate principles is ahistorical and largely apolitical. By and large, this group is not aware of the dialectics and contradictions in the news industry that created them as a distinct cadre of journalists. They have only a partial consciousness of their role and their social position. In my PhD I called this group the "grey collar journalists" caught up in the dynamics unleashed by the commodity form of news and caught in a class location between the ruling class and the working class. This contradictory class location is a product of economics and ideology. The majority of journalists are waged workers with no capital stake in the news industry; but the dual nature of the news "product" allocates them to contra-dictory class locations with resulting ambivalence in their consciousness. There is in fact an emotional dialectic at play that drags news-workers in the direction of one or the other of the major social classes. They vacillate and sometimes change sides, but they also reflect and expose, to the careful reader, listener or viewer, the unsolvable contradictions within the system as a whole; whether economic, legal, social, cultural or political (Hirst 2002: iv).

The *Guardian* newspaper is perhaps the best-known, globally, in the group of Fourth Estate Idealist publications, though there are many others, particularly online. *The New York Times* and its staff would also consider themselves to be in this camp, but if so, they would be on the conservative fringes. It would be absurd to think that the politics of each of these publications lines up exactly, or that they share a common ideological thread beyond the most basic and broad ideals. *Salon* is one online outlet that comes to mind that is broadly representative of this group, which, by and large, eschews formal political identification beyond being in favor of progressive social causes, such as women's and LGBTQI rights, and against racism, sexism and homophobia. Of the more recent additions to the online pantheon, the *Huffington Post, Buzzfeed* and *Vox* would place themselves in the Idealist camp.

In November 2017, *The Guardian*'s editor-in-chief, Katharine Viner, gave a landmark speech in which she set out "a mission for journalism in a time of crisis." In her remarks, Viner outlined the values which underpin the Fourth

Estate's idealist liberalism. She began by acknowledging that the political, economic and social turbulence the world is experiencing today requires of journalism "nothing less than a serious consideration of what we do and why we do it" (Viner 2017). In a classic iteration of Fourth Estate principles, Viner argued that *The Guardian* is socially "progressive" and exist to hold power to account and uphold "liberal values": "We believe in the value of the public sphere; that there is such a thing as the public interest, and the common good; that we are all of equal worth; that the world should be free and fair.

This is fine as a statement of liberal values, but it also fails to put flesh on the bones or address the real inequalities in wealth and power that actually divide "the public" and the "public sphere." *The Guardian* lays claim to "championing the public interest," but what exactly constitutes the public's interest is not explained. Viner's ideals do not address the practicalities—economic, political, cultural and ideological—that create the circumstances in which the powerful elite actually gets to exercise power in the first place. When it comes to addressing the crisis of trust which is undermining the value of the Fourth Estate, Viner's comments draw out some of the problems, which she is candid enough to admit also affect *The Guardian*. The crisis of trust extends across the whole of public life—business and politics, in particular—and for the news media it is a crisis in which it risks "becoming wholly part of the same establishment that the public no longer trusts." In part this is because journalists "are increasingly drawn from the same, privileged sector of society" as the powerful elites. In Katharine Viner's eyes the solution is for organizations like *The Guardian* to employ more reporters from "diverse" backgrounds, but this is no more than tokenism. In order to get onto *The Guardian*'s payroll these "diverse" reporters will have undergone the same screening and training—in the ways of the News Establishment—as anyone else. Such a proposal is largely hollow and only serves to highlight the lack of real substance in the liberalism of the Fourth Estate Idealists. The very real problems—addressed in the following chapter—are systemic and having a quota of ethnically and gender diverse staff members is not going to solve them.

In her 2017 remarks, Katharine Viner attempted to address how *The Guardian* should respond to the social crisis that threatens the break-up of the current world order, but her solutions fall short of embracing real revolutionary change which she dismisses in an off-hand way as "despair" and "just another form of denial." All that we are left with, in terms of a *Guardian* strategy for change, is the offer of "hope," which Viner defines as "a faith in our capacity to act together to make change." But what kind of change, and who is the "we" that will take action? *The Guardian*'s role is to sit squarely in the middle, being careful not to offend anyone. According to Viner the publisher will "embrace as wide a range of progressive perspectives as possible ... We will also engage with and publish voices from the right." This is liberal middle-of-the-roadism at its very worst. Embracing the worst of conservative thought—shading over into authoritarian and overtly racist argument—is fence-sitting, not actively advocating for radical solutions.

There is no doubt that *The Guardian* sits on the "left" and progressive end of the political spectrum of the News Establishment; as such I am a supporter. However, I also think it is important to critique the Fourth Estate Idealists as they are trapped inside the dynamics, dialectics and contradictions of commodified journalism. In my view, Kathrine Viner—and her Fourth Estate colleagues—do not have a full understanding of what the commodification of journalism is all about (see the next chapter for my outline of the "political economy of news"). Katharine Viner addressed "commodification" in a 2013 speech delivered while she was working for *The Guardian* in Australia. Her understanding is superficial and ahistorical, limiting the idea of commodification to "churnalism," "rewriting [agency] wires, press releases and each other" (Viner 2013). Yes, this is a problem, but it is not the commodification of journalism. The news has been commodified since late in the seventeenth century and it has been a commodity produced on an industrial scale from the mid-nineteenth century to today. In her 2013 remarks, Katharine Viner's comments about commodified journalism end with a justification that *The Guardian*'s coverage of "the serious stuff" is "getting away from commodified news" and "doing something different." But *The Guardian* is actually systemically frustrated in this regard. It exists within a mediasphere that is totally reliant on the commodity form and all the contradictions that this entails. No matter how much of a "progressive voice" the editor wants *The Guardian* to be, it is restricted by the limitations of the news industry which operates according to the profit principle and which privileges this over any notion of the public interest. My key criticism of the Fourth Estate Idealists is their failure to fully understand the political economy of the news industry.

As a January 2018 analysis of *The Guardian*, by the radical Media Lens collective, tends to show, more often than not, the Idealist media takes a centrist, or slightly left-of-center position that does not fundamentally challenge the status quo, particularly on economic, or hard ideological grounds. According to Katharine Viner (2018), *The Guardian* is "thoughtful, progressive, fiercely independent and challenging," but the Media Lens critique is just as thoughtful and fierce about the publisher's claims:

> "Fiercely independent and challenging"? When the Guardian Media Group is owned by The Scott Trust Limited, a "profit-seeking enterprise"? (In other words, it is *not* a non-profit trust, with many readers still mistakenly holding a romantic vision of benign ownership.) When the paper is thus owned and run by an elite group of individuals with links to banking, insurance, advertising, multinational consumer goods, telecommunications, information technology, venture investment, corporate media, marketing services and other sectors of the establishment? When the paper remains dependent on advertising revenue from corporate interests, despite the boast that "we now receive more income from our readers than we do

from advertisers." When the paper has actually ditched journalists who have been "fiercely independent and challenging"?

(Media Lens 2018)

According to Media Lens, *The Guardian* is a "liberal pillar of the establishment" that plays an important role in the" manufacture of consent" (Herman and Chomsky 1988)—the process by which the media helps to inculcate the subordinate classes and social groups with ideas that benefit the real interests of the elites and the ruling class. Noam Chomsky explained how this process works in a 1989 speech, just after his book with Edward Herman, *Manufacturing consent*, was published:

> The liberal bias is extremely important in a system—in a sophisticated system of propaganda. In fact, there ought to be a liberal bias. The liberal bias says, thus far and no further, I'm as far as you can go, and look how liberal I am. And of course, it turns out that I accept without question all the presuppositions of the propaganda system. Notice that that's a beautiful type of system. You don't ever express the propaganda, that's vulgar and too easy to penetrate, you just presuppose it. Unless you accept the presuppositions, you're not part of the discussion. And the presuppositions are instilled, not by, you know, beating you over the head with them, but just by making them the foundation of discussion. You don't accept them, you're not in the discussion.
>
> (Chomsky 1989)

The openly left-wing journalist John Pilger continues this theme with his observation that even in the most liberal of media any critique of politics is limited to "that which takes place inside, or within a short cab journey of the Palace of Westminster" (Pilger 1992: 13). In this passage, Pilger is talking about the limits of parliamentary democracy as also demarcating the limits of permissible discussion of politics. In his 1992 book, *Distant Voices*, Pilger argues that the Fourth Estate Idealist is a liberal-minded journalist who becomes a guardian of social norms and attempts to strike a balance between opposing extremes. They are ultimately unsure of their own position, because they occupy a contradictory class location between capital and labor, and they vacillate and report on the opposing social forces that power the contradictory dialectic of their time. Pilger's acerbic comment is that such people can be relied on to protect the interests of the establishment "during difficult times, such as when established forces go to war," is a template for some of the criticism that can be levelled at publications like the *New York Times* and *The Guardian* in recent years over Iraq, Iran and Syria, among other conflicts. In the same passage, Pilger also notes the ahistoricism of much journalism that is "faithful to the deity of 'impartiality'." He says such work "rejects the passion and moral imagination

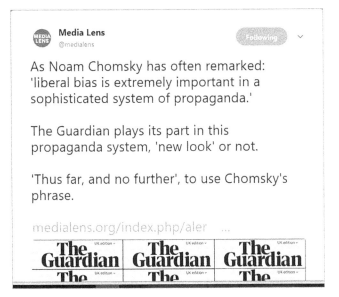

Media Lens
@medialens

Following ⌄

As Noam Chomsky has often remarked: 'liberal bias is extremely important in a sophisticated system of propaganda.'

The Guardian plays its part in this propaganda system, 'new look' or not.

'Thus far, and no further', to use Chomsky's phrase.

medialens.org/index.php/aler ...

FIGURE 1.1   Media Lens Tweet re *The Guardian*.

that discern and define the nature of criminality and make honest the writing of narrative history" (Pilger 1992: 13). The Media Lens critique of *The Guardian*, coupled with Chomsky's and Pilger's comments, adds weight to my grey collar thesis that any media criticism of the ruling class is bounded by the emotional dialectic of the front page, the ideological limits of representative democracy and the hegemonic ideology of the market system.

American media critic Daniel Hallin has neatly expressed the dialectic of the Fourth Estate as both an economic and ideological contradiction that is journalism's "ambivalent identity" (Hallin 1994: 1). This is similar to what I have called the contradictory emotional dialectic of news *as work*. I agree with Hallin's formulation that this is a struggle against the internal and external limits of the "professionaliza-tion" of journalism that threatens to upset the balance between "the public-interest culture of journalism and the culture of commodity-production" (ibid.: 4). Media institutions attempt to contain the contradiction between public interest and profit within the "sphere of legitimate controversy" sanctioned by liberal democratic elites, "the region where [the ideology of] objective journalism reigns supreme: here neutrality and balance are the prime journalistic virtues" (ibid.: 54). At the same time the news media play a containing role, "excluding from the public agenda those who violate or challenge consensus values, and uphold the consensus distinction between legitimate and illegitimate political activity" (ibid.).

As a group, the Idealists believe in the notion of public interest and seek to undertake the Fourth Estate function of speaking truth to power—in other words, in terms of the News Establishment, they are the good guys. However, their critical consciousness is necessarily limited by their commitment to the commodity form. They are insiders and therefore largely dependent on the system. While they do exercise freedom of thought and action—within the limits of editorial hierarchies— their freedom is self-limited and they hew to the normative traditions and cannot conceive of any practical alternative to the commodity form, or the capitalist system. Given that this group is perhaps the most intellectually active of all the cohorts of Establishment journalist, it is perhaps not surprising that there is an overlap between this group and the fourth sector, the Normative Scholars of journalism.

Normative Scholars of the News Establishment

Since about the turn of the twentieth century—120 years ago—journalism education has been housed in the modern university, at the center of the production of systemic intellectuals. Joseph Pulitzer, perhaps the first newspaper mogul, funded the Columbia Journalism School in 1912. For many decades, journalism educators have been reliant on their Establishment benefactors to hire their graduates, which is a necessary KPI for their tenure-track success. This has led to a situation where, both formally and informally, the news industry has been able to dictate the terms of engagement, including the parameters of curriculum and, in some cases, academic hiring decisions. Journalism scholars are also almost entirely dependent on Establishment sources for research funding. As governments cut back their investments in non-essential research —that which does not lead to direct commercialization—academics are increasingly reliant on industry funding. Journalism has mostly been a poor cousin within the social sciences, and the social sciences have never attracted the funding allocated to the hard sciences. In the United States this has led to institutions relying on generous benefactors to fund journalism research—the Knight Foundation, the Poynter Institute and the other big news corporates, for example—often leading to a skewing of research towards industry goals. The American experience is now being globalized, Reuters funds a research institute at that most establishment of universities, Oxford in the UK.

Journalism teachers and scholars are also usually recruited directly from Establishment newsrooms. They are products of Establishment institutions, they are likely graduates of a university journalism program and have been internalizing the normative rules and values of Establishment News since their late teens. They are now part of the Establishment and promote its values; they also seek to sustain it in its current form. There is very little critical scholarship done within this cohort, which is evident from the literature reviewed for this book. The bulk of research from Normative Scholars does not explore journalism beyond the commodity form and, when it does, I have found that it attempts to bring alternative forms back within the fenced enclosure of the normative corral. Scholarship on alternative forms is by and large framed from an Establishment perspective. The key journals in journalism studies are dominated by normative and non-critical studies. I have gone outside of this Establishment scholarship to find critical works, particularly in the political economy of media and journalism, and critical media studies.

The academic stake in the system is not something new, or limited only to journalism scholars. It is an essential element of loyalty demanded by the chief executives and trustees of most universities around the world, and certainly in the Western tradition. As Chomsky points out, within the communications disciplines—including journalism—there is a long tradition of leading scholars helping to formulate elite propaganda, based on the convenient, but fundamentally flawed premise, that the mass of the population was (for various reasons) unable to think clearly for itself. This idea itself has a long and ignoble history among elite intellectuals, it goes right back to the birth of Fourth Estate Idealism during the English revolution (Patching and Hirst 2014). Over a period of several hundred years—as the Fourth Estate model became the norm—this view was enhanced, modified and made palatable via a largely compliant media. It perhaps reached some sort of peak of perfection around the time of the First World War when the United States government required public opinion to support its intervention in distant Europe:

> Walter Lippmann, who was the dean of American journalists, is the man who invented the phrase manufacture of consent. He described the manufacture of consent as a self-conscious art and a regular organ of popular government. This, he said, is quite important, this is a revolution in the practice of democracy, and he thought it was a worthwhile revolution. The reason is, again, the stupidity of the average man. The common interests, he said, very largely elude public opinion entirely, and they can be managed only by a specialized class whose personal interests reach beyond the locality.
>
> *(Chomsky 1989)*

The democracy deficit is not really new, communication scholars were aware of it and proposing solutions in the 1920s. Social theorist John Dewey wrote about it in *The Public and its Problems* in 1927. Dewey was worried that governments found it convenient to keep the public in relative ignorance, in order to carry out the duties of state unencumbered by the democratic niceties. In the 1920s and 30s, the time in which the real industrial model of modern journalism came of age Lippmann and Dewey were engaged in an important debate around the issue of how the news media and journalism—as well as other information industries—might best serve the ideals of representative democracy.

A number of challengeable assumptions underlie this debate, perhaps most importantly the idea that representative democracy as it existed in the 1920s and 1930s was the most effective, or the ideal form of government. With some minor qualifications—mainly recognizing that it is not perfect—the same assumption holds today. In this normative system, the dialectic posits that there should exist a fully informed public, capable of making rational decisions in its own interests and the interests of the whole society, as embodied in government (Celmer 2014). In essence the discussion between Lippman and Dewey was a debate within the Establishment of the day over methods, rather than aims and purpose.

> What Dewey and Lippmann agree on is that contemporary society is too fragmented for the public to fully comprehend. But while Lippmann suggests an elite group of intelligent individuals to solve that problem, Dewey believes that it is possible to empower the public with tools that will allow them to critically think about the problems confronting them. Open communication and associations amongst the public will contribute to the expansion of knowledge.
>
> *(Celmer 2014: 53)*

Lippman favored a system of elite experts to make decisions because, he argued, the general mass of the public was too ignorant and passive to be relied upon beyond voting every few years for elite and expert leaders. Dewey's main difference was that he felt that through education and careful preparation of media messages, the public could reach a sufficient level of enlightenment to be trusted with decision making. Dewey was in favor of more creative ways of presenting information—including the news—to the public. The "Lippmann–Dewey" debate, has periodically resurfaced in journalism and media studies, but media scholar Michael Schudson, for one, believes the differences between the two have been historically exaggerated: "What turned the Lippmann-Dewey discourse into a "debate" were liberal intellectuals in the 1980s and 1990s, writing at another moment of democratic disillusion as they sought to take stock and seek hope" (Schudson 2008: 1032).

One of the legacies of this debate—real or not—is a highly bureaucratic and instrumental version of democracy that dovetails normatively with the political economy of advanced capitalism. It is a view of democracy that emphasizes elite decision-making over meaningful public participation and favors "stability, bureaucratic decentralization, and the competitive election of elites" (Whipple 2005: 156).

One legacy of the Dewey–Lippmann debate of nearly a century ago is the birth and growth of a public relations industry that today dwarfs journalism in terms of its ability to craft messages for the public. Messages that, all too often, carry a commercial value greater than their democratic value. It is no coincidence that in most universities in which journalism is taught and researched there is usually an equivalent number of faculty dedicated to the propagation of public relations as a profession and an academic discipline. The PR industry and its academic enablers are also now part of the News Establishment—thanks to the growth of so-called "native advertising" and marketing, thinly veneered with news values. This cohort owe their existence to the propagandists who emerged in the United States as a result of the First World War, including the godfathers of modern public relations, Edward Bernays and Harold Laswell.

Laswell was a pioneer of the professionalization of the communications industry, and influential in establishing public relations as an academic discipline. Like Bernays before him, Laswell was a firm believer in the need for propaganda in ostensibly democratic societies. Laswell argued that the role of the media was to mitigate discord that was potentially threatening to the social order of the day. His answer was to "replace public discourse with democratic propaganda" (Naveed 2016). Of course, the very idea of democratic propaganda is a nonsense; propaganda is only, and always, a tool of social control through the application of psychological sleight of hand against the public consciousness: "the management of collective attitudes by the manipulation of significant symbols" (Laswell 1927: 627). Communication scholarship today is broadly established on the principles enumerated by Lipmann, Bernays, Dewey and Laswell (among others) and it continues to rest on empirical and normative research traditions laid down by the middle of the last century. It is predicated on assumptions that might no longer hold (Nerone 2012)—the relative autonomy of the media from the apparatus of the State and from pressures to bend editorial decisions to economic necessity (profitability). In this regard, an influential and highly normative text—which John Nerone believes is making a comeback since the collapse of the Soviet Union—is *Four Theories of the Press*, published at the height of the Cold War, and which normalized all the assumptions underlying the so-called free market model as the ideal for Western journalism. Normative theories of the press are idealized and focus on what the news media should do under so-called normal conditions—which are usually assumed to be market-oriented and free from state interference (Benson 2008).

Hallin's spheres of consensus and limited controversy also play out in the scholarship of journalism and are part of the academic infrastructure that makes normative approaches appear routine and benign. Part of the problem of the News Establishment is that the reality of crisis has rendered this normative and idealistic view of the news industry, and of the social practices of journalists, incapable of providing any real solutions. Normative values no longer hold, or provide any explanatory or solution-focused assistance, but the News Establishment has, on-the-whole, shown itself lacking in any capacity to move beyond its embedded ideological assumptions. There are exceptions to this rule; however, I argue strongly that, to move beyond the crisis, we have to investigate more critical theoretical perspectives and more radical solutions. While figures within the journalism establishment attempt to control the boundaries of limited controversy and maintain the core elements of consensus, the reality is that the public sphere is, to some extent, now beyond such control efforts. They days of a dominant mainstream consensus providing the news narrative within the limits of acceptable controversy are over. The disruptive technologies of social media have created some space in which alternative narratives can gain traction, often contradicting, and occasionally overturning the mainstream consensus. Alternative news outlets, existing outside the economic constraints of commodity journalism are also beginning to exercise some influence. I do not want to argue that this new digital public space is perfect—there are many flaws to discuss in the following pages—but it is clear that social media is a space where non-commercial and even anti-commercial social journalism might flourish.

Social Journalism—the New Alternative?

So, if I am right—and I believe I am—the news industry, mainstream journalism and many journalism scholars constitute the News Establishment, and they are part of the problem. This means we have to do something different, because repeating the same mistakes over and over again is, in some quarters, the very definition of madness. The thesis of this book is that perhaps we need to look to "alternative" forms of journalism for some answers to the democracy deficit problem; I have decided to call my version of the alternative "social journalism." I spend some time in the following pages defining and defending this proposition, but in short, what I mean by it is this:

> "Social journalism" is a form of journalistic practice that occurs outside of the news industry and outside the professional confines of journalism. Social journalism involves non-journalists in the news production and distribution chain, above and beyond engaging with professional newsrooms. It is not a form of journalism that—in political economy terms—is bound by the *relations of production* that pertain to commodity-form news. It is a set of news-gathering, production, consumption and dissemination practices that largely occur in, through and on social media platforms, channels and devices.

Social journalism incorporates the ideas of citizen journalism, and it can involve collaborations between non-journalists and professionals. It can be imagined as both an educational opportunity—to increase critical media literacy—and also a powerful tool for energizing civil society (Caton-Rosser and McGinley 2006). Social journalism involves ordinary people having some level of training in the skills and aptitudes of journalism—for example in the techniques of mobile journalism, or "mojo" (Burum and Quinn 2016)—while retaining their independence. It will mainly be not-for-profit, but if individuals can make a living from it in the "gig economy" then good for them. The key aim of social journalism is to address the democracy deficit through both information-sharing and activism. It is a necessary component of the movement known as "monitorial democracy" (Schudson 1998), and it has implications at scale from the hyperlocal to the global. The starting point for this book—both the theoretical first section and the more practically oriented second half—is an observation by the British journalism scholar, Tony Harcup:

a mixture of an alternative viewpoint with a level of journalistic skill may in fact still be necessary if non-professional journalists are to become investigators into or monitors of the powerful and not merely shouty propagandists or bloggers about cupcakes.

(Harcup 2016: 654)

In "Alternative Journalism as Monitorial Citizenship?," Harcup argues that citizens need knowledge and training to carry out journalistic functions within the context of their communities and their everyday lives. I agree, and in chapter 7 I expand on this idea using the work of Italian Marxist, Antonio Gramsci who coined the term "integral journalism": a type of reporting and editorial decision-making that "seeks not only to satisfy all the needs … of its public, but also to … arouse its public and progressively enlarge it" (Forgacs 2000: 383). I hope, that after reading the rest of this book, you will agree that I have provided the means for you to acquire both an "alternative viewpoint"—about the news industry and journalism—and "a level of journalistic skill," such that you will be able to confidently begin thinking of yourself as a social journalist helping to overcome the democracy deficit and who helps to hold the powerful—including the News Establishment—to account in a meaningful way.

References

Atton, Chris, and James F. Hamilton. 2008. *Alternative Journalism*. London: Sage.

Beharrel, Peter, and Greg Philo. 1977. *Trade Unions and the Media*. London: Macmillan.

Bell, Emily, and Taylor Owen. 2017. "The Platform Press: How Silicon Valley Reengineered Journalism." Tow Center for Digital Journalism. Accessed April 19, 2017. www.cjr.org/tow_center_reports/platform-press-how-silicon-valley-reengineered-journalism.php.

Benson, Rodney. 2008. "Journalism: Normative Theories." In *The International Encyclopedia of Communication*, edited by Wolfgang Donsbach, 2591–2597. London: Wiley.

Berberoglu, Berch. 2016. *The Global Capitalist Crisis and its Aftermath: The Causes and Consequences of the Great Recession 2008–2009*. New York: Routledge.

Burum, Ivo, and Stephen Quinn. 2016. *MOJO: The Mobile Journalism Handbook: How to Make Broadcast Videos with an iPhone or iPad*. Burlington, MA: Focal Press.

Caton-Rosser, Mary, and Jennifer A. McGinley. 2006. "Alternative media and the learning culture of civil society: Outreach and teach strategies." *InterActions: UCLA Journal of Education and Information Studies* 2(1): 1–19. https://escholarship.org/uc/item/9ws9n9c5.

Celmer, Matthew. 2014. "The Solution to the Dewey/Lippmann Debate." *The Graduate Research Journal* (Indiana University) 1: 49–55. Accessed January 23, 2018. https://scholarworks.iu.edu/journals/index.php/iusbgrj/article/view/12754.

Champagne, Patrick. 2005. "The 'Double Dependency': The Journalistic Field between Politics and Markets." In *Bourdieu and the Journalistic Field*, by Rodney Benson and Erik Neveu, 48–63. Cambridge: Polity. Accessed August 3, 2017.

Chomsky, Noam. 1989. "Manufacturing Consent: The Political Economy of the Mass Media." Speech delivered at the University of Wisconsin–Madison, March 15. Accessed January 22, 2018. https://chomsky.info/19890315/.

Faraone, Roque. 2011. "Economy, Ideology, and Advertising." In *The Handbook of Political Economy of Communications*, edited by Janet Wasko, Graham Murdock and Helen Sousa, 187–205. Malden, MA: Blackwell.

Fontaine, Paul. 2013. "Diversity of Media Ownership Literally Non-existent in Canada." J Source. Accessed March 2, 2018. http://j-source.ca/article/diversity-of-media-owner ship-literally-non-existent-in-canada/.

Forgacs, David. 2000. *The Gramsci Reader: Selected Writings, 1916–1935*. New York: New York University Press.

Frase, Peter. 2016. *Four Futures: Life after Capitalism*. London: Verso.

Friedman, Uri. 2018. "How's Democracy Holding Up After Trump's First Year?" *The Atlantic*. January 14. Accessed January 14, 2018. www.theatlantic.com/international/ archive/2018/01/trump-democracy-ziblatt-levitsky/550340/.

Fuchs, Christian. 2010. "Alternative Media as Critical Media." *European Journal of Social Theory* 13(2): 173–192.

Graves, Lucas. 2017. "The Monitorial Citizen in the "Democratic Recession." *Journalism Studies* 18 (10): 1239–1250. doi:10.1080/1461670X.2017.1338153.

Hallin, Daniel. 1994. *We Keep America on Top of the World*. London: Routledge.

Harcup, Tony. 2016. "Alternative Journalism as Monitorial Citizenship? A Case Study of a Local News Blog." *Digital Journalism* 4(5): 639–657. doi:10.1080/21670811.2015.1063077.

Herman, Edward, and Noam Chomsky. 1988. *Manufacturing Consent: The Political Economy of the Mass Media*. New York: Random House.

Hirst, Martin. 2002. *Grey Collar Journalism: The Social Relations of News Production*. Prod. Charles Sturt University. Bathurst. Accessed January 20, 2018. https://espace.library. uq.edu.au/view/UQ:10922.

Hirst, Martin. 2011. *News 2.0: Can Journalism Survive the Internet?* Crows Nest, NSW: Allen and Unwin.

Laswell, Harold. 1927. "The Theory of Political Propaganda." *The American Political Science Review* 21(3): 627–631.

Leong, Lewis. 2017. "Fighting Fake News: How Google, Facebook and Others are Trying to Stop it." *Tech Radar*. May 25. Accessed November 8, 2017. www.techradar.com/ news/fighting-fake-news-how-google-facebook-and-more-are-working-to-stop-it.

Media Lens. 2018. "A Liberal Pillar of the Establishment—'New Look' *Guardian*, Old-Style Orthodoxy." *Media Lens*. January 18. Accessed January 18, 2018. http://media lens.org/index.php/alerts/alert-archive/2018/861-a-liberal-pillar-of-the-establish ment-new-look-guardian-old-style-orthodoxy.html.

Moore, Jason W. 2014. "The End of Cheap Nature. Or How I Learned to Stop Worrying about "The" Environment and Love the Crisis of Capitalism." In *Structures of the World Political Economy and the Future of Global Conflict and Cooperation*, edited by Christian Suter and Christopher Chase-Dunn, 285–314. Berlin: Lit Verlag.

Naveed, Fakhar. 2016. "Harold Lasswell's Propaganda Theory." *Mass Communication Talk*. October 17. Accessed January 22, 2018. www.masscommunicationtalk.com/harold-lasswells-propaganda-theory.html.

Nerone, John. 2012. "The Historical Roots of the Normative Model of Journalism." *Journalism* 14(4): 446–458. doi:10.1177/1464884912464177.

Patching, Roger, and Martin Hirst. 2014. *Journalism Ethics: Arguments and Cases for the Twenty-First Century*. London: Routledge.

Persily, Nathanial. 2017. "Can Democracy Survive the Internet?" *Journal of Democracy* 28 (2):63–76. Accessed January 13, 2018.

Pilger, John. 1992. *Distant Voices*. London: Verso.

Rappler. 2018. "Media Watchdogs Slam Malacañang Ban on Rappler Reporter." *Rappler*. February 23. Accessed February 24, 2018. www.rappler.com/nation/196690-media-watchdogs-malacanang-ban-rappler-reporter.

Schudson, Michael. 1998. *The Good Citizen: A History of American Civic Life*. New York: The Free Press.

Schudson, Michael. 2008. "The "Lippmann–Dewey Debate" and the Invention of Walter Lippmann as an Anti-Democrat 1986–1996." *International Journal of Communication* 2: 1031–1042. Accessed January 24, 2018. doi:1932-8036/20081031.

Simon, Joel. 2017. "The New Face of Censorship." Committee to Protect Journalists. April 25. Accessed January 20, 2018. https://cpj.org/2017/04/introduction-the-new-face-of-censorship.php.

Tucker, Joshua A., Yannis Theocharis, Margaret, E. Roberts and Pablo Barberá. 2017. "From Liberation to Turmoil: Social Media and Democracy." *Journal of Democracy* 28 (4): 46–59. Accessed January 14, 2018.

Viner, Katharine. 2013. "The Rise of the Reader: Journalism in the Age of the Open Web." *The Guardian*. October 9. Accessed March 21, 2018. www.theguardian.com/commentis free/2013/oct/09/the-rise-of-the-reader-katharine-viner-an-smith-lecture.

Viner, Katharine. 2017. "A Mission for Journalism in a Time of Crisis." *The Guardian*. November 16. Accessed March 21, 2018. www.theguardian.com/news/2017/nov/16/a-mission-for-journalism-in-a-time-of-crisis.

Viner, Katharine. 2018. "Welcome to a New Look for the Guardian." *The Guardian*. January 15. Accessed January 18, 2018. www.theguardian.com/media/2018/jan/15/guardian-new-look-online-katharine-viner.

Watts, Duncan J., and David M. Rothschild. 2017. "Don't Blame the Election on Fake News. Blame it on the Media." *Columbia Journalism Review*. December 5. Accessed December 28, 2017. www.cjr.org/analysis/fake-news-media-election-trump.php.

Whipple, Mark. 2005. "The Dewey–Lippmann Debate Today: Communication Distortions, Reflective Agency, and Participatory Democracy." *Sociological Theory* 23(2): 156–178. Accessed January 24, 2018.

2
JOURNALISM AND THE INTERNET OF THINGS

The Relationship between Journalism and Technology

This chapter explores how the future of journalism is being impacted by the technological development commonly referred to as the "Internet of Things" (IoT). The IoT, we are told, is about the connection of objects to the Internet and making greater use of the immense datasets that this provides. The IoT is about artificial intelligence and the future of work. For the news industry, the "Internet of Things" means robots creating news without human intervention, perhaps leading to a further breakdown of our already fractured trust in journalists. One implication of the IoT is that it will lead to even more uncertainty about the business of journalism, and maybe even more chaos, both inside and outside the newsroom. There is no escaping that this is the landscape in which journalism operates today. I have been a journalist and journalism educator for the best part of four decades, never have I seen or experienced so much turmoil in the news industry as we are witnessing today.

Despite nearly a decade of discussion and experimentation, the world's leading news experts—whether media executives, award-winning editors, or the brightest of scholars—have not yet figured out how to save the news industry, or journalism, from what I regard as a self-imposed crisis. As discussed in Chapter 1, the News Establishment cannot solve the problems it has created for itself. The rest of this book takes up these themes in various ways; beginning with a mapping of the current tumultuous landscape and the issues it throws up for journalists, their audiences and for producers of news operating outside of the news business. This mapping and analysis is then extended with an exploration of the ways in which what I choose to call "social journalists" can either intervene in the professional production of news, or operate independently of it.

There is no doubt that journalism and the news industry are under pressure and this is the focus of the first four chapters of this book. The pressure on the profession of journalism and on the business of news gathering and distribution, is often said to be the result of the same technologically disruptive forces that have created the Internet of Things. In this narrative, technology is responsible for the newly emerged social media behemoths like Facebook, and search engine giants like Google. For many observers, the disruption we are experiencing—changing how we live, work, consume, love and communicate—is purely, or predominantly, the result of digital technologies. The creation of the Internet at the beginning of the 1990s is posited as the starting point for all the disruption we've seen since then. From this perspective the second phase of the digital revolution—mobile devices and the tens of thousands of applications (apps) created to take advantage of them—has only served to speed up the process of collapse of what seemed once like permanent institutions of society and the economy. Certainly, technological revolution is an important factor in digital disruption, but it is really only part of the picture.

For some analysts and commentators, disruption is seen as being entirely positive in its consequences. The view that digital technology—the microchip and subsequent developments—is the primary, if not the only, cause of the disruption, chaos and remaking of society that we are witness to, is a technologically "determinist" position. In relation to journalism, it is summed up in this observation:

> [The] technological potentialities of the internet and digital-related technologies were perceived as the means to direct journalism into its heralded societal function of serving the people by fostering increased accountability and transparency as well as by establishing dialogical and participatory models of communication.
>
> *(Spyridou et al. 2013: 80)*

In other words, digital technologies would democratize journalism and help journalists to help us overcome the growing democracy deficit. In this technologically determinist view, the process of disruption within the field of journalism is attributed to the impact of technology itself in a mono-causal fashion. This is a theoretical tradition known as "technological determinism." While it can be appealing because it appears to offer a simple, common sense, explanation for the cause of all the disruption we see in society in general and in the news industry, there are fundamental flaws in the determinist position.

A Necessary Critique of Technological Determinism

Technological determinism is the belief that progress is driven by scientific-technological development, that such progress is inevitable and, to a large extent, beyond human control. It is particularly associated with the "digital revolution" predicated on the microchip and it received a boost with the birth of Internet culture in the 1990s. It has been associated with what critics have labelled the "California ideology" that permeates Silicon Valley and the hi-tech world of Internet-era companies, such as Google, Uber and Facebook: "the Californian ideology is held by IT entrepreneurs and clearly linked to techno-determinism and American neoliberalism. It has become a buzzword for the business culture Google and other IT companies perform" (Mager 2014: 28).

Astrid Mager describes the "Californian ideology" as a form of digital utopian thinking that treats the algorithms at the heart of powerful search engines as almost infallible or God-like entities that need to be nurtured, protected and tightly held as corporate secrets. Privacy concerns, problematic surveillance of users and the commercialization of users' data are dismissed as low order issues, while the power of the machines is celebrated.

The utopian view of technology also permeates journalism studies (Steensen 2011), just as technological determinism is a strong ideology within the News Establishment. Two key reasons have been put forward to explain the strong attraction journalists feel towards determinism:

> ... in the digital age, recently-commercialized technologies are central to the work journalists do, making them seem naturalized and essentialized in the news ecosphere ... [and] the explanatory paradigm for examining change in journalism as practice and in the news industry is historically heavily influenced by determinist tropes in media and communication scholarship.
>
> *(Örnerbring 2010)*

In closing this chapter, I will examine how technological determinism is demonstrated in the news media's coverage of the Internet of Things. In doing so, I don't wish to suggest that every article promotes a utopian view of the IoT, only that it is the predominant perspective, in which problematic issues—such as privacy breaches, data surveillance and the commodification of leisure time—are either ignored completely, or minimized in the coverage. Interestingly, it seems that the tide of utopian thinking may be turning, slowly, but surely. In 2017, leading web guru, Rick Webb, made an astonishing Christmas Day discovery about himself and fellow utopian spruikers—they were wrong!

> For the last twenty years, I believed the internet prophets of old. I worshipped at the altar of Stewart Brand and Kevin Kelly. I believed that the world would be a better place if everyone had a voice. I believed that the world would be a better place if we all had no secrets.
>
> But so far, the evidence points to an escapable conclusion: we were all wrong.
>
> *(Webb 2017)*

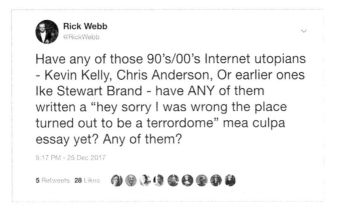

Rick Webb
@RickWebb

Have any of those 90's/00's Internet utopians
- Kevin Kelly, Chris Anderson, Or earlier ones
Ike Stewart Brand - have ANY of them
written a "hey sorry I was wrong the place
turned out to be a terrordome" mea culpa
essay yet? Any of them?

9:17 PM - 25 Dec 2017

5 Retweets 28 Likes

FIGURE 2.1 Web Entrepreneur and Reformed Utopian Calls for a Collective "Mea Culpa."

For Webb, a telling feature of the misplaced optimism is the technical rationality of the Silicon Valley tech companies, who peddle in technological determinism: a belief that the machines can make it right; can overcome human fallibility; and can create a utopian global village: "It's quite possible that the premise is completely false. And I'm not sure we ever considered for a moment that it could be wrong" (Webb 2017).

Technological determinism has several variants that differ in intensity from "hard" to "soft," but its essential feature is that technology is given an autonomous role in historical development. The progress seemingly brought about by technological change is posited as beyond the control or will of human actors, and free from any influencing social relations, such that "technology itself exercises causal influence on social practice" (Bimber 1990: 338). This view represents a "hard" determinist position: technology drives change and there is little we can do to intervene, moderate its influence, or stop it; even if we wanted to. A variation on this theme is a softer version that Bruce Bimber calls the "unintended consequences account" of technological determinism. In this view, technology creates problematic consequences that were unforeseen at the time of its invention, but is overall beneficial and represents "progress." This approach argues that technology is only "partially autonomous" (ibid.: 339). Most determinist accounts of technology follow what Bimber calls the "logical sequence account" in which it is held that "society evolves along a fixed and predetermined path, regardless of human intervention" (ibid.: 341). This is an approach most often associated with discussions of technological disruption in relation to media and its attendant technologies. A good example of this is provided in a 2010 journal article exploring how the use of Twitter might change sports journalism. The authors explicitly adopted a determinist position, based on the work of Marshall McLuhan, to frame their study: "Technological determinism ... suggests that new media technologies such as Twitter could create changes in the culture that trigger a corresponding change in journalism practice" (Schultz and Sheffer 2010: 238).

The primacy of technology in this process of change is clearly signaled in this sentence. Other scholars have also adopted this technology as change-agent discourse in their discussions of how journalistic standards have been consistently falling since at least the late 1980s (see, for example Ursell 2001). However, as Gillian Ursell argues, it is the socio-economic and political climate of increased competition for eyeballs and revenues, in which the new media technologies have been introduced, that effectively determines how they are deployed: "It is this competition which appears to be the immediate cause of organizational and technological change." This is a social constructivist view, rather than deterministic and it is more helpful for our purposes (see below and Spyridou et al. 2013).

A clear and contemporary example of determinism in action was media coverage the so-called "Twitter revolution" across the Middle East in 2010–2011. Many commentators embraced a deterministic view of the events of the "Arab Spring" and argued that there would be an inevitable and unstoppable progression towards liberation as a result of millions of people taking to the streets in Egypt and other Arab nations. Unfortunately, they were wrong and were seduced by "a heady brew of social media activism; scarce official pronouncements and revolutionary romanticism that coursed through the souks and through social media" (Hirst 2012a). The horror of subsequent events in Syria, Libya and Egypt itself make it abundantly clear that, despite its momentary power, the technologies of social media are, in themselves, not sufficiently powerful to change the course of history. Syria and Libya are being torn apart by bloody civil war and the al Sisi regime in Egypt is now closing down opposition media, arresting activists and journalists, and launching a full-scale attack on the rights of LGBTQI people. Miriyam Aouragh (2012) has written eloquently against the determinism of what she calls the "celebratory" accounts of the "Facebook revolution" which promoted the view that Western technologies, not the actions of participants themselves, would liberate the Arab world from dictatorship and repression. It is important that these overly optimistic analyses (Lindgren 2013) are countered by more sober assessments of the power of so-called online mobs to affect the course of history without coming out from behind their screens.

Rather than assess new information against what we know of the past, in order to make sense of the present, the determinist narrative is formed around only the available facts, and a poorly understood "common sense" view of the world. This is a "bias of convenience" which can only produce "an easy to digest narrative based on available facts and not requiring any difficult historical contextualizing" (Hirst 2012a). Accounts privileging a determining role for social media in the events of the Arab Spring have taken on a life of their own; they have become useful "mini-fables" that direct attention away from the historical genesis of events to look only at consequences. As Aouragh notes, these myths take the form of "wishful thinking" that somehow social media would effectively undermine brutal and heavily armed state regimes (ibid.: 529). The fact that most of the actual organizing of the uprising, particularly in Egypt, took place offline had escaped the mainly foreign press contingent that descended on Cairo. To them it appeared that the revolution was indeed started on social media, and the real centers of resistance were "rarely noted by the internet-obsessed reporters" (ibid.: 532).

In my view, the reason why so many journalists and so many media scholars fall into the trap of even a "soft" form of determinism is because they live in a "perpetual present" in which every new development is seen only in a linear fashion, unrelated to the past, and not essentially linked to it by history or social relations. Like technological determinism, the "perpetual present" is a feature of the belief system that permeates the News Establishment. Thinking only in the short-term and present tense is a feature of journalistic decision-making that helps to simplify the world, making it easier to report as new and exciting—two of the main features of "the news." As Adam Rothstein points out when discussing our fascination with drones, technological determinism tends to view historical narratives in a linear fashion that all move towards a better future, as such "we simply need to stay the course" (Rothstein 2015) and live in the present moment confident that things have improved (on the past) and will improve (in the future).

In most determinist theories, there is, in effect, a "before and after narrative" that empowers technology as "a virtually autonomous agent of change" and that creates a "popular discourse of technological determinism," whose "internal logic" strongly suggests that technology takes on "a life of its own" in a "seemingly predetermined sequence" (Marx and Smith 1998: ix). Such ideological memes have become a pervasive theme in today's mediasphere and, subsequently, in much media and journalism scholarship. Daniel Chandler argues that there is an academic variant of technological determinism he calls "media determinism" in which media institutions, technologies and processes are presented as autonomous causal actors in social life: "determinists interpret technology in general and communications technologies in particular as the basis of society in the past, present and even the future" (Chandler 2002). As Steensen (2011: 311) observed in a critical review of determinism in media and journalism studies, "researchers, scholars, business executives and practitioners alike all participate in a game of prophesying revolution" whenever a new technology appears on the scene. This is the very definition of media determinism in which any change is deemed, at least initially, to be beneficial, and only beneficial. In relation to social media, this view does not acknowledge the tension and contradictions—the dialectic—between the platforms and applications and commodified sites of profit for their owners and the uses to which activists (as in the "Arab Spring") might put them: "there is a direct mismatch between the commercial logic and activist use of social media as public information infrastructures" (Aouragh 2012: 530).

To counteract this reductive and determinist view of media, and of historical change, we need to argue for the primacy of social relations; which are the concrete, daily relations between people in their material circumstances. We have to recognize and account for relationships of unequal power, and the complexity of relations between people and things (material objects in time and space). In this conceptualization of historical development, technology is the servant, or the tool, of change, not the primary cause. A view of technology that situates change within the realm of social relations and human agency, recognizes that change is directed by "associated systems of socio-political directives" (Heilbroner 1998: 76); that is historical change is the result of human-made decisions about how the economy and society are to be managed, and whose social interests will be paramount. As Karl Marx noted in this famous opening passage from his pamphlet *The Eighteenth Brumaire of Louis Bonaparte*: "Men make their own history, but they do not make it as they please; they do not make it under self-selected circumstances, but under circumstances existing already, given and transmitted from the past" (Marx 1852).

Therefore, and in opposition to a purely determinist view of history and change, a more nuanced and perhaps a more useful approach is to place technology into a dialectical relationship with human agency. This is the space of "mediation" in which there is a process of combined and uneven development existing between technology and human agency. Rather than reducing complex social developments to a single causal explanation—which technological determinism attempts to do—an approach based on "mediation" emphasizes the idea that a society is a complex totality in which many forces combine with human agency to produce any given set of structures and relationships at a particular moment in time. This process of combination is uneven because there is inequality within various power relationships; and because at certain times one factor may exert a stronger influence than another; but it does so within the constraints imposed by even a weak countervailing force. Viewed through this lens, combined and uneven development means that the forces of technology and human agency interact with one another in a way that affects both. The end result—the change in circumstances—is the result of this interaction and the dependency that each has on the other. The social relations and the technology—in the form of machinery, software and apps, for example—exist in a mutually constructive dialogue. Society is formed, and therefore changes, through the interaction of human agency and technology "in ways that humans both intend and do not intend, anticipate and do not anticipate, control and do not control" (Bell 1995: 625). This social constructivist approach is adopted in this book, along with a political economy perspective (see Chapter 3). This epistemology views journalism as a social phenomenon that takes place within specified relations of production that include economic, technological, political and ideological factors which are mutually constituted. In the news industry, the application of new technologies is therefore shaped by the decisions made by executives, editors and journalists, but under conditions over which they have little or no control. However, in order to see this clearly, we need to move out of the fog and excitement of what Vincent Mosco (2005) calls the "digital sublime"; that rose-tinted and determinist vision of disruptive technologies as benign, progressive and to be celebrated, rather than critically assessed.

If we approach the current situation of crisis in the news industry without being blinded by the digital sublime, we notice that Facebook and Google are among a handful of new media companies that can, and will, challenge the legacy power of the traditional news industry. Many news organizations feel threatened by these relative newcomers and are struggling to find ways of either competing, or joining forces with them that secures their own future financial viability (Hutton 2017).

As we discuss in the following chapters, this battle for economic supremacy has already weakened the former giants of print and broadcasting. Google and Facebook are no longer "just" technology companies; they are also publishers (Bell 2017) and this threatens what used to be a cozy monopoly held by the news media companies. What we are seeing in this epic struggle is the latest form of a war that has been fought before—between print and radio; between radio and television, between the VCR and the Betamax recorder, and between vinyl and the CD. Now digital downloads and music streaming are challenging the hegemony of the CD and video streaming threatens the business model for broadcast television and the cinema. Digital technologies, based on the microchip, the Internet and mobile telephony represent the new media version of this continuous and mutually constitutive interplay of new and old technologies enmeshed in old and emerging social relations (Hirst and Harrison 2007).

The reasons why Google and Facebook have become so powerful have little to do with the technology, and a lot to do with economics. As two of the richest companies in the new media landscape, the power of Google and Facebook is based on their huge market capitalization and this, in turn, is based on calculations about their future profitability (Fuchs 2012: 726). While the tensions between the legacy media and the tech-giants are new, the scenario that is playing out is no more than a new contradiction within the global media industries based on long-standing dialectic of "tension between new technological potentialities on the one hand and economic concentration on the other" (Murdock and Golding 1973: 207). A concrete manifestation of this unavoidable tendency towards a new dialectic in the digital economy is the so-called "Internet of Things" and, as we shall see, it is likely to cause further disruption to journalism and the news industry. However, before exploring this emerging dialectic, I need to outline the theoretical propositions that underpin my approach within a scholarly the tradition of political economy of communication.

What is the Political Economy of News?

The mass media—at least in the form that dominated the twentieth century—appears to be in decline. We are not consuming as much live broadcast media as we did even a decade ago and print circulations are in probably terminal decline; time-shifting, podcasts and online delivery of news have forever changed the media ecology we inhabit. In an attempt to explain this, techno-logical determinism points to a new form of communication, the "network society" (Castells 1996) based on "distributed media" (Wittel 2012) in which many producers vie for attention in a crowded, but necessarily more democratic marketplace. Political economy argues that this is only a partial explanation. Political economists have formed the view that the social totality is developed out of the complex of dialectical relationships between technologies, the forces of production and the actions of human beings struggling to survive and thrive in the material world and against sometimes difficult odds. This is the theoretical approach—the epistemology—of political economy. In the next few pages, a political economy analysis will be outlined and then in the following four chapters it will be applied to the digital media landscape in order to critique the determinist view and posit an alternative interpretation of a networked and "distributed" media ecology. In particular, this analysis will be brought to bear on the news industry and journalism to explain the crises of trust and profit-ability which confront it today (Hirst 2011), and to suggest an alternative approach based on the idea of a more "social" journalism, and less reliance on the News Establishment.

Political economy is not new; in fact, it predates what we now call "orthodox" economics by almost 100 years. Adam Smith and Karl Marx, while poles apart politically, are seen as two influential founders of its theories and applications. The political economy tradition embraces a wider view of economic activity than simple supply and demand within an otherwise unpro-blematic market economy Political economy places issues of control, power and inequality at the center of its analysis (Browning and Kilmister 2006: 1). Thus, I situate myself in this tradition, which Browning and Kilmister would define as "critical political economy," requiring a "radical revision of conventional economic concepts in the light of their inadequacy in dealing with the questions generated by that context" (ibid.: 2). When it comes to understanding commu-nication and the media, this approach is useful because it has a focus on the social rather than the technological, or purely economic. It is also historical, in that it tries to understand the past and the present on a continuum of "transformations, shifts and contradictions that unfold over long loops of time" (Wasko, Murdock and Sousa 2011). In recent years, the political economy of communication has been updated and revised to account for the digital revolu-tion and subsequent developments; including to theorize the emergence of social media and user-generated content (Fuchs and Mosco 2012). As a founding editor of the journal *Political Economy of Communication*, I have played a small role in this work, but also rely on contributions from many colleagues, particularly in the Political Economy section of the International Association for Mass Communication Research (IAMCR).

Political economy approaches are an antidote to the technological determinist view previously discussed, because they privilege social relations over the artefacts of technology in proposing an explanation of the process of historical change and transition. This is important if we are to put the "digital revolution" into perspective, and not just fall for the easy seduction and reductivism of the "digital sublime." For instance, an analysis based on the principles of political economy, allow us to understand that the news industry has colonized social media spaces for the purposes of extracting profit from them, rather than for the fuzzy, warm notion of engaging with audiences. The economic imperative of profitability—to secure subscriptions and eyeballs for advertisers—is driving engagement strategies, not public interest (Hirst 2011: 126).

I have been using a political economy approach now for more than 30 years and it forms the core theoretical and methodological ideas of my research and my writing (see, for example, Hirst and Harrison 2007; Hirst 2011; Patching and Hirst 2014). I can claim little originality in this, apart from one or two ideas in relation to the news commodity; I am essentially standing on the shoulders of giants (see Wasko, Murdock and Sousa 2011) and the political economy tradition is well established in communication studies. However, it is not so widely applied in scholarship about journalism where a more normative and empirical tradition, which falls back on determinism, has taken root. Some communication scholars have applied a political economy approach to journalism and it is to these sources that I turn for inspiration and support (see McChesney 2003, for example).

One of the first serious academic works in the political economy of communication was an essay by Graham Murdock and Peter Golding published in 1973. This seminal paper outlines the foundations of a political economy approach based on a recognition that the "mass media" is made up of companies that are "first and foremost industrial and commercial organizations which produce and distribute commodities" (Murdock and Golding 1973: 206). This is important, but perhaps no more so than the recognition that these media companies are essential elements of a modern capitalist market economy subject to the same laws, dynamics and contradictions that beset the system as a whole. These commonalities include periodic boom and bust cycles, a tendency towards concentration and eventual monopoly conditions, an ethos built on the profit motive, and putting shareholder interests before those of society or the general public. It is on this basis that I made my arguments about the News Establishment in chapter one. With this in mind, Murdock and Golding argued that political economy must consider changes in the media industries as symptomatic of, and interlinked with, "more general economic changes." In turn, to theorize and analyze the media industries "requires an historical perspective which will locate changes in the mass media within the general context of industrialization" (ibid.). This approach must also be applied to a study of the post-Internet mediasphere because it still functions within the over-arching paradigm of commodity capitalism. In other words, the digital revolu-tion has not taken society beyond capitalism, the networked society and distributed media forms still function within the governing rules of exploitation, profit and social control (George 2012). We only need to mention the activity of "phishing"—fraudulent activity to separate online consumers from their money—to see how capitalism takes advantage of new platforms to continue deceptive economic practices forged in the days of the carpetbaggers of the Wild West (Klikauer 2016).

A key insight from Murdock and Golding's pioneering work that I have developed in my own work on journalism and news is the secondary function of media, that it disseminates "ideas about economic and political structures" and therefore has an "ideological dimension" (Murdock and Golding 1973) and a role in creating a sense of popular culture. I have come to call this twin problematic of journalism, as both economic and ideological product, the "duality of the news commodity," which symbolizes "the dialectical tension between private profit and public interest" (Hirst 2011: 74). It is the central contradiction in a system of industrial journalism; it is also a key feature of news in the online realm and, as such, one of the reasons why the old business models are seen to be failing so badly.

At the heart of a political economy method and analysis of journalism is the concept of the social relations of news production; which is simply a way of talking about the totality of relationships—economic, political, cultural, tech-nological, ideological and inter-personal—which govern the way in which news is produced. Examining social relations within the political economy of journal-ism means examining the duality of structure and action. In concrete terms this translates into understanding the role of journalists as "actors who produce content," but who do so within an institutional system of "rules, procedures, structures and technologies" (Fuchs 2010: 175). To understand this dialectically simply means understanding that the structures of the news media impose their own constraints on the journalist-actor. In a capitalist society the structures and institutions of the news industry are overdetermined by unequal control over resources—both the physical and intellectual means of production.

Social relations of production cover everything; from the way that news production is financed, to the technologies employed in gathering, reporting and distributing news, to the ways in which reporters and editors actually think about the stories they produce and publish. The social relations of news production govern the way that newsrooms are organized, how editorial decisions are made, and how the news industry is structured. In other words, this assemblage of social relations creates the conditions in which the News

Establishment emerged on the cusp of the twentieth century in the form of the first "news barons"—Pulitzer and Hearst, for example. Inside newsrooms, the process of thinking about editorial decisions forms what I call an "emotional dialectic," which mirrors the social relations and contradictory duality of the news commodity. In news media, the "interplay" of opposing forces—the emotional dialectic—carries over into the news agenda and decisions about how and why a story should be reported. The "emotional dialectic" in journalism situates reporters and editors as public intellectuals who shape the news narrative from within an ideological bubble that manifests as a belief in the innate objectivity of their position and disguises the real interests represented in the coverage they produce. The "emotional dialectic" is a product of the balance of class forces at any given historical juncture. It is a function of the economic location that journalists occupy within the capitalist production process and it shapes their political and their ideological conditioning. As members of the News Establishment, news workers—journalists, editors and producers—occupy a contradictory class location between labor and capital; this is the principal economic determinant of their "in between" status that gives rise to the ideology of Fourth Estate journalism. They are not owners of the means of production; they are wage-laborers who perform some ideological and political control functions of Capital. However, journalists are not the owners of Capital, nor are they members of the ruling class (in general). They are bound by the duality of the news commodity, but also exercise more agency than many workers due to the intellectual nature of their daily labor (Hirst 2012b). They work on ideas and therefore must be free enough to form opinions, but not so free that they wander too far from the purpose of most news, which is to "manufacture" the consent of the subordinate classes to the rule of the dominant class (Herman and Chomsky 1988). It is the contradictions inherent in the news economy that place journalists in the News Establishment, not their individual thinking.

My political economy approach, methodology and outlook can be summarized in point form as follows and each will be relevant in the following chapters.

- In a broad sense news is a commodity produced according to the rules of capital accumulation. Therefore, news workers, including journalists, subeditors, etc., are also workers in the political economy sense of being labor organized to produce and circulate surplus value and profits for the owners of the enterprise.
- Journalism is a labor process that is defined by the generalized social relations of commodity production. By analyzing the nature of journalism as "work," and the contradictory class locations occupied by news workers it is possible to develop a better critical understanding of how the emotional attitudes of news workers are formed and of the politics of journalism.

- The duality of the news commodity and the attendant emotional dialectic means that the ideological positions of news workers are necessarily contradictory. The news discourse does not always follow the "rules" of the News Establishment, and can sometimes be in opposition to the hegemonic social order.
- By the "politics of journalism" I mean the role of news workers—and the News Establishment—in the framing, construction and dissemination of ideas in the public arena. In this sense, journalists are "public intellectuals" who help shape the emotional dialectic of their time and place and to popularize or naturalize what is actually a contested interpretation of fact and history.
- As public intellectuals, journalists are subject to the ideological pressures imposed on the news by the ruling class—the News Establishment—but it is dialectical pressure, meaning there is always some level of resistance (i.e. Fourth Estate ideals).
- The emotional dialectics of news work are the product of the interplay of competing social forces, but subject to the hegemony (control) of the Establishment. This allows us therefore, to characterize the role of journalist-as-public intellectuals who play an active role in the manufacture of consent.
- The major ideological functions of the media are to normalize and disguise the true class nature of capitalist social systems; the amelioration of an ongoing crisis of legitimation surrounding "late capitalism" (Jameson 1991); and to assist the ruling class to maintain its global hegemony (Hesmondhalgh 2008).
- The hegemonic emotional attitudes in journalism today are grounded in the dialectics and contradictions of the liberal-democratic "free market" paradigm. However, this paradigm has been put under pressure at various times in its history from emergent cultural forms, such as the "new journalism" of the 1960s and perhaps even more "postmodern" forms of journalism today.
- News reporting has both explicit and implicit ideological consequences for the process of social legitimation. As we come to in chapters six and seven, it is possible that social journalism, practised independently of the news industry might challenge the hegemony of the newsroom in framing the news discourse.
- The disruption caused by the overwhelming tide of digital technologies and the pressure they have exerted over existing social relations of news production represents the biggest threat to the established (legacy) news media and to its advertising-based "free market" model. We are witnessing a period of instability in journalism and the news industry that is unprecedented.

Confusion about how to cover the fall-out from the "Brexit" referendum in the United Kingdom, and the election of Donald Trump in the USA, are typical examples of how destabilized the system has become. The Trump election has pushed the political news media in the US is into disarray; open hostilities have erupted between the more "liberal" news media (CNN, *The New York Times*, etc.) and the pro-Trump Fox News network. Similar fault lines are opening up in many national news ecospheres and across the global media landscape. The usually hidden politics of journalism are on display and subject to wide public debate as a result of this disruption to business as usual.

While there is little doubt that the business model supporting journalism is in disarray, this does not, in my view, represent a fundamental shift away from the advertising-supported model that sustained it successfully throughout the twentieth century. Instead, there has been a shift in how the model is calibrated. Aggregating an audience that can then be auctioned off to advertisers is still fundamental to media profitability. The change is that now the commercial odds are in favor of the advertisers; the cost of advertising online is a fraction of the costs in print and broadcast media. News publishers are losing out as their share of revenue from advertising sales has fallen dramatically in the past decade (Fuchs 2012). The political economy insight that explains this is the concept of audience as commodity. This idea is fundamental to understanding how the mass media operated for nearly 100 years in its print and broadcast forms, and it is crucial also to understanding how the economics of the digital media operate. The function of Facebook, Google and all commercially operational social media platforms is to aggregate and sell an audience to advertisers. In the digital media ecology, we can add to this the sale of vast amounts of highly accurate data about the audience, right down to individual members. A second insight that underlines the importance of this approach is that within the social media context audiences also "work" themselves, in an unpaid capacity to support the profits of Facebook, etc. The study and understanding of this unpaid labor aspect of social media has taken on a new significance in the context of user-generated content, which is provided free to social media platforms, but which is then monetized by them without the producers receiving any financial reward (Brown and Quan-Hasse 2012). This will be further discussed in chapter five, where it lays the foundations for an analysis of how social journalism is being operationalized inside mainstream and some alternative newsrooms.

Journalism as Business versus Journalism as a Public Good

There is a simple truism in the business of journalism: "Without robust financial returns, serious journalism is threatened—and in the current media landscape that threat seems very serious indeed" (Oldroyd 2017). If this little bit of business common sense is ignored, the profession of journalism may well end sooner, rather than later, because without the news industry there would most likely be no organized news reporting, no newsrooms to speak of. Nobody who has been paying attention to what's happening in journalism and the news business today could argue with this statement, but what about the proposition that without a functioning news media, our democracy is threatened? Is this just as true?

The answer depends very much on who you ask and how they are inclined to view what it means to have a "functioning" news media. For commentators like Rachel Oldroyd (ibid.), the link between a viable news industry and the Fourth Estate role of journalism is an unbreakable nexus: "An independent press informs, educates, scrutinizes and questions. It provides the facts that help citizens better understand their world and it holds to account those that wield the power."

But is this unbreakable nexus between *industry* and *journalism* the only way that a democratic media can be organized? This is the central concern of political economy in any discussion of news and journalism. As McChesney points out, one key feature of the news industry as currently constituted is its manifest failure to provide "something approximating democratic journalism" (McChesney 2003: 299). In addressing this failure, political economy makes an important distinction between the news media as an industry and the role of journalism in informing our democratic decision-making and in providing a watchdog over the rich and powerful.

News has a public interest function as a source of information that is meant to "animate democracy" according to ethical ideals (MEAA 1999). This ethical principle is based on an idealized notion of the "public sphere" and "public interest" is predicated on a misreading of the German communication scholar, Jürgen Habermas and his work on the bourgeois public sphere. Habermas is quite clear that in a society divided along class lines, it is the ruling class that determines the values and limits of "public opinion": "The self-interpretation of the bourgeois public sphere crystallized in the idea of 'public opinion'" (Habermas 1991: 89).

However, in an uncritical re-interpretation of Habermas, class divisions in the public sphere—between Capital and labor, for example—are ignored. A central premise of the political economy approach is not to assume that the interests of the News Establishment and the interests of a democratic public sphere are the same thing, or even closely aligned. We see this clearly present in the dual nature of the news commodity. The production and circulation of news in its commodity form is a source of profit for those who control the means of production. Maximizing this profit for shareholders is the raison d'être of the news business and if this means cost-cutting, or sacking journalists, so be it. In addition, news functions to legitimize elite narratives and a ruling class world-view. A second constraint on the purely "democratic" version of how the news media is supposed to operate is that news information is not politically neutral. Instead, the spin on news tends to favor the viewpoints of the social, political and economic elites (Keane 2013). There is a conflict—a contradiction—between shareholder values and public interest values and journalists are inevitably caught up in this process of dialectical entanglement (Patching and Hirst 2014). As we shall see in the next chapter, this duality, embedded in the very form of journalism, also plays a role in the spread of so-called "fake news." In Chapter 5, I will demonstrate that this duality, and the unstable dialectic it creates, are also at the very heart of the problems news companies are having finding a profitable method of publishing through all the chaos and disruption imposed on the industry by our reactions to the digital revolution.

The news industry is like most other industries in a capitalist economy, the economic function of news is to provide a return on investment (ROI) to capitalist investors. The famed American investor, Warren Buffett began investing in newspapers in 2012, but not because he had become a champion of American democracy in his old age, as a shrewd capitalist, he believed it would provide him with an ROI that would enrich him even further. He stood to make a cool $US 20 million on the deal (Greenslade 2012). By early 2017, Buffett had changed his mind about the newspaper business, declaring it "doomed" apart from one or two global brands, such as the *New York Times*. This should not really come as a surprise; the future for newspapers does look particularly grim, and after all, Buffett is "a billionaire known primarily for his interest in making money, not journalism" (Ingram 2017). We will return to the news business in chapter five. In the remaining pages of this chapter, I will apply insights from the analysis outlined here to media coverage of the Internet of Things (IoT). The purpose is to demonstrate the value of political economy and to illustrate how the News Establishment is, largely, enmeshed in the myths and fables of technological determinism.

News and the Internet of Things

You may have heard of the Internet of Things, it's pretty hard to avoid it these days. But do you know what the Internet of Things actually is, or what it actually does?

A working definition of the IoT is that it is billions of electronic devices, tools, gadgets and objects embedded with computer chips and sensors, such as WiFi, that allow them to be connected to the Internet. The software and network connections built into these devices allow them to collect data and then to exchange that data with other gadgets—fridges, robots, cars, and so on—or humans. These "smart" objects can also transfer data into the "cloud," the nebulous and (apparently) almost limitless space where data is stored remotely (not on your laptop, for example). We are only just beginning to grasp just how huge the IoT is likely to become; the iWatch is a good example of an early "wearable" device that begins to harness the potential of powerful computers in small objects; so-called "smart" homes is another example (IIA 2015). Link the "smart" home with the iWatch—to turn appliances on and off, for example—and you have some idea of what is possible with the IoT.

If you were to just go with the hype, you could be forgiven for thinking that the IoT is going to solve all of humanity's problems, particularly those necessary, but irritating, domestic chores like cooking, cleaning the apartment or walking the dog. According to newspaper columnist Malcolm Maiden, we arrived at our starting point for this journey—the Internet of Things—sometime around May 2016. But, Maiden also warned that the IoT could be a double-edged sword. Yep, according to its enthusiastic backers, the IoT is going to make your life, my life and our lives more efficient, simpler, happier and less crowded with the awful mundane tasks like actually taking care of personal hygiene. But, as Maiden writes, it could also be after your job.

The news media's general approach to the IoT mirrors the "Californian ideology" mentioned previously. If there's not already a robot or an app that will take care of business, then it's only a matter of time before some bright Silicon Valley type invents, builds and markets the digital solution to your quotidian dilemmas. By mid-2016, for example, driverless cars were being incessantly hyped even as their testing prior to their release on the roads and highways revealed how dangerous they could be to pedestrians. Driverless cars navigate and steer using GPS and motion sensors that govern speed and distance between the car and other objects in the environment (Maiden 2016). The driverless car is a bit like the "Holy Grail" of the IoT, so much so that rumors began circulating in August 2015 that Apple was secretly working on an autonomous vehicle project, as were tech-giant Google and the Japanese car manufacturer, Honda (News.com.au 2015). In December 2016 the rumors were given a boost when a letter was leaked which purported to show that Apple was working on the driverless car more seriously; it was even dubbed the "iCar" (Painter 2016). A May 2016 report in the *Wall Street Journal* suggested that most major car companies, ride-sharing providers like Uber and technology companies are all competing to bring driverless cars onto a road near you (Wakabayashi and MacMillan 2016). Like many over-hyped predictions, there is no certainty about when driverless cars will be commercially available. Despite numerous and heavily promoted trials of automated passenger vehicles, as of August 2018 driverless vehicles had not got past the trial stage.

The IoT is more than Jetsons' style futuristic transport; the supply chain for everything from groceries to medical procedures can be connected to the web allowing for the remote monitoring of inventory and health status. The boosters say that this will be a boon for the economy as many mundane jobs can be automated and whole factories can be managed by a handful of humans connected to a grid of machines and computers. Robot assembly lines are already here, robot doctors are diagnosing remotely, and robot journalists are not far away.

Of course, the digital reality is never as bright, shiny or covered in bling as the digital promise. As Vincent Mosco reminds us, we have to be wary of the digital sublime—the tendency to over-hype the liberating potential of digital

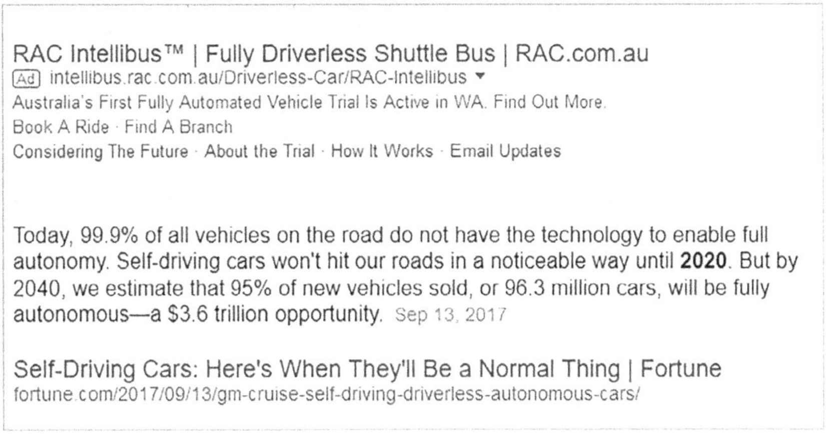
RAC Intellibus™ | Fully Driverless Shuttle Bus | RAC.com.au
Ad intellibus.rac.com.au/Driverless-Car/RAC-Intellibus
Australia's First Fully Automated Vehicle Trial Is Active in WA. Find Out More.
Book A Ride · Find A Branch
Considering The Future · About the Trial · How It Works · Email Updates

Today, 99.9% of all vehicles on the road do not have the technology to enable full autonomy. Self-driving cars won't hit our roads in a noticeable way until **2020**. But by 2040, we estimate that 95% of new vehicles sold, or 96.3 million cars, will be fully autonomous—a $3.6 trillion opportunity. Sep 13, 2017

Self-Driving Cars: Here's When They'll Be a Normal Thing | Fortune
fortune.com/2017/09/13/gm-cruise-self-driving-driverless-autonomous-cars/

FIGURE 2.2 Predictions about the Driverless Car Show a Preoccupation with Technology as Progress.

technologies and to invest them with almost magical powers of healing and upward, linear *progress*. The Internet of Things *is* progress, it *must* be. Logic alone tell us that connecting things via the web so that these things can exchange data with each other is something we couldn't do 20 years ago. We can now, and that means progress has occurred. Right? We have moved from point A (before the IoT) to point B (living with the IoT). Within the world of IT and engineering, the IoT is almost always seen as a boon to business and consumers alike; it is seen as a "promise" to revolutionize "the way we live and work," and "saving time and money" (Palettella et al. 2016). Given that reporters will often rely on such expert opinion, we should not be surprised when their optimistic and enthusiastic endorsements find their way into the news media. Often it is the positive-sounding aspects of the technology that get priority and the headlines, as this lead paragraph from an Australian news story highlights: "Technology that can track bushfires, monitor horny pandas, and order beers for the fridge is set to become available across the whole state" (Sheperd 2017).

This makes the IoT seem like a benign and progressive force for good. How could anyone possibly not agree that a technology with these mundane-sounding attributes is a good thing? The article reinforces this view, quoting a representative of the French company supplying the technology saying that only people who don't know how the IoT works would be "afraid" of it: "But those who do embrace it can see big benefits." The story is datelined "France," but there is no mention that the French supplier of the technology may have contributed to the journalist's travel from the state of South Australia to France. I did email the reporter to ask her, I did not get a response. That's progress for you!

However, progress must be about more than simply moving from A to B as if life was meant to be lived along straight and narrow lines. Progress must also be about quality of life as much as quantity. According to the World Economic Forum over 50 billion devices will be connected to the Internet by the time you are reading this book. It's likely you're reading it electronically and that you've probably downloaded it to an e-reader, iPad or tablet. Promoters of the IoT also assume that most of us will soon be connected to a 3D printer, and that we will download the software to print household objects, rather than go to a store or buy them online. However, injecting a note of realism into the debate about the IoT, the WEF also predicts that while enjoying its many benefits, we will be subject to even greater levels of surveillance. In other words, to access the so-called benefits of the IoT, we will have to trade away our privacy (WEF 2015). We have to ask if this is too high a price to pay for convenience. How much are we willing to give up in order to have our whole world connected by "ubiquitous" computing? Interestingly, when these questions are raised, they are typically framed in terms of national security, perhaps forgetting that one nation's security might be another nation's insecurity.

A good example of this is a story from late in 2017 about the use of Chinese-manufactured surveillance technology. It is an example that highlights another salient aspect of the News Establishment belief system; nationalism. "My" country is always right, even when it's wrong, is a strongly embedded ideological meme that replaces logic and intellectual curiosity when it comes to reporting world affairs. In the Chinese technology story, the threat is not framed as the surveillance itself, but rather as a scenario in which foreign actors might gain access to sensitive data.

> Simply put, we're all going to be using Chinese technology and devices as a critical component of our connected lives moving forward. How consumers, companies, and governments effectively manage that reality will have widespread implications for digital security and privacy protection.
>
> *(Lowmaster 2017)*

The headline frames China's involvement as "insidious," but does not make any negative comments about surveillance being problematic. A *Forbes* magazine article about how the IoT will play out in coming years relies entirely on a pro-business research firm to underpin several predictions, none of which address privacy or other possible concerns (Press 2017).

When discussing the IoT, we have to ask questions about the world of work. In a capitalist market economy, for most people not working means not eating, not having a place to live and not having much of a social life. But when robotics and artificial intelligence moves from science *fiction* to science *fact*, will machines replace humans in the workforce? What happens to the millions of people who work in factories or in the transport industry when their jobs are outsourced to the IoT? Economists are already telling us that today's jobs will be gone in a few years as machine intelligence replaces humans in many areas of production and distribution. We should be worried about this because it is unlikely that the productivity gains from the IoT will outstrip job losses. According to some pundits, while the IoT provides opportunities for efficiency, it could also have a downside—such as increasing unemployment. Perhaps the best we can say about the IoT is that it will be disruptive in economic, social, political and cultural terms. Like taking a trip in a driverless car, the IoT could be the start of a wild ride.

The Internet of Things is built on what we have come to know as "disruptive" technologies. These are applications or gadgets that harness digital technologies, usually in devices that are getting smaller and smaller, but more and more powerful at the same time. Our working lives are an area of intense disruption thanks to the application of robotics and artificial intelligence to tasks that were once only able to be done through human labor. Not only could driverless cars, buses and truck lead to the loss of jobs for professional drivers; jobs are disappearing in other industries too as robots and AI become more sophisticated. Some estimates suggest that up to 40 percent of the workforce of 2017 could become redundant over the next 20 to 30 years.

One highly experimental and statistical paper written in 2013 by Oxford University academics Carl Benedikt Frey and Michael Osborne predicted that it would be mainly low-wage and unskilled manual workers who might be most affected by the first waves of robots entering the workforce. However, their list of the top 10 occupations most likely to be affected over time is quite diverse and includes some surprises: telemarketers, insurance underwriters, watch repairers, accounting clerks; legal secretaries, models, estate agents, cooks and dental technicians (Frey and Osborne 2013). The authors predicted that more creative types of work would be less susceptible to automation and you might think that journalism would therefore be immune—at least for some time—but that is not the case.

There already robots doing journalism. As scary as that might sound if you're considering a career in the news industry, you need to get your head around it, it is a fact and it's happening in a surprising number of places. (You can read more about this in Chapter 12.) We will hear a lot more about the IoT in coming months and years; much of it will be celebratory and couched in terms of the benefits, rather than the problems it presents. As I've attempted to outline in this chapter, the explanation for this is partly revealed by journalists" own propensity to technological determinism and also because of the news industry's own deep connections to, and reliance on, IoT style technologies. For example, in the same week that the IoT was hyped in its news coverage, the Australian arm of News Corporation also announced a deal to gift a Google Home smart speaker device to anyone who took out a 12-month subscription to one of its print and/or online titles.

What this tells us is that the news media—particularly as it is industrially organized—has trouble dealing with the liquidity and flux of modern life, what philosopher Zygmunt Bauman (2000) calls "liquid modernity," a state of permanent revolution and social volatility that has its roots in the unstable political economy of capitalism. As media scholar Mark Deuze notes, the news media is not immune from this unsettling tendency in modern life:

> Media as social institutions do not escape the sense of accelerated, unsettling change permeating liquid modern life, and it is exactly this notion of volatile, uncertain (global and local) flux that professional journalism fails to come to terms with.
>
> *(Deuze 2008: 856)*

Bauman tell us that self-actualization, the becoming of a free individual, necessitates a first step, that of becoming an active citizen who takes responsibility and action to change the world around her or him (Bauman 2000: 40). This is a premise of this book, a starting point for our exploration of what social journalism *might* be, and our starting point for a further exploration of the failure of the news media—both as a set of institutions and as the practice of journalism—to concretely address the current volatile times with any sense of certainty as to how we should respond, or what the outcomes are likely to be for democratic citizenship.

References

Aouragh, Miriyam. 2012. "Social Media, Mediation and the Arab Revolutions." *Cognition, Communication, Co-operation* 10(2): 518–536. Accessed June 8, 2016. www.triple-c.at/index.php/tripleC/article/view/416.

Bauman, Zygmunt. 2000. *Liquid Modernity*. Cambridge: Polity Press.

Bell, Emily. 2017. "Technology Company? Publisher? The Lines Can No Longer be Blurred." *The Guardian*. April 2. Accessed June 7, 2017. www.theguardian.com/media/2017/apr/02/facebook-google-youtube-inappropriate-advertising-fake-news.

Bell, Michael M. 1995. "The Dialectic of Technology: Commentary on Warner and England." *Rural Sociology* 60(4): 625–632.

Bimber, Bruce. 1990. "Karl Marx and the Three Faces of Technological Determinism." *Social Studies of Science* 20(2): 333–351. www.jstor.org/stable/285094.

Brown, Brian A., and Anabel Quan-Hasse. 2012. "'A Workers' Inquiry 2.0': An Ethnographic Method for the Study of Produsage in Social Media Contexts." *Cognition, Communication, Co-operation* 10(2): 488–508. Accessed March 19, 2017. www.triple-c.at/index.php/tripleC/article/view/390.

Browning, Gary, and Andrew Kilmister. 2006. *Critical and Post-Critical Political Economy*. New York: Palgrave Macmillan.

Castells, Manuel. 1996. *The Rise of the Network Society*. Oxford: Blackwell.

Chandler, Daniel. 2002. "Technological or Media Determinism." Accessed July 18, 2016. 1www.aber.ac.uk/media/Documents/tecdet/tecdet.html.

Deuze, Mark. 2008. "The Changing Context of News Work: Liquid Journalism for a Monitorial Citizenry." *International Journal of Communication* 2: 848–865. doi:1932-8036/2008FEA0848.

Frey, Carl Benedict, and Michael A. Osborne. 2013. *The Future of Employment: How Susceptible are Jobs to Computerisation?* Oxford: Oxford Martin School, University of Oxford. September 17. Accessed November 29, 2016. www.oxfordmartin.ox.ac.uk/downloads/academic/The_Future_of_Employment.pdf.

Fuchs, Christian. 2010. "Alterntive Media as Critical Media." *European Journal of Social Theory* 173–192. Accessed January 12, 2018.

Fuchs, Christian. 2012. "Dallas Smythe Today—the Audience Commodity, the Digital Labour Debate, Marxist Political Economy and Critical Theory. Prolegomena to a Digital Labour Theory of Value." *Cognition, Communication, Co-operation* 10(2): 692–740. Accessed June 8, 2017. www.triple-c.at/index.php/tripleC/article/view/443.

Fuchs, Christian, and Vincent Mosco. 2012. "Introduction: Marx is Back—The Importance of Marxist Theory and Research for Critical Communication Studies Today." *Cognition, Communication, Co-operation* 10(2): 127–140. Accessed March 19, 2017. www.triple-c.at/index.php/tripleC/article/view/421.

George, Pleios. 2012. "Communication and Symbolic Capitalism. Rethinking Marxist Communication Theory in the Light of the Information Society." *Cognition, Communication, Co-operation* 10(2): 230–252. Accessed March 19, 2017. www.triple-c.at/index.php/tripleC/article/view/376.

Greenslade, Roy. 2012. "The Real Reasons for Warren Buffett's Newspaper Deals." *The Guardian*. May 21. Accessed July 12, 2016. www.theguardian.com/media/greenslade/2012/may/21/warrenbuffett-newspapers.

Habermas, Jürgen. 1991. *The Structural Transformation of the Public Sphere: An Enquiry into a Category of Bourgeois Society*. Translated by Thomas Burger and Frederick Lawrence. Boston, MA: MIT Press.

Heilbroner, Robert. 1998. "Technological Determinism Revisited." In *Does Technology Drive History? The Dilemma of Technological Determinism*, by Leo Marx and Merritt Roe Smith, 67–78. Boston, MA: MIT Press.

Herman, Edward, and Noam Chomsky. 1988. *Manufacturing Consent: The Political Economy of the Mass Media*. New York: Random House.

Hesmondhalgh, David. 2008. "Neoliberalism, Imperialism and the Media." In *The Media and Social Theory*, by David Toynbee, Jason Hesmondhalgh, 95–111. Abingdon: Routledge.

Hirst, Martin. 2011. *News 2.0: Can Journalism Survive the Internet?* Crows Nest, NSW: Allen and Unwin.

Hirst, Martin. 2012a. "One Tweet Does Not a Revolution Make: Technological Determinism, Media and Social Change." *Global Media Journal* 6(2). Accessed July 15, 2016. www.hca.westernsydney.edu.au/gmjau/archive/v6_2012_2/martin_hirst_RA.html.

Hirst, Martin. 2012b. "The Cultural Politics of Journalism: Quotidian Intellectuals and the Power of Media Capital." In *Scooped: The Politics and Power of Journalism in Aotearoa, New Zealand*, edited by Martin Hirst and Sean, Rupar, Verica Phelan, 48–64. Auckland: AUT Media.

Hirst, Martin, and John Harrison. 2007. *Communication and New Media: From Broadcast to Narrowcast*. Melbourne: Oxford University Press.

Hutton, Will. 2017. "Are We Finally Reacting to the Disruptive Supremacy of Facebook and Google?" *The Guardian*. March 26. Accessed June 7, 2017. www.theguardian. com/commentisfree/2017/mar/26/finally-reacting-disruptive-supremacy-of-face book-and-google.

IIA. 2015. *The Internet of Things: Opportunities and Applications across Industries*. International Institute for Analytics. Accessed November 29, 2016. www.sas.com/content/dam/ SAS/en_us/doc/research2/iia-internet-of-things-108110.pdf.

Ingram, Mathew. 2017. "Warren Buffett Says Most Newspapers, Including His Own, Are Doomed." *Fortune*. February 28. Accessed November 8, 2017. http://fortune.com/ 2017/02/28/buffett-newspapers-doomed/.

Jameson, Frederic. 1991. *Postmodernism, or the Cultural Logic of Late Capitalism*. Durham, NC: Duke University Press.

Keane, John. 2013. *Democracy and Media Decadence*. Cambridge: Cambridge University Press.

Klikauer, Thomas. 2016. "Reflections on Phishing for Phools: The Economics of Manipulation and Deception." *Cognition, Communication, Co-operation* 14(1): 260–264. Accessed March 15, 2017. www.triple-c.at/index.php/tripleC/article/view/751.

Lindgren, Simon. 2013. "The Potential and Limitations of Twitter Activism: Mapping the 2011 Libyan Uprising." *Cognition, Communication, Co-operation* 11(1): 207–220. Accessed July 14, 2016. www.triple-c.at/index.php/tripleC/article/view/475.

Lowmaster, Kaelyn. 2017. "China's Insidious Surveillance Army: The Internet of Things." *The Hill*. November 21. Accessed November 23, 2017. http://thehill. com/opinion/cybersecurity/361300-chinas-insidious-surveillance-army-the-internet-of-things.

Mager, Astrid. 2014. "Defining Algorithmic Ideology: Using Ideology Critique to Scrutinize Corporate Search Engines." *Cognition, Communication, Co-operation* 12(1): 28–39. Accessed November 23, 2017. www.triple-c.at/index.php/tripleC/article/ view/439.

Maiden, Malcolm. 2016. "The Internet of Things: it's arrived and it's eyeing your job." *The Age*. Melbourne. May 21. Accessed May 21, 2016. www.smh.com.au/business/ innovation/the-internet-of-things-its-finally-arrived-and-its-eyeing-your-job-20160520-gozz1f.html.

Marx, Karl. 1852. *The Eighteenth Brumaire of Louis Bonaparte*. Accessed February 21, 2017. www.marxists.org/archive/marx/works/1852/18th-brumaire/ch01.htm.

Marx, Leo, and Merritt Roe Smith. 1998. *Does Technology Drive History? The Dilemma of Technological Determinism*, ix–xv. Boston, MA: MIT Press.

McChesney, Robert. 2003. "The Problem of Journalism: A Political Economy Contribution to an Explanation of the Crisis in Contemporary US Journalism." *Journalism Studies* 4(3): 299–329. doi:10.1080/1461670032000099688.

MEAA. 1999. *MEAA Journalist Code of Ethics: Media, Entertainment and Arts Alliance*. Sydney: MEAA. Accessed November 29, 2016. www.meaa.org/meaa-media/code-of-ethics/.

Mosco, Vincent. 2005. *The Digital Sublime: Myth, Power and Cyberspace*. Boston, MA: MIT Press.

Murdock, Graham, and Peter Golding. 1973. "For a Political Economy of Mass Communications." *The Socialist Register* 10: 205–234.

News.com.au. 2015. "Apple Rumoured to be Showing Interest in Car Testing Facility." News.com.au. August 17. Accessed December 13, 2016. www.news.com.au/technol

ogy/innovation/motoring/apple-rumoured-to-be-showing-interest-in-car-testing-facility/news-story/8751ca2b8923d1e9ff113651414c31c1.

Oldroyd, Rachel. 2017. "Foundations and the Foundation of a New Way of Funding Journalism." Journalism.co.uk. January 4. Accessed January 5, 2017. www.journalism.co.uk/news/foundations-and-the-foundation-of-a-new-way-of-funding-journalism/s2/a697598/.

Örnerbring, Henrik. 2010. "Technology and Journalism-as-Labour: Historical Perspectives." *Journalism* 11(1): 57–74. doi:10.1177/1464884909350644.

Painter, Lewis. 2016. "iCar Release Date Rumours, Features and Images." *MacWorld*. December 9. Accessed December 13, 2016. www.macworld.co.uk/news/apple/icar-apple-car-release-date-rumours-news-caros-evidence-concept-images-patents-december-update-2016-3425394/.

Palettella, Rita, Mischa Dohler, Alfredo Greico, Gianluca Rizzo, Johan Torsner, Thomas Engel and Latif Ladid. 2016. "Internet of Things in the 5G Era: Enablers, Architecture and Business Models." *IEEE Journal on Selected Areas in Communications* 34(3): 1–17. doi:10.1109/JSAC.2016.2525418.

Patching, Roger, and Martin Hirst. 2014. *Journalism Ethics: Arguments and Cases for the Twenty-First Century*. Abingdon: Routledge.

Press, Gil. 2017. "10 Predictions For The Internet Of Things (IoT) In 2018." Forbes. November 9. Accessed November 23, 2017. www.forbes.com/sites/gilpress/2017/11/09/10-predictions-for-the-internet-of-things-iot-in-2018/#2780ab4735e7.

Rothstein, Adam. 2015. *Drone*. New York: Bloomsbury Academic.

Schultz, Brad, and Mary Lou Sheffer. 2010. "An Exploratory Study of How Twitter Is Affecting Sports Journalism." *International Journal of Sport Communication* 3: 226–239.

Sheperd, Tory. 2017. "The Internet of Things Coming to South Australia after French Firm Sigfox Makes Deal with State Government." *The Daily Telegraph*. November 21. Accessed November 23, 2017. www.dailytelegraph.com.au/news/the-internet-of-things-coming-to-south-australia-after-french-firm-sigfox-makes-deal-with-state-government/news-story/491c667a631824eae11e5f8450c86e56.

Spyridou, Lia-Paschalia, Maria Matsiola, Andreas Veglis, George Kalliris and Charalambos Dimoulas. 2013. "Journalism in a State of Flux: Journalists as Agents of Technology Innovation and Emerging News Practices." *International Communications Gazette* 75(1): 76–98. doi:10.1177/1748048512461763.

Steensen, Steen. 2011. "Online Journalism and the Promises of New Technology: A Critical Review and Look Ahead." *Journalism Studies* 12(3): 311–327. doi:10.1080/1461670X.2010.501151.

Ursell, Gillian D. M. 2001. "Dumbing Down or Shaping Up? New Technologies, New Media, New Journalism." *Journalism* 2(2): 175–196.

Wakabayashi, Daisuke, and Douglas MacMillan. 2016. "Apple's Latest $1 Billion Bet Is on the Future of Cars." *The Wall Street Journal*. May 14. Accessed December 13, 2016. www.wsj.com/articles/apples-1-billion-didi-investment-revs-up-autonomous-car-push-1463154162.

Wasko, Janet, Graham Murdock and Helen Sousa. 2011. "The Political Economy of Communications: Core Concerns and Issues." In *The Handbook of Political Economy of Communications*, by Janet Wasko, Graham Murdock and Helen Sousa, 1–10. Oxford: Wiley-Blackwell.

Webb, Rick. 2017. "My Internet Mea Culpa." NewCo Shift. December 27. Accessed January 2, 2018. https://shift.newco.co/my-internet-mea-culpa-f3ba77ac3eed.

WEF. 2015. *Deep Shift: Technology, Tipping Points and Societal Impacts*. Geneva: World Economic Forum. Accessed November 29, 2016. www3.weforum.org/docs/WEF_GAC15_Technological_Tipping_Points_report_2015.pdf.

Wittel, Andreas. 2012. "Digital Marx: Toward a Political Economy of Distributed Media." *Cognition, Communication, Co-operation* 10(2): 313–333. Accessed March 27, 2017. www.triple-c.at/index.php/tripleC/article/view/379.

3

JOURNALISM IN A "POST-TRUTH" WORLD

A "Post-Truth" World?

Just a week after reality TV "star" and self-described "billionaire" Donald J. Trump unexpectedly won the 2016 United States Presidential election on November 9, Oxford Dictionaries announced that "post-truth" was "word of the year for 2016." In a media release issued on November 16, the president of Oxford Dictionaries, Casper Grathwohl, said that the choice of "post-truth" was "fuelled by the rise of social media as a news source and a growing distrust of facts offered up by the establishment." Mr Grathwohl added that "*post-truth* as a concept has been finding its linguistic footing for some time." For good measure, he then added: "I wouldn't be surprised if *post-truth* becomes one of the defining words of our time" (Oxford Dictionaries 2016).

The timing of Oxford Dictionaries' release of the word of the year was not contingent on Donald Trump being president-elect (at the time) of the United States. It makes sense to release the announcement towards the end of the year, rather than, say, in March. However, the company press release makes a reference to Trump: "We first saw the frequency [of 'post-truth' being used in the media] really spike this year in June with buzz over the Brexit vote and again in July when Donald Trump secured the Republican presidential nomination," Mr Grathwohl said. He then noted that since "post-truth" has come into the media lexicon, "usage of the term hasn't shown any signs of slowing down" (ibid.).

One now commonplace feature of a "post-truth" environment is so-called "fake news," but what, really, is it? Today, "fake news" has spread to all parts of the media landscape. In fact, some political operators, like the Republican Governors' Association in the USA, have adopted the false news approach as their default position. The RGA launched a highly partisan "news" website called *Free Telegraph*, designed to make readers think it is a genuine breaking news site (Holloway 2017). So today we have to ponder what it means to live in a world where, for some people and under some circumstances, *truth itself has become irrelevant.* If you're reading this book because you have an interest in navigating the world of social journalism, or perhaps of one day being a social journalist, then a time in which truth becomes meaningless might present some challenges. It certainly raises the very difficult question: *If truth is now irrelevant, what is the point of journalism and journalists?*

The concept of "truth" is central to the mission and values of journalism; particularly for the Fourth Estate elements of the News Establishment. Audiences must also be able to rely on the veracity of information circulating in either news channels or via social media. If what journalists report is not the "truth," then what is the point? How can we be expected to navigate the complexities of politics—such as a presidential or parliamentary election—if the news we are reading is "post-truth"? Does it mean that as journalists we can write whatever we like? Or, that if we write something that is not true when it's written that it somehow becomes the truth, or at least *a version of* the truth when it is published? Perhaps not, but it does mean that as consumers of news we have to be alert to the possibility that the news we are seeing, hearing or reading may not be a true representation of the world. Many of us struggle with the post-modernist notion that "truth" can somehow be relative, or that differing versions of an event can somehow compete to be "true," or somehow all be "true" at the same time. It defies both logic and the laws of physics. As management theorist Professor Bill McKelvey wrote about postmodern theories of truth, history and science: a "flagrant disregard of justification logic leaves their belief generation little different from that of witchdoctors" (McKelvey 2002: 23). In a sense, we've always had this problem, so "post-truth" journalism is nothing new on one level. The notorious supermarket checkout titles, like *National Inquirer* and the *Daily Star*, have thrived on the publication of fake news, some of it so outrageous it is hard to conceive that anyone reading it would think it anything other than a farrago of lies and nonsense—think "Elvis is alive and living on Mars" as a headline.

However, we don't even need to go to the extreme of the *Daily Star* to find versions of "fake news," there has always been bias in journalism; right from the very first attempts at transmitting news from one person to another. There are several reasons why the reported truth may vary from a wholly accurate rendering of the actual event being reported on. Photographs, or audio and video recording are technological attempts to deal with the problem of truth in journalistic accounts. However, history shows us that sound and images (still and moving) can be doctored or edited in a way that conceals reality; or in a way that presents a skewed, or even totally false, picture of what happened. The latest iteration of this is likely to make the current fake news problem seem

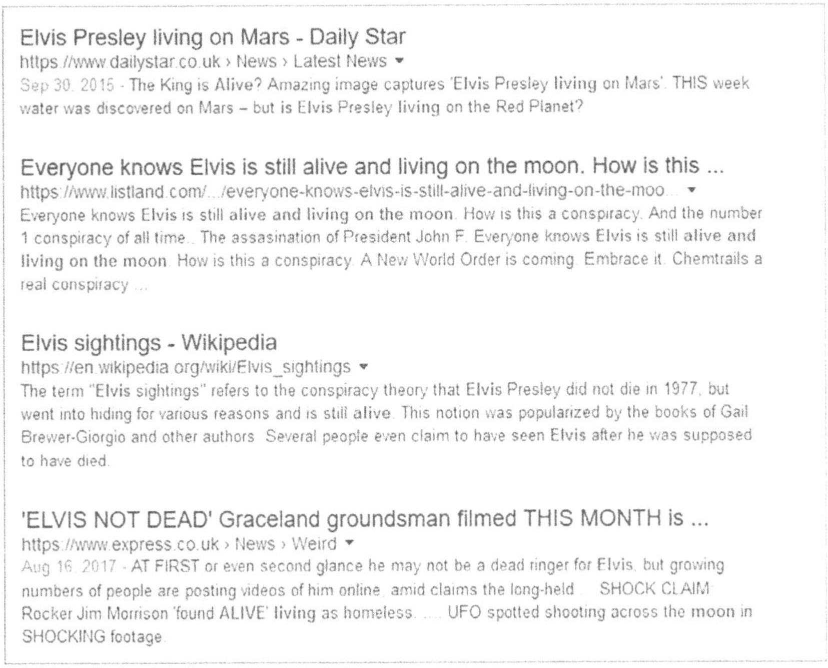

Elvis Presley living on Mars - Daily Star
https://www.dailystar.co.uk › News › Latest News ▾
Sep 30, 2015 - The King is Alive? Amazing image captures 'Elvis Presley living on Mars'. THIS week
water was discovered on Mars – but is Elvis Presley living on the Red Planet?

Everyone knows Elvis is still alive and living on the moon. How is this ...
https://www.listland.com/.../everyone-knows-elvis-is-still-alive-and-living-on-the-moo... ▾
Everyone knows Elvis is still alive and living on the moon. How is this a conspiracy. And the number
1 conspiracy of all time... The assasination of President John F. Everyone knows Elvis is still alive and
living on the moon. How is this a conspiracy. A New World Order is coming. Embrace it. Chemtrails a
real conspiracy ...

Elvis sightings - Wikipedia
https://en.wikipedia.org/wiki/Elvis_sightings ▾
The term "Elvis sightings" refers to the conspiracy theory that Elvis Presley did not die in 1977, but
went into hiding for various reasons and is still alive. This notion was popularized by the books of Gail
Brewer-Giorgio and other authors. Several people even claim to have seen Elvis after he was supposed
to have died.

'ELVIS NOT DEAD' Graceland groundsman filmed THIS MONTH is ...
https://www.express.co.uk › News › Weird ▾
Aug 16, 2017 - AT FIRST or even second glance he may not be a dead ringer for Elvis, but growing
numbers of people are posting videos of him online, amid claims the long-held   SHOCK CLAIM
Rocker Jim Morrison 'found ALIVE' living as homeless. .... UFO spotted shooting across the moon in
SHOCKING footage.

FIGURE 3.1   Elvis Living on Mars, Says *Daily Star.*

trivial by comparison. A University of Washington research team has used artificial intelligence (AI) to create a very realistic and almost undetectable way of digitally manipulating audio and video to simulate real motion and speech. In July 2017 the team unveiled a video of Barack Obama speaking, but it was a digital recreation, not the video recorded when Obama actually spoke. According the news reports, the technique seems fairly simple: "The realistic results put words in Obama's mouth by converting audio sounds into mouth movements and blending them onto an existing video of speech" (McGoogan 2017). Of course, there is more to it than that, but it is clear that the technology could be used to create very misleading videos that might—no, they will—find their way into a news broadcast or viral meme very soon.

A further difficult problem that has plagued journalism from the very beginning of time is that eye-witness reports are notoriously unreliable. Two people witnessing the same event may later have totally different recollections of what they saw. The problem with eye-witnesses is that memory is fallible. Memories are constructed and reconstructed in the brain, they are not just lodged at the time they are created. Over time memories can fade and the recreation of them can involve certain aspects of the memory being altered—often subconsciously, but sometimes due to the influence of third parties and the power of suggestion (Arkowitz and Lilienfeld 2010). This means that reporters have to check the facts and seek some form of verification—usually by asking more than one or two witnesses about what they think they saw. Cross-checking, or the process of "triangulation" of the facts involving three or more reliable sources can help to ensure a reasonably accurate version of the truth is presented in reportage. However, as we will examine in the chapter on the new ethical standards for verification, we have to keep in mind that this is not an infallible process that guarantees "the truth, the whole truth, and nothing but the truth."

The *Oxford English Dictionary* has offered up a definition of "post-truth" that makes it clear that feelings and emotions play a part in determining what we believe—what we hold to be the truth:

> post-truth *adjective*
> Relating to or denoting circumstances in which objective facts are less influential in shaping public opinion than appeals to emotion and personal belief.
>
> (*Oxford Dictionaries 2016*)

Is there any wonder that we have a democracy deficit when we can't even agree on basic facts? Never in modern times has functional media literacy been more important. In a helpful brief essay that accompanies the Oxford Dictionaries announcement of the 2016 word of the year, British journalist Neil Midgley offers a few more insights into what "post-truth" actually means. He points out that it is very close to the made-up word "truthiness" invented by American comedian Steve Colbert. "Truthiness" was Oxford Dictionary word of the year in 2005. So, the definition of "truthiness" is also important to our discussion: "the quality of seeming or being felt to be true, even if not necessarily true" (Midgley 2016). Colbert's use of "truthiness" in his comedy —he played a very conservative news host to satirize American conservatism— related to statements from politicians and other public figures that were designed to persuade people about an issue, but not necessarily by telling the truth. It was a way for Colbert to make clear to his audience that the statements he was questioning were perhaps a *version of the truth*, not *the truth*.

So "truthiness" in Colbert's satirical use is related to another word used in political discourse to denote that the version of the story being presented is painted in a light favorable to one particular side. This word is "spin" and it is very common to hear that a politician or a journalist is "spinning" a story a particular way in order to deliver a particular message. Spinning a story is a slippery slope to "truthiness" and, ultimately, to "post-truth" politics. From "spin" we get "spin doctors" and "spin room." The *Oxford English Dictionary* defines spin in this context as "the presentation of information in a particular way; a slant, especially a favourable one" and the term "spin doctor"—meaning someone adept at spinning a story to suit their agenda—has been around for at least 30 years, but it really didn't become common until the late 1990s (Wick 2015).

Spin doctors are the architects of spin. They are the officials or public relations operatives who help candidates, politicians or companies to work out which particular line is going to be most beneficial to them or cause the least amount of damage when used publicly. The "spin room" is usually a place where media briefings are held—typically following a major political speech or announcement—where the designated spin doctors, or "surrogates" in presidential election terminology, talk at greater length with journalists to give them more detailed and nuanced versions of the spin they want on the event or issue.

You can see that with all this spin and truthiness going on, and when you add in a reporter's own bias, sometimes the truth can be hard to come by. This is made all the more difficult in the "post-truth" world when "spin" and "truthiness" combine to create an even more difficult to detect category, so-called "fake news." We will return to the issue of bias towards the end of this chapter, but for now we need to explore the "fake news" phenomenon that came to prominence throughout 2017.

Truthiness, Post-Truth and Fake News

2017 ended the same way it began, with consumers of journalism unable to easily tell "real" news from "fake." The problem was not just that so-called "fake news" had saturated our social media feeds, we were also confronted with everyone—from left to right on the political spectrum—accusing the mainstream media of publishing "fake" news too. Supporters of Donald Trump, who was inaugurated as the 45th president of the United States on January 20, 2017, accused the mainstream media, but in particular the *New York Times* and *Washington Post* in print, MSNBC and CNN in broadcast news of an ever-present bias against their president. On the other hand, respected independent websites, such as *The Intercept*—while not supporting Trump—accused mainstream outlets of promoting false pro-Clinton stories without foundation. For his part, Donald Trump seemed to take great delight in the term "fake news," even ludicrously claiming at one point that he invented the term; a claim the *Los Angeles Times* debunked as "fake news about fake news" (Schaub 2017).

One confusing story, which began late in 2016 and came to dominate the American news agenda throughout 2017 and 2018, was an allegation that Russian hackers, backed by the Putin government, had interfered in the US Presidential election to the benefit of Donald Trump and the detriment of his Democratic opponent Hillary Clinton. The accusation, carried prominently in stories leaked to the *New York Times* by un-named government sources, was that cyber-attacks on the Democratic Party's national organization could be directly linked to hackers operating with the help of Russian spy agencies. Reports by the CIA and the Department of Homeland Security were cited as sources by the *NYT*. However, there was no "smoking gun" and officials admitted that the allegation of Russian government involvement was their best guess, not a certainty. Cyber-security experts were always skeptical about allegations of Russian government interference in the election while acknowledging that hacking did occur. Writing for *Medium*, cyber-security analyst Trent Lapinski wrote that the claims were not backed by any hard evidence or sources: "What has been released so far is entirely circumstantial, and if anything is evidence that the US Government does not have the proof required to make a strong enough case against Russia or anyone else" (Lapinski 2016).[1]

In January 2017, the *Washington Post* made an additional claim in relation to Russian hacking—that a malicious virus (malware) linked to the alleged election hacking had also been found on a computer linked to the Vermont power grid. This story was disturbing and indicated that the Russian hacking campaign—if that's what it was—went further than political parties and could be targeting vulnerable electricity infrastructure. The *WaPo* story began with this alarming claim: "A code associated with the Russian hacking operation dubbed Grizzly Steppe by the Obama administration has been detected within the system of a Vermont utility, according to US officials."

However, within 48 hours the *WaPo* story was discredited. The virus was on a laptop that had not been connected to the grid and could therefore pose no threat. As Glenn Greenwald pointed out for *The Intercept*, this was another piece of "fake" news spread by the *Washington Post* without the proper journalistic checks and placing too much trust in officials with an agenda to push. The truth was "undramatic and banal," Greenwald wrote, but it served a purpose, to further promote the idea that Russia was somehow undermining American democracy through coordinated cyber-attacks (Greenwald 2017). As it turned out, this was just the beginning of the "fake news" saga in 2017. As the year progressed and a series of inquiries probed allegations of Russian interference in the 2016 election, President Trump attempted to deflect accusations of collusion between his campaign and Russian agents by claiming that the whole episode was a case of manufactured "fake news." However, by the end of the year Twitter, Google and Facebook had to face tough questions about how their algorithms had promoted fake news—and possibly Russian propaganda—during the 2016 election cycle and how this might have benefited now President Trump. For example, in October 2017, it was confirmed Russian sources funded thousands of provocative campaign advertisements that were shared millions of times on Facebook (Wagner 2017). In early 2018 information began to emerge about the extent of Russian penetration of Twitter using mainly robotic fake accounts to promote pro-Trump and anti-Clinton messages during the 2016 election. Twitter launched a "purge" of fake and "bot" activity on its platform, taking down hundreds of thousands of accounts (Lorenz 2018).

FIGURE 3.2   Three Tweets in 48 Hours from Donald Trump, Each Accusing the Media of Promoting Fake News about Him.

"Fake news" is not just about the American election; it is generally getting harder and harder for consumers of news and news-like information to discern fact from fiction; the real from the unreal; and truth from deception, As consumers, we are faced with the difficulty of having to work out if a news item our friend has posted into our Facebook timeline, or shared via Twitter, is believable or not. Our friend might be a trustworthy person who only has good intentions, but what if they've been fooled? Fakes are getting harder to unmask and when the stakes are high—as in, for example an American Presidential election—some people might go to any length to pass off a fake news report as the truth.

Did "Fake News" Win the White House for Donald Trump?

We may never know for sure if a campaign of false news stories promoted in the conservative media and via social channels helped Trump's campaign. What we can say is that plenty of examples of "fake news" surfaced during and just after the 2016 Presidential election. Social media and social journalists were important sources of political information about both candidates, but sometimes the reports they carried or created were more confusing than helpful. It turns out, some of it was designed to be misleading.

One writer and marketer of fake news stories actually claimed in a *Washington Post* interview that he helped put Donald Trump in the White House. It seems like an incredible claim, and it's certainly hard to prove or disprove, but the fact that one person can make such a claim shows just how widespread the problem of "fake" news has become. Paul Horner was a serial hoaxer who claimed to have made a very good living from writing and publishing fake news on his website *National Report*. In a 2016 interview with *WaPo*'s digital culture critic, Caitlin Dewey, Horner, who said he was the founder and chief reporter for *National Report*, said he believed Donald Trump was president "because of me."

The *National Report* was a satirical website, but it looked convincingly like a respectable news outlet, even though headlines like "President-elect Trump asks that all his intelligence briefings have pictures," or "Trump to nominate Chris Christie to Supreme Food Court" are hard to take seriously. However, some of Horner's faked election news items were picked up by other news outlets and shared millions of times via social media. Many of them ended up on Facebook and it was this that attracted the most intense scrutiny from investigators

GREATEST HITS

Trump to Nominate Chris Christie to Supreme Food Court

1 year ago | 1 comment

TRUMP TOWER – President-Elect Donald J. Trump has reportedly assured NJ Governor Chris Christie that, despite recent reports, he has not been banished [...]

Man Shouts 'Allahu Akbar!' Before Photobomb

1 year ago | 1 comment

Amsterdam, Netherlands – According to Dutch police, a crazed man detonated a devastating photobomb on an unsuspecting newlywed couple visiting [...]

Area Mall Offering 10% Discount to Non-Active Shooters

1 year ago | 2 comments

Appleton, WI – The Fox Valley Mall has come under fire (pun intended) for an ad placed in Sunday's Press Gazette newspaper offering a mall-wide [...]

FIGURE 3.3 Classic Headlines from *National Report*.

probing the "collusion" story. In September 2016 Paul Horner died after an accidental drug overdose (White 2017). The real issue is why were so many of Horner's stories picked up by more serious media outlets and not properly fact-checked before republication? Horner said he got away with it because Trump's supporters were prepared to believe his anti-Clinton stories and "don't fact-check anything—they'll post everything, believe anything" (Dewey 2016). It is difficult to know if the *National Report* website is still active or only archival; when I checked in early 2018 many stories were months-old and it did not appear that much content had been posted since late in 2017. I emailed the site's listed contact person for clarification, but at time of publication had not received a response. After the election, Facebook and other social media companies came under fire from some critics for allowing the fake news about the election to be posted and promoted intensely. Some fake stories were satirical, like those posted by Horner, but some had a more malicious intent, and some were generated from tweets by Trump himself, including a story that news outlets were ignoring information damaging to his opponent, Hillary Clinton.

The efforts of Paul Horner and other hoaxers prompted one prominent commentator, CNN's media editor, Brian Stelter, to describe the amount of fake news stories about the election as a "plague" and to advise everyone to "triple check before you share" (Stelter 2016). Others went even further and accused Trump's supporters on the far right of American politics of deliberately seeding false news stories into social media. A few days after the election, pop culture writer Hannah Jane Parkinson suggested in *The Guardian*, that social media providers and technology companies were powerless to stop fake news from being planted on and shared from their sites. Parkinson wrote that the "'alt-right' (aka the far right) ensnared the electorate" by planting false stories on social media. She also noted that Google, Facebook and Twitter "seem unwilling to admit there's a problem" (Parkinson 2016). However, the tech giants were forced to address these allegations when it became clear during 2017 that the issue would not go away and that their failure to respond to criticism was damaging their brand image. By the middle of 2017 both Google and Facebook had announced a new protocol for fact-checking news items that would use both algorithms and human fact-checkers, but critics argued it was too little, too late (Leong 2017). By the end of the year both companies had faced inquiries in the USA, Germany and Australia, among other nations, in which they were forensically cross-examined by politicians and pressed to fix the problems quickly. The German government even threatened to introduce punitive fines if they did not clean up their act. At the heart of these concerns was a sentiment that Russia had played a role in American politics to subvert the democratic process. True, or not, it is an alarming accusation with overtones of Cold War paranoia.

Did Russia Hack the 2016 Presidential Election?

The most damning allegations of interference in the 2016 Presidential election cycle were directed at the Russian government and President Vladimir Putin. One cybersecurity company claimed it had evidence that Russian government agents had been actively soliciting and planting fake news items to help the Trump campaign (Strohm 2016). The claim that Russia "weaponized" social media and fake news reports is hard to prove or disprove and the company making the claim, FireEye Inc, has a commercial interest in promoting such claims. However, they were widely reported at the time. FireEye Inc manufactures cybersecurity hardware and software and has an interest in generating sales leads via such alarming stories. The Pulitzer Prize-winning website *Politifact* claimed that its investigation was not able to find conclusive evidence of Russian government involvement in vote-hacking or the publication of fake news. *Politifact* was able to confirm that some Russian news agencies did publish false stories about the election that were effectively pro-Trump (Carroll 2016); but this is hardly a smoking gun.

The FBI began examining alleged Russian meddling in the 2016 election after it was revealed in October that Russian expertise may have been behind the hacking of Democratic National Committee (DNC) servers which resulted in Wikileaks releasing thousands of emails, some of which were damaging to Clinton's campaign. By the end of 2016, the allegations surrounding Russian interference in the Presidential election were dominating the news cycle, and this continued well into 2018, too. Trump and his supporters dismissed the rumors and a proposed Congressional investigation of the allegations as the complaints of "bitter" Clinton supporters (Viebeck 2016). The interference story overshadowed the Trump White House all the way through 2017 and into 2018 as well. Several Trump associates, including serving and former White House employees, found themselves at the center of a scandal that, it seems, was not going to go away. At the heart of the allegations of Russian interference, from the beginning, was a top-secret intelligence briefing from the CIA that was leaked to the *Washington Post* soon after the election. According to the *WaPo* report, not only did Russians promote pro-Trump fake news items, they also released stolen and hacked emails damaging to the Clinton campaign with the express aim of helping Trump (Entous, Nakashima and Miller 2016). A second leak to the *New York Times* also asserted that Russian hackers also broke into Republican databases to "disrupt" and "discredit" the election campaign (Sanger and Scott 2016). However, respected investigative journalist, Glenn Greenwald, argued that these leaks were themselves a type of fake news because the sources for the claims of systemic Russian interference remained anonymous and, therefore, beyond public scrutiny. Greenwald went further than this, accusing sections of the American news media of being uncritical and "Lost partisans" dismayed at the Trump victory and looking for any excuse to claim the result as tainted (Greenwald 2016). Greenwald is right—up to a point—but his critique of the US news media's pro-Hillary blind spots does not, in my view, take away from the substantial circumstantial evidence of Russian meddling in US politics, beginning in 2015 and extending through the election cycle.

In January 2017 US the intelligence community issued a report which concluded that Russian agents had been involved in election interference. The FBI inquiry was initially led by director James Comey, whom Trump fired under unusual circumstances. In May 2017 Special Counsel Robert Mueller took over the investigation, which he was still running in August 2018, despite persistent rumors that President Trump wanted to fire him too (Price 2017). The conservative media attempted to discredit Mueller, but by the end of 2017 several of Trump's senior aides and former administration officials had been charged with offences uncovered by the investigation (Manchester 2017). Throughout 2017 President Trump continuously denied any collusion between his campaign and Russian agents, he dedicated dozens of tweets to the issue and made the claim in his many campaign-style rallies. However, this did not stop the fact-checking outfit, *Politifact* from calling Trump's denials the "lie of the year" for 2017.

Politifact's Angie Drobnic Holan (2017) wrote that there was a "mountain of evidence" to support credible assertions that "Russian President Vladimir Putin ordered actions to interfere with the election,: including "cyber-theft," "propaganda against particular candidates," and efforts to "undermine public faith in

FIGURE 3.4 CNN's Brian Stelter Tweets the *Politifact* Story about "the Lie of the Year" in 2017.

the US democratic process." Drobnic Holan noted that this allegation had been consistently denied by Trump who, "continually asserts that Russia's meddling in the 2016 election is fake news, a hoax or a made-up story, even though there is widespread, bipartisan evidence to the contrary" (ibid.).

At the end of August 2018, as this manuscript was being prepared for publication, there was no clear resolution of the hacking allegations, but there was a confusing amount of evidence that appeared to confirm some Russian meddling. Four Trump associates had been charged at that point, along with 13 Russians, a UK-based lawyer and a California man also pleaded guilty to minor charges; several other senior White House staff and former staff had also been interviewed by various committees investigating the allegations of interference (Prokop 2018). However, a number of alarming stories alleging interference had also been debunked. Glenn Greenwald, of *The Intercept*, blew giant holes in the allegation that Russia had hacked into electronic voting systems in 21 states and remained a leading sceptic about some of the more outlandish claims about Russian interference. A timeline of events linked to the hacking allegations, produced by CNN (CNN Library 2017), certainly provides circumstantial evidence, including statements by Donald Trump both before and after the election. At the same time, a respected and exiled Russian journalist, Masha Gessen, convincingly argues that if there was meddling by the Kremlin, it was "ad hoc" and not seriously coordinated. There was certainly some effort to distribute disruptive propaganda during the campaign and several Russians associated with the so-called "troll factories" have admitted to their handiwork, but it is not clear how effective it was in swaying voters one way or another (Gessen 2017). Proof of its effectiveness may be almost impossible to find, but evidence that it happened has been provided.

Ironically, and perhaps as an over-reaction to the criticism it received, in early 2018 Facebook announced it would reduce the amount of commercially published news it fed into people's timelines and replace it with more "personal" content. To me, this seems like a dumbing down of Facebook that is hardly going to address the democracy deficit. Replacing news feeds with more funny cat videos and cute baby pictures might keep you moderately entertained while the world collapses around you; it certainly won't stop the collapse from happening. News publishers were understandably upset at the news, having invested heavily in producing Facebook-friendly content they now risked losing any commercial benefit from engagement with the site (Constine 2018). Only weeks after Mark Zuckerberg made this announcement, Facebook was embroiled in another scandal relating to alleged Russian "collusion" in the Trump election campaign. A shadowy global data company, Cambridge Analytica, was exposed for taking billions of bits of data about perhaps more than 50 million Facebook users and using the profile information to target voters in the 2016 election. The Cambridge Analytica CEO was also secretly recorded boasting about helping the Trump campaign, even claiming to have given the candidate his line about "Crooked Hillary":

> "We just put information into the bloodstream of the internet and then watch it grow, give it a little push every now and again over time to watch it take shape," said the executive. "And so this stuff infiltrates the online community, but with no branding, so it's unattributable, untrackable."
>
> *(Graham-Harrison and Cadwalladr 2018)*

It was also widely reported that Facebook executives knew what Cambridge Analytica was doing and were prepared to keep quiet about it until two whistleblowers leaked details about Facebook's knowledge of the massive breach of its privacy values. Chris Wylie worked for CA and provided the media with documents and statements that exposed his former employer and Facebook to serious criticism. Facebook's first response seems like a petty act of revenge—it deleted Wylie's accounts on its servers and on Instagram: "'This is the power Facebook has,' Wylie said Tuesday [March 20, 2018] during an onstage interview at the Frontline Club in London. 'They can delete you from the internet'" (Nieva 2018).

The second whistleblower was a former Facebook employee and his allegations suggest that the company was willing to allow third parties access to user data on a regular basis, in contravention of its own stated privacy regulations. Sandy was responsible for data security at Facebook in 2011–2012 and claimed he warned company executives repeatedly about problems with its approach to third party access to users' data: "My concerns were that all of the data that left Facebook servers to developers could not be monitored by Facebook, so we had no idea what developers were doing with the data" he said (Lewis 2018).

There is no doubt that Facebook took a hit over this scandal, its share price dropped when news broke, but more importantly, it is another heavy blow against the credentials of social media companies who claim to be all about protecting users' privacy and caring about open and democratic communication practices:

> The problems this story raises go beyond the Trump campaign, Cambridge Analytica, and even Facebook; they cast a shadow on the integrity of our democratic systems and expose the eroding privacy of individual citizens in democratic societies.
>
> *(Gal 2018)*

As Uri Gal pointed out, what happened in this instance was really an example of Facebook's business model in action, rather than an anomaly: Facebook is all about harvesting and monetizing user data. As a result of the revelations, a social media campaign using the hashtag #deleteFacebook was initiated by WhatsApp founder Brian Acton. The Cambridge Analytica scandal certainly added fuel to the dumpster fire of as-yet unanswered questions about the role of social media during the 2016 American presidential election.

Was Social Media the Main "Fake News" Channel?

In the aftermath of the "fake news" scandal surrounding the 2016 campaign, Facebook seemed to take the problem seriously—at least till the CA scandal broke—and it was widely reported that many of the more outrageous "alt-right" Twitter accounts were disabled soon after the election. A research director at the Tow Center for Digital Journalism, Claire Wardle, told *The Guardian* that Facebook "stumbled into the news business" and did not have "editorial frameworks and editorial guidelines" in place to deal with the deluge of news and news-like information that inundated the site during the 2016 election (Solon 2016). Facebook founder Mark Zuckerberg was criticized for initially not recognizing that there was an issue, but he backtracked after a near-revolt by some of his staff. Writing on his own Facebook page, Zuckerberg acknowledged that "identifying the "truth" is complicated" and

FIGURE 3.5 The Hashtag #deleteFacebook Rated Highly on Twitter.

pledged to restrict how fake news producers can access to the site's advertising revenue. However, as NPR's Aarti Shahani pointed out, Facebook makes money from the eyeballs it draws when fake news items are shared into people's news feed (Shahani 2016).

What these incidents and responses show quite clearly is that perhaps social media companies like Facebook and Twitter are not ready for, or equipped to handle, the rise in social journalism. But neither, it seems, are our political leaders. In his final months in office President Barak Obama weighed into the debate about the rise of fake news on the Internet and how to deal with it. Speaking at a media conference with German Chancellor, Angela Merkel, a week after the election, Mr Obama said fake news presents a problem for democracy. "If we are not serious about facts and what's true and what's not, if we can't discriminate between serious arguments and propaganda, then we have problems," the President said on his final visit to Europe before handing over to Donald Trump in January 2017. This was not President Obama's first foray into the debate about "curating" news on the Internet. In October 2016—before the fake election news story broke—Mr Obama called for the "wild, wild west" online media landscape to be tamed. "We are going to have to rebuild within this wild-wild-west-of-information flow some sort of curating function that people agree to," the President said at an innovation conference in Pittsburgh. However, the President's conservative critics were quick to jump on this idea as "Leftist" censorship and a "Goebbelsesque" attack on freedom of speech (Geller 2016).

Trump's Appropriation of "Fake News"

Since the now infamous squabble about the size of the crowds attending his January 2017 inauguration (Robertson and Farley 2017), Donald Trump has deployed "fake news" as a collective noun to label much of the American Fourth Estate. Trump uses it constantly to deride news stories and outlets he doesn't like; this extends to any news that does not accord with his narrative of achievement and fabulousness. His attacks on the *Washington Post*, the *New York Times* and the CNN network prompted some White House correspondents to boycott the annual presidential Christmas meet-and-greet in December 2017. The fact that a prominent black journalist and a gay reporter were pointedly not invited also signaled Trump's feud with the news media is likely to continue (Shugerman 2017a).

As of the time writing this chapter, the political crisis swirling around an embattled President Donald J. Trump continues to be fueled by his almost daily references to "fake news." Inside the Trump bubble "fake news" means any of the mainstream media reporting of his presidency that he doesn't like. It began with the newly installed POTUS taking issue with media coverage of his inauguration; disputing crowd estimates. Within only weeks the "fake news" narrative from the White House was being applied to any criticism of the President, the White House and Trump-appointed officials. In 2017 alone, between January 10 and November 2, Trump had called the mainstream media collectively "fake news" 146 times on Twitter and dozens of times in speeches. FactCheck.Org estimated from public records that Trump used the "fake news" slogan over 300 times in 2017 (Kiely 2018). He made repeated attacks on the *New York Times*, the *Washington Post*, and all of the major TV networks by name. In mid-2018 the President began openly refering to the news media as "the enemy of the people" in tweets and speeches. On the other hand, he praised Fox News and retweeted stories from the network constantly. After seeing how successful Trump has been at energizing his supporters through constantly claiming that bad news is "fake news," politicians from around the globe have echoed his sentiments whenever they are faced with embarrassing or damaging coverage they don't like. The US President can take some credit for increasing the global democracy deficit by giving the green light to politicians to dismiss legitimate criticism and to normalize lying as a strategy for political survival.

There is a lot to be said and more research to be conducted on the broader effects of Trump's war with the American news media across the public sphere. However, there is not much doubt about his motivations. On one side Trump is appealing to his shrinking base among American voters; there seems to be a hardcore of about 30 percent who will support him no matter what. To supporters, Trump's comments feed into their anger and distrust of the "elite" Washington media corps and they reinforce his (fake) outsider status as a new type of political leader who has promised to "drain the swamp." His angry, and at times violent rhetoric towards the media deflects attention from the simple fact that Trump has not kept his promises and that his policies, if enacted are likely to harm, not help his base. This reflects what appears to be Trump's "base only" strategy. He knows he cannot win votes among more liberally minded groups, so he focuses his propaganda efforts on his conservative base (Rosen 2017).

In a bizarre, Orwellian twist, which reflects Rosen's thinking, Trump actually made the outlandish claim that he invented the term "fake news." "The media is really, the word, one of the greatest of all terms I've come up with, is 'fake,'" Trump said during a softball interview on a Christian television network (Cillizza 2017). The parallels with "newspeak" and George Orwell's *Nineteen Eighty-four* are not without merit. Comments implying Trump—like "Big Brother"—is always right are frequently heard from Trump surrogates. Orwell's chillingly prescient book also foreshadows fake news. The hero of *1984* is Winston Smith, a journalist whose job —which he does reluctantly—is to rewrite news stories appearing in "*The Times*" whenever the previous version might contradict the propaganda of the ruling party:

> Day by day and almost minute by minute the past was brought up to date ... But actually [Winston] thought as he re-adjusted the Ministry of Plenty's figures, it was not even forgery. It was merely the substitution of one piece of nonsense for another.
>
> *(Orwell 1988 [1949]: 35)*

This is not so different from White House counsel Kellie Ann Conway invoking the idea of "alternative facts" when called on to defend claims that the January 2017 inauguration crowd had been perhaps the largest ever when it clearly was not (Fandos 2017). While the comment outraged most serious observers, it only strengthened the belief, among Trump supporters, that the Washington media elite was conspiring against him. Ironically, in late November 2017 President Trump presented a textbook example of the deployment of this category of fake news when he retweeted anti-Muslim stories promoted by a British fascist outfit known as Britain First. The content of the viral tweets is contested and most likely the videos do not actually contain what they are purported to. Trump retweeted three times material from Britain First and then his spokesperson, Sarah Huckabee Sanders, defended him by arguing that it didn't matter if the videos were fake.

> "Whether it's a real video, the threat is real," Press Secretary Sarah Huckabee Sanders told reporters. "His goal is to promote strong border security and strong national security." "I'm not talking about the nature of the video," she said. "The threat is real, what the President is talking about—the need for national security and military spending—those are very real things, there's nothing fake about that."
>
> *(Shugerman 2017b)*

Such comments might be astonishing to some, but they go largely unchallenged and certainly appear to only energize Trump's base. While Trump and his media surrogates attempted to impose their own control mechanisms over the phenomenon and concept of "fake news," analysts and commentators are now beginning to question the motivations driving the President and his surrogates to make such outrageous comments that seem to bend reality to suit their will. This represents the symbolic content of the "fake news" narrative emanating from the White House and Trump's media surrogates. The question is: Why are they doing this?

A War on Reality?

Donald Trump's obsession with the "fake media" narrative may be one of his many psychological weaknesses and a sign of psychiatric disorder (Pachelli 2017), but this is, at best, only part of the picture. Attacking the news media also serves a logical purpose for the Trump White House. By sowing the seed of doubt, through endless accusations of the media lying and distorting things to attack him, Trump is able to achieve two objectives. The first is to simply appeal to his base of rusted-on supporters who are willing to believe that he is the victim of a media-led conspiracy. The second is to muddy the water so that it is almost impossible for the media to keep track of his own lies and thereby allow Trump to reach out to his base with a narrative of his own outstanding successes. Analysis by the *Washington Post* and other media outlets confirmed that between his inauguration in January and the November 18, 2017, Trump had made verifiably false statements more than 1600 times; it jumped to over 3000 by August 2018. It is obvious that Trump's lies are mostly calculated—he may or may not believe them himself—but, as suggested in *Salon*: "Now he's using lies to keep himself from being removed from office" (Truscott 2017).

As noted, the White House has tried to control the "fake news" narrative to mobilize Trump's base against the political forces he believes are aligned to derail his presidency. According to this version of events, the president is under attack from the entrenched media and political elites who are being discomforted by Trump's efforts to "drain the swamp" in Washington DC. This is a crude, but seemingly effective, technique of propaganda that appeared to work for Trump in the first months of his presidency; but that has perhaps lost its shine, in part because of the repetition and the childish ways in which Trump throws around the term "fake news" as an accusation.

The constant criticism of journalists and news outlets by Trump and his surrogates, which began when the now disgraced Sean Spicer was running White House briefings, draws attention to concerns that the President is moving American political discourse away from the bedrock of truth into a semi-Fascist epistemology in which truth is what the President says it is and facts don't matter. Things have become so alarming in American politics, and Trump's disconnect from reality so noticeable, that the debate has become wider than the state of the President's mental health. As *New York Times* columnist Michelle Goldberg noted in an early December 2017 op-ed: "He might be delusional, or he might simply be asserting the power to blithely override truth, which is the ultimate privilege of a despot" (Goldberg 2017).

Writing in *Salon*, executive editor Andrew O'Hehir (2017), argued that "reality is losing" under Trump's endless assaults. Like many other serious and thoughtful commentators, O'Hehir believes—and it's hard to disagree—that Trump's "assault on democracy goes hand-in-glove with his assault on *truth*." There is real danger here, if truth becomes notional and contingent, it becomes harder to resist the anti-democratic agenda that Trump is pursuing. The techniques employed here, if they are a deliberate strategy from the President and his supporters, are an example of what has become known as "gaslighting," the process of deliberately disorienting and confusing someone in order to gain a psychological advantage over them. According to one popular definition, to "gaslight" is lying to someone and manipulating them emotionally in a deliberate attempt to "deceive [them] into questioning their own perception of reality" (Gibson 2017).

This leads to the third problem, a further erosion of trust among readers and viewers seeking an authentic news experience. As trust levels continue to fall, the real fakers benefit because when cynicism overtakes the audience, fabrications become almost indistinguishable from real news. More importantly, the audience begins to care even less about politics as they lose the ability to easily tell truth from falsehood. This process of disengagement creates the psychological effect that Hannah Arendt (1951: viii) describes so well in *The Origins of Totalitarianism*; when authoritarian leaders can engender deep cynicism among the public, their lies and brutalities are less likely to be challenged. As Arendt put it in the Preface to the first edition; there is a "curious contradiction" between the "avowed cynical 'realism'" of totalitarian politics and its "conspicuous distain" for reality itself. It is these psychological conditions that lead to cynicism and passivity on the part of citizens. It is perhaps not surprising that we can begin to detect this sentiment now emerging among disillusioned American voters, even those who supported Trump in 2016. A Trump voter in West Virginia, interviewed for a feature in *The Intercept*, says she has very little time for, or interest in politics, but she has also adopted some of Trump's views about the news media:

> "Every little decision, every little thing that's done in politics that's released to the public—it's made a big deal of," she says. "Even if he does something good, they portray it in a way to make it seem negative against him. Everybody's against Trump, it seems like."
>
> *(Kranitz and Speri 2017)*

At the end of 2017, Trump's gaslighting and his "war on reality" began to take a sinister turn with his allies and media surrogates, including the Fox News network, openly disparaging the FBI and suggesting that it had been captured by pro-Clinton forces and in need of dismantling. Pro-Trump lobbyist Tom Fitton used an appearance on Fox to call for the FBI to be dissolved because it had been "turned into a KGB-style operation by the Obama administration" (Schwartz 2017). The following day, Donald Trump repeated this talking point himself in a brief exchange with journalists: "It's a shame what's happened with the FBI, but we're going to rebuild the FBI. It'll be bigger and better than ever," he said in a clear signal that he was going to continue his rhetoric disparaging the agency's investigation of his alleged collusion with the Kremlin. As noted, a key plank of this gaslighting strategy is that the allegations are "fake news" being circulated in by journalists and news organizations hostile to the President. At the end of Trump's first year in the White House, even conservative commentators were calling this a "desperate effort to stave off the investigation" (Schindler 2017).

There are two possible and mutually exclusive propositions in play here: either, Trump is delusional, or he's playing a strategic long game of disinformation and chaos to entrench himself in the White House. There are even suggestions that he has adopted the Putinesque strategy of *dramaturgia*—the staging of deliberate provocations to destabilize politics in order to take advantage of the resultant confusion.

> What if all the Trumpian chaos that the "mainstream media" have come to take for granted as pugilism and vanity was part of a more cunning plan? … While Trump may not have state-controlled media at his disposal, as Putin does, to serve as 24-7 propaganda organs both domestically and abroad, his team is finding ways to shrewdly approximate Putin's capacity to shape narratives and create alternative realities.
>
> *(Mariani 2017)*

This is another theory that takes, as its start point, the Russian interference meme and builds on Trump's alleged deep ties to Putin and the Kremlin. While there is evidence of collusion between the Trump camp and Russian agents during the campaign, there is no definitive proof that Trump himself is actively cooperating with Putin. It is important that critical progressives don't get sucked into the conspiracy theories because they are, in themselves disarming.

To define "fake news" as only a Trump-related issue, or as a conspiracy to spread Russian influence in the West, does not provide a lens for examining the broader issue of truth and meaning in the public sphere. Political economy needs a broader understanding of fake news that moves beyond the normative belief in objective Fourth Estate journalism as practiced in liberal-democratic capitalism. We need a category that allows for a challenge to the idea that news in general can be taken as an objective approximation of reality, without any overt or embedded bias. This is what is generally known as the Fourth Estate view—founded on outmoded concepts of objectivity—that asserts that independent journalism in the marketplace of ideas is a necessary precondition of liberty and democracy.

From a political economy perspective, the Fourth Estate view is an ideological position that assumes the current socio-economic system is unassailable and represents the best that we can expect. The legitimacy of institutional forms of liberal-democratic journalism is assumed, but all of its in-built biases—for example, against progressive politics and the legitimacy of trade unions and workers" struggle—are never challenged. Political economy needs to approach the fake news debate with the understanding that most categories of news— particularly about politics, economics and controversial social issues (such as the Black Lives Matter movement)—are embedded with ideology that may be either deliberate and explicit, or implicit and a form of unconscious bias. This is a deep-rooted bias that creates distortions in news coverage that often go undetected. It is the bias that defines the News Establishment and its belief system predicated on commodification and the profit motive being the unassailable cornerstones of market democracies. In fact, the news industry sought to further profit from Donald Trump's demonization of the News Establishment as

FIGURE 3.6 *The New Yorker* Capitalizing on the Fake News Label.

"fake news." Throughout the first year of Trump's presidency, *The New Yorker* was not the only media organization to attempt to monetize the issue through marketing its subscription services.

The first step in dealing with the fake news problem is to have a fuller understanding of why the fake news phenomenon has gained such a strong foothold in the media, particularly online and in social channels. In the next chapter, we will explore this using the lens of political economy to look at how the growth of fake news is linked to the recent history of change and disruption in the news industry.

Note

1 As of August 2018, the investigation into alleged Russian state-sanctioned interference into the 2016 US presidential election—and the extent to which there was "collusion" with the Trump campaign—is ongoing and highly politicized. No definitive proof or conclusion is yet possible about these events, despite mounting circumstantial evidence.

References

Arendt, Hannah. 1951. *The Origins of Totalitarianism*. New York: Harcourt.
Arkowitz, Hal, and Scott O. Lilienfeld. 2010. "Why Science Tells Us Not to Rely on Eyewitness Accounts." *Scientific American*. 1 January. Accessed September 8, 2017. www.scientificamerican.com/article/do-the-eyes-have-it/.
Carroll, Lauren. 2016. "Russia and its Influence on the Presidential Election." *Politifact*. Washigton DC, December 1. Accessed December 2, 2016. www.politifact.com/truth-o-meter/article/2016/dec/01/russia-and-its-influence-presidential-election/.

Cillizza, Chris. 2017. "Donald Trump Just Claimed He Invented 'Fake News.'" *The Point*, CNN Politics. October 26. Accessed December 4, 2017. http://edition.cnn.com/2017/10/08/politics/trump-huckabee-fake/index.html.

CNN Library. 2017. "2016 Presidential Campaign Hacking Fast Facts." October 31. Accessed December 15, 2017. http://edition.cnn.com/2016/12/26/us/2016-presidential-campaign-hacking-fast-facts/index.html.

Constine, Josh. 2018. "Facebook Feed Change Sacrifices Time Spent and News Outlets for 'Well-Being'." *TechCrunch*. January 11. Accessed March 3, 2018. https://techcrunch.com/2018/01/11/facebook-time-well-spent/.

Dewey, Caitlin. 2016. "Facebook Fake-News Writer: 'I Think Donald Trump is in the White House Because of Me'." *The Washington Post*. November 17. Accessed November 18, 2016. www.washingtonpost.com/news/the-intersect/wp/2016/11/17/facebook-fake-news-writer-i-think-donald-trump-is-in-the-white-house-because-of-me/.

Drobnic Holan, Angie. 2017. "2017 Lie of the Year: Russian Election Interference is a 'Made-Up Story.'" *Politicfact*. December 12. Accessed December 13, 2017. www.politifact.com/truth-o-meter/article/2017/dec/12/2017-lie-year-russian-election-interference-made-s/.

Entous, Adam, Ellen Nakashima and Greg Miller. 2016. "Secret CIA Assessment Says Russia was Trying to Help Trump Win White House." *The Washington Post*. December 9. Accessed December 13, 2016. www.washingtonpost.com/world/national-security/obama-orders-review-of-russian-hacking-during-presidential-campaign/2016/12/09/31d6b300-be2a-11e6-94ac-3d324840106c_story.html?hpid=hp_hp-top-table-main_russiahack-745p%3Ahomepage%2Fstory&utm_term=.21.

Fandos, Nicholas. 2017. "White House Pushes 'Alternative Facts.' Here Are the Real Ones." *The New York Times*. January 22. Accessed December 2, 2017. www.nytimes.com/2017/01/22/us/politics/president-trump-inauguration-crowd-white-house.html.

Gal, Uri. 2018. "Cambridge Analytica Scandal is Not a 'Breach'. It is Facebook's Business Model in Action." *ABC News*. March 23. Accessed March 23, 2018. www.abc.net.au/news/2018-03-22/facebook-cambridge-analytica-digital-surveillance-data-privacy/9575160.

Geller, Pamela. 2016. "Obama: Internet News Needs to be 'Curated.'" *The Geller Report*. October 17. Accessed November 18, 2016. http://pamelageller.com/2016/10/obama-internet-news-needs-to-be-curated.html/.

Gessen, Masha. 2017. "Russian Interference in the 2016 Election: A Cacophony, Not a Conspiracy." *New Yorker*. November 3. Accessed December 15, 2017. www.newyorker.com/news/our-columnists/russian-interference-in-the-2016-election-a-cacophony-not-a-conspiracy.

Gibson, Caitlin. 2017. "What is 'Gaslighting'? And How Does It Relate to Donald Trump?" *The News & Observer*. January 27. Accessed April 19, 2017. www.newsobserver.com/news/politics-government/article129199504.html.

Goldberg, Michelle. 2017. "Trump Is Cracking Up." *The New York Times*. December 1. Accessed December 3, 2017. www.nytimes.com/2017/12/01/opinion/trump-is-cracking-up.html.

Graham-Harrison, Emma, and Carole Cadwalladr. 2018. "Cambridge Analytica Execs Boast of Role in Getting Donald Trump Elected." *The Guardian*. March 21. Accessed March 23, 2018.

Greenwald, Glenn. 2016. "Anonymous Leaks to the WashPost About the CIA's Russia Beliefs Are No Substitute for Evidence." *The Intercept.* December 10. Accessed December 13, 2016. https://theintercept.com/2016/12/10/anonymous-leaks-to-the-washpost-about-the-cias-russia-beliefs-are-no-substitute-for-evidence/.

Greenwald, Glenn. 2017. "Russia Hysteria Infects WashPost Again: False Story About Hacking US Electric Grid." *The Intercept.* January 1. Accessed January 3, 2017. https://theintercept.com/2016/12/31/russia-hysteria-infects-washpost-again-false-story-about-hacking-u-s-electric-grid/.

Holloway, Kali. 2017. "Republican Governors Have Created a Fake News Site Masquerading as a Legitimate Publication." *Alternet.* September 19. Accessed October 15, 2017. www.alternet.org/media/republican-governors-have-created-fake-news-site-masquerading-legitimate-publication.

Kiely, Eugene. 2018. "Trump's Phony 'Fake News' Claims." FactCheck.Org. January 16. Accessed March 9, 2018. www.factcheck.org/2018/01/trumps-phony-fake-news-claims/.

Kranitz, Stacey, and Alice Speri. 2017. "A Year in the Ohio River Valley: Hard Times in Trump Country." *The Intercept.* December 17. Accessed December 18, 2017. https://theintercept.com/2017/12/16/hard-times-in-trump-country/.

Lapinski, Trent. 2016. "Evidence of Russian Election Hacking Is Inconclusive." *Medium.* December 31. Accessed January 3, 2017. https://medium.com/@trentlapinski/evidence-of-russian-hacking-is-inconclusive-d485726b962f#.uz7x533zm.

Leong, Lewis. 2017. "Fighting Fake News: How Google, Facebook and Others Are Trying to Stop it." *Tech Radar.* May 25. Accessed November 8, 2017. www.techradar.com/news/fighting-fake-news-how-google-facebook-and-more-are-working-to-stop-it.

Lewis, Paul. 2018. "'Utterly Horrifying': Ex-Facebook Insider Says Covert Data Harvesting was Routine." *The Guardian.* March 20. Accessed March 24, 2018. www.theguardian.com/news/2018/mar/20/facebook-data-cambridge-analytica-sandy-parakilas.

Lorenz, Taylor. 2018. "Inside Twitter's Bot Purge." *The Daily Beast.* February 21. Accessed March 3, 2018. www.thedailybeast.com/inside-twitters-bot-purge.

Manchester, Julie. 2017. "Timeline: Mueller's Russia probe." *The Hill.* November 28. Accessed December 13, 2017. http://thehill.com/homenews/administration/357639-timeline-muellers-russia-probe.

Mariani, Mike. 2017. "Is Trump's Chaos Tornado a Move From the Kremlin's Playbook?" *Vanity Fair.* March 28. Accessed December 5, 2017. www.vanityfair.com/news/2017/03/is-trumps-chaos-a-move-from-the-kremlins-playbook.

McGoogan, Cara. 2017. "Scarily Convincing Fake Video Tool Puts Words in Obama's mouth." *The Telegraph.* July 12. Accessed September 7, 2017. www.telegraph.co.uk/technology/2017/07/12/scarily-convincing-fake-video-tool-puts-words-obamas-mouth/.

McKelvey, Bill. 2002. "Postmodernism in Management Theory." In *Postmodernism and Management: Pros, Cons, and Alternatives,* by Ed Locke, 1–28. Amsterdam: Elsevier.

Midgley, Neil. 2016. "Word of the Year: Post-Truth." Oxford Dictionaries. November 16. Accessed November 16, 2016. https://en.oxforddictionaries.com/word-of-the-year/word-of-the-year-2016.

Nieva, Richard. 2018. "Whistleblower Wylie: Facebook Can 'Delete You from the Internet.'" CNet. March 20. Accessed March 24, 2018. www.cnet.com/news/cambridge-analytica-whistleblower-facebook-can-delete-you-from-the-internet/.

O'Hehir, Andrew. 2017. "Donald Trump is Waging War on Reality — So Far, Reality is Losing." *Salon*. December 3. Accessed December 3, 2017. www.salon.com/2017/12/02/donald-trump-is-waging-war-on-reality-so-far-reality-is-losing/.

Orwell, George. 1988 [1949]. *Nineteen Eighty-Four*. London: Penguin.

Oxford Dictionaries. 2016. "Oxford Dictionaries Word of the Year 2016 is Post-Truth." November16. Accessed November 18, 2016. www.oxforddictionaries.com/press/news/2016/11/17/WOTY-16.

Pachelli, Nick. 2017. "The Conversation About Trump's Mental Health Is Finally Changing. But Is It Too Late?" *Esquire*. October 13. Accessed December 16, 2017. www.esquire.com/news-politics/a12820137/trump-mental-health-conversation/.

Parkinson, Hannah Jane. 2016. "Click and Elect: How Fake News Helped Donald Trump Win a Real Election." *The Guardian*. November 14. Accessed November 18, 2016. www.theguardian.com/commentisfree/2016/nov/14/fake-news-donald-trump-election-alt-right-social-media-tech-companies.

Price, Greg. 2017. "Will Trump Fire Mueller? Democrats Want to Protect Special Counsel Amid FBI Bias Cries." *Newsweek*. December 6. Accessed December 13, 2017. www.newsweek.com/mueller-trump-fire-fbi-bias-740094.

Prokop, Andrew. 2018. "All of Robert Mueller's Indictments and Plea Deals in the Russia Investigation So Far." *Vox*. March 1. Accessed March 4, 2018. www.vox.com/policy-and-politics/2018/2/20/17031772/mueller-indictments-grand-jury.

Robertson, Lori, and Robert Farley. 2017. "The Facts on Crowd Size." FactCheck.org. January 23. Accessed December 2, 2017. www.factcheck.org/2017/01/the-facts-on-crowd-size/.

Rosen, Jay. 2017. "His Campaign to Discredit the Press is a Permanent Feature of Trump's Political Style." *PressThink*. July 16. Accessed December 5, 2017. http://pressthink.org/2017/07/campaign-discredit-press-permanent-feature-trumps-political-style/.

Sanger, David E., and Shane Scott. 2016. "Russian Hackers Acted to Aid Trump in Election, U.S. Says." *The New York Times*. December 9. Accessed December 13, 2016. www.nytimes.com/2016/12/09/us/obama-russia-election-hack.html?hp&action=click&pgtype=Homepage&clickSource=story-heading&module=first-column-region&region=top-news&WT.nav=top-news&_r=0.

Schaub, Michael. 2017. "Trump's Claim to Have Come Up with the Term 'Fake News' is Fake News, Merriam-Webster Dictionary Says." *Los Angeles Times*. October 9. Accessed November 23, 2017. www.latimes.com/books/jacketcopy/la-et-jc-fake-news-20171009-story.html.

Schindler, John. 2017. "The Trump-Putin War on American Intelligence Is in Overdrive." *The Observer*. December 15. Accessed December 16, 2017. http://observer.com/2017/12/trump-putin-attack-american-intelligence-fbi/amp/?__twitter_impression=true.

Schwartz, Ian. 2017. "Sudicial Watch's Fitton: Was FBI Turned Into A KGB-Type Operation Under Obama Administration?" RealClear Politics. December 14. Accessed December 16, 2017. www.realclearpolitics.com/video/2017/12/14/judicial_watchs_fitton_was_fbi_turned_into_a_kgb-type_operation_under_obama_administration.html.

Shahani, Aarti. 2016. "Facebook, Google Take Steps to Confront Fake News." *All Tech Considered*. National Public Radio. November 15. Accessed November 18, 2016. www.npr.org/sections/alltechconsidered/2016/11/15/502111390/facebook-google-take-steps-to-confront-fake-news.

Shugerman, Emily. 2017a. "Black and LGBT Reporters Respond after Being Left Off White House Christmas Party Guest List for First Time in Years." *The Independent*.

November 30. Accessed December 1, 2017. www.independent.co.uk/news/world/americas/us-politics/white-house-christmas-party-guestlist-black-lgbt-reporters-april-ryan-chris-johnson-a8085086.html.

Shugerman, Emily. 2017b. "White House Defends Trump and Says it Doesn't Matter if Video He Retweeted was Fake: 'The Threat is Real.'" *The Independent*. November 29. Accessed November 30, 2017. www.independent.co.uk/news/world/americas/us-politics/trump-muslim-retweet-real-threat-white-house-defence-sarah-huckabee-sanders-latest-a8082891.html.

Solon, Olivia. 2016. "Facebook's Failure: Did Fake News and Polarized Politics Get Trump Elected?" *The Guardian*. November 11. Accessed November 18, 2016. www.theguardian.com/technology/2016/nov/10/facebook-fake-news-election-conspiracy-theories.

Stelter, Brian. 2016. "The Plague of Fake News is Getting Worse—Here's How to Protect Yourself." CNN Money. Accessed November 18, 2016. http://money.cnn.com/2016/10/30/media/facebook-fake-news-plague/.

Strohm, Chris. 2016. "Russia Weaponised Social Media in US Election, Company Says." *The Age*. December 2. Accessed December 2, 2016. www.theage.com.au/world/russia-weaponised-social-media-in-us-election-company-says-20161201-gt29u7.html.

Truscott, Lucian, K. 2017. "Why Trump Lies." *Salon*. November 19. Accessed November 28, 2017. www.salon.com/2017/11/18/why-trump-lies/.

Viebeck, Elise. 2016. "Trump Spokesman Says Russia Talk Coming from People 'Bitter' Clinton Lost." *The Washington Post*. December 12. Accessed December 13, 2016. www.washingtonpost.com/news/powerpost/wp/2016/12/12/trump-spokesman-says-russia-talk-coming-from-people-bitter-clinton-lost/?utm_term=.6c923f0a6bd2.

Wagner, Kurt. 2017. "These Are Some of the Tweets and Facebook Ads Russia Used to Try and Influence the 2016 Presidential Election." *Recode*. October 31. Accessed December 13, 2017. www.recode.net/2017/10/31/16587174/fake-ads-news-propaganda-congress-facebook-twitter-google-tech-hearing.

White, Kalia. 2017. "Report: Drug Mixing Killed Fake-News Writer Paul Horner." *USA Today*. December 6. Accessed December 13, 2017. www.usatoday.com/story/news/nation-now/2017/12/06/report-drug-mixing-killed-fake-news-writer-paul-horner/928412001/.

Wick, Julia. 2015. "Where Does the Term 'Spin Doctor' Come From?" *Longreads*. February 15. Accessed November 18, 2016. https://blog.longreads.com/2015/02/15/where-does-the-term-spin-doctor-come-from/.

4

THE POLITICAL ECONOMY OF FAKE NEWS

"Fake News" and Political Economy

Fake news should be a serious topic in the political economy of communication because it brings into sharp relief a critique of the news industry and of journalism from a critical theory perspective. As noted in chapter two, political economy approaches have the advantage of a focus on unequal power relations in the field of communication, including news and journalism (Mansell 2004). Given there is a growing interest in political economy within communication studies (Fuchs and Mosco 2012), it is timely to focus attention on the apparent epidemic of fake news to explain and historicize it. As it continues to evolve through the media ecosphere, fake news appears to be a period-specific construct that has application only within the context of the 2016 US Presidential election and the subsequent chaotic freak show that the Trump presidency has become. President Donald Trump has weaponized the term—with echoes of the Nazi slogan, "*Lügenpresse*" the "lying press"—to attack media outlets that he doesn't like (Noak 2016). More broadly, the fake news issue is a debate about who gets to define "truth," and associated with that, it throws into relief the role of journalists and journalism in liberal democracies (McNair 2018).

There is no doubt that fake news is at the heart of a profoundly political debate, centered in the United States, but with echoes across Europe following the "Brexit" negotiations and the French election of 2017. A study from the Internet Institute at Oxford University in April 2017 reportedly found that perhaps a quarter of political news circulating on social media in France was from suspect sources and could be designated as fake or "junk news" (Howard et al. 2017). News reports at the time were quick to also blame Russian state-sanctioned propaganda actions as being behind many of the false anti-Macron and pro-Fillon stories, alleging they were being promoted by the Sputnik and Russia Today news services (Gilbert 2017). The moral panic about Russian interference in western nations also surrounded the fraught "Brexit" debate in the UK. Throughout 2017 allegations were raised in the media about so-called Russian propaganda being circulated to cloud the "Brexit" debate and to favor a "leave" position (Grice 2017). In another parallel with the post-election inquiries into "fake news" in the United States, Facebook came under fire for not doing "enough"—whatever that might mean—to curtail the influence of algorithmically promoted false stories during the Brexit referendum (Week 2017).

While it is tempting to take allegations of Russian interference in Western politics at face value, it is important to step back and ask why Putin and Russia would be the culprits and the target of such claims. To some degree, it can be argued that it is Western media and political operatives falling back onto an old Cold War trope reminiscent of the 1950s, or the Cuban missile crisis of 1962. While alleged Russian meddling and propaganda efforts are the subject of inquiries in the US, France and Britain—and perhaps with good reason—it is simplistic and reactionary to buy into the conspiracy theory as the full, or the only, explanation of what is happening in this contested arena. We should be particularly cautious when one of the political figures promoting the line that Russia created the "fake news" problem is former UK Prime Minister Tony Blair, one of the architects of the fake 2003 dossier that launched cruise missiles against the civilian population of Baghdad. As Glenn Greenwald (2017a) has pointed out in *The Intercept*, there is also plenty of "fake news" around that overstates possible Russian interference in the US presidential election. By the time you're reading this, the Russian interference story may have reached its conclusion, but as of August 2018 it seems to have some way to go, with more revelations to play out before it is over.

A political economy inquiry into fake news can begin with an analysis of contemporary American, British and French events—particularly as they have global significance and impact—but it cannot end there. To the extent it can, our approach must distance itself from current hyperbolic accounts of contemporaneous events to examine the category of fake news dispassionately, historically and through a lens of materialist political economy. In particular, our focus in this chapter needs to be on the structural and procedural relationships of power that are articulated in the digital media landscape, which include questions of production, the allocation of resources and the controlling role of capital in the media and not just on the "symbolic content" of the messages (Mansell 2004: 77).

Categories of Fake News

The unprecedented chaos surrounding Donald Trump's presidency is the immediate context for a discussion of the political economy of fake news, but it should not distract us from a more serious, scholarly and forensic examination of what the category of fake news means within the scholarship of journalism and communication studies. The issue of fake news goes much further than the simple politico-cultural binary frame through which the Trump presidency is being viewed and it also has extensive historical precedents, even though the term itself may not have been in common usage prior to the 2016 US campaign season.

The renewed interest in fake news as a category has led to several attempts to arrive at a workable definition. Some, attempt a broad approach, while others, like this one by researchers at Trend Micro, are quite limited:

> Fake news is the promotion and propagation of news articles via social media ... in such a way that they appear to be spread by other users, as opposed to being paid-for advertising ... [and] designed to influence or manipulate users' opinions on a certain topic towards certain objectives.
>
> *(Gu, Kropotov and Yarochkin 2017)*

This narrow definition is operationalized in the Trend Micro report from which it is taken because it suits the analysis and evidence presented. In short, the report argues that fake news is the commercial weaponization of information, largely by elements operating in the shadows of the Dark Net, most likely with the backing of one or more States, notably Russia and China.

While this is useful and relevant to the potential use of fake news in the 2016 US election, it is a narrow and ahistorical definition, which is unsuited to a wider discussion of fake news. It does not, for example, account for fake news that is not disseminated through social media; nor does it account for well-established forms of false information such as public relations astroturfing. Fake news—as a generic name for false or misleading news-like information—can be spread by word of mouth, or through traditional print and broadcast channels and it has been distributed via those means for hundreds, if not thousands of years (Burkhardt 2017: 5). Therefore, we need either a much broader definition of fake news, or we need several specific definitions that are suitable for deployment in different arenas.

In simple terms, fake news can be broken down into the following sub-categories:

- Fake news used as a synonym for "false stories," that is stories that are "intentionally fabricated," but can be proven as factually incorrect and that "could mislead readers" (Allcott and Gentzkow 2017: 213).
- Fake news as stories that originate on satirical websites, such as *The Onion*, "but could be misunderstood as factual when viewed in isolation," particularly through a social media lens (ibid.: 213).
- News-like content that is advertorial and commercial that is selling a service or product, also known as "native advertising."

- The term "fake news" used in political discourse as an accusation against information being promoted by your opponents. Fake news is deployed as pejorative term for any item of news that you disagree with, or that paints your cause, position, candidate, leader, or president in an unfavorable light.
- Fake news as a form of propaganda. In this context, deliberately faked information is deployed via a news-like interface in order to deceive readers or viewers for political or commercial advantage, also known as "gaslighting"—the use of emotional undermining, and other manipulative techniques to hold power over someone, or a group of people (Sarkis 2017).
- Fake news that is highly ideological and misleading, but which appears to have some basis in verifiable objective reality and therefore contributes to the manufacture of consent within subaltern groups.

Political economy helps to explain and contextualize each of these distinct categories, which are all derived from the dialectic of contradictions within journalism as practiced in liberal democratic polities founded on the capitalist mode of production. As argued here, there is an inevitability about fake news, given that a wholly truthful media is almost categorically impossible in capitalist societies.

Fake News through a Historical Lens

Fake news existed long before Donald Trump claimed to have invented the term in 2017. Hoaxes have also been an integral part of the news landscape for the last 500 years, and while reporters might have insisted they were based on truth, often they were far from it. So, an important question that political economy can provide an answer to is: Where has the current tsunami of fake news come from? A simple answer is that there is a level of deception involved in the news process and it's always been there. Sometimes it is conscious and at others represents a largely unconscious, but systemic bias. One researcher has likened the news "ballads" of the sixteenth century to the tabloid press of today; using sensationalism and outrage to sell, and not being too particular about the truth. "Like the tabloid news coverage of today, news ballads were always sensationalist, covering topics that were sure to appeal to the attention of shoppers in busy marketplaces" (McIlvenna 2017).

One of my favorite examples is an early-seventeenth-century news report of dragons in southern England. No doubt the idea of dragons would be terrifying to people in the region, and they were unlikely to venture out to see for themselves. In more recent time, hoaxes have taken in everything from supposed landings on the moon in 1835 to Orson Welles's radio broadcast of H. G. Wells's novel *War of the Worlds* a century later in 1938. These are amusing hoaxes, designed to entertain rather than convince. Satirical news programs also relied on an element of fakery, such as the famous BBC prank story about Italian spaghetti trees on April Fool's Day in 1957. Such hoaxes play on a certain ignorance or naivety in the audience, but they are not malicious. However, there are clear examples, both contemporary and historical, where false news stories have been used to great effect. One incident, which some suggest is merely apocryphal, concerns the media baron William Randolph Hearst during the US–Mexico war. According to some accounts Hearst demanded that his correspondent and war artist Frederic Remington stay in Havana even though he felt that there would be no conflict: "You furnish the pictures, I'll furnish the war," Hearst is supposed to have cabled in January 1898. While the telegram story is now considered a hoax, there is no doubt that Hearst used an incident involving a mysterious explosion aboard a US navy vessel in Havana harbor to create a pretext for war. Hearst's newspapers blamed a Spanish bomb planted on the USS *Maine*, but there has never been any evidence to counter the accepted view that it was an unfortunate accident in the ship's ammunition lockers that caused the explosion (Campbell 2011). This incident has been called the "WMD episode" of its time. History provides many such examples which are worth recounting because they help to put contemporary concerns about the fake news phenomenon into useful context.

The current crisis of trust in traditional news sources can probably be traced back to the Iraq invasion of 2003 and the way news outlets uncritically reported the WMD lie as pretext for war (Hirst 2011). Since then the crisis has only deepened, in 2017, only a little over half of American voters said they trust mainstream media (Barthel and Mitchell 2017); a Reuters Foundation study reported that about one-third of respondents across 36 countries felt they could trust the news media (Goldsmith 2017). Ironically, both surveys found that trust levels for social media are even lower, hovering in the mid-20s. The crisis in media profitability and the failure of the audience-commodity advertising model to cover rising production costs is the second structural component of the rise in fake news. There has been a steady rise in the amount of non-news content being shoehorned into a news-like template and format and splashed across the websites of major news organizations. The polite term for such content is "native advertising," it is sales copy written to resemble news content, but usually with a brand-specific message. This type of content is popular among key advertisers and it is a growing market; some analysts say the amount of native advertising online has tripled since 2015 (Main 2017).

Fake News and Commodity Journalism

The News Establishment creates its own versions of "fake news" for a variety of reasons; some are purely commercial—for the profitable clicks, views, likes and shares it generates—and others are highly political—for deliberate and systemic propaganda effect. Both involve the deliberate deception of the news-consuming public, and this is what unites them. In his book, *Post-Truth: How Bullshit Conquered the World*, James Ball (2017) makes an important point about the wider problematic category of fake news; there's a "whole range" of stories that are, for one reason or another, false but are believed by people who either accept that they might be true, or "convincingly pretend" to believe them. This last point is important in relation to Donald Trump; his predilection for both shaming the news media as fake and generating his own tsunami of fake news is buttressed by his convincing act of self-belief in his own rhetoric. "Trump's versatility in generating half-truth, untruth and outright spectacular mendacity borders on genius" (ibid.).

Ball invokes a non-academic term to describe the easily spoken untruths now routinely part of political discourse; he calls it "bullshit" (adopted from a 2005 book, *On Bullshit*, by Harry Frankfurt). The media's spreading of this "bullshit" is the outcome of a state of affairs in which politicians no longer care about telling the truth, but only about the "optics"—how a given situation will play out in the media and the "narrative" that is constructed around it. "Bullshit" is a useful phrase because it encompasses more than deliberately concocted false stories; it also applies to the half-true statement that is passed off to journalists who are too lazy, too poorly resourced, or too ill-equipped intellectually to challenge it. The "culture and norms" (Ball 2017) of the newsroom are not sufficiently robust to filter out the bullshit and so it enters public life as a first-draft of history and becomes normalized through unchallenged repetition. It is also useful to be reminded that before President Trump, the term "fake news" had other meanings, including as a label for a category of broadcast news that made use of public relations material known as a "video news release": "A VNR presents a client's message, using a format and tone that mimic actual TV news. Nothing in the material for broadcast identifies the PR firm—or, more importantly, the paying client or clients— behind the VNR" (Farsetta and Price 2006: 5).

From a progressive political economy perspective, the symbolic content of "fake news," such as represented in VNRs, or even by Trump supporters, has a long and political history that is intimately and dialectically bound to the commodity form of journalism in a capitalist market economy. A Fourth Estate-inflected approach would attempt to explain fake news using a normative, yet highly ideological, media markets model in which fake news is theorized as "distorted signals uncorrelated with the truth" about the state of the world that arises in the market because it is "cheaper to provide than precise signals," and "may generate some utility for some consumers" (Allcott and Gentzkow 2017: 212). This explanation does not examine the power and control issues that actually shape the market and it leaves the focus on the symbolic, rather than address structural and procedural issues which make the production and distribution of fake news an attractive proposition to some actors.

In the eyes of his supporters at least, Trump has successfully appropriated a term that was first applied to news stories mostly supportive of his campaign, that were spread widely on social media that proved to be fake (Coll 2017). The obvious false story about the Pope endorsing Trump is the paradigm example.

The fake Pope endorsement story began life on a now defunct satirical news website; and spread virally, highlighting the symbolic and memetic process of people believing what they would like to be true, and circulating it within sympathetic echo chambers of like-minded social media friends. However, a more puzzling and complicated picture emerged when a so-called fake news epicenter was discovered in the isolated Macedonian town of Veles where approximately 100 pro-Trump sites were registered and operated. It is hard to think of this as a coincidence, but it certainly highlights the valuable nexus between fake news and the profit motive. According to a report in *Wired*, some of the teens behind the fake news sites were making US$8,000 per month, more than 20 times the average wage in Veles at the time (Subramarnian 2017). The article does not explore the possibility that there was Russian influence behind the entrepreneurial teens, but other examples of alleged Russian promotion of dubious news during the American election have been reported. The most serious is that Russian agents bought US$100,000 or more in advertising on Facebook with the clear aim of promoting false election stories and targeted at voters in crucial swing states. These stories were then amplified by a coordinated wave of reposting and tweeting by fake "bot" accounts, according to news reports (Shane 2017).

Ball (2017) makes some very good points about how the economics of the news industry encourage the production of fake news, not just deliberate fakes, but clickbait headlines and ideologically charged front page stories designed to provoke audiences into emotional responses to situations where facts are ignored, manipulated, or misrepresented to create the desired effect. A March 2017 report from the Tow Center for Digital Journalism makes a similar point about the profitability of fake news. According to the authors, "the structure and economics of social platforms incentivize the spread of low-quality content over high-quality material" (Bell and Owen 2017: 10). This observation underscores the importance of the commercial motive behind journalism—the very profit motive of capitalism—it is to make money from the sale of the news commodity, and to do this via the redistribution of surplus value from labor to capital. This transaction occurs through the vehicle of advertising, which transfers surplus value from the advertiser to the publisher via the commodification of audiences. Thus, we cannot separate the social, cultural, political and ideological functions of news from the simple function of capital accumulation. This principle is still the driving force behind the news business in the digital realm, even though the business models that underpin it are broken, perhaps irrevocably. As Bell and Owen (ibid.: 11) acknowledge, the spread of "fake news" online is a symptom of "the commercialization and private control of the public sphere."

To understand this requires a return to one of political economy's central concerns, the transfer of value (as profit) from advertisers to media companies via a process known as audience commodification. A simple explanation of this concept is that media audiences (whether, for print, broadcast or online products) are aggregated by the publisher and then sold to advertisers; the price depends on the size and quality of this audience commodity. The act of viewing the content becomes a form of "work," or commodified labor performed without any monetary compensation and therefore "free" to the publisher/seller (Smythe 2006). As Fuchs (2012) and others have demonstrated, the audience as commodity is still a key category in the political economy of communication. However, in the digital mediasphere this commodification takes two forms, both of which are crucial to the discussion of "fake news": the first is the simple aggregation of eyeballs that involves the audience in the active "work" of viewing content; the second is the category of audience labor that actually creates content which is then appropriated by media capital without payment.

Both types of labor are essential to the circulation, commodification and valorization of fake news via digital channels and platforms. There are several reasons for this, and most are predicated on the low barriers to entry that allow individuals and organizations to establish and monetize web content for a small capital investment. Secondly, the ease with which algorithmic "bots" can be established to mimic human social media accounts creates a low-cost and effective means to disseminate information virally, whether it is reliable, or not. To a substantial degree, news publishers are now "at the mercy of the algorithm" (Bell and Owen 2017: 10). Finally, once bots have initiated a release of information it is easily amplified through friend networks, often without it being easily detectable that it originated with bot accounts (Burkhardt 2017: 15). As the fake news drama has unfolded throughout 2017, the algorithms employed by Facebook and Google—which appear to be open to manipulation by well-programmed "bot" armies—have also been subject to scrutiny. While I am not prepared to blame these companies for the spread of fake news, or hold them entirely responsible, it is clear that they are now giants in the communication game and are largely determining the parameters of the digital public sphere. For that reason, it is important for political economists to continue the work pioneered by Christian Fuchs into the financialization of these media giants and the ways in which their vertical and horizontal integration creates new monopoly conditions within the global media industries (Fuchs 2012).

The algorithmic amplification of fake news, which enriches Google and Facebook more than it does young bored Macedonian entrepreneurs, is made possible by the deeply embedded structures of surveillance and big data within the digital economy. User information is collected cheaply by the bots, it is further processed by other algorithmic and machine-learning techniques and then assembled into commodified batches that are on-sold to content distributors and used to direct content back to the original user. Often a human end-user will not even be aware that the content they are seeing has been specifically chosen for them based on their previous browsing or social media history. Thus, it becomes possible to almost entirely automate the generation and distribution of content—whether reliable or not—using algorithms with the ability to mimic human natural language on social media. As Joanna Burkhardt notes in a moment of bleak humor: "the bot is not interested in the truth or falsehood of the information itself" (Burkhardt 2017: 15).

A number of other factors contribute to the economics of fake news and each, when coupled with one or more of the others, tends to compound the problem even further. The blurring of the once sacrosanct separation between advertising and editorial is a factor in the ability of fake news to slip undetected into the news agenda. A further factor that links fake news to the digital news industry is the use of provocative and often misleading "clickbait" headlines. Clickbait headlines often feature a sensational claim, but they are not always backed up in the article. Globally, the *Daily Mail* brand is notorious for such headlines, which can stretch across three or four lines. Fake news generators have adopted similar tactics to draw in readers. This is effective because research has shown that most people who share news on social media will often do so after only reading the headline. Rarely, it seems, do we check the whole story before clicking like, or send.

Advertising blurring into editorial provides another incentive for the purveyors of fake news. Popular sites, which aggregate the largest audiences for on-selling to advertisers, are rewarded with a larger share of the online advertising pie, creating incentives to push more of the same types of popular content. Online display advertising and click-rate accounting models encourage publishers to generate large audiences for low-cost articles with controversial headlines and outrageous claims. When speed is important, false or misleading claims are published anyway and corrected later if there is enough of an outcry. Either way, the bigger the outrage the higher the click rate and the publisher's goals of generating revenue are achieved. In this way, real news outlets also benefit from fake news that is deliberately created to mislead. By injecting themselves into this already compromised space, the purveyors of fake news can monetize their content and hide it among similarly sensational stories. To some extent, this shows how fake news relies on the psychology of the spectacle and sensation to gain traction.

Newsroom resourcing is also an issue affecting journalists' ability to filter out fake news or "bullshit." Tight deadlines and a 24-hour news clock limit the number of hours a reporter can spend on a story. Shrinking news budgets also mean fewer reporters on any given shift leading to rostered staff having to produce more copy to fill an ever-expanding online news hole. Not only does this allow blatant fabrication to slip through unattended gates, the news hole is also filled with commercial "native advertising" that masquerades as news copy to mimic the "natural" ways in which audiences engage with such content (Sharethrough 2018). Mainstream outlets benefit from native advertising and the passing off of paid content as news-like information.

Finally, the very nature of social media lends itself to the manifestation of false information as truth due to several in-built technological and social factors.

1   Speed: One of the most compelling attractions of social media is speed. Operating at a level of near physical instantaneity, social media allows for the rapid dissemination and peer-to-peer sharing of information. As has been well documented in relation to fact-checking of broadcast and online news, speed has replaced accuracy as a necessary intrinsic value of news-like information. Being first to tell others has replaced being right and accurate as the holy grail of digital journalism.

2   Aggregation: News and news-like information is shared multiple times in second and third-hand posts, reposts and interpretations. Like Chinese whispers, the detail can change over the various retellings.

3   Monetizing the clickstream: We have moved well beyond the first blush and thrill of our relationship with digital media. We have progressed from the digital sublime to the digital mundane. Social media is now the quotidian. Not being connected via social media is now the outlier behavior for people under 75 and this creates large audiences that are available to sell to advertisers, and to create further free content that can be monetized.

4   The problematic "Fourth Estate" ideology of journalism as practiced in western liberal democracies also tends to promote a culture of fake news because the systematic failures of journalism to secure the trust of audiences leaves them cynical, dis-engaged and receptive to fake news generated for both profit and for propaganda.

Fake News Makes the "Post Truth" World Possible

Fake news is hard to define, but I believe it comes in three main flavors: the obviously fake, the easy-to-spot deliberate fake and the subtle fake that almost passes undetected.

The obviously fake should not fool too many people, but it still does. If you have ever read the satirical news website *The Onion* you have come across very clever fake news. It is deliberately outrageous and often quite funny. The best of this category of fake news offers a sharp commentary on real events, but it should not be too hard to spot it as fake. Having said that, a now infamous case of *The Onion* fooling supposedly clever people has gone down as one of the greatest journalistic hoaxes, so far, of the twenty-first century. In 2012 *The Onion* posted a satirical story describing North Korean dictator Kim Jong-un as the site's "sexiest man alive." A few days later the official Chinese government website, *The People's Daily*, reported the story as fact reproducing almost the entire *Onion* article alongside several photographs of the Korean leader. *The*

New York Times was also fooled by an *Onion* piece and reported as fact a fake news item about Barack Obama "singing in the shower" to make himself popular with younger voters (Fallon 2012).

As we discussed earlier, the timing of Oxford Dictionaries' announcement about "post-truth" being 2016's word of the year and the election of Donald Trump was coincidental; but it seems likely that when rival Collins decided that "fake news" would be its word(s) of the year in 2017, they had the president firmly in their sights. In a widely quoted media release, Collins's head of content said the term had dominated political discourse throughout the year:

> "Fake news," either as a statement of fact or as an accusation, has been inescapable this year, contributing to the undermining of society's trust in news reporting: given the term's ubiquity and its regular usage by President Trump, it is clear that Collins' Word of the Year "fake news" is very real news.
>
> *(Hunt 2017)*

We can add to this that the increase in "fake news" being cynically manufactured for propaganda purposes certainly adds to the democracy deficit. We got a stark reminder of this in early 2018 when the National Cybersecurity Center reported that Russian-controlled "bot" accounts had been provoking both pro-gun and anti-gun activists in the wake of yet another tragic school shooting incident in the US (Cybercenter 2018).

Donald Trump was able to bypass much of the mainstream media during the 2016 election season. He delivered his messages straight to his supporters, who were then able to amplify these sound and sight bites via their own social media channels. This was certainly helpful to his campaign, but he also avoided scrutiny on serious issues by turning the election cycle into an emotion-filled circus. By making outrageous and unverifiable claims—that Hillary Clinton was "crooked" for example—Trump spoke directly to the emotional core of his base. Many Trump supporters were silent during the campaign, but they were listening to his key phrases about being the "forgotten" Americans, about how the so-called "elites" and political "insiders" had been ignoring "real" people for decades and how he would "drain the swamp" of Washington politics if he was elected.

Canadian journalism professor Alfred Hermida argues that Trump's victory was built on the media value-add of his supporters "spreading and amplifying subjective and emotional affective news—designed to provoke passion, not [to] inform" (Hermida 2016). There is some truth in this observation that also speaks to the fragmentation of the formerly dominant mainstream news model and the diaspora of news flows that no longer reflect the top-down world of morning newspapers and evening bulletins. Audiences are now circulating news horizontally—between themselves—and in this maelstrom the original source may be lost or simply overlooked. What once appeared to be careful "fact-checking" by trusted news outlets (it often wasn't) meant that information had to go through at least a minimal verification process; but on social media platforms this step is poorly performed, or simply ignored.

Social media platforms are now a space of "news-like" information rather than hard, verified news (Hirst 2011) This "news-like" information is not rigorously fact-checked; instead audiences "find, support and share, facts, false-hoods and feelings" through their Facebook and Twitter feeds. The very essence of social media is that it is a space "designed to envelop users in the cosy embrace of the familiar, not [to] challenge misinformed views or address unsubstantiated rumours" (Hermida 2016). In the expanding mediascape of social journalism the problem of feelings and falsehoods outweighing actual facts is exponentially greater. As we have seen in this chapter, a lie can spread on the Internet, or via Twitter, faster than a journalist can muster the time or the energy to fact-check it. Today the feedback loop between social media and the mainstream news media is also so fast that a lie can become a news headline before anybody bothers to verify it.

Today everybody needs to take the issue of verification seriously. Whether they are news producers working at the *New York Times* or CNN, social journalists tweeting out news as it happens, or even just an audience member who share news-like information via Facebook and other platforms. In a post-truth world where fake news is difficult to spot at first glance everybody must be a fact-checker. We will return to this issue in chapters eight and nine, in which the possibility for greater efforts to verify news and news-like informa-tion is a focus.

A further issue in the ongoing debate about "fake news" and journalistic truth-telling is the bias of the reporter. We can do nothing about the bias of our sources; we can only be aware of their bias and hope to counter that where necessary with other points of view. The bias of the journalist is something that we can deal with, particularly if we are that reporter. If we are honest with ourselves and we are prepared to behave ethically in our role as social journal-ists, we should have no trouble admitting to our prejudices. Most of the time we don't want to change them, but we should be able to acknowledge how they influence our reporting. Our bias may well inform our motive for wanting to be a reporter, whether in a large news organization like the *New York Times*, the Fox News network or MSNBC, or even if we're working for a small-town news website or print outlet. Bias certainly plays a role in social journalism, in blogging and in partisan political reporting. In these situations, bias is really just another word for our belief system.

The emotional dialectics of journalism—fueled by the dual nature of the news commodity—create a level of unconscious bias in editors and reporters. I have characterized this as the belief system of the News Establishment. Despite this structural impediment, a thoughtful journalist and a media literate lay person should at least be aware of their own views, beliefs and bias. How would you classify yourself? Are you "liberal," "progressive" or "conservative" in the American context; would you consider yourself "left" "center" or "right" on the political spectrum? Do you believe that global warming is "man-made" or are you in the "deniers" camp? Where do you stand on the major social issues of the day, whatever they are, wherever you are? Even if you identify as "apolitical" you have taken a stand. Are you Christian, Jewish, Muslim or a member of the Plymouth Brethren? Do you belong to an Evangelical church? If you identify with a particular faith, how observant are you? These are only some of the religious choices we make; some of us are agnostic (neither believing, nor disbelieving in the existence of a God) and some are atheists (choosing to have no God). Wherever you fall, or choose to put yourself, on any of these religious and/or political continua, you have beliefs and these beliefs will necessarily inform how you think about the world, how you choose to act in the world and, like it or not, often how other people will judge you. Keeping an "open mind" is not the same as having no core beliefs.

What's all that got to do with journalism in a "post-truth" world? Everything actually. Our belief system—what sociologists and political scientists call an ideology—will also help determine our attitudes to what we believe about the external world and therefore our perceptions of both *truth* and *post-truth*. Bias is also an issue of trust, which appears to be in short supply these days. The rise of fake news also makes it harder for audiences to place trust in the news media. If news consumers feel betrayed by either deliberate or inadvertent fake news stories they are less likely to trust journalists to get it right. In a sense this creates a downward spiral; as we trust media sources less, we tend to rely more on peer-to-peer sharing and information verification. But, as the research shows, a lot of what gets shared in peer-to-peer social media networks is inherently unreliable to begin with. Audience psychology—wanting to feel connected by sharing—combined with high circulation speeds and algorithms that promote popular content, provides a fertile ground for the spread of what one group of researchers called the "digital catnip" of fake news (Carey 2017).

How Are We Going to Deal with "Fake News"?

The problem of fake news is one all of us are going to have to face, whether we are consumers, professional journalists or working in the social journalism space. What we have to understand is that dealing with conspiracy theories and the people who push them is not easy. For those who hold to conspiracy theories any attempt to debunk, or disprove, them usually leads them deeper into their own beliefs. For example, the bizarre story about alleged pedophile rings operating from a popular pizza parlor in Washington DC, with the blessing of senior Democratic Party officials and Hillary Clinton, was able to gain traction among right-wing Trump supporters who were already primed to believe wild conspiracy theories about their political enemies. In 2017, when credible journalists exposed the alleged Comet Ping Pong pedophile ring as fake news, those who really wanted it to be true began circulating another theory—this time, that 28-year-old Edgar Welsh from North Carolina was a "false flag" operative sent in by Clinton's backers to shoot up the pizza parlor in order to hide the truth of the allegations. One blog site that promoted this new theory was *NewsInsideOut.com*, which claimed that the "false flag" operation was done to discredit those making the accusation, to hide existence of the pedophiles, and to deflect from the activities of the "Global Satanic Ritual Abuse Pedophile Ring." The website also claimed that the "false flag" operation was managed by the same government "PsyOps team" that had exploded the IEDs during the 2013 Boston marathon (Webre 2016). Another site, with obvious pro-Trump leanings, *Conservative Daily Post*, also carried the "false flag" narrative adding the detail that a CTV camera on the street outside Comet Ping Pong had been moved and peppering its report with tweets supporting the conspiracy theory (Bougis 2016).

The #PizzaGate conspiracy was also an active sub-Reddit thread in the main "conspiracy" thread where Welch's brief career as an actor was discussed, alongside more wild accusations of pedophile rings and Satanic rituals.

While it is nearly impossible to counter the most ridiculous conspiracy theories and fake news memes that emerge in social media and blog posts, there should be some way of dealing with other categories; particularly when they are based in reporting by news organizations that are supposedly more reliable than the highly partisan blogs on the fringes of political discourse. The promotion of fake news, either wittingly or unwittingly, is a big issue for the News Establishment and mainstream news organizations whose reputations have suffered over the past decade as their credibility and reliability have fallen in the eyes of consumers. As we know, readers, listeners and viewers are deserting mainstream media, or are so cynical that they choose not to believe anything. As one contributor to the debate following the 2016 US election pointed out,

Purpose of Pizzagate false flag shooting explained

NewsInsideOut.com

By Alfred Lambremont Webre

BLAINE, WA. – The shooter Patsy in the Comet Pizzagate False Flag Shooting is identified as Edgar Maddison Welch, who played the part of the SHOOTER in the Movie "Something About Pizza!" Welch's acting chops and history qualify him as a "Crisis actor" in the Pizzagate false flag "psyop" operation.

FIGURE 4.1   The False Flag Narrative Was Carried on Sites Like NewsInsideOut.com.

FIGURE 4.2 Sub-Reddit Group in the Main "Conspiracy" Thread Discussing #PizzaGate.

some individuals and groups are so dissociated from what is real or factual that they don't even see fake news as problematic: "Some people really don't see that they have been duped or finding out later that it is fake as a problem" (Nelson S 2016).

Despite recognizing fake news as a problem, there are few workable solutions being offered in the marketplace. The obstacles to dealing with fake news appear huge at the moment; not only is it hard to eradicate, as we've been discussing, it is actually quite difficult to identify.

The first issue is deciding what constitutes fake news and what is merely bias in reporting. On overtly partisan sites—such as those of the avowedly left and the right—the bias is usually obvious to astute readers, but it is not so easy to spot on more mainstream news outlets. Added to this is the volume of "advertorial" or sponsored content that appears in the guise of news. Such content is not always clearly labelled and if it looks like news many are likely to see it as such and not take into account built-in commercial bias.

The second problem, linked to the issue of partisanship is "objectivity." Is there really any objectivity in the news media today? It is certainly hard to find news that is entirely impartial or that is *only* factual. News has never really been without bias; there is an element of interpretation in every news story and with interpretation comes the privileging of one viewpoint over another. Allied to the problem of objectivity is the obvious issue of news that is poorly sourced or invalidated because it is badly written and perhaps from an unreliable news outlet. Linked to this issue is the very real psychological divide between "rationalist" and "intuitionist" thinking. Rationalists are willing to take on board empirical data and facts, then to apply logic and reason in order to arrive at a rational worldview. On the other side, intuitionists are prone to emotive responses gut feelings and metaphor, which we sometimes call "motivated reasoning," or even "magical thinking" (Swan 2016). As we've been discussing, conspiracy theories work with intuitive thinking, rather than a rational exposition of facts and data. These intuitions are then confirmed through what psychologists call "confirmation bias"—that is, we tend to gravitate towards people and ideas that confirm our own prejudices, or reinforce our core beliefs (Malcolm and Willis 2016). Increasing our digital media literacy and developing our rational thinking capabilities are ways in which we can become more attuned to bias in the news.

The third dilemma is sorting out who and how fake news is to be called out. Who can be trusted to be the "umpire"? Fact-checking is an expensive and time-consuming task in any news organization and when resources are difficult to come by, fact-checking is one of the first activities that gets cut. On social media sites like Facebook the problem is made more complex by the sheer volume of material being shared among users. As we noted, Facebook came under fire following the 2016 US election because of the number of fake news items allegedly spread via "likes" and "shares." According to an analysis by *Buzzfeed*, fake news was shared more than real news items and as more fake stories were shared, the number of verified news stories being shared fell (Silverman 2016). The backlash prompted Facebook executives to face up to the issue and the public pressure seemed to lead to divisions within the company. While CEO Mark Zuckerberg defended Facebook, engineers at the social media giant were telling the media that a technical fix might be possible—if the company would face up and take ownership of the problem.

Facebook's head of AI research, Yann LeCun, was reported as saying that the artificial intelligence necessary to filter fake news was either ready or could be made ready for deployment if the company chose to do so (Gershgorn 2016). Other experts told *The Guardian* that Facebook was unlikely to block fake news because the financial returns generated by the volume of sharing was too tempting to executives and shareholders (Solon 2016).

It seems that reliable AI—algorithms that can filter the "good" from the "fake" news—is still some way from being perfected and deployed. There are several technical problems with AI which can be summarized as it is not yet capable of inference and detecting nuanced meaning in the sentences it reads. Also, in the final instance, AI relies on humans building the extensive databases it needs to verify the material it is cross-checking. In the end though, I think we'd all prefer to trust humans to be the gatekeepers and curators. The problem is, our trust in the gatekeepers of twentieth-century journalism is waning (Swift 2016) and is likely to run out before a suitable replacement can be deployed. In 2016, Facebook considered hiring more human fact-checkers, but found the cost too high. Instead, Facebook's fact-checking has been outsourced to so-called partner organizations, but it is underfunded and woefully inadequate. Efforts are ongoing, but even the scheme's supporters acknowledge they are only "scratching the surface" and that thousands of false stories are not checked due to lack of resources (Sharockman 2017).

At the same time, as the wild allegations about Russian hacking of the election or planting malware in the Vermont electricity grid show, the problem of "fake" news is not confined to social media. The speed at which news circulates today, combined with competition for stories and eyeballs, means that even respectable and mainstream news organizations, like the *NYT*, the *WaPo* and Reuters news agency can be gamed into promoting fake news items that gain traction because of the legitimacy of these famous brands. Towards the end of 2017 a number of media organizations were caught out in covering stories that they could not back up, or that turned out to be false. A string of mistakes led to some high-profile journalists losing their jobs. A number of the mis-reported stories were about Donald Trump, his associates and the FBI investiga-tion into the Russian meddling allegations. The end result of this was that Donald Trump was able to renew his attacks on the mainstream news media and its credibility suffered yet another severe blow (Greenwald 2017b). If we cannot rely on the once reliable news media to effectively weed out unreliable news any more, what can we do?

Media Literacy as One Answer to the Spread of "Fake News"

I am not, at this point, offering a cure to the problem of fake news, though others have attempted to do so, notably within a normative framework that privileges the liberal democratic notion of the Fourth Estate (McNair 2018). No doubt, there is need of an antidote to the spread of anti-democratic false narratives in journalism, but I doubt that the Fourth Estate paradigm holds the answers. Rather, I assert here that the ideological paradigm in which the Fourth Estate operates makes the News Establishment part of the problem and compli-cit—even if unwittingly—in the growth and spread of fake news. The solution is a much more radical overhaul of the news production process—with workers' control at its heart (Hirst 2011)—but there is not the space to explore that here. The seriousness with which a variety of American commentators—from Trump's own conservative side of politics, as well as "liberals"—are now calling into question the very premise of American democratic norms and processes shows just how toxic Trump has become to the body politic. His ongoing tirade of abuse towards the American news media, and his characterization of them as "fake news," is reason enough to take the issue seriously. However, for political economy of communication there is a deeper, underlying issue: How did it come to this?

As argued in this chapter, to answer this question requires an understanding of media and communication that goes beyond normative scholarly approaches and that combines political economy and critical theory. The explosion of "fake news" that we've experienced since 2016 is the result of several inter-twining and dialectical factors. It is both a manipulation of symbolic content to suit a particular political agenda—the Trump factor—and also an almost inevitable by-product of the collapse of the old media news paradigm. The combination of audience cynicism, falling levels of trust in news media, linked to the news media's own problems (rush to publish, lack of resources, etc.), and a growing reliance on algorithms, all contribute to the rise in fake news distribution (Himma-Kadakas 2017). There is—to re-introduce a term from chapter one— a process of mutual constitution and mediation occurring, between the political forces of Trump's rhetorical fixation and operationalization of the "fake news" meme, and the imploding news industry desperate to cling to its own dwindling social, cultural and economic power; as conceptualized in the "Fourth Estate" model and practiced by the News Establishment.

The role of ideology—as reflected through the media's Fourth Estate model—is to normalize this ignorance through the "manufacture of consent" (Herman and Chomsky 1988) and to a great extent it is consent based on false representations of the reality of capitalism. Manufactured consent is, at the same time, and necessarily, manufactured ignorance. Consent is manufactured on the back of a series of lies, which must be maintained in order for the underlying system to be maintained: "This situation is partly a function of ideological blindness, and partly a reflection of the all-too-human desire to believe in positive scenarios such as the well-known, but hypothetical, 'free lunch'" (Betancourt 2010).

However, as I've argued here, the Fourth Estate model—as an ideological safety-valve that normalizes commodity journalism and the News Establishment—is itself problematic and disintegrating under the pressures of economics and technology. Only a critical political economy approach can adequately deal with this fact, and explain how the social system of capitalism relies on general and mass ignorance for its survival. As Betancourt notes there is a "social dynamic of misinformation" in play, which can be recognized as a key dialectic and contradiction in the manufacture of consent, and which, when played out in full, can eventually lead to the unmasking of the lies at the core of pro-capitalist ideology.

It seems, as Trump's desperate clinging on to the trope of "fake news" shows, the spread of lies and the techniques of "gaslighting" are effective for periods of time, particularly when repeated in a directed way at an audience pre-conditioned to be receptive. In this context, they sow confusion and cynicism, leading to an effective disarming of any potential psychological resistance: "The creation of systemic unknowns where any potential 'fact' is always already countered by an alternative of apparently equal weight and value renders engagement with the conditions of reality ... contentious and a source of confusion" (Betancourt 2010).

Trump's conservative forces are reliant on this confusion and the disengagement it engenders to mask the seriously undemocratic and anti-worker agenda that is at the core of his "Make America Great Again" project. It is important to criticize both MAGA and Trump's use of the fake news trope in order to arm the resistance to it. Progressive political economy should play a role in this.

I have argued here that while constant chants of "fake news" from the Trump White House are real and important—in the way that they can lead to a de-activation of citizenship and therefore reinforce his "base only" strategy—they are not the only category of fake news worth investigating. Importantly there are economic factors in play which generate a market for fake news—such as the Russian and Chinese "dark net" services that provide automated promotional social media activities on a commercial basis (Gu, Kropotov and Yarochkin 2017)—and which extend to the commercial activities of Facebook and Google, among others.

I've also suggested that an over-emphasis on Trump's operationalization of fake news, without a deeper critical understanding of fake news, weakens any critique and serves to reinforce the ideology of the Fourth Estate. The problematic nature of the Fourth Estate model is highlighted by the number of mistakes made by mainstream reporters in covering the Russian interference stories throughout 2017. As we noted in the previous chapter, over-zealous reporters were too reliant on official sources and too readily believed information they were given without being able to fully verify it for themselves. This only served to reinforce Trump's fake news narrative and it can only further erode trust in the Fourth Estate news media. Conservative *New York Post* columnist David Harsanyi made an interesting point that American political reporters were damaging their own credibility—and that of their publisher—by rushing to publish stories that turned out to be false:

> The fact that many political journalists (not all) have a political agenda is not new, but if they become a proxy of operatives who peddle falsehoods, they will soon lose credibility with an even bigger swath of the country. They will have themselves to blame.
>
> *(Harsanyi 2017)*

At the core of this problem for the mainstream media was an over-reliance on official sources, and a willingness to believe, rather than actually checking facts for themselves. Such elementary mistakes can only lead to more cynical disengagement by citizens in the public sphere, at a time when we need to be encouraging more active participation in politics and communicative actions by marginalized and dispossessed citizens. The additional mistake of not being transparent with audiences about how the mistakes were made in the first place (Greenwald 2017b) adds to the news media's problems. Deepening our understanding of fake news is a precursor to helping establish effective strategies to defeat it and prevent its corrosive impacts of the public sphere. As suggested in this chapter, "fake news" is a symptom of the current twin crises afflicting modern mainstream journalism; the declining trust factor, and the broken business models. It is to these issues that we turn in the next chapter to ask: Can journalism be saved from itself?

References

Allcott, Hunt, and Matthew Gentzkow. 2017. "Social Media and Fake News in the 2016 Election." *Journal of Economic Perspectives* 31(2): 211–236. Accessed August 19, 2017. doi:10.1257/jep.31.2.211.

Ball, James. 2017. *Post-Truth: How Bullshit Conquered the World*. Kindle Edition. London: Biteback Publishing. Accessed November 27, 2017.

Barthel, Michael, and Amy Mitchell. 2017. "Americans' Attitudes About the News Media Deeply Divided Along Partisan Lines." Pew Research Center. Accessed November 28, 2017. www.journalism.org/2017/05/10/americans-attitudes-about-the-news-media-deeply-divided-along-partisan-lines/.

Bell, Emily, and Taylor Owen. 2017. "The Platform Press: How Silicon Valley Reengineered Journalism." Tow Center for Digital Journalism. Accessed April 19, 2017. www.cjr.org/tow_center_reports/platform-press-how-silicon-valley-reengineered-journalism.php.

Betancourt, Michael. 2010. "Immaterial Value and Scarcity in Digital Capitalism." CTheory. Accessed December 2, 2017. www.ctheory.net/articles.aspx?id=652.

Bougis, Elliot. 2016. "Comet Pizza EXPOSED In Huge Mainstream Media Coverup, Top Officials Implicated In Pedo Ring." *Conservative Daily Post*. December 5. Accessed December 13, 2016. https://conservativedailypost.com/comet-pizza-exposed-in-huge-mainstream-media-coverup-top-officials-implicated-in-pedo-ring/.

Burkhardt, Joanna M. 2017. "Combatting Fake News in the Digital Age." *Library Technology Reports* (American Library Association)53(8). Accessed November 28, 2017. https://journals.ala.org/index.php/ltr.

Campbell, W. Joseph. 2011. "The 'Anniversary' of a Media Myth: 'I'll Furnish the War'." Media Myth Alert. January 13. Accessed December 5, 2017. https://mediamythalert.wordpress.com/2011/01/13/the-anniversary-of-a-media-myth-ill-furnish-the-war/.

Carey, Benedict. 2017. "How Fiction Becomes Fact on Social Media." *The New York Times*. October 20. Accessed December 15, 2017. www.nytimes.com/2017/10/20/health/social-media-fake-news.html.

Coll, Steve. 2017. "Donald Trump's 'Fake News' Tactics." *The New Yorker*. December. Accessed December 4, 2017. www.newyorker.com/magazine/2017/12/11/donald-trumps-fake-news-tactics.

Cybercenter. 2018. "Russian Bots vs. the Gun Debate." *Cyber-Brief*. March 5. Accessed March 9, 2018. https://cyber-center.org/russian-bots-vs-the-gun-debate/.

Fallon, Kevin. 2012. "Fooled by *The Onion*: Nine Most Embarrassing Fails." *The Daily Beast*. September 29. Accessed November 18, 2016. www.thedailybeast.com/articles/2012/09/29/fooled-by-the-onion-8-most-embarrassing-fails.html.

Farsetta, Diana, and Daniel Price. 2006. *Fake TV News: Widespread and Undisclosed*. Madison, WI: Center for Media and Democracy. Accessed December 18, 2017. http://documents.routledge-interactive.s3.amazonaws.com/9780415517713/STUDENTS/chapter2/iw/dig_deeper/Fake_TV_News.pdf

Fuchs, Christian. 2012. "Dallas Smythe Today—the Audience Commodity, the Digital Labour Debate, Marxist Political Economy and Critical Theory. Prolegomena to a Digital Labour Theory of Value." *Cognition, Communication, Co-operation* 10(2): 692–740. Accessed June 8, 2017. www.triple-c.at/index.php/tripleC/article/view/443.

Fuchs, Christian, and Vincent Mosco. 2012. "Introduction: Marx is Back—The Importance of Marxist Theory and Research for Critical Communication Studies Today." *Cognition, Communication, Co-operation* 10(2): 127–140. Accessed March 19, 2017. www.triple-c.at/index.php/tripleC/article/view/421.

Gershgorn, David. 2016. "Facebook Has the Technological Capability to Fix Fake News, According to its Chief AI Researcher." Quartz. December 1. Accessed December 2, 2016. http://qz.com/850695/facebooks-fb-chief-ai-researcher-says-the-social-net work-has-the-technology-to-fix-fake-news/.

Gilbert, David. 2017. "Russia's Fake News Machine is Targeting the French Elections." *Vice News*. April 21. Accessed December 5, 2017. https://news.vice.com/story/russias-fake-news-machine-is-now-targeting-the-french-election.

Goldsmith, Belinda. 2017. "Trust the News? Most People Don't, Social Media Even More Suspect—Study." June 22. Accessed Novemeber 28, 2017. www.reuters.com/article/us-media-news-survey/trust-the-news-most-people-dont-social-media-even-more-suspect-study-idUSKBN19D015.

Greenwald, Glenn. 2017a. "Yet Another Major Russia Story Falls Apart. Is Skepticism Permissible Yet?" *The Intercept*. September 9. Accessed December 5, 2017. https://theintercept.com/2017/09/28/yet-another-major-russia-story-falls-apart-is-skepti cism-permissible-yet/.

Greenwald, Glenn. 2017b. "The US Media Suffered Its Most Humiliating Debacle in Ages and Now Refuses All Transparency Over What Happened." *The Intercept*. December 10. Accessed December 15, 2017. https://theintercept.com/2017/12/09/the-u-s-media-yesterday-suffered-its-most-humiliating-debacle-in-ages-now-refuses-all-trans parency-over-what-happened/.

Grice, Andrew. 2017. "Fake News Handed Brexiteers the Referendum—and Now They Have No Idea What They're Doing." *The Independent*. January 18. Accessed December 5, 2017. www.independent.co.uk/voices/michael-gove-boris-johnson-brexit-euro sceptic-press-theresa-may-a7533806.html.

Gu, Lion, Vladimir Kropotov and Fyoder Yarochkin. 2017. "The Fake News Machine: How Propagandists Abuse the Internet and Manipulate the Public." Trend Micro. Accessed May 30, 2017. www.google.com.au/url?sa=t&rct=j&q=&esrc=s&source= web&cd=2&cad=rja&uact=8&ved=0ahUKEwjmxNvY_N_XAhUCE5QKHTq LARkQFggvMAE&url=https%3A%2F%2Fdocuments.trendmicro.com%2Fassets% 2Fwhite_papers%2Fwp-fake-news-machine-how-propagandists-abuse-the-internet.p.

Harsanyi, David. 2017. "The Media Are Killing Themselves with Botched Anti-Trump Reporting." *The New York Post*. December 15. Accessed December 16, 2017. https://nypost.com/2017/12/15/the-media-are-killing-themselves-with-botched-anti-trump-reporting/?utm_campaign=applenews&utm_medium=inline&utm_source=applenews.

Herman, Edward, and Noam Chomsky. 1988. *Manufacturing Consent: The Political Economy of the Mass Media*. New York: Random House.

Hermida, Alfred. 2016. "Trump and Why Emotion Triumphs over Fact When Everyone is the Media." *The Conversation*. November 17. Accessed November 29, 2016. http://theconversation.com/trump-and-why-emotion-triumphs-over-fact-when-everyone-is-the-media-68924.

Himma-Kadakas, Marju. 2017. "Alternative Facts and Fake News Entering the Journalistic Content Production Cycle." *Cosmopolitan Civil Societies: An interdisciplinary journal* 9 (2): 25–40. Accessed December 16, 2017. doi:10.5130/ccs.v9i2.5469.

Hirst, Martin. 2011. *News 2.0: Can Journalism Survive the Internet?* Crows Nest, NSW: Allen and Unwin.

Howard, P. N., Samantha Bradshaw, Bence Kollanyi, Clementine Desigaud and Gillian Bollsover. 2017. *Junk News and Bots during the French Presidential Election: What Are French Voters Sharing Over Twitter?* Oxford: Oxford Internet Institute. Accessed

December 5, 2017. www.oii.ox.ac.uk/blog/junk-news-and-bots-during-the-french-presidential-election-round-ii.

Hunt, Julia. 2017. "'Fake News' named Collins Dictionary's Official Word of the Year for 2017." The Independent. 2 November. Accessed December 15, 2017. www.independent.co.uk/news/uk/home-news/fake-news-word-of-the-year-2017-collins-diction ary-donald-trump-kellyanne-conway-antifa-corbynmania-a8032751.html.

Main, Sami. 2017. "New Study Shows That the Number of Native Ad Buyers Increased by 74% in Just One Year." *AdWeek*. July 10. Accessed November 28, 2017. www.adweek.com/digital/new-study-shows-that-the-number-of-native-ad-buyers-increased-by-74-in-just-one-year/#/.

Malcolm, Lynne, and Olivia Willis. 2016. "The Psychology of Conspiracy Theories." All in the mind. Australian Broadcasting Corporation. February 17. Accessed December 13, 2016. www.abc.net.au/radionational/programs/allinthemind/the-psychology-of-conspiracy-theories/7177962.

Mansell, Robin. 2004. "Political Economy, Power and New Media." *New Media and Society* 6(1): 74-83.

McIlvenna, Una. 2017. "Why Fake News Is Anything but New." *Pursuit*. December 10. Accessed December 18, 2017. https://pursuit.unimelb.edu.au/articles/why-fake-news-is-anything-but-new.

McNair, Brian. 2018. *Fake News: Falsehood, Fabrication and Fantasy in Journalism*. Abingdon: Routledge.

Nelson S. 2016. "What is Fake News?" *Medium*. December 2. Accessed December 2, 2016. https://medium.com/@phalaris27/what-is-fake-news-eb6d15f19245#.qti65pt11.

Noak, Rick. 2016. "The Ugly History of 'Lügenpresse,' a Nazi Slur Shouted at a Trump Rally." *The Washington Post*. October 24. Accessed March 9, 2018. www.washingtonpost.com/news/worldviews/wp/2016/10/24/the-ugly-history-of-luegenpresse-a-nazi-slur-shouted-at-a-trump-rally/?utm_term=.c69efc8cc016.

Sarkis, Stephanie A. 2017. "11 Warning Signs of Gaslighting." *Psychology Today*. January 22. Accessed March 9, 2018. www.psychologytoday.com/blog/here-there-and-every where/201701/11-warning-signs-gaslighting.

Shane, Scott. 2017. "The Fake Americans Russia Created to Influence the Election." *The New York Times*. September 7. Accessed December 5, 2017. www.nytimes.com/2017/09/07/us/politics/russia-facebook-twitter-election.html.

Sharethrough. 2018. "Native Advertising—the Official Definition." Accessed March 9, 2018. https://sharethrough.com/nativeadvertising/.

Sharockman, Aaron. 2017. "We Started Fact-Checking in Partnership with Facebook a Year Ago Today. Here's What We've Learned." *PolitiFact*. December 15. Accessed March 9, 2018. www.politifact.com/truth-o-meter/article/2017/dec/15/we-started-fact-checking-partnership-facebook-year/.

Silverman, Craig. 2016. "This Analysis Shows How Fake Election News Stories Out-performed Real News On Facebook." Buzzfeed. November 17. Accessed December 13, 2016. www.buzzfeed.com/craigsilverman/viral-fake-election-news-outper formed-real-news-on-facebook?utm_term=.spE61G8py#.rbpGmqopA.

Smythe, Dallas. 2006. "On the Audience Commodity and its Work." In Media and cultural studies: Keyworks, by Meenakshi, Gigi Durham and Douglas Kellner, 230-256. Oxford: Blackwell.

Solon, Olivia. 2016. "Facebook's Failure: Did Fake News and Polarized Politics Get Trump Elected?" *The Guardian*. November 11. Accessed November 18, 2016. www.

theguardian.com/technology/2016/nov/10/facebook-fake-news-election-conspi
racy-theories.

Subramarnian, Samanth. 2017. "Inside the Macedonian." *Wired*. February 5. Accessed
December 5, 2017. www.wired.com/2017/02/veles-macedonia-fake-news/.

Swan, Thomas. 2016. "10 Reasons Why People Believe Conspiracy Theories." Owlca-
tion. May 13. Accessed December 13, 2016. https://owlcation.com/social-sciences/
10-Reasons-Why-People-Believe-In-Conspiracy-Theories.

Swift, Art. 2016. "Americans' Trust in Mass Media Sinks to New Low." Gallup.
September 14. Accessed December 2, 2016. www.gallup.com/poll/195542/ameri
cans-trust-mass-media-sinks-new-low.aspx.

Webre, Alfred Lambremont. 2016. "Comet Ping-Pong Pizzagate False Flag Shooter
"Crisis Actor" Meme Exposed!" NewsInsideOut.com. December 6. Accessed December 13, 2016. https://newsinsideout.com/2016/12/comet-ping-pong-pizzagate-false-
flag-shooter-crisis-actor-meme-exposed/.

Week. 2017. "Facebook Faces 'Fake News' Inquiry over Brexit." *The Week*. October 25.
Accessed December 5, 2017. www.theweek.co.uk/brexit/89229/facebook-faces-fake-
news-inquiry-over-brexit.

5

CAN JOURNALISM BE SAVED?

A Question that Won't Go Away

The question of journalism's survival has been around for at least a decade. In 2011 I wrote a book with the title *News 2.0: Can Journalism Survive the Internet?* At the time, I offered a cautious "yes," but this was heavily qualified with arguments that what might survive would not be the same the journalism that had existed throughout most of the Twentieth Century. It is interesting to me, though also a little sad, that in the intervening years things have got worse for journalism and journalists, not better. A central theme of *News 2.0* was that journalism faced two distinct but related crises; they are still here and they are getting deeper.

   The first crisis impacted directly on the profession itself and was a crisis of credibility and public trust. I argued that journalists were rapidly losing credibility because of their complicity in some of the most misleading stories of the previous decade, including the now infamous Saddam Hussein weapons of mass destruction lie about Iraq, that was used as a pretense for launching an unprecedented attack on a sovereign nation that the world is still paying for today in untallied quantities of blood and treasure. This story, and others like it before and since, have severed the bond of trust between journalists and their publics. My thesis in *News 2.0* was that the news audience would turn away from the mainstream media because of this trust and credibility issue and, instead, turn to alternative sources of information, including peer-to-peer sharing via social media networks. We have seen this become incontrovertible fact. Journalists today are still struggling to win back the trust of audiences and have to prove their credibility anew every day, on every new story. One lasting positive from this tale of mistrust is that the public today is perhaps more skeptical and less accepting of news reporting at face value and, perhaps also more equipped to carry out its own fact-checking. In this book I have taken my critique a step further to argue that the News Establishment is part of the problem and that we need to develop an alternative. Perhaps that alternative is "social journalism."

What we can also perhaps add today is that the trust problem is worse and there are two important reasons for this. The first is the avalanche of fake, or at least highly suspicious, news and news-like information now in circulation. The impact of this is not only on news publishers, who become suspect, but also on the platforms on which the fake news circulates. As the Tow Center report, *The Platform Press*, highlights, fake news is symptomatic of a "structural problem" related to Facebook's business model—to monetize popular content—and its reliance on algorithmic automation (Bell and Owen 2017: 59). Algorithms cannot process information based on its accuracy, only on its popularity; and this is where the second reason for declining trust emerges; the emergence of "click-bait content" using emotional hooks, "OMG" headlines, or sexual innuendo, to push otherwise unremarkable material. Such viral content is driving the revenue of platforms like Facebook and Google, but it is also increasingly important for new entrants (for example, *Buzzfeed*) and legacy news publishers who rely on it to drive traffic (ibid.: 45). How to best monetize this type of content and increase their market share is the problem that most worries the financial wizards of the News Establishment.

The second crisis affecting journalism in the twenty-first century is the crisis of profitability in the news industry itself. Today we can see that this crisis is in the process of ripping the News Establishment apart. Declining rates of profit have been a problem for some time, even perhaps from the mid-1970s on; but the relatively high rate of return on investment in the news industry, and the perception that advertisers were somehow captive to the publishers and broadcasters who delivered the audience for the advertised products, had masked the underlying problems. The cold hard truth was that the arrival of the Word Wide Web in the late 1990s changed forever the dynamic between publishers and audiences, between publishers and advertisers and between advertisers and audiences. Even more important, it was also beginning to change the relationships between audience members too. The Internet allowed a direct connection between members of the audience that had not previously existed. It shifted the news from a one-way model of communication into a dialogue and it put some power (not all of it) in the hands of the previously passive consumers. More importantly, it has shifted most of the economic power from the traditional news publishers towards the two giant technology platforms that have emerged in the last two decades. Google is the world's largest search engine, reaching an 80 percent market share since it was first conceived in 1995 (Heitzman 2017), and Facebook is the global equivalent of a large nation state with over 1.6 billion users. It's hard to remember a time before Facebook, but it has only

been around for about 15 years. Google and Facebook are effectively mono-
polies, even though it might not appear that way given that their products are
intangibles but they share many of the same characteristics, including both
vertical and horizontal integration and the ability to set terms for their clients
and their competitors. Google is also now moving to consolidate its market
power by also shifting into manufacturing objects that connect to the Internet of
things (see Chapter 1). Facebook is on a slightly different trajectory, it is seeking
to monopolize the distribution and monetization of content and advertising,
thereby compelling the media companies to meet its terms (Bell and Owen
2017: 46). Facebook is also in the data business and alarmingly seems willing to
burn its users in return for commercial relationships with third parties. The
centrality of data-mining to the profitability of Facebook was highlighted by the
Cambridge Analytica scandal in March 2018: Facebook's share price took a
steep dive as the company's indiscretions were gradually disclosed over the
period of several days. The drop of about 3.4 percent was reported to have seen
Mark Zuckerberg's holdings fall by about US$9 billion in in less than 72 hours
(Independent.ie 2018).

Publishers are reliant on the platform giants, but only take a small slice of the
revenue pie while giving up valuable data about their customers and, so far,

FIGURE 5.1   Facebook Share Price Tumbles on the Nasdaq Following the Cambridge
Analytica Scandal.

subscription models or even begging readers for charity contributions—as *The Guardian* does—have not been enough to fill the rapidly emptying coffers of the traditional news companies.

Today, if I ask "Can journalism survive the Internet?," or, as I titled this chapter, "Can journalism be saved?" my answer is not quite as optimistic as it was in 2011, and even then, I was ambivalent. Now, an air of realistic pessimism seems appropriate and it is shared by many of the reports and academic analyses I've read while writing this book. The depths of the crisis, and the lack of viable solutions to the problem of the news industry's economic survival, lead me and many other observers to rather pessimistic conclusions. When the most optimistic and Establishment-friendly language is "hopeful"; when the most successful experiments are described as being on the "fringes," and when US\$24 billion platform and mobile IPOs are failing to turn a profit (Bell and Owen 2017: 52), it is hard to see a way out of this economic hole.

In *News 2.0* I treated the crises of trust and profitability as separate categories for the sake of my argument and narrative, but I also made it clear that they were inextricably linked together in a tense relationship of contradiction and mutual need. I based my arguments in the tradition of political economy of communication. I was standing on the shoulders of giants when I made my observations. It is the same vantage point adopted in this book because the problems are almost identical, though more intractable and the contours sharper today than they were in 2011. The same issues are being discussed and they revolve around the same basic questions about the business model of the news industry and whether or not the News Establishment can continue to support public interest journalism, even though it helps to legitimize the system by reinforcing the Fourth Estate mythology of adversarial and power-shaming reporting. Political economy is fundamentally concerned with these issues and also incorporates a holistic and social view of technology, as outlined in Chapter 1. This means I do not adopt a deterministic position that says that digital technologies are the sole disruptor of the previous model. An historic view suggests that the seeds of the current crises were sown decades ago and, indeed that they are inherent in the commodity form of the news industry within a market-defined capitalist economy. However, before we venture into the economics of the news industry—present and future—a more fundamental question needs to be answered: "Do we actually need news and journalism to have a functioning democracy?" In other words, we need to ponder the issue of whether or not journalism is worth saving before we attempt to answer the questions surrounding how we might achieve its salvation.

Credibility and Crisis: Does Democracy Need Journalism?

Does democracy need journalism? It seems to be a reasonable question, and the instinctual answer is a resounding "yes." After all, isn't the raison d'être of the Fourth Estate to hold those in power to account for their deeds and their misdeeds? There is no doubt that this *watchdog* role is an essential feature of good journalism that claims to be in the public interest but so much of what we consider to be news today is no more than a sorry parade of gossip and public curiosity. Also, as I argued in chapter 1, the News Establishment today protects elites from too much public scrutiny, rather than speaking truth to power. There is also plenty of public disappointment with the news and with journalists because of the rise of so-called "fake news" (however you define it) and there are plenty of complaints about bias and the ways in which opinion has over-taken fact as the basis for much of what passes for reporting. Things are so bleak, it would seem, that there might even be a case to be made for the proposition that the media today is responsible for a weakening of democracy and a consequential rise in authoritarian politics. As John Keane has argued, a decadent media makes itself complicit with unscrupulous politicians to subvert democracy in favor of a "mediacy," an age of "organised political fabrication," which is aided and abetted by "accredited journalists and other public relations curators" (Keane 2013: 172).

Perhaps we have, to some extent, fetishized the role of the media in creating, supporting and protecting "democracy" and perhaps we've placed too much emphasis on the "Fourth Estate" model. According to classic interpretations of how the Fourth Estate is supposed to work, it has a watchdog role and is supposed to "speak truth to power." However, there is a mountain of evidence, both empirical and anecdotal, that in many instances, the news media colludes with power, rather than critiquing it and calling out abuses. The "Fourth Estate" is compromised by the commodified nature of journalism itself and the structure of the news markets. Critics of the news media and its supposed watchdog role have long argued that it is too close and too aligned with centers of power, and that "market forces coupled with public policy have tended to opt for private gain over the public interest" (Dahlgren 1991: 10). This same criticism is now being made about the new electronic public sphere ushered in by the opening up of the Internet in 1993. At that time, there was an air of promise and optimism that would align the open access design of the World Wide Web to the "civic purpose of journalism." However, today even the most optimistic acknowledge that the Internet we have is "a far cry from the open web of Tim Berners-Lee" and has become "dominated by a small number of platform companies" and not a space of democratic creation, free from com-mercial control or governmental interference (Bell and Owen 2017: 17). In fact, Berners-Lee himself made calls for greater "regulation" of the tech giants and called on Mark Zuckerberg to fix the problems with Facebook exposed by the Cambridge Analytica scandal. In an open-letter, Berners-Lee said that some tech companies had become "too powerful" because they could "control which ideas and opinions are seen and shared" (Solon 2018). In a series of tweets around the same time, Berners-Lee called on Web users to take action to secure their data:

What can web users do? Get involved. Care about your data. It belongs to you. If we each take a little of the time we spend using the web to fight for the web, I think we'll be OK. Tell companies and your government representatives that your data and the web matter.

(Ghosh 2018)

At the heart of the question about the relationship between journalism, the social web and democracy is the central ideal of the "Fourth Estate" – journalism's watchdog role, which theoretically holds those in powerful position responsible to the public. However, the history of the Fourth Estate and the material reality today show that the contemporary news media no longer represents a truly oppositional force to the powerful economic and political elite. The Fourth Estate was forged in the crucible of the revolutions that brought the bourgeoisie to power in Europe and later created the most powerful capitalist nation, the United States. The original Fourth Estate was a highly partisan form of journalism that excoriated the royal families and aristocracies of old Europe at a time when merchants, manufacturers, bankers and businessmen were fighting to release the yoke of feudal political rule exercised by Kings, Bishops and Popes. The political atmosphere was very different from that of today. In the Seventeenth and Eighteenth centuries, and indeed till the middle of the Nineteenth, the bourgeoisie was in the process of becoming the new ruling class and the newspapers of the day were important centers of agitation, exciting new ideas and revolutionary propaganda (Kaplan 2006: 178).

Once the bourgeois class had cemented its place at the center of economic and political power, it no longer needed an oppositional press. Instead, what it needed was a press that would support its continued rule and that would pacify the increasingly restless proletariat that the rise of capitalism both needed and feared in equal measure (I have written extensively on this in a previous book— see Patching and Hirst 2014—so this is a very brief summary of the full argument). Suffice to say that the Fourth Estate today is a vestigial reminder of what the press fought to become 200 years ago. Journalists cling to the ideal of being oppositional and of being gallant servants of the public who challenge the more outrageous deeds of corrupt rulers and economic tyrants; but, to be brutally honest, they are today paper tigers whose roar and fangs are ineffectual against the power of wealth and nation states. Today, the Fourth Estate is part of the News Establishment that resists, rather than promotes, fundamental and systemic change.

Journalists today effectively work to keep the system going, by providing ideological comfort to the subordinate social classes who labor under a veneer of democratic form, but whose economic exploitation is never fundamentally questioned by the Fourth Estate press. This is what Edward Herman and Noam Chomsky (1988) meant by their timeless phrase "the manufacture of consent." As Géraldine Muhlmann (2010) writes in *Journalism for Democracy*, the public only sees what journalism puts in front of them, but their "seeing" is interrupted by "structures which reflect the material domination of the moment, and hence confirm it." Thus, Fourth Estate journalism produces an ideological account of the world which, ultimately "serves to smooth over the differences, the gulf and the struggle between the dominant and the dominated." Further, Muhlmann argues, this type of journalism effectively "prevents any point of view that is truly challenging to the current domination in society from being made to emerge or being made visible" (ibid.: 118). The institutions of journalism, journalists, and their daily practices, are embedded in a social, economic and political culture which takes for granted certain assumptions about the world, about the nature of democracy and about the nature of capitalism that are all held within the ideology of "objectivity." This view presumes the neutrality of journalism and tends to hide or ignore the material features of journalism as a business which make it a supportive feature of the system overall, and it makes it difficult for news audiences to see the operations of the News Establishment clearly on a day-to-day basis. Objectivity has become the marker of an ideological view of journalism as professionalist, technocratic and somehow outside politics; it has removed from public expression all notions of classes and class struggle, in favor of a party-based approach to politics that privileges only "the policies and pronouncements of 'important' legitimate speakers from formal political institutions" (Kaplan 2006: 182).

Thus, it is possible to argue that "Yes," democracy does need journalism, but it must be clarified to specify that representative democracy, as exemplified in most Western capitalist nations, needs a particular kind of journalism. Representative democracy needs a journalism that will help it maintain the consent-producing fictions of formal equality and rights, while allowing the underlying inequalities of class, race and gender to be maintained in a mediated form that does not threaten the profitability of the system as a whole. In short, in order for it to survive as an economic and political system, capitalism requires the News Establishment to be on its side. The contradictions within the Fourth Estate model have led to what senior editor Janine Gibson (2017) has called a "relevance crisis" that does not lend itself to "simple answers." She is right; journalism cannot solve this problem while it is stuck in the paradigm of the fourth Estate:

> journalism is having a relevance crisis. Everyone else is utterly polarized, why wouldn't the Fourth Estate be just as divided? Journalism as we used to know it was split as to whether it was an honest trade or an honorable profession.
>
> *(Gibson 2017)*

Neither of these bi-polar paths can solve the crisis, they are two sides of the same dialectical coin. A different kind of journalism is needed under different circumstances; including under conditions of flux and change. It is hard for us to imagine what this might be like, but in chapter seven I attempt at least a partial imagining and explanation of the democratic role that social journalism might play. What we might see, and perhaps we already are seeing it in the fragmentation of audiences and the development of so-called "opinion bubbles," is a return to a more partisan form of media. This would be a media landscape in which objectivity is abandoned and journalists—whether amateur or professional—clearly profess for one viewpoint or another.

It is a contradiction of representative democracies that politicians rely on the media to provide them with symbolic support and to encourage the governed to lend their consent; but simultaneously, this is a role that tends to conflict with the symbolic role of the media as an oppositional Fourth Estate. It gives rise to a lot of ambiguity within the field of journalism which has its feet firmly rooted in capitalist commodity relations and its head in the idealistic clouds of democratic discourse (Bourdieu 1998). The Fourth Estate is symbolically oppositional to political power, but at the same time it is dialectically dominated by powerful economic and political factors (Champagne 2005), from which it cannot escape in any meaningful way. A study detailed in the *Columbia Journalism Review* highlights this in relation to coverage of the 2016 US Presidential election. It found that the most influential sources were not so-called "fake news," but the incomplete and, at times biased coverage of the campaign in the mainstream news media. The report's authors describe this as a broader failure of mainstream journalism to inform audiences of the very real and consequential issues at stake (Watts and Rothschild 2017). This can only lead to further disengagement among citizens who feel let down by the news media. In terms of Trump and his "war on the media," the more mistakes that the mainstream press and journalists make, the more effective his rhetoric becomes (Shafer 2017).

We can argue that social media has contributed to the crisis in trust, relevance and credibility now afflicting mainstream News Establishment organizations. Fake news in social media channels contributes to the rise in cynicism and mistrust. On the other hand, the rise of social media has facilitated a greater level of public scrutiny into the mainstream media system. This is how the contradictions and mutual constitution of journalism and social media play out dialectically. Therefore, it is difficult to know, at this point in time, if social media can play a more positive role in improving our democracies and assisting the prevention what some are suggesting is a backwards trajectory into authoritarianism and less democracy.

> At present, the authoritarianism business is booming. According to the Human Rights Foundation's research, the citizens of 94 countries suffer under non-democratic regimes, meaning that 3.97 billion people are currently controlled by tyrants, absolute monarchs, military juntas or

competitive authoritarians. That's 53 percent of the world's population. Statistically, then, authoritarianism is one of the largest—if not *the* largest— challenges facing humanity.

(Kasparov and Halvorssen 2017)

I would argue that journalism as presently constituted is—for the reasons outlined above—almost incapable of being a strong countervailing force against the "authoritarianism business," because it is compromised by its own profit-oriented institutions that tend to proffer systemic propaganda as news. In a capitalist society, journalism is dominated by market forces, including a heavy dependence on advertising and the support of governments to provide conducive regulatory and tax regimes that allow news companies to prosper. However, when the advertising model is broken and no longer provides guarantees of profits and shareholder returns, the news industry faces a second, and perhaps insurmountable, crisis. Today, the News Establishment is in the grip of this economic crisis: the question is "Can it recover?"

Why is the News Business Model Broken?

The advertising model has been breaking for some time, perhaps even since the 1970s when news and media companies were floated on the stock exchange and were no longer predominantly held by single family groups (Meyer 2009). Others have suggested that the decline in newspapers began when they hired large numbers of graduates with business degrees, but no real affinity with journalism (Underwood 1993). The consensus is that newspapers, in particular, but news media more generally, were in decline long before the Internet threw a giant spanner into the works of the printing press. The Internet, mobile devices and apps, have only accelerated the process of decline. Online media are slowly but surely killing newspapers in print; and perhaps podcasts and video streaming have already fatally undermined broadcasting. There is no going back, but also, the road ahead seems to be unmade, rocky, full of potholes and lined with bandits. The advertising model is still dominant, but it is not providing the large returns it used to for publishers and broadcasters. Instead it is a terrain defined by technologies that favor the largest platforms—Facebook and Google—and which undercuts the profitability of the legacy media at every turn (Bell and Owen 2017: 43).

To be effective, advertising has to be seen and then be a motivator to action. However, when the average viewer is spending less than 50 seconds on a web page or viewing content on a mobile device (Bilton 2017), the effectiveness of any advertising is decreased. This small insight is one key to the crisis of profitability in both legacy and emerging online news media models. The eyeballs are there, but they are not paying attention to the display advertising alongside the copy they are reading, or video they are watching. Publishers and the advertising industry have both been forced to the conclusion that "brand advertising" is a failing model that is being replaced by online direct marketing. The broken bond between advertisers and content publishers, through which the advertising previously subsidized the cost of producing news, is the big lesson of how the Internet has disrupted the twentieth century business model that once funded public interest journalism. There can be no return to the past; that road is permanently closed and the consensus is that advertising revenue will continue to fall. The Internet and mobile apps have created a new hybrid form of advertising that is not tied to content creation; classifieds and display advertising are losing ground, publishers are no longer in the driver's seat (Anderson, Bell and Shirky 2012).

We have known for some time—perhaps the last 25 to 30 years—that newspapers were a failing business model, but they were able to compete reasonably effectively with radio and television while ever these were the only platforms for news. The disruption caused by the arrival of digital media technologies has thrown all of that out the window. News has always been expensive and while it provided a means of attracting and holding audiences' loyalties to print and broadcast real estate, media capitalists tolerated the costs. The morning newspaper, delivered to tens of thousands of households, had a captive audience, at least until morning television began to steal away eyeballs. The evening television bulletin, usually broadcast in the strategic 6pm to 7pm timeslot was also a winning formula that set up evening viewing patterns well into what used to be considered "prime time" the period from about 7.30pm to 11pm. While networks competed against each other, the basic formula was to have successful news and current affairs shows in the early evening—fronted by telegenic and non-threatening "likeable" hosts—followed by a series of blockbuster programs; dramas, movies, variety shows and quiz games. Online streaming has effectively destroyed that model, with implications far beyond the news industry.

In hindsight, the twentieth-century media landscape resembles a lost Golden Age, and one that print and television executives look back on wistfully and with some regret. The first assault on free-to-air television's dominant position in broadcast news was the arrival of Ted Turner's upstart 24-hour news channel Cable News Network (CNN) in 1980. Cable and satellite subscription television punched a hole in prime time and the networks have never recovered. In order to stem the losses (at least temporarily) the television networks had to copy some aspects of their cable and satellite rivals; thus morning lifestyle "magazine" shows with chatty and annoying hosts jumping from segment to segment and much more opinion feeding into the news agenda, much like the formula pioneered by Fox News under the stewardship of disgraced former CEO Roger Ailes.

The basic problem in the news industry today is that the costs of production are greater than the revenues collected in the commodity exchanges that occur between advertisers and publishers and between publishers and consumers. As pointed out in previous chapters, the news commodity has a dual form. Part of the cost recovery occurs when a consumer pays for an item of news or media, in the form of outright purchase, or renting in the case of a subscription broadcast or narrowcast service. The second aspect of cost recovery is via the advertising transaction through which an advertiser buys access to a segment of a given audience. The problem for both legacy and new, digital, media is that the gap between income (the revenue stream from consumer purchases and advertisers) and costs of production has grown so wide that it is causing a collapse of media companies' bottom lines. As the political economy of news shows us, if a commodity is not profitable then capitalists will attempt to cut production costs to restore their rate of return. If this proves too difficult, they will simply stop producing it and move their investment funds to some other commodity form, location or industry till they find a satisfactory rate of return.

We are today faced with just such a crisis of production in what's left of the news industry. It is a problem that has affected the legacy media for perhaps a decade or more and is the major cause of job losses among journalists and other news employees. However, the logic of general adoption means that even new and emerging digital news media are faced with the same necessity to keep costs down. This is now a universally recognized position, even among supporters of public interest journalism inside the News Establishment.

> The broadly negative turn in the fortunes of legacy news businesses leads us to two conclusions: News has to become cheaper to produce, and cost reduction must be accompanied by a restructuring of organizational models and processes.
>
> *(Anderson, Bell and Shirky 2012: 11)*

Make no mistake, "restructuring" mean job cuts and smaller production budgets. The desired outcomes are that the cutting of costs will restore profitability and therefore lead to more investment in journalism; and, that restructuring will mean that journalists can be relieved of the trivial and menial tasks they are (supposedly) doing and, instead, be set to work on more important public interest reporting. While this sounds like a sensible plan, there is no proof that it will lead to the outcomes desired by the reformers. In fact, it appears that some of the digital start-ups, founded on this cheaper model, are already beginning to fail. Both the *Huffington Post* and *Buzzfeed* have been forced into redundancies and into cutting the number of journalists they employ; other start-ups have either closed or been forced into mergers in order to survive. The user-controlled site *Digg*, once valued at over $160 million, shut ignominiously in 2012 (CIO Insight 2012). Even the much-lauded pioneer of citizen journalism Andy Carvin was not a sufficient drawcard to keep his site, *Reported.ly*, alive after First Look Media cut its funding in 2016 (Ingram 2016). These closures and failures are not the only ones, just among the most prominent; they should not come as a surprise; the logic of competition and accumulation pushes all media companies in this direction.

The problem is that when such measures have been suggested and implemented across other industries and professions, the results have not been more and better jobs, but less workers, longer hours and smaller pay packets. There really is no way to sugar-coat this. The news industry is bound by the same logic of capital accumulation and periodic crisis that governs all sectors of the economy. For example, the technology revolution has not created a generation of young tech-savvy and well-paid IT professionals; jobs in computing have become proletarianized, down-graded, outsourced and underpaid. While the market value of the top tech companies has steadily increased over the past decade, they are actually employing less workers and on lower average salaries than they were in the year 2000 (Algaze 2017). The threat of lay-offs hangs over many tech workers, particularly if they are over 40 (Bort 2015). The experience of the digital news industry over the same period has been very similar; all the major national and international news organizations—from the *New York Times* down—have shed jobs in editorial and all supporting areas, including advertising sales. Despite some offsets, the growth of digital newsrooms has not matched the pace of lay-offs in legacy journalism. While exact figures are hard to quantify, globally, the news industry has shed tens of thousands of employees; this is no surprise when the global newspaper industry alone is losing advertising revenues of nearly US$3 billion annually (PWC 2017). The outlook across the new media news industry is also a pessimistic one. Many methods have been tried to raise revenues and replace the income lost from the decline in display and classified advertising—subscriptions, pay walls, pay-per-view mobile apps and micropayments—according to the experts they are failing, or underperforming (Anderson, Bell and Shirky 2012). A key report from the international peak body for newspaper publishers from 2017 suggests that as advertising revenue declines, print and online news media are looking to replace it with more subscribers. Of course, this has to have a friendly-sounding name, so it has become "audience-focused"—which simply means that newspaper publishers (in print and online) are now getting more revenue from sales than they are from advertising (Henriksson 2017).

Are Paywalls and Subscriptions a Savior for News Media?

In September 2017, the *Washington Post* announced it had reached a subscription base of one million readers for its online product, bringing it close to its competitor, the *Wall Street Journal* with just over 1.27 million subscriptions (Stelter 2017). The number of *WaPo* subscribers had doubled in the first six months of 2017—perhaps attributable to the Trump factor experienced by other news outlets who noticed a surge in subscribers following the 2016 election and January 2017 inauguration of Donald Trump. The *New York Times* reported it was signing up around 10,000 new subscribers every day in the weeks following Trump's swearing in ceremony. By May 2017 it had 2.5 million digital subscribers, setting a new record (Doctor 2017a). The *NYT* got to three million subscribers by the end of 2017, but it has admitted to a degree of "churn"—that is short-term subscribers who don't renew but are replaced by new ones. The cost of retaining subscribers is also high and has forced organizations like the *Times* to substantially increase its sales and marketing spend. It is going to take the *New York Times* at least another five years to get to its stated target of 10 million subscribers (Moses 2017).

Some commentators argued that this spike in subscriptions meant that paywalls are working and that people are willing to pay for quality journalism. But what happens if we take out the "Trump bump" from digital subscription figures? It is unlikely that American newspapers would have seen such a spike in readers willing to pay for online access if Hillary Clinton had won the November 2016 poll. Analysts have shown that globally only the bigger news brands have really benefited from solid growth in digital subscriptions, while smaller and regional outlets have shown only modest growth, or none at all. For newspapers, subscriptions to the print edition still dominate, in some cases in a ratio of 90 to 10 percentage points (Doctor 2017b). With these numbers and estimates that only three to four percent of the online news audience is actually paying for what it consumes, it is hard to see how paywalls and subscriptions are going to replace advertising revenue and help to keep sections of the legacy media afloat for much longer. Already the costs of printing a daily—or even a weekly—newspaper far outweigh the revenues generated from subscriptions. Advertising covers the shortfall, as it always has, but that avenue is closing fast for all the reasons we've discussed.

On the other hand, at the end of 2017, some commentators were beginning to see holes in the paywall and suggested that they might not be the savior we previously thought they were (Howard 2017). Writing on the *Newco Shift* blog, Rob Howard argued that paywalls are another flawed business model that are "doomed to fail" because it they are "inherently in conflict with journalism's primary goal," which is "to educate and inform the public about important issues." This is perhaps a controversial and unpopular view, but it is one I have some sympathy for. Howard's argument is that porous paywalls eventually lead to readers who won't pay to bypass it leaving for other free content. So, for most sites, Howard argues, a subscription model only really works with a hard paywall—that is, a paywall that does not allow any breaches.

Recent studies show that paywalls are not a savior for the news publishing industry. Digital subscriptions are accounting for only 20 to 30 percent of revenue for many large legacy publishers who have installed paywalls. In 2017, researcher Merja Myllylahti found that "paywalls provide additional revenue for newspaper publishers, although it is not substantial enough to sustain newsroom structures as print advertising and circulation continues to shrink" (Myllylahti 2017: 171). Myllylahti argues that if newspapers were funded by paywall revenue alone, they could only sustain "substantially smaller" newsrooms (ibid.: 173). Many newspapers are softening their digital paywalls because they need more readers. The most common paywalls are "freemium" paywalls in which some content is freely accessible, and the premium content is behind a paywall. Publishers have adopted this approach because they have to attempt to balance subscriptions with advertising revenues. If they take their content off-site, for example placing it in searchable Google caches, or on Facebook, they lose control over their audience and any income it might provide directly, or indirectly in the form of saleable data (Bell and Owen 2017). By allowing readers a limited amount of free access they are able to inflate their on-site numbers to maintain higher advertising rates. One example is a so-called "diamond" paywall introduced in 2017 at the Finnish daily, *Helsingen Sanomat*. The paper's diamond level subscription provides exclusive content that is not available behind its five free stories per week "soft" paywall (Hazard Owen 2017). For most readers, *Helsingin Sanomat* has a metered model, not hard paywall. It has introduced the diamond paywall for its digital-only, exclusive stories, and this is close to a hard paywall. A metered model allows people to read 5 to 10 stories on the *Helsingin Sanomat* site for free; after which they have to subscribe to access more content.

For mostly historical reasons, the of majority paywalls at legacy media—mainly newspapers that have shifted online—are at least a little bit porous. Some offer a limited number of articles for free before a cookie prevents you from any further access; but unless the freebie limit is set very low (at only a handful of articles per month) then for most readers it does not create a barrier. For some publications, paywalls are also breached by free services such as links shared to Facebook; Apple News on iOS devices, and by Google's similar news service which aggregate copy from many mastheads and present it free to viewers. These automated services collate news and organize it according to user preferences and many publishers feel the need to make their newsfeeds available to Apple and Google in order to boost their audiences. They do this to please their advertisers who like to reach as many eyeballs as possible, but it is a bit self-defeating because it cannibalizes their pay-to-view content protected behind a paywall, available (theoretically) only to subscribers. Even though these aggregator services are relatively new, they are attracting big audiences. Apple News reached over 40 million users after just a year of operation (Greenberg 2016).

Rob Howard has another argument against paywalls, and again, it is hard for me to disagree:

> The Internet business models reward future traffic rather than the author-
> ity and prestige that come from years of honest, serious reporting. They

push for more news, trendier news and faster news, and they discourage calm, thoughtful, responsible journalism.

(Howard 2017)

This comment highlights the inherent contradictions and the force of the dialectic pushing publishers towards third-party platforms. What initially seemed like a good idea actually ends up hurting the business even further. Publishers are now facing a further threat to their revenues, the rise of the platform giants, in particular Google and Facebook, which are capturing their audiences and the valuable metrics data that they generate.

Will Video Kill the News Websites?

The 1970s British pop group The Buggles famously sang that video would "kill the radio stars." It's a catchy tune and an infectious lyrical hook, but it is not a statement of fact. It certainly is not, with hindsight, all that historically accurate either. Ironically, the video of the song has had over 16.5 million views on YouTube since it was uploaded in January 2008. Today, a similar lament is being sung about the impact of the so-called "pivot to video" that became a newsroom mantra from about late 2015 and peaked less than two years later. "Publishers must acknowledge the pivot to video has failed, find out why," wrote Heidi Moore in a September 2017 column for *Columbia Journalism Review*. The evidence from audience measurement sites, such as comScore, seem to support the "video has failed" argument, showing that sites which moved heavily to video in 2016 were hemorrhaging page views (Moore 2017). The problem was compounded for some websites, analysts suggested, because they had to fire writers in order to pay for the more expensive video stories (Tani 2017). The so-called "pivot" to video was predicated on the demands that Facebook began to place on news publishers to monetize their content on the platform and to feed the all-powerful algorithms. However, for publishers, video proved to be expensive and difficult to produce in sufficient quantities to satisfy the demands put on them by third-party platforms (Bell and Owen 2017: 37–38). By the end of 2017, the influential Nieman Labs had written off the pivot as "a Hail Mary attempt to ease economic and investor pressure by pandering to ad buyer preferences," that had failed (Banikarim 2017). *Gizmodo* editorial director Susie Banikarim pronounced it dead in a piece headlined "RIP Pivot to Video (2017–2017)." Like many other fads promoted by the gurus of the News Establishment, this one too was DOA.

On the other side of the ledger, one of the companies that comScore highlighted as losing up to 60 percent of its traffic hit back at the suggestion that it was in trouble because of its emphasis on video. According to a *Mic* executive most of the audience for its videos was on other social media channels that comScore's measuring failed to pick up. *Mic* is not unique in this regard; it is a service aimed at younger "millennial" audiences, and the company believes that this demographic is more open to video stories (Shields 2017). A number of major players, particularly among the newer digital-only news publishers who also have millennials as their target, have also embraced the shift to video and laid of editorial writers. The business model of these new entrants is well captured by the *Mic* "about" statement:

> *Mic* was born out of the recognition that the old models of journalism had become less engaging and relevant. While maintaining the rigor and commitment to original reporting and championing essential fact-finding, *Mic* has sought to give voice to critical news stories from modern and diverse perspectives.
>
> *(Mic 2017)*

As well as hosting content on its own site, *Mic* (and similar services) also make extensive use of social media channels where video content has more traction. For example, *Mic* has over 3.5 million Facebook followers. However, the pivot to video is not all about creating more exciting and viewable content. Despite its confident approach in 2017, by early in 2018 *Mic* was having to deflect rumors that it was in financial trouble and looking for a buyer and, it seems, the "millennials-focused" site was in the midst of another "pivot":

> *Mic* feels as if it's found the type of journalism that works. If the company once aspired to be a newfangled CNN, now it has a new role model: "60 Minutes" for the social-video generation.
>
> [*Mic* CEO Chris] Altchek said *Mic* had found a sweet spot by shooting videos focused on social justice, diversity, women's issues, and other progressive causes. It cranks out roughly 2½ hours of video a month. "We produce much less content that we used to," he said. "But it's much higher-quality journalism."
>
> *(Shields 2018)*

The "pivot" had to be invented because news executives had known for some time that banner advertisements at the top of web pages were no longer working, "and the solution, handed down by frantic media executives, is video" (Schonfeld 2017). As with most decisions impacting on staffing, resources and outputs in the news business today, this one is driven by simple economics.

> Why this is happening is simple: The web has a surplus of copy versus advertising. Companies have decided that sticking an ad at the front of a video makes it less ignorable than putting a similar ad next to an article.
>
> *(Curtis 2017)*

As Bryan Curtis points out in the piece this quote is taken from, perfecting the pivot did not prove easy for those, like MTV and Fox Sports among others, who tried it throughout 2016. However, this does not mean that video is not important. On social media and particularly on phone screens, the short vertical video—shot in portrait mode, not landscape—is still vitally important for eye-witness accounts, breaking news and topical "filler" pieces (Ferne 2017).

The video pivot was just one of several formatting experiments being trialed across mobile devices and social platforms such as SnapChat to try and win and retain younger audiences for news. The platform distribution model is here to stay, for the time-being at least, along with the native advertising model in which marketing is disguised as news-like information, but nobody is suggesting that they have found the solution. Instead there is a push towards a "three tier" model of "advertising, subscriptions and not-for-profit" (Bell and Owen 2017: 51). However, this hybrid is also fraught with contradictions; for example, how should a publication like *The Guardian* be viewed? While it claims to be a not-for-profit publication and says it is proud to not have adopted a paywall/subscription, it accepts native advertising, or what it coyly calls "paid content" and it also has a pleading (and annoying) pop-up at the end of every article, soliciting donations from readers. I like *The Guardian*, at least compared to some news outlets, but I find its approach to fundraising to be misleading. The company is run according to the rules of the news business—to all intents and purposes it is a highly commercial enterprise that operates its newsroom according to cost-recovery principles. *The Guardian* is a not-for-profit in name only and it is effectively marketing subscriptions/donations as a way of keeping itself afloat in a commercial sense. However, we should consider the not-for-profit sector that is funded by foundation money or wealthy individuals as it has become a key player in public interest reporting.

Market Failure and Philanthropy

There is no doubt that the advertising market has failed the news industry, and this applies across all media. In fact, it is a recurring feature of the political economy of capitalism, the news media is not immune, despite some believing it to be a special category of industry that might, somehow, escape the logic and contradictions of capitalism. The heart of the failed market is that production costs are high and the rate of return is low: the news industry has become "inefficient, expensive, wasteful and it hinders our resources to create the best

FIGURE 5.2   *The Guardian* Solicits Donations from Supporters to Pay for its Journalists.

journalism possible" (Gautier 2017). Executives in the news industry, academics from several disciplines and armchair experts from around the globe have been trying to fix the problem with various proposals to "redesign" the news economy and re-imagine the news industry at the level of production, distribution and consumption. For Teun Gautier, the solutions are quite simple and he has distilled them down to five key points:

1 **Brand proposition:** Content is only a part of the total publisher proposition—a sense of belonging, connection to peers, events, retailing, selection and other elements are possibly of more value.
2 **Single article sales:** Content consumption is increasingly content driven ... Publishers should re-design their infrastructure to adopt this new potential and focus on targeted selling of single articles.
3 **Industry-wide micropayment standard:** In order to monetise the single article sales, we need an industry-wide micropayment capacity.
4 **Syndication:** Creating one's own content and distributing it only on one platform is a huge waste of our industry's capacity ... Publishers should re-sell their content to others and buy existing content in return.
5 **Freelancers:** Freelancers will, expectedly, produce up to 70 per cent of all journalistic content ... Publishers could capitalise on this distributed production ecosystem by innovating their relationships with freelancers.

(Gautier 2017)

The result of the changes outlined above, Gautier argues, will be a "fundamentally different" news ecosystem: "Creating a fundamentally different networked ecosystem will generate lower cost, higher efficiencies, higher revenues and, as a result, more vital, sustainable and relevant journalism."

Unfortunately, nothing in Gautier's list is all that new, or innovative. Networking news has only resulted in the industry's problems being transferred to a new terrain, it has not turned around costs, efficiency or revenues. Engagement strategies have been in place now for over a decade with mixed, but mostly limited beneficial results; micro-payments have a similar history and, so far, have not provided anything like a sustainable yield to publishers. If you do the math, as I did in *News 2.0*, it is clear that micro-payments have to be averaged over tens of millions of transactions before any kind of profitability is established. Syndication of copy has been around for two centuries; buy-ins now dominate some news outlets who can no longer afford their own networks of correspondents; and freelancers have long been the exploited underbelly of the news industry. Freelance rates are dropping like stones. A good union rate might be around US$1.00 a word on paper, but no publishers are paying this rate today. I regularly see freelance jobs advertised in my large metropolitan market with a going rate of 10 cents per word. Not only is that insulting to hard working freelancers, it is a wage well below the poverty line. It is hard to see any freelancer supporting herself on that kind of return, even if they work 80 hours a week and never turn down a job. It is against this background that we have seen a renewal of interest in not-for-profit (or non-profit) models and an emphasis on philanthropy. Even *The Guardian* and *The New York Times* have now established executive positions to generate income from so-called philanthropic giving. Similarly, freelancers are attempting to find charitable income sources and to finance their work via online giving sites like Paetron and GoFundMe, with limited success. Journalism schools now have a focus on "entrepreneurial journalism," which is really preparing graduates for a life of under-employment poverty in the "gig economy" (EFJ 2017). The problem with this approach, like with Gautier's suggestions above, is that it cannot overcome the fundamental political economy of the news industry and it is virtually impossible to sit outside it with any kind of success, because the dialectic of the commodity form is too powerful. The market might be failing, but its grip is still strong at the institutional level and also in the ideology of the News Establishment, which is predicated on a flawed "marketplace of ideas" philosophy.

Not-for-profit news media must be able to cover their costs somehow, and many of them fail because it is difficult to do so (Westpahal 2017). Most American non-profit media are small with budgets under US$500,000 and many are attempting to work in small, local markets, which is difficult in itself (Rosenstiel et al. 2016). Whether they recover a portion of their costs through subscriptions, by selling stories to other outlets, and/or a paywall is irrelevant in a sense. If the aim to produce and promote public interest journalism, then somebody has to pay for it. One method of covering the cost of producing public interest reporting that has come to prominence in recent years is the appeal to philanthropic individuals and foundations to support journalism.

In recent years—Perhaps the last 10 to 15—There has been a growth in the number of non-profit news organizations that have sprung up with the support (usually) of a generous (and rich) philanthropist. Some of these were short-lived and tended to go as quickly as they came once the benefactor either ran out of money or fell out with the editorial team. One of these was the Australian-based publication, *The Global Mail*, which arrived with a fanfare and sank without trace less than five years later. Other outfits have had more staying power, either because they have been able to diversify the sources of their funding—*The Conversation* is one that comes to mind—or because they have found a business model that appears to be sustainable and stable enough to weather the ridges and troughs of the business cycle. For some newspaper owners, turning their once profitable money-burning operations over to a not-for-profit seems like a way of saving the journalism. Geoffrey Lenfest, octogenarian owner of the *Philadelphia Inquirer*, made just such a move in 2016.

According to a report in the *Columbia Journalism Review* there were more than 100 established news outlets in the USA that were funded by philanthropists at the end of 2017 (Westpahal 2017) The not-for-profit model seems to be doing well in the United States where a 2013 Pew Research Center report found over 150 NFP outfits were doing some form of journalism. But the report's authors were also quick to point out that, while some were doing well, the sector as a whole was fragile and facing problems going forward (Mitchell et al. 2013). Others are more optimistic, insisting that there is room for more philanthropy in the journalism business (Westpahal 2017). Indeed, American not-for-profits have banded together to lobby for their collective interests and to promote effective investigative, public interest journalism (INN 2017). This is a welcome endeavor and it has already produced some impressive results—The Panama Papers and other large-scale investigations—but how sustainable is it in the long run? The News Establishment is not running a charity, and if a journalistic activity does not produce a return on investment (ROI) it will be discarded, just as the pivot to video was abandoned when it no longer worked.

While philanthropic funding of journalism seems to be an altruistic approach to fixing the business model crisis, it is not without its own problems. A research paper by Professor Rodney Benson, published online in August 2017, is the most comprehensive assessment to-date of the trend towards philanthropy-supported journalism. Unfortunately, Professor Benson's analysis is not very promising. Two notable findings from his project are worth highlighting upfront because they encapsulate very nicely the essence of the problem. Professor Benson notes firstly that "financial elites' tend to dominate decision-making structures at board level in commercial news organizations, not-for-profit news organizations and philanthropic foundations. Secondly, and perhaps, at least partially, as a consequence of the first finding, philanthropic support tends to reinforce an "upper middle-class, pro-corporate orientation in mainstream American journalism" (Benson in press: 2).

To say I'm not surprised by this is an understatement. It is precisely what I would have expected, even if Benson had found that the boards were not dominated by the "financial elites." Predominance of elites on the boards of these organizations is to be expected; it is what elites do and what makes them elite. However, structural political economy factors, as I outlined above, are just as, if not more, important. Financial elites are invested in the profit motive and, as Benson (ibid.: 2) points out, attempting to conjoin this with public interest journalism has never really worked. It was, Benson points out, already "unravelling" at the turn of the last century. There is a fundamental series of tensions between profit and public interest that are inherent in the capitalist mode of production. Journalism and, more importantly, the news industry are not immune to these pressures which form an inescapable dialectic vacuum which forces philanthropic models into the contradiction between wanting to be economically sustainable (that is, turn a profit and return on investment) and to act in the public interest. As Benson notes (ibid.: 1), this means non-profits will inevitably "reproduce dominant commercial media news practices" or be doomed to serve only small "elite" audiences. This is a big problem for non-profits attempting to compete with the mainstream news media. Inevitably, like *The Guardian*, they will be drawn into the contradictions inherent in the market-driven model. Clinging hopefully to the troubled Fourth Estate model is unlikely to save either the not-for-profits, or the commercial news media. However, the political economy dialectics of the news industry compels them to keep trying to save themselves, and this is the bottom line for all of the experimentation with social media applications and techniques. As we've seen in this chapter, the news media has a conflicted relationship with the platform giants, but at the same time it is forced to engage with them and with other social media channels because, increasingly, this is where the audience is to be found. The following chapter explores the ways in which news organizations have attempted to harness social media to engage audiences and to monetize these interactions.

References

Algaze, Ben. 2017. "What Happened to the Tech Job Boom?" Extreme Tech. September 20. Accessed September 28, 2017. www.extremetech.com/computing/256056-where-is-the-tech-job-boom.

Anderson, C. W., Emily Bell and Clay Shirky. 2012. *Post-Industrial Journalism: Adapting to the present.* New York: Columbia Journalism School/Tow Center for Digital Journalism.

Banikarim, Susie. 2017. "RIP Pivot to Video (2017–2017)." NiemanLab Predictions for 2018. December. Accessed March 9, 2018. www.niemanlab.org/2017/12/r-i-p-pivot-to-video-2017-2017/.

Bell, Emily, and Taylor Owen. 2017. *The Platform Press: How Silicon Valley Reengineered Journalism.* New York: Tow Center for Digital Journalism. Accessed April 19, 2017. www.cjr.org/tow_center_reports/platform-press-how-silicon-valley-reengineered-journalism.php.

Benson, Rodney. In press. "Can Foundations Solve the Journalism Crisis?" *Journalism* [online first: August 31, 2017]: 1–19. Accessed September 11, 2017. doi:10.1177/1464884917724612.

Bilton, Ricardo. 2017. "Publishers are Seeing Real Performance Gains from Google AMP and Facebook Instant Articles (but $$$ Remains a Question Mark)." NiemanLab. September 27. Accessed September 28, 2017.www.niemanlab.org/2017/09/publishers-are-seeing-real-performance-gains-from-google-amp-and-facebook-instant-articles-but-remains-a-question-mark/.

Bort, Angela. 2015. "Some Tech Workers over 50 are Literally Working Themselves to Death — and Other Things We Discovered about Their Careers." *Business Insider.* November 14. Accessed September 28, 2017. www.businessinsider.com/stressful-lives-of-older-tech-workers-2015-11?IR=T.

Bourdieu, Pierre. 1998. *On Television and Journalism.* London: Pluto Press.

Champagne, Patrck. 2005. "The 'Double Dependency': The Journalistic Field between Politics and Markets." In *Bourdieu and the Jounalistic Field*, edited by Rodney Benson and Erik Neveu, 48–63. Cambridge: Polity.

CIO Insight. 2012. "How Not To Run a Social News Site: The Demise of Digg." *CIO Insight*. June 16. Accessed August 3, 2017. http://search.ebscohost.com/login.aspx?direct=true&db=bah&AN=89810581&site=ehost-live.

Curtis, Bryan. 2017. "What 'Pivoting to Video' Really Means." *The Ringer*. July 3. Accessed July 4, 2017. www.theringer.com/2017/7/3/16045198/fox-sports-mtv-news-vocativ-layoffs-pivot-to-video-77e441a49cb7.

Dahlgren, Peter. 1991. "Introduction." In *Communication and Citienship: Journalism and the Public Sphere*, edited by Peter Dahlgren and Colin Sparks, 1–25. London: Routledge.

Doctor, Ken. 2017a. "Behind the *Times*' Surge to 2.5 Million Subscribers." *Politico*. May 12. Accessed May 14, 2017. www.politico.com/media/story/2016/12/behind-the-times-surge-to-25-million-subscribers-004876.

Doctor, Ken. 2017b. "Newsonomics: Our Peggy Lee Moment: Is That All There is to Reader Revenue?" NiemanLab. September 26. Accessed September 28, 2017. www.niemanlab.org/2017/09/newsonomics-our-peggy-lee-moment-is-that-all-there-is-to-reader-revenue/.

EFJ. 2017. "Studies Find Precarious Employment Tied to Digitalisation and the Gig Economy." European Federation of Journalists. November 6. Accessed March 9, 2018. https://europeanjournalists.org/blog/2017/11/06/studies-find-precarious-employment-tied-to-digitalisation-and-the-gig-economy/.

Ferne, Tristan. 2017. "Beyond 800 Words: New Digital Story Formats for News." BBC News Labs. September 20. Accessed October 4, 2017. https://medium.com/bbc-news-labs/beyond-800-words-new-digital-story-formats-for-news-ab9b2a2d0e0d.

Gautier, Teun. 2017. "Redesigning the Journalistic Economy as if Starting from Scratch." Journalism.co.uk. November 20. Accessed January 2, 2018. www.journalism.co.uk/news-commentary/redesigning-the-journalistic-economy-as-if-starting-from-scratch/s6/a713512/.

Ghosh, Shona. 2018. "The Web's Creator Has Some Advice for Mark Zuckerberg—and Said He Sometimes Feels Devastated by His Own Invention." *Business Insider*. March 23. Accessed March 24, 2018. www.businessinsider.com.au/tim-berners-lee-mark-zuckerberg-cambridge-analytica-2018-3?r=US&IR=T.

Gibson, Janine. 2017. "A Crisis of Relevance." *Columbia Journalism Review*. Fall. Accessed December 28, 2017. www.cjr.org/special_report/news-janine-gibson-newspapers-audience.php.

Greenberg, Julia. 2016. "Apple Wants All Publishers to Join Apple News (And Look Good) Now, Too." *Wired*. March 15. Accessed September 28, 2017. www.wired.com/2016/03/apple-wants-publishers-join-apple-news-look-good-now/.

Hazard Owen, Laura. 2017. "Don't Try Too Hard to Look Cool (and Other Lessons from European Newsrooms' Digital Experiments)." NiemanLab. September 26. Accessed September 26, 2017. www.niemanlab.org/2017/09/dont-try-too-hard-to-look-cool-and-other-lessons-from-european-newsrooms-digital-experiments/.

Heitzman, Adam. 2017. "How Google Came To Dominate Search And What The Future Holds." *Forbes*. June 5. Accessed August 21, 2017. www.forbes.com/sites/forbesagencycouncil/2017/06/05/how-google-came-to-dominate-search-and-what-the-future-holds/#709bd3283872.

Henriksson, Teemu. 2017. "World Press Trends 2017: The Audience-Focused Era Arrives." WAN-IFRA Blog. June 8. Accessed March 9, 2018. https://blog.wan-ifra.org/2017/06/08/world-press-trends-2017-the-audience-focused-era-arrives-0.

Herman, Edward, and Noam Chomsky. 1988. *Manufacturing Consent: The Political Economy of the Mass Media*. New York: Random House.

Hirst, Martin. 2011. *News 2.0: Can Journalism Survive the Internet?* Sydney: Allen and Unwin.

Howard, Rob. 2017. "Why Paywalls Don't Work." Newco Shift. December 19. Accessed December 29, 2017. https://shift.newco.co/why-paywalls-dont-work-7e658576e311.

Independent.ie. 2018. "Facebook Chief Takes $9bn Hit as Share Price Falls." *The Independent*. March 23. Accessed March 24, 2018. www.independent.ie/business/technology/facebook-chief-takes-9bn-hit-as-share-price-falls-36727319.html.

Ingram, Mathew. 2016. "Andy Carvin Talks About First Look Media Shutting Down His Social News Wire." *Fortune*. August 15. Accessed August 3, 2017. http://search.ebscohost.com/login.aspx?direct=true&db=bah&AN=117498743&site=ehost-live.

INN. 2017. "About." Institute for Nonprofit News. Accessed December 28, 2017. https://inn.org/about/.

Kaplan, Richard K. 2006. "The News About New Institutionalism: Journalism's Ethic of Objectivity and Its Political Origins." *Political Communication* 23: 173–185. doi:10.1080/10584600600629737.

Kasparov, Gary, and Thor Halvorssen. 2017. "Why the Rise of Authoritarianism is a Global Catastrophe." *The Washington Post*. February 13. Accessed August 3, 2017. www.washingtonpost.com/news/democracy-post/wp/2017/02/13/why-the-rise-of-authoritarianism-is-a-global-catastrophe/?utm_term=.d1ec459e8aba.

Keane, John. 2013. *Democracy and Media Decadence*. Cambridge: Cambridge University Press.

Meyer, Philip. 2009. *The Vanishing Newspaper: Saving Journalism in the Information Age*. 2. Columbia, MO: University of Missouri Press.

Mic. 2017. "About." Accessed October 4, 2017. https://mic.com/about#.q1JIvITFy.

Mitchell, Amy, Mark Jurkowitz, Jess Holcomb, Jodi Enda, and Monica Anderson. 2013. "Nonprofit Journalism: A Growing but Fragile Part of the U.S. News System." Pew Research Center. June 10. Accessed January 5, 2017. www.journalism.org/2013/06/10/nonprofit-journalism/.

Moore, Heidi N. 2017. "The Secret Cost of Pivoting to Video." *Columbia Journalism Review*. September 26. Accessed September 28, 2017. www.cjr.org/business_of_news/pivot-to-video.php.

Moses, Lucas. 2017. "To Get to 10 Million Subscribers, The New York Times is Focusing on Churn." DigiDay. October 26. Accessed March 9, 2018. https://digiday.com/media/get-10m-subscribers-new-york-times-focusing-churn/.

Muhlmann, Géraldine. 2010. *Journalism for Democracy*. Translated by Jean Birrell. Cambridge: Polity.

Myllylahti, Merja. 2017. "Newspaper Paywalls and Corporate Revenues: A Comparative Study." In *The Routledge Companion to Digital Journalism Studies*, edited by Bob Franklin and Scott Eldridge II, 166–175. Abingdon: Routledge.

Patching, Roger, and Martin Hirst. 2014. *Journalism Ethics: Arguments and Cases for the Twenty-First Century*. Abingdon: Routledge.

PWC. 2017. "Global Entertainment and Media Outlook 2017–2021." PriceWaterhouse-Cooper. Accessed September 28, 2017. www.pwc.com/gx/en/industries/entertainment-media/outlook/segment-insights/newspapers.html.

Rosenstiel, Tom, William Buzenberg, Marjorie Connelly, and Kevin Loker. 2016. "A Look at the Landscape of Nonprofit Journalism." American Press Institute. April 20.

Accessed December 28, 2017. www.americanpressinstitute.org/publications/reports/look-nonprofit-journalism/.

Schonfeld, Zac. 2017. "MTV News—and Other Sites—Are Frantically Pivoting to Video. It Won't Work." *Newsweek*. June 30. Accessed October 4, 2017. www.newsweek.com/mtv-news-video-vocativ-media-ads-pivot-630223.

Shafer, Jack. 2017. "Who's Winning Trump's War With the Press?" Politico. December 27. Accessed December 28, 2017. www.politico.com/magazine/story/2017/12/27/trump-press-war-winning-216160?cid=apn.

Shields, Mike. 2017. "Millennial Publisher Mic.com Says comScore Data Showing a Shrinking Audience is Wrong—and it Exposes a Critical Disagreement in Digital Media." *Business Insider*. September 20. Accessed September 21, 2017. www.businessinsider.com.au/miccoms-video-pivot-has-comscore-data-showing-audience-dropping-2017-9?r=US&IR=T.

Shields, Mike. 2018. "Digital Media Startup Mic Says it's Doing Just Fine Despite Talk of an Industry Armageddon." *Business Insider*. March 8. Accessed March 9, 2018. www.businessinsider.com/digital-media-startup-mic-wants-to-set-the-record-straight-2018-3/?r=AU&IR=T.

Solon, Olivia. 2018. "Tim Berners-Lee: We Must Regulate Tech Firms to Prevent 'Weaponised' Web." *The Guardian*. March 12. Accessed March 24, 2018. www.theguardian.com/technology/2018/mar/11/tim-berners-lee-tech-companies-regulations.

Stelter, Brian. 2017. "Washington Post Digital Subscriptions Soar Past 1 Million Mark." CNN Media. September 26. Accessed September 28, 2017. http://money.cnn.com/2017/09/26/media/washington-post-digital-subscriptions/index.html.

Tani, Maxwell. 2017. "Mic is Laying Off Staff as it Prepares for a Pivot to Video." *Business Insider*. August 8. Accessed October 4, 2017. www.businessinsider.com.au/mic-staff-layoffs-pivot-to-video-2017-8.

Underwood, Derek. 1993. *When MBAs Rule the Newsroom: How the Marketers and Managers are Reshaping Today's Media*. New York: Columbia University Press.

Watts, Duncan J.,, and David M. Rothschild. 2017. "Don't Blame the Election on Fake News. Blame it on the Media." *Columbia Journalism Review*. December 5. Accessed December 28, 2017. www.cjr.org/analysis/fake-news-media-election-trump.php.

Westphal, David. 2017. "Journalism's New Patrons: California Nonprofit Targets Individual Donors." *Columbia Journalism Review*. October 30. Accessed December 28, 2017. www.cjr.org/business_of_news/calmatters-nonprofit-journalism-california.php.

6

SOCIAL JOURNALISM AND THE NEWS ESTABLISHMENT

Social Journalism in the Newsroom

Discussion in this chapter is focused on a definition of social journalism that situates it as an adjunct to the work of professional journalists. Julia Haslanger notes that the term "social journalist" can apply to people both inside and outside the traditional newsroom structure. She writes that it can apply "to many journalists in different roles" (Haslanger 2016), but as I've argued previously (Hirst 2011), we need to be fairly precise and consistent in using terms like *citizen journalism, alternative journalism, social journalism, social news*, and so on; otherwise our language becomes too broad and our definitions lose their value for analytical purposes. In this and the next chapter I attempt to sort out a clear definition, beginning inside the News Establishment, and moving beyond it in the next.

"Social media" is the first term we need to be clear about What is it? Most of us would understand it intuitively as a series of networked platforms on the Internet and applications on our mobile devices, through which we connect with friends, family, colleagues, associates and random strangers (Hermida 2016). Our connections can have a multitude of purpose:

- to trade gossip, images, videos, personal information or news (Facebook, WhatsApp, Snapchat, Twitter, Pinterest, Instagram, etc.);
- to play games and connect with like-minded gamers anywhere in the world;
- for professional engagement (LinkedIn, Academia.edu);
- to engage in random acts of consensual sex (Tinder, Grind'r) or to find ever-lasting love (dating websites); and
- to keep up with news from other sources, either mainstream news feeds, or alternative sites and reporters we like.

Through social media we have the ability to connect (at least superficially) with a lot more people than can possibly fit into our real-world circles of friends, family, work colleagues and acquaintances. Using social media can make us feel connected and that we are engaging with a large group of people. Social media can feel like breaking down the isolation of six degrees of separation. When it comes to news, many of us are now interpreting mainstream news, and making sense of it, through the lens of social media sharing (Steensen 2016: 115). Social media has many functions, from education and collaboration that can be professionally useful; to entertainment that can be distracting, or even addictive to some. The bottom line with social media is communication and engagement (Safco and Brake 2009: 2). Various sites and applications within the realm of social media have different functions, some are purely for social networking, for meeting people and staying connected; others are more useful for the news industry and for journalists (both professional and amateur). The useful sites enable sharing of content, words, images or video, and some are actually publishing platforms hosting original content, blogs, news or other useful information. Some are also "live" and are useful for on-the-scene broadcasts or face-to-face video communication (the most useful apps are discussed in Chapters 9, 10 and 11).

Increasingly, however, our engagement is being monetized, not necessarily by us, but by someone, or some corporation. Gaming apps have what they call "in-game purchases" that can lead to inadvertent spending on upgrades or accessories; news apps are increasingly accessed only by subscription or by micro-payments for articles downloaded; most free apps have an upgrade, paid version that unlocks more features and work on annual subscriptions; and on free apps, like Twitter, we get advertisements dropped into our timelines. There's nothing we can do about it. Did you read the T&Cs? Increasingly, as I've pointed out already, our data is also valuable and highly prized. Social media is fantastic for making and maintaining connections, but our engagement has a price, and that price is that we give up data about ourselves, as well as some of our online privacy; ultimately, we end up as disembodied eyeballs sold and traded in the digital advertising market. An alternative option to the reality of the mainstream turning user-generated content into another profit center, is for the former audience to take on more of an active role in producing, circulating and curating news of, for and by itself. The platform(s) for this is (are) already primed; social media provides a space where citizens can organize and share without any controlling intervention by professional journalists Perhaps this is the future and the true meaning of the term "social journalism," and we will explore it in the next chapter. However, like many such new terms it is still fluid; an agreed definition has not yet been pinned down. Before we can talk too much about what it *might* be, we need to have a better understanding of what social journalism is, and *what it is not*, in the here-and-now.

Innovation, Audiences and the News Establishment

The News Establishment's push towards co-opting audience members into *some form* of participation in newsroom activities has accelerated over the past decade or so, largely driven by the economics of newspapers. The failure of the twentieth-century print journalism business model—expensive newsrooms funded by advertising revenues and sales of "dead tree" newspapers—is the real driving force in experiments at "crowdsourcing" news, or enlisting readers as reporters. The results of these experiments are mixed, but my survey of examples tends to show that most have had minimal success at best, and some have been complete failures at worst. One study of attempts to engage readers as reporters at a local English newspaper concluded that "newspapers need citizen journalists more than citizen journalists need newspapers" (Sutcliffe 2016). However, that realization has not halted experiments and the almost relentless drive to "innovate" in an attempt to save the industry. It's hard not to think of a cat chasing its own tail and to see such "innovations" as a sinkhole of diminishing returns.

In what seems like a never-ending—and never quite succeeding—search for a financial solution to the crisis of profitability, the News Establishment is embracing innovation in virtually all areas of its business. In earlier chapters I may have painted the picture of this process as just "grasping at straws," as the inevitable decline continues unabated. While this is true for many failed experiments such as the "pivot to video," overall the goal of such innovation is often to improve the bottom line. This may or may not work in the short-term, and in the long-term it may only be capable of postponing collapse; but innovation can also be used for non-commercial gains. A 2017 report from the Reuters Institute found that some news companies were embracing digital technologies for reputational reasons; to increase organizational flexibility, and even to showcase their willingness to embrace change and experimentation for its own sake (Cornia, Sehl and Nielsen 2017).

One key focus of newsroom innovation is the attempt to harness the power of social media to both enhance the news product and to grow a paying audience through subscriptions, or even donations. It is this intersection of professional and amateur news-gathering and publishing that has given rise to one definition of social journalism. This chapter explores the history and future of this hybrid model that is often associated with attempts by news organizations to build audiences in their immediate communities, an approach that is often labelled the "hyper-local" model. Newsrooms are also making efforts to innovate and harness audience members in other ways too. One method is known as "crowdsourcing," which is a journalistic variation on James Surowie-ki's idea that there is wisdom in collective approaches to problem-solving, which he wrote about in his 2005 book *The Wisdom of Crowds*. In a news-gathering sense, crowdsourcing takes advantage of the reach of social media to engage audience members in researching stories, or in suggesting to the newsroom which stories they want covered (Onuhoa, Pinder and Schaffer 2016). "Data journalism" is another area in which the wisdom of the crowd is harnessed to assist journalists to craft stories from massive amounts of raw data that might otherwise be too complex, or too expensive, to sort into recognizable and reportable information.

News organizations need grist to feed the great churning mill of daily journalism, but the need is more of an economic necessity, than a burning desire to cover every conceivable story, or to democratize the news process. Now, with newsrooms shrinking and outlets proliferating online, mainstream news media are finding it necessary to outsource their own news-gathering activities. Many names have been conjured for the reality that newsrooms are increasingly relying on content provided by members of their audience, either wittingly or not. "Social" journalism has become one of the latest fad words for this phenomenon, but it is not the first.

"Social Media News Gathering"

BBC reporter Lisette Johnston did a PhD study at City University in London on how the BBC was using "citizen journalists" to cover the conflict in Syria in 2011–2012. She says that her research showed the importance of on-the-ground "eyewitnesses" in difficult-to-access conflict zones like Syria, which in many ways resembles a news "black hole" (Johnston 2016a). Getting accurate news from war zones is never easy, but in the context of an "asymmetric" civil war, fought largely in inaccessible parts of the country, reliance on amateur, social journalists is now standard operating procedure for many news organizations. Johnston's colleague, Stuart Hughes, a journalist with the BBC World Service, coined the phrase "social media newsgathering" to describe his interaction with audience members to source material for his stories (Johnston 2016b). Johnston, too, describes a number of problems with managing citizen journalists working in a conflict zone, most notably their tendency to have their own political agenda, or to exaggerate details in order to favor their "side" in the fighting. Using so-called citizen journalists in war zones is an extreme example of social media newsgathering, but it can be effective in other areas too.

Stuart Hughes says he came to rely more on Twitter than traditional newswires when searching out story ideas: "The way I use social media has completely changed the way I gather news. I used to wait for stories to drop on the wires. That was the first indication that something was happening." (Stuart Hughes, cited in Hahn 2013: 11). Social media is now thoroughly embedded in the suite of technologies available to journalists and which they are expected to use with some level of mastery and skill; but this does not mean that everyone in the newsroom is embracing social media or finding it helpful for completing their daily tasks. It is clear from the Cision social journalism report of 2017 that not all journalists are as enthusiastic about social media as the

BBC's Stuart Hughes. In fact, one of the take-out conclusions from the 2017 *Global Social Journalism Study* is that after a decade of Twitter, many journalists are ambivalent about its value to their work. Journalists might feel they need to be on several social media platforms (the average is more than five), but they also feel that the platforms and apps are not necessarily of any great, or lasting value. More than half of the respondents to Cision's social media usage survey fell into the categories of "observer," or "skeptic" identified by low use and "more negative" attitudes around social media.

There is no doubt that social media is a key platform for publishing, distribution and promotion and a clear 90 percent of respondents said they used social media daily for these purposes (Cision 2017: 9). Social media is also commended by respondents for bringing them closer to their audiences—the Holy Grail of engagement—but at the same time, journalists are also contributing less to content communities and crowdsourcing sites in 2017 than they were five years ago (ibid.: 10). Engagement, in this sense, seems to be a pro forma and a hollowed-out experience for both journalists and their audience with very little focus on "information gathering and sourcing" from audience members (ibid.: 12).

What also become clear from reading the Cision report, though it is not explicit in the findings, is that journalists are still overly reliant on public relations practitioners, experts and official sources to generate their copy and for quote-worthy material (86 percent of the time): reporters use mainly "traditional" methods to communicate with these official sources too, "email, telephone or face to face" (ibid.: 14). Paradoxically, while there is a heavy reliance on PR operatives, more than half of respondents also felt that they could not always be trusted (ibid.: 37). This also points to the trust problems within journalism itself and between journalists and audiences.

It's not surprising then that nearly half of respondents felt that using social media does not make them any more productive than before and that it might "add to their workload, rather than ease it" (ibid.: 16). Personally, I am not surprised by these findings; my experience of journalists on Twitter—with a handful of exceptions—is that they are "engaged" with their audience, but not listening to them. Furthermore, I would also argue that for many journalists, being on Twitter is of no more use than as a platform to bicker among themselves and insult each other, usually over ideological differences. Sometimes this even extends to vicious trolling of other reporters and individuals who attempt to correspond with them via the platform. In general, it seems that reporters have a dialectical—and somewhat paradoxical—relationship with social media. For the majority perhaps, there is a professional imperative to be involved, and an expectation from employers that editorial staff will be engaged via Facebook, Twitter, and other platforms. There is also a positive aspect, which is the ability to publish, distribute and promote their stories or personal branding; it is this which, in my view, leads to the general feeling—still only 48 percent of Cision's 2017 respondents—that social media is now an essential element of journalistic practice. However, there is also uncertainty.

According to the Cision report over 70 percent of respondents were "unsure" about the idea that "automation and algorithms make their work easier and more interesting" (ibid.: 17). Another aspect of the report that caught my attention was the finding that "constant use of social media may counteract some positive impact of the platforms on journalists' work" (ibid.: 18). Of the two most active groups of respondents ("Architects" and "Promoters" in Cision's lexicon) most spent between five and eight hours per day on social media, and a majority of the rest spent between three and four hours per day. This seems an extraordinary amount of time and could be indicative of an unhealthy relationship, bordering on addiction. This is difficult to tell beyond this anecdotal inference, but it seems, to me, to be a reasonable assumption given what we know about the addictive nature of screen-based activities and the endorphin rush of satisfaction people get from monitoring the "likes," "shares," "retweets" and "comments" their social media posts receive.

What is more solidly concluded from the Cision report is that social media is impacting on the profession of journalism, "altering traditional values and practices" (ibid.: 20), but not always in a good way: "Less than half of the respondents agreed that overall social media has had a positive impact on journalism" (ibid.). The respondents expressed concern about "fake news," the focus "on speed rather than analysis" and "undermining traditional journalistic values such as objectivity" (ibid.). The percentage of respondents who agreed with this proposition has steadily increased over the last few years, from 49 percent in 2013 to 57 percent in 2017 (ibid.: 21). The Cision report also shows a decline in the number of very active social media users among respondents. The most active groups (Promoters and Architects) accounted for 56 percent of respondents in the 2012 survey and only 21 percent in 2017. The least active groups (Skeptics and Observers) grew from 29 percent in 2012, to 54 percent in 2017 (ibid.: 23). My observation is that this is perhaps the effect of early enthusiasm for social media wearing off over time—the lifting of Mosco's veil of the "digital sublime"—as the realization dawns that perhaps the value of social media and its positive transformative effects have been somewhat overhyped.

As might be expected, Cision's data reflects this in some ways too. Among the Architects and Promoters (the heaviest users, and a declining group numerically) there is a strong belief in the positive impacts of social media on journalism. The reverse is true among Observers and Skeptics, who overwhelmingly believe "traditional" journalism is being undermined by reliance on social media (ibid.: 33). In fact, the Cision report concludes from this data that "a large section of media professionals tend not to be very proactive on social media" (ibid.: 34). Overall, the Cision report, while not providing any great definitional insights into the term "social journalism," does tend to confirm

both the centrality of social media in the modern digital newsroom, but also—
and perhaps, inadvertently—the ambivalent nature of the relationship between
journalists and social media tools. In my view it also points to a disconnect
between what industry insiders think of the value of social media in a newsroom context and the often-enthusiastic ways in which social media has been
embraced within the academic community. I have already made the case that a
soft form of technological determinism underpins much of the normative
research into social media take up and impacts within the news industry. Some
of the academic analyses that, in my view, tend to promote a (mistaken)
determinist theory that exhibits and confirmatory bias towards extolling the
benefits and ignoring or downplaying the dialectical contradictions and paradox
of social media's penetration of the news industry.

NowThis: Social Journalism from Social Media

One very good example of journalists leveraging social media to gather and
report breaking news is the social-only service *NowThis*, which has pioneered
the use of short videos with superimposed text to tell its stories and the clips are
designed for distribution via Twitter, Instagram, Facebook and other social
media apps, rather than from an aggregated web source.

As a start-up, *NowThis* is yet to turn a profit, or monetize its offerings, but it
has the financial backing of a large and established media company, Discovery
Communications, which owns the cable giant Discovery channel as well as
other brands (Ha 2016). The *NowThis* model is to use its reporters to source
material from social media feeds and to supplement this with its own journalists
"on the ground" in locations where news is breaking. *NowThis* is also moving

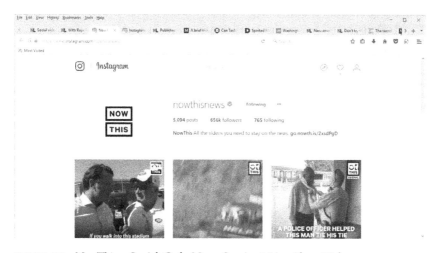

FIGURE 6.1   *NowThis*: a Social-Only News Service Using Short Videos.

into longer-form videos and short documentaries as part of its expansion planning—let's hope they don't get taken down by a pivot away from the "pivot to video." A key figure at *NowThis* is reporter Andy Carvin who first made a name for himself by harnessing the power of social media to report on the 2011 uprisings in the Middle East known as the "Arab Spring." Carvin went on to work for a similar service, *Reported.ly*, until its parent company, First Look Media, shuttered it in the summer of 2016. According to Carvin, the biggest advantage to the distributed reporting model used by *NowThis* is that it gives the illusion that the organization has more reach than it perhaps really does. It can cover breaking news in many locations by harvesting social media feeds, rather than having boots on the ground (Bilton 2017). Despite its early success and the way in which it leverages existing content on social media, it is not clear where *NowThis* fits into a definition of social journalism. The presence of professional journalists and editors on its staff, and the start-up's association with the Discovery brand means that the company more resembles a news aggregator that is trying to monetize itself through inserting repackaged and original content into a free distribution network through social channels. The monetization of *NowThis* content is also achieved through brand partnerships, such as with Chase Bank to promote financial services to millennials (Shields 2017). This is a form of native advertising dressed as news-like content, which is certainly stretching the definition of social journalism.

The *NowThis* example suggests that to qualify as social journalism an enterprise or activity must be more than harvesting content from social media that has been posted by other users in order to (eventually) monetize it, or at least leverage it towards monetizing a brand. Collaboration with a large operator

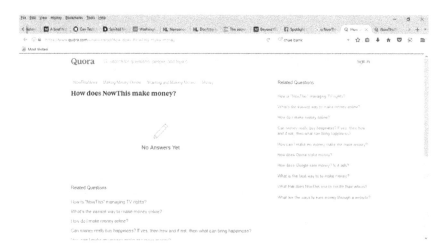

FIGURE 6.2 A Very Good Question that Everyone is Searching for an Answer to.

like the Discovery group is also a feature of the political economy of this emerging sector of the News Establishment and fits the predictive curve of developments in this space. Certainly, for some, monetization is a key goal, but social journalism must have other qualities too. *NowThis* is an aggregation site that is also a good example of the "appropriation" model that relies on "crowdsourcing," the finding, appropriating and contextualizing of amateur video material sourced via social media (Usher 2017).

Crowdsourcing—Computer-Assisted Reporting Comes of Age

One avenue for eventually creating a sustainable space for social journalism is crowdfunding to cover costs or crowdsourcing both content and resources. Crowdsourcing and data journalism are two relatively recent developments in the field that opened up about 20 years ago and was then called "computer-assisted reporting," or "CAR." CAR was what early adopters recognized as an important breakthrough in the symbiotic, if sometimes chaotic, relationship between computing and journalism (Quinn 1997). Today crowdsourcing and data journalism are the sophisticated teenaged offspring of this marriage of convenience. They are discussed side-by-side in this chapter, because many of the early crowdsourcing projects in journalism were heavily reliant on data and resulted in some of the first important data journalism stories of the early twenty-first century. The relationship is perhaps best personified in the famous crowdsourced data journalism project initiated by *The Guardian* newspaper in relation to what became known as the MPs expenses scandal in the UK in 2009.

Crowdsourcing news is relatively new, but it promises to be an important aspect of news-gathering in years to come. However, it is not easy to master and developing a "crowd" from which to source news requires time and patience. Many promises have been made about the value of crowdsourcing news and how it would help to transform journalism in the digital age (Van Der Haak, Parks and Castells 2012), but what is the truth of such claims? There have been some successes, but as we've discussed in relation to business models, after an initial wave of enthusiasm, there is little lasting benefit or much evidence of a sustainable and proven model that represents a beacon of hope for the future of news. A 2016 report for the Tow Center suggested that crowdsourcing has not yet become mainstream within large news organizations, rather it is still in its infancy and only a "handful" of reporters and editors are "standard bearers" for its benefits (Onuhoa, Pinder and Schaffer 2016).

At its simplest, crowdsourcing refers to the ways in which journalists and news organizations can encourage members of their audience to get involved in the news-gathering and reporting process. Crowdsourcing usually begins with a news organization, or an individual reporter making a call for people to help out with a particular reporting task. From there, members of the public might send in tips or leads for a journalist to follow-up; or at a more sophisticated level, people might involve themselves in the research, analysis and reporting of the story. An important aspect of crowdsourcing in journalism is that, ultimately, the reporter and editors decide what information will be used or rejected when submitted from the crowd (Onuhoa, Pinder and Schaffer 2016). Thus, crowdsourcing is not the same as a Wiki where the collaboration extends the role of publisher to members of the crowd. Further, crowdsourcing is not the same as "citizen journalism," it is the harnessing of members of the public for specific reporting tasks directed by the recruiting news organization (Agapie, Teevan and Monroy-Hernandez 2015).

At a crude level, crowdsourcing is just another way of gathering material at the research stage of reporting or locating potential interview subjects via social media channels populated by individuals motivated to help out on a story that bears directly on their personal experience. Some news executives also see it, in somewhat cynical terms in my view, as just another method of harvesting data about their readers and marketing the news service to an expanded customer base. If that is all crowdsourcing means to a news organization, then it must surely eventually drive the crowds away, not encourage them to be engaged. To be successful, the goal of crowdsourcing must be to harness what the audience knows and to use this information to deepen the coverage of important, public interest issues. Crowdsourcing also has to be more than simply repackaging "user-generated content" (UGC) into commercial products.

Over the past decade or so, major global news organizations have been collaborating on big data-driven investigations and also making their datasets available for amateurs and non-professionals. Crowdsourcing has become a way for news organizations to harness a form of collective brainpower to help with difficult subjects, or huge datasets that require hours of forensic digging, which is often beyond the resources of a small newsroom staff.

Data journalism is a technique of reporting and analysis that works with large data sets, using the power of network computing, to explain complex stories using graphics to explore the data and make it accessible to readers. It is a form of journalism that has become popular as the ability of individuals to crunch massive troves of data in meaningful ways has become easier, thanks to cheaper processing power and the availability of applications able to manage huge amounts of information quickly. Data journalism has developed out of older forms of reporting, often referred to as "computer-assisted journalism," or "precision journalism." It is the application of scientific and social scientific methods to reporting (Appelgren and Nygren 2014).

One famous example that combined crowdsourcing with data journalism was a project initiated by *The Guardian* in 2009 to investigate publicly available documents recording the expenses claims of members of the UK Parliament. Over a million documents were released by the UK government and this presented obvious logistics and resource problems for news organizations who wished to dig into the detail. *The Guardian* enlisted readers to help sift through the documents using proprietary software to check the claims of their own local MPs. Over 25000 readers became involved, and the investigation uncovered many instances of MPs abusing the system with false or exaggerated claims. As a result of *The Guardian* and other newspapers uncovering the scandal, MPs began paying back the money they had claimed and some were even prosecuted for fraud (Daniel and Flew 2010). Investigative and data journalism are among the hardest areas of reporting and news-gathering and not easy for the social journalist to break into and being involved in a crowdsourcing exercise might be one way to make the leap.

Involving the Audience through "Ambient Journalism"

Even though the term "ambient news"—meaning that the news is available everywhere—is nearly 20 years old, former BBC journalist and now professor of journalism at the University of British Columbia, Alfred Hermida can be credited with popularizing the term "ambient journalism" in a series of papers and book written in the last decade. In simple terms, Hermida (2010) explained, "ambient news" simply means that news is all around us in everyday life; we don't have to look very far to find it. However, even when news is all around us and easily accessible, audiences are still passive. It is not until audience members, individually and/or collectively, begin to participate in the circulation of news that we see the birth of "ambient journalism." Audience members "become part of the news process, but they tend to do so in multi-faceted and fragmented ways that produce small pieces of content that can be collectively considered as journalism," usually produced or circulated via social media (ibid.). Hermida's initial focus was on the use of Twitter as a site for the generation of short bursts of news-like information around events as they were happening; he expanded on this in a 2014 book, *Tell Everyone: Why We Share and Why it Matters* (Hermida 2014), which argues that ambient journalism—in which almost everyone on social media participates in the telling and retelling of news—is now an essential strand of the social nervous system. "The news is a constant buzz in the background, available at any time, on any device, in just about any place, and it is produced by both professionals and the audience itself" (ibid.: 2).

While Hermida is right on some of the essentials, I think that he is almost too enthusiastic about social media and its potential to turn everyone into a social journalist. He has been accused of "boosterism" and overstating his case (Beattie 2015) and, while it might not be intentional on his part, I think this is essentially correct. Perhaps, like the reporters covering the Arab Spring, Alfred Hermida has become disoriented by the seemingly invincible discourse of technological determinism. In 2011, reporters were soaking up the ever present "ambient journalism" (Hermida 2010) in Egypt; but it was a confusing mixture of inexperienced youth activism; scarce official pronouncements and revolutionary romanticism that coursed through the souks and markets of the region and through social media. Throughout the Arab Spring the use of social media by the overwhelmingly young activists, to provide a crowdsourced commentary and even to organize their actions, became one obvious and easily understood trope that could enliven a news narrative and connect with Western audiences. The situation also took on the appearance of being an occasion of "ambient journalism," in which the audience itself had become part of the news process and was producing small pieces of content on an hourly basis that both informed and activated the crowds in Tahir Square and other centers of resistance. There is some truth in the idea that social media contributed to the various uprisings that constituted the Arab Spring, but it is far from the whole and complex truth. It has led to the danger that in writing the first *rough draft* of the history of the Arab Spring, reporters could privilege technology, rather than the actions of the many and varied participants.

Technological determinism enters Hermida's thesis via the argument that social media enhances "the formation of social ties" by virtue of its inherent design characteristics. This is a one-sided view that denies the dialectical nature of social media and confuses electronic interaction with real engagement. I think this is also clear in Hermida's use of the "Arab Spring" example in *Tell Everyone*. Hermida makes the common mistake of generalizing from this specific set of circumstances—particularly as it relates to events in Egypt before the fall of Hosni Mubarak—to extrapolate a set of principles that do not hold outside of the context of their creation. Hermida was working as reporter in the 1990s covering the Middle East at a time when the Mubarak regime was at the height of its repressive powers. In observing the changes between "now and then," Hermida notes that the change "illustrates how social media helps to shift power away from the state and into the hands of its citizens" and that social media "helped to tip the scales away from the machinery of repression" (Hermida 2014: 4, 5).

However, this was not even true when Hermida wrote it. By the time *Tell Everyone* was published in 2014, the repressive Egyptian state, under a thinly disguised martial law, was back in full control of the country and the people. In 2013, reformist-Islamist President Mohamed Morsi was replaced in a coup which then led to the massacre of hundreds of his supporters (Kingsley 2013). Since then the regime of former field marshal Abdel Fatah el Sisi has imprisoned activists, unionists, journalists and academics who challenge its iron-fisted rule. According to a July 2017 report by Al Jazeera, more than 60,000 political prisoners languish in Egyptian prisons. President Sisi has built 16 new jails since he came to power in the July 2013 coup (Al Jazeera 2017). It is difficult to know with any certainty why Hermida would have ignored this information, but by dismissing it he is able to maintain the fiction that, somehow, social media has made the lives of ordinary Egyptians better since 2011. Hermida's account privileges the technologies of social media as the liberators of Egyptian citizenry, but it fails to take into account the ongoing situation and, instead, presents the Arab Spring as if it is a frozen-in-time moment; a perpetual present without a past, or a future. In this it reflects much of the journalism around the events of 2011, reporting that was suffused with technological determinism, and lack of context. The myth of the Arab Spring and the liberatory power of social media has become, like the contemporary reportage of the event itself, "an easy to digest narrative based on available facts and not requiring any difficult historical contextualizing" (Hirst 2012). There were many brave examples of activists using social media to good effect during the uprisings of 2011, but we do not honor their memory by pretending that the pendulum has not swung decisively back in favor of the despots of the region. The situation in Egypt in 2011, and in other Middle Eastern nations caught up in the Arab Spring represent an unusual situation, so too do the circumstances in war zones, such as Syria, and it is perhaps not surprising that global news giants—like the BBC—come to rely on citizens to be their eyes and ears on the ground. But what role is there for so-called "citizen journalists" under more normal, average and everyday conditions? Does it have a role in local news?

Reciprocal Journalism and Hyperlocalism

The term "reciprocal journalism" was created in 2014 and first appeared in the journal *Journalism Practice*. It is one of many contemporaneous Establishment-oriented responses to the well-worn trope that professional journalism "lost touch with its community" (Lewis, Holton and Coddington 2014) sometime between 1993 and 2003. Reciprocal journalism was theorized as a method for newsrooms to move "beyond mere engagement and participation," and to assist community journalists to achieve "connectedness and embeddedness" (ibid.: 232). Reciprocal journalism is built on the idea of reciprocity—the mutual exchange of actions, or gifts—as a means of strengthening community ties, and it is supposed to encourage "two-way and multi-way forms of value exchange in and through online and offline social networks" (ibid.). Reciprocity, it is argued, can take several forms: "direct reciprocity" occurs when journalists "retweet each other's content," or respond to non-journalists via Facebook or Twitter (ibid.: 233). There is no doubt that this happens, but it is hardly revolutionary; nor is it particularly a form of community building. This type of interaction is now part of the digital mundane, and it hasn't led to any major breakthroughs in engagement. "Indirect reciprocity" is more amorphous and the example given in *Journalism Practice* is Twitter hashtags—again nothing startling or innovative about this common practice. In the academic literature "reciprocal journalism" has been linked to another recently enumerated topic the "hyperlocal journalist" and both are linked to small, often not-for-profit efforts to create community-based publications, or more commonly websites (Harte, Williams and Turner 2017).

Localism, or even the grander-sounding "hyperlocalism" has been around for a decade or so and it is an editorial philosophy that seeks to ground a news outlet (usually, but not always a web-only publication and, occasionally a small print-run newspaper) in a local community that is not well-served by larger, more corporate media outlets. But does it work? The results are very mixed. In some regions and territories, it is reportedly working well, while in others, experiments in hyperlocal news have been poorly received and eventually shuttered. One company that initially appeared to be doing well in the hyperlocal news business is also unusual because it operates as a not-for-profit trust. Independent News Media Incorporated operates 25 local newspapers in markets largely abandoned by metropolitan dailies. The company manages titles in Florida, Delaware, Maryland and Arizona. However, INMI is not immune from the advertising downturn, some of its titles have pulled back from daily to bi-weekly, or tri-weekly publication in order to save money. The papers in the company's portfolio cover school boards and other local events, as well as issues that don't get a run in the larger news outlets (Nesmith 2016).

Writing in *Journalism Practice*, Harte and his co-authors make a bold claim that there is "economic value" and an "ability to play traditional democratic roles" inherent in hyperlocal news ventures; but, frankly I have not come across much evidence of this. The examples and case studies noted by Harte, Williams and Turner do not provide much comfort either and the caveats around their success are many: "widespread economic insecurity," "potential unsustainability," their "variable nature" and quality and the lack of "scale and reach" due to the small communities they are serving (either geographic, or interest-based) (Harte, Williams and Turner 2017: 161). The potential for hyperlocal journalism to be a democratizing force is limited due to these constraints, despite the efforts of academic observers to talk up its prospects. The authors note that commercial attempts to develop hyperlocal outlets commercially in the USA and the UK "have largely failed" in monetary terms, and in terms of engaging audiences. Even the most optimistic of assessments are qualified by doubts. Harte et al. (2017: 164) suggest that journalists are no longer just "content creators," but also "community builders," but they offer no argument as to why this should be the case, apart from the fact that the "communication architecture of social media" makes such a shift possible. It is, in my view, a case of mistaking a *necessary* condition, for a *sufficient set of conditions*. The data provided appears to support this proposition. Of the more than 1900 pieces of content analyzed, readers appeared to engage with less than 20 percent of them in terms of using the enabled comments function:

> ... in 9 per cent [of the analyzed content pieces] readers commented about the comment, but did not engage in conversations with anyone; in 4 per cent readers conversed with each other and in 6 per cent of posts hyperlocal publishers also participated in comment thread conversations ($N = 1941$).

> *(Harte, Williams and Turner 2017: 167)*

These are hardly the numbers that reflect high, or even modest levels of community engagement, or participation by the audience, even when measured against a low standard, such as commenting on an article. However, I am never one to throw out a baby with the bathwater and there is one aspect of "reciprocal journalism" that may provide some insights into how a more robust form of social journalism might be introduced and sustained. The idea of "sustained reciprocity" which extends both "direct" and "indirect" reciprocity over a longer time scale may well provide a template for the slow, but sustainable development of more useful and independent forms of social journalism, based on "sustained and continually growing relational trust and goodwill"; it might be a "difficult task," but if it is successful it may have a "significant long-term payoff" (Lewis, Holton and Coddington 2014: 235). We will return to this topic in the next chapter.

Corporate Journalism and "Owned Media"

The terms "corporate journalism," "brand media" and "owned media" can cover a multitude of variations on a theme, but the theme is very basic— corporations can produce their own "news" and by-pass the gatekeepers in the newsroom. In an analogue world, this type of communication was managed in the form of newsletters sent to clients with updates about new products, important new hires or other changes in the business; but today corporate journalism has moved beyond this brief to include corporations sponsoring publications that appear to be a bit more independent of the bottom line, but still promote the company's values and market position.

This model has become known as "owned media," or "brand media" as opposed to "paid media," which might have included advertorial or straight advertising. Owned media means corporations producing their own news-like information, often sourced from freelancers or the now ubiquitous "content farms" which aggregate freelancers to sell their work to clients, and that have notoriously contributed to falling freelance rates in most markets. Many large companies across most industries, but particularly in finance, banking and insurance are now also in the tailored news and "owned media" business (Korporaal 2015). Owned media is very common across most global and national sporting codes, for example Major League Baseball, most English Premier League soccer teams and many other clubs or competitions throughout the world. While these sites target specific audiences with content geared to their interests, they also host advertising for third parties, which may also include advertorial content.

An interesting case study of "owned media" is a company whose main line of business is manufacturing and selling mattresses but which attempted to turn itself into a news service. In 2015, the multinational mattress and bedding company, Casper, launched a news website dedicated to "the science, culture and curiosities of sleep" called *Van Winkle's*. The site didn't carry any explicit advertising for Casper products or much in the way of branding; instead it pitched itself as being full of weird and offbeat stories "dedicated to exploring the relationship between sleep and the rest of our lives" (Casper 2017).

> "Building Van Winkle's was a great experience. But the question is if that is a viable business pursuit," said Koyen. "Generally speaking, being an independent brand publication is not going to work. At the end of the day, brands are performance marketers. If you don't deliver business results, they will let you go."
>
> *(Chen 2017)*

The strategy of Van Winkle's parent company was to become a leading voice in the world of sleep-related information; "and part of owning that category is owning the best content related to it" Casper CEO Philip Krim told the *Wall Street Journal* (Marshall 2015). Initially, *Van Winkle's* took its mission seriously and was managed by experienced editors who commissioned exclusive sleep-related content to keep the site current. However, the experiment was short-lived. In between my drafting this chapter in October 2017 and completing it in March 2018 Van Winkle's was closed down. According to a former editor, Jeff Koyen, the site did not generate sales or advertising revenues and it was abandoned as an expensive, but failed, experiment.

To succeed, sites like *Van Winkle's* needed the credibility of journalistic presentation in order to mask its inherently commercial intent, which in this case is to create a "feel good" link between the news-like content and the Casper brand. In this guise, this "social" journalism is a form of paid content

FIGURE 6.3   Van Winkle's Signs Off after only Two Years Online.

that straddles the boundary between journalism and advertorial. According to the American Press Institute, the purpose of what it defines as "sponsored content" is to "alter public perceptions" of the sponsoring company and to help it "achieve its branding goals" (Sonderman and Tran 2013). There is nothing unusual about this practice today, it is common to many large organizations, including banks and other major commercial institutions. The razor and shaving accessories company the Dollar Shave Club founded an online "magazine" dedicated to covering fashion, relationships and sex topics "from a male point of view" (Schollmeyer 2017). This is now hosted on the free content-sharing platform, *Medium*. Despite its potentially "politically incorrect" approach, *MEL Magazine* was still going strong in October 2017, with articles on viruses in semen, herpes, a profile of Kiefer Sutherland and an astrologer's guide to sex. Similar start-up media outlets with a focus on women, and with links to global lifestyle brands, have also surfaced in the past two to three years, for example Disney's *Babble*. Some, like Goop, a brand of cosmetic and beauty products launched by the actress Gwyneth Paltrow have even ventured into a print product (Bereznak 2017).

Not all attempts at creating branded media sites failed as quickly as *Van Winkle's*. In Australia one of the nation's largest banks, ANZ, has maintained its branded news site *BlueNotes* for over four years providing well-written copy that promotes the bank's business through subtle connections, rather than "in-your-face" content. Significant global brands are also maintaining a presence in this field on the basis that "thought leadership" is an important tool of differentiation and also a point of contact for potential customers. It is marketing by another means; "In a nutshell, brand journalism is marketing through journalism" (Newman 2015). The use of traditional journalistic techniques— honesty, trust, being useful, and story-telling—can make it hard to differentiate news from brand journalism.

Before we get too carried away and think that this branded journalism is likely to be the whole future, or some sort of savior for the news industry, it is important to remember that sponsored content has a purpose—essentially it is a form of disguised advertising. This means that the commercial goals of the publisher are the likely dominant reason any particular title will continue. If the corporate goal of selling more product is no longer being met; or, as more typically happens, the costs of production outweigh the brand-related benefits, the publication is likely to close, or to be pared back as happened with Van Winkle's within two years of its ambitious start up (Bereznak 2017). In a sense, brand journalism is a type of "social news," it is news-like information presented in a conventional news-like format, but its purpose is as much to persuade as it is to inform.

The phenomenon of "brand journalism" also reminds us of the importance of political economy when it comes to modelling variations on the theme of social journalism. As Nikki Usher has pointed out, there is an imbalance between the institutional forces of the News Establishment and the still relatively weak field of user-generated news-like content, including social journalism. There is a disconnect between the "promise" and the "reality" of amateur journalism (Usher 2017: 248), and "brand journalism" sits across this divide.

Social Journalism and the Gig Economy

I know from experience that the unvarnished truth today is that it is almost impossible to make a living from freelance journalism. Not only has digital disruption irreparably damaged the advertising-reliant business models of legacy media, it has introduced the practice of aggregation with its attendant side-effect of appropriation of content without paying. In political economy terms, this tendency is driving down the price of journalism more generally, which is a contributing factor in the rise of "content farms" and the attendant misery of "low pay" and even "no pay" work for journalists (Bakker 2012). This means it is hard for professional reporters outside the newsroom, and even harder for social journalists to make a living from their passion. Monetizing your own work or marketing your own brand might sound like it's fun and free from the hassle of having to please a boss, but most freelancers know that the reality is a tough grind. Unfortunately, this is the reality of the so-called "gig economy" where nominally independent contractors sell their wares or ply their trade from home, or from collective workspaces. It is a tough way to make a living. Not only do you have to research and write your material, often you have to pitch it to unsympathetic editors, or even do your own website maintenance, tout for subscribers and market your own work (Watkins 2017).

The downside of the gig economy for journalists is that content becomes cheaper and freelancers become impoverished. Many editorial functions have been outsourced to content farms, which offer very low rates on a per-word basis and afford no employment protections to the workers who sign up to them. One Melbourne-based crowdsourcing platform for news-like content is offering AU$10.5 cents per word, which means, on average a 700-word piece is worth AU$75.00 to the writer. On average it would probably take a writer between four and six hours to write and edit such a piece to a publishable standard. When you factor in the time it takes to actually pitch for each job— approximately an hour—a journalist is earning around AU$15.00 per hour, which is below the legally mandated minimum wage of AU$17.70 per hour. To make any sort of living wage—set at AU$672.70 per week, for 38 hours work, by Australian law—a freelance journalist would need to work a minimum of 45 hours per week. The union rate for freelancers—set by the Media, Entertainment and Arts Alliance—is AU$1.14 per word for the first 1000 words and then AU$93 cents for each additional word. For daily and hourly hire of freelancers the rates are AU$998.00 per day, or AU$249.00 per hour. Even a level-entry full-time journalism job pays better than the content farm rate; at AU$19.76 per hour it is above the minimum rate. Average salaries for junior to mid-level journalists in Australia are between AU$60,000 and AU$80,000 per year. Somebody is making money from these content farm operations, but it is not the freelancers who actually produce the copy.

Journalism has become a precarious occupation; freelancers have always been aware of this, but word rates and commissions from busy editors were relatively bankable. These days those certainties are gone. Freelance rates are tumbling and work that once might have attracted a union rate of close to a dollar per word have fallen to around 10 cents a word. Mass layoffs, particularly in the English-speaking world have not been compensated for by new hires at digital start-ups. Most new start-up newsrooms are tiny—having less than 20 staff—when compared to the hundreds of journalists once employed by the mainstream news outlets. Journalists are increasingly told they need to be "entrepreneurial," to seek out their own niche and turn it into a profitable news beat. Research shows that such entrepreneurs are few and far between and that for most, success is illusory. In many ways, the focus on this market-oriented myth of the enterprising individual "making it" is closing down the space in which more socially and collectively organized responses to the crisis in journalism might get a hearing (Cohen 2015). The reality is that most social journalists are not going to earn a living from their work—it is more of a hobby at this time—but perhaps there's an upside, the freedom to set your own agenda. I am certain that as the crisis of the News Establishment deepens, more space will open up outside of mainstream newsrooms as audiences seek out new channels for informing themselves about the world around them.

The Failure of Integration

The News Establishment is taking necessary steps to defend its monopoly and to shore up its profit rates in a declining market and as Usher notes, the "utopian view" from the Ivory tower of academia is not matched by the empirical reality discussed in the research literature: "most efforts to incorporate citizen journalism into traditional journalism have failed" (Usher 2017: 249). However, I am of the view that this failure is actually of little consequence to the financial masters of the news industry. For these entrenched Establishment figures the fact that there is, as Nikki Usher says "little room for citizen journalism to flourish on its own," is less important than the metrics of "engagement" which demonstrate additions to the bottom-line. As I've demonstrated in the first half of this book, the News Establishment is happy with a limited form of shallow "engagement" that translates into eyeballs and subscription revenues. News managers have little concern that the engagement they prefer is not the same as real "participation" in the news "conversation." Nor are they worried that the much-feted "collaboration" touted in the promise of hyperlocal partnerships and "community-building" is only beneficial—in their terms—if it adds to income streams. As Nikki Usher argues, most news organizations are happy to "appropriate" user-generated content, and often without even asking permission or paying for the usage rights and to integrate it with their own material, *if* it enhances their coverage and leads to more eyeballs: "appropriation is a key word because the content—though created by an ordinary non-journalist, becomes the content of the news organisation" (ibid.: 255).

Participation and collaboration that amount to nothing more than submitting UGC to be monetized by the News Establishment is not "citizen journalism"; it just another form of audience exploitation in which the "user's subjective creations are commodified" (Fuchs 2012: 704) for the benefit of media capital. Across the communication and media vectors, capitalism takes advantage of voluntary "peer-to-peer" labor to create commodities—UGC—that, in turn, deliver surplus value back to the beneficiary owners—the shareholders (Bauwens 2005). These relationships of appropriation and exploitation mirror generalized relations of production in a commodity-producing capitalist economy, and this means that the products created in this way cannot be "social journalism." If it is to mean anything at all, social journalism must mean actually doing the reporting, gate-keeping and curating of news content for the benefit of the audience, on our own and, most likely, outside the newsroom and outside both the economic and ideological control of the News Establishment. Social journalism must be self-actualizing and take the cultural, political economy form of an "alternative media that questions the status quo" (Fuchs 2012: 699). We have some way to go before this aspiration is realized, but in the following chapter—and in the rest of this book—we begin to explore the possibility of this happening and ways in which enhanced media literacy may help pave the way forward.

References

Agapie, Elena, Jaime Teevan, and Andres Monroy-Hernandez. 2015. "Crowdsourcing in the Field: A Case Study Using Local Crowds for Event Reporting." *Proceedings of the Third AAAI Conference on Human Computation and Crowdsourcing*, November 8–11,San Diego, CA. Palo Alto, CA: AAAI Press. www.aaai.org/Library/HCOMP/hcomp15 contents.php.

Al Jazeera. 2017. "What is it Like to Live under President Sisi?" *Al Jazeera*. July 4. Accessed January 11, 2018. www.aljazeera.com/indepth/features/2017/04/live-president-sisi-170403084015718.html.

Appelgren, Ester, and Gunnar Nygren. 2014. "Data Journalism in Sweden." *Digital Journalism* 2(3): 394–405. doi:10.1080/21670811.2014.884344.

Bakker, Piet. 2012. "Aggregation, Content Farms and Huffinization: The Rise of Low-Pay and No-Pay Journalism." *Journalism Practice* 6(5–6): 627–637. doi:10.1080/17512786.2012.667266.

Bauwens, Michel. 2005. "The Political Economy of Peer Production." ctheory.net. Accessed November 6, 2017. https://journals.uvic.ca/index.php/ctheory/article/view/14464/5306.

Beattie, Stephen W. 2015. "Review: Tell Everyone: Why We Share and Why It Matters." Quill and Quire. Accessed August 17, 2016. https://quillandquire.com/review/tell-everyone-why-we-share-and-why-it-matters/.

Bereznak, Alyssa. 2017. "Can Tech Startups Do Journalism?" *The Ringer.* September 26. Accessed September 27, 2017. www.theringer.com/2017/9/26/16364548/casper-snapchat-airbnb-startup-publications.

Bilton, Ricardo. 2017. "With Reported.ly Vets, NowThis Wants to Make Social Reporting Core to its Original Content Ambitions." NiemanLabs. March 23. Accessed April 7, 2017. www.niemanlab.org/2017/03/with-reported-ly-vets-now this-wants-to-make-social-reporting-core-to-its-original-content-ambitions/?relatedstory.

Casper. 2017. "Van Winkles." Accessed October 3, 2017. https://vanwinkles.com/about.

Chen, Yuyu. 2017. "Casper's Shutdown of Van Winkle's Shows the Limits of 'Brand Journalism.'" DigiDay. November 13. Accessed March 10, 2018. https://digiday.com/marketing/caspers-shutdown-van-winkles/.

Cision. 2017. "2017 Global Social Journalism Study." Cision. Accessed January 8, 2018. www.cision.com/us/resources/white-papers/global-social-journalism-study/?clid=whitepaper-ty.

Cohen, Nicole S. 2015. "Entrepreneurial Journalism and the Precarious State of Media Work." *South Atlantic Quarterly* 114(3): 513–533. Accessed October 19, 2017. doi:10.1215/00382876–3130723.

Cornia, Allessio, Annika Sehl, and Rasmus, Kleis Nielsen. 2017. "Developing Digital News Projects in the Private Sector." Oxford: Reuters Institute. Accessed October 4, 2017. http://reutersinstitute.politics.ox.ac.uk/risj-review/innovation-digital-news-not-always-exclusively-tied-pursuit-clearly-defined-editorial.

Daniel, Anna, and Terry Flew. 2010. *The Guardian Reportage of the UK MP Expenses Scandal: a Case Study of Computational Journalism.* Sydney: Communications Policy & Research Forum.

Fuchs, Christian. 2012. "Dallas Smythe Today—the Audience Commodity, the Digital Labour Debate, Marxist Political Economy and Critical Theory. Prolegomena to a Digital Labour Theory of Value." *Cognition, Communication, Co-operation* 10(2): 692–740. Accessed June 8, 2017. www.triple-c.at/index.php/tripleC/article/view/443.

Ha, Anthony. 2016. "Thrillist, NowThis, The Dodo and Seeker form a New, Discovery-Backed Holding Company." TechCrunch. October 13. Accessed March 8, 2017. https://techcrunch.com/2016/10/13/group-nine-media/.

Hahn, Nadja. 2013. *What Good is Twitter? The Value of Social Media to Public Service Journalism. Eurovision and POLIS.* London: London School of Economics. Accessed February 23, 2017. http://eprints.lse.ac.uk/59881/.

Harte, David, Andy Williams, and Jerome Turner. 2017. "Reciprocity and the Hyperlocal Journalist." *Journalism Practice* 11(2–3):160–176. Accessed November 1, 2017. doi:10.1080/17512786.2016.1219963.

Haslanger, Julia. 2016. *Social Journalism: The Who, What, Where, When, Why and How.* New York: The Tow-Knight Center for Entrepreneurial Journalism. Accessed November 28, 2016. http://towknight.org/research/social-journalism-who-what-when-how/.

Hermida, Alfred. 2010. "From TV to Twitter: How Ambient News Became Ambient Journalism." *M/C Journal* 13(2). Accessed June 5, 2016. www.journal.media-culture.org.au/index.php/mcjournal/article/view/220.

Hermida, Alfred. 2014. *Tell Everyone: Why We Share and Why it Matters*. eBook. Torotnto: Doubleday Canada.

Hermida, Alfred. 2016. "Social Media and the News." In *The Sage Handbook of Digital Journalism*, edited by Tamara Witschge, C. W. Anderson, David Domingo and Alfred Hermida, 81–94. London: Sage.

Hirst, Martin. 2011. *News 2.0: Can Journalism Survive the Internet?* Crows Nest, NSW: Allen and Unwin.

Hirst, Martin. 2012. "One Tweet Does Not a Revolution Make: Technological Determinism, Media and Social Change." *Global Media Journal* 6(2). Accessed July 15, 2016. www.hca.westernsydney.edu.au/gmjau/archive/v6_2012_2/martin_hir st_RA.html.

Johnston, Lisette. 2016a. "How is Citizen Journalism Transforming the BBC's Newsroom Practices." Open Democracy. January 8. Accessed February 23, 2017. www.open democracy.net/ourbeeb/lisette-johnston/how-is-citizen-journalism-transforming-bbc-s-newsroom-practices.

Johnston, Lisette. 2016b. "Social News = Journalism Evolution? How the Integration of UGC into Newswork Helps and Hinders the Role of the Journalist." *Digital Journalism* 4(7): 899–909. Accessed December 31, 2017. doi:https://doi.org/10.1080/21670811.2016.1168709.

Kingsley, Parrick. 2013. "Egyptians Grieve for Loved Ones as Massacre Continues." *The Guardian*. August 17. Accessed January 11, 2018. www.theguardian.com/world/2013/aug/16/egypt-massacre-morsi-clashes-mosques.

Korporaal, Glenda. 2015. "ANZ Blue Notes and GE Reports Pioneer 'Owned Media.'" *The Australian Business Review*. June 17. Accessed December 16, 2016. www.theaustra lian.com.au/business/the-deal-magazine/anz-bluenotes-and-ge-reports-pioneer-owned-media/news-story/12b6e262b85baf500b13240a23200c33.

Lewis, Seth C., Avery E. Holton, and Mark Coddington. 2014. "Reciprocal Journalism." *Journalism Practice* 8(2): 229–241. Accessed September 9, 2017. doi:10.1080/17512786.2013.859840.

Marshall, Jack. 2015. "Mattress Company Casper Launches Sleep-Focused Publication 'Van Winkle's.'" *The Wall Street Journal*. June 9. Accessed October 3, 2017. https://blogs.wsj.com/cmo/2015/06/09/mattress-company-casper-launches-sleep-focused-publication-van-winkles/.

Nesmith, Susannah. 2016. "A Chain of Small Newspapers Hits on a Formula for Growth." *Columbia Journalism Review*. December 5. Accessed December 13, 2016. www.cjr.org/united_states_project/newspaper_nonprofit_growth_journalism.php.

Newman, Daniel. 2015. "The State Of Brand Journalism: Are Brands Becoming The Media?" Forbes. December 8. Accessed March 10, 2018. www.forbes.com/sites/danielnewman/2015/12/08/the-state-of-brand-journalism-are-brands-becoming-the-media/#382bfe621fba.

Onuhoa, Mimi, Jeanne Pinder, and Jan Schaffer. 2016. *Guide to Crowdsourcing*. New York: Tow Center for Digital Journalism.

Quinn, Stephen. 1997. "Learning the Four Rs of Computer-Assisted Reporting in Australia." *Asia-Pacific Media Educator* 3(9): 131–141.

Safco, Lon, and David K. Brake. 2009. *The Social Media Bible: Tactics, Tools & Strategies for Business Success*. New York: Wiley & Sons.

Schollmeyer, Josh. 2017. "Note from the Editor." *MEL Magazine*. Accessed October 3, 2017. https://melmagazine.com/about.

Shields, Mike. 2017. "NowThis is Partnering with Chase to Help Millennials Feel Better about Banks." *Business Insider.* July 27. Accessed July 30, 2017. http://uk.businessinsi der.com/nowthis-is-partnering-with-chase-to-help-millennials-with-money-2017-7? op=1&r=US&IR=T.

Sonderman, Jeff, and Millie Tran. 2013. The Definition of 'Sponsored Content'. American Press Institute. November 13. Accessed August 24, 2017. www.americanpressinstitute. org/publications/reports/white-papers/the-definition-of-sponsored-content/.

Steensen, Steen. 2016. "The Intimization of News." In *The Sage Handbook of Digital Journalism,* edited by Tamara Witschge, C. W. Anderson, David Domingo and Aldred Hermida, 113–127. London: Sage.

Sutcliffe, Chris. 2016. "Newspapers Need Citizen Journalists More than Citizen Journalists Need Newspapers." *The Media Briefing.* November 25. Accessed December 1, 2016. www.themediabriefing.com/article/newspapers-need-citizen-journalists-more-than-citizen-journalists-need-newspapers.

Usher, Nikki. 2017. "The Appropriation/Amplification Model of Citizen Journalism." *Journalism Practice* 11(2–3): 247–265. doi:10.1080/17512786.1223552.

Van Der Haak, Bregtje, Michael Parks, and Manuel Castells. 2012. "The Future of Journalism: Networked Journalism." *International Journal of Communication* 6(16): 2923–2938. Accessed September 13, 2017.

Watkins, Emily. 2017. "How are Australian Freelance Journalists Funding their Work?" Crikey Insider. October 9. Accessed October 9, 2017. http://tinyurl.com/y9wab7uc.

7
SOCIAL JOURNALISM REIMAGINED

Collaboration as Social Journalism

Social journalism is a term that has only recently come into common usage, but what is it? The best definition is hard to pin down, but several people have made a valiant attempt at answering the "What is social journalism?" question. The definition of "social media" is quite settled; but when it comes to "social news" and "social journalism," there is a lot more equivocation, overlap and confusion in attempts to agree on a useful definition. The terms "social news" and "social journalism" are proving to be problematic and difficult to quantify. The phrase "social journalism" does not appear at all in *The Sage Handbook of Digital Journalism*, published in 2016. The closest reference is in the phrase "social and citizen journalism" on page 30 (Owen 2016). In this chapter we will try to settle some definitional issues, as well as explore the ways in which social journalism might be able to compete with the failing News Establishment.

Julie Haslanger (2016) has provided one of the most comprehensive summaries in a report for the Tow-Knight Center for Entrepreneurial Journalism at CUNY in New York. Haslanger begins with social media which is a good place to start, but social journalism is more than just journalism plus social media. Social journalism is about more than simply sharing news clips on Twitter, Instagram or Facebook. For Haslanger, though, the whole point of social journalism is what mainstream news organizations are doing in order to better engage with their audience(s). As we discussed in the previous chapter, this seems like a great idea in theory, but it is proving elusive in practice. What Haslanger and others are referring to loosely as social journalism is an extended and idealized form of "collaborative journalism" through which professional newsrooms seek the cooperation of audience members to bring stories to life, or to help with research and corroboration. According to a September 2017 report from the Center for Cooperative Media, this collaboration model has moved from the fringes to the mainstream and constitutes the latest "revolution" in journalism techniques. The report author, Sarah Stonbely, says optimistically that collaborative journalism has shifted from being largely experimental to "common practice" (Murray 2017).

Collaborative journalism involves reporters working more closely with their audience through a variety of techniques: crowdsourcing, events, interactions on social media, just to name a few. According to Julie Haslanger, collaboration involves reporters finding the right readers, active listening skills, and solid analytical skills to capitalize on the feedback loop from interactions with readers (Haslanger 2016). In other words, collaboration appears to be no more than a heightened from of appropriation, similar to that identified by Nikki Usher. The focus of collaborative journalism is on journalism *for* the audience, or perhaps journalism *with* the audience, but it is not journalism *of* the audience. Julie Haslanger's research was looking only at what existing news organizations are/were doing; which she found amounted to "spending the majority of their time and energy helping their news organization meet its business goals." This also appears to be a consistent feature of the six types of collaborative reporting outlined in Sarah Stonbely's research, where the sharing of editorial and other production resources can reduce the publishers' costs.

Sarah Stonbely's investigation of collaborative practice covers a range of interactions between cooperating newsrooms, and between newsrooms and audience members that might result in published or broadcast stories:

- Temporary and separate collaborations are single-use and rely on individual collaborators to produce content that may, or may not, be published at the discretion of editors. This provides flexibility for the publisher but can also run into problems because there is little or no central editorial direction applied to the projects. In this type of collaboration, a newsroom will typically partner with a non-news organization, such as a university journalism school, or a community organization.
- Temporary and co-creation collaborations are single-use but are more directed by the publisher and content is created through close cooperation. While this type of collaboration may produce more focused and useable stories, there can also be problems. Newsrooms and the collaborating organization or individuals may have competing interests and priorities. This type of collaboration is more resource-intensive for the publishing newsroom.
- Temporary and integrated collaborations are usually between cooperating news organizations—for example the global consortium that published simultaneously on the Panama Papers in 2016—and are therefore capable of producing more complex and data-rich stories. These complex projects require organization to organization cooperation, a shared commitment to the story and the allocation of commensurable resources by each collaborator.

- Ongoing and together collaborations are complex, require trust and are resource-heavy. Typically, one or both cooperating organizations will need to hire a dedicated manager to oversee the project. The benefit is a deeper level of coverage and greater audience engagement for all partners, beyond what they could typically achieve on their own.
- Ongoing and integrated collaborations are most commonly used where linked editorial offices can use a shared back office to streamline administration and sales functions. They can also be used to share journalistic outputs across titles or platforms.
- Ongoing and separate collaborations are typically content-sharing arrangements between news organizations. In such cooperative ventures each party retains their own editorial independence and resources are not typically shared beyond an agreement to republish.

In some ways, collaborative journalism attempts to embrace the citizen reporter in cooperation with the more traditional newsroom model. In this context, use of the term "social journalism" refers to a hybrid of mainstream and citizen reporting. As Julia Haslanger defines and describes social journalism it is about connecting professional journalists with the audiences and communities they serve through sharing stories, finding stories and involving community members with the news product.

This definition sees social journalism as an extension of newsroom practice, rather than something different in nature. According to brand strategist and newsroom advisor, Woody Lewis, social journalism is an adjunct to social media practice, and "an essential component of any news organization's strategy" (Lewis 2009). In Lewis view, the "legacy media"—newspapers and broadcast outlets—need to embrace the "citizen journalist" in order to remain relevant and to harness the "network effect" of people sharing news among themselves. They also need to recognize the differing editorial perspective, "the watchdog or advocacy role" that also defines citizen journalism. However, this is still a professional view, written with one eye on the bottom line and aligned to Usher's appropriation model. Even though Lewis was writing this advice nearly a decade ago, it is still the approach taken by the more mainstream media; the audience that Julia Haslanger was writing for in 2016. As noted in the previous chapter, this is an approach that privileges and supports the News Establishment, and that is designed to help it navigate a path through the current crises of profitability and trust.

Citizen Journalism, Social News and Social Journalism

While they are widely used in the academic literature, the terms "social news" and "social journalism" have been fluid since at least 2003 and, so far as I can tell, there are few if any agreed and settled boundaries. The difficulty perhaps began with attempts to define "citizen journalism" using a broad-brush approach. Early definitions of citizen journalism included re-posting, tagging or linking to content; the use of audience-shot footage in professional news publications, participation in comments threads, or the actual production of news and "news-like" content (Hirst 2011) and items created by non-professionals. Luke Goode (2009: 1288) provides one starting definition of "citizen journalism," but it seems to cover all the activities just mentioned: "a range of web-based practices whereby 'ordinary' users engage in journalistic practices." In *News 2.0* I tried to refine this overly broad definition of citizen journalism by arguing that it should really only be used to label "news" and "news-like" information directly produced by non-professionals for the specific purpose of advancing a social or political cause. In this sense "citizen journalism" is a "subset" of a broader category that I called "user-generated news-like content" or "UGNC" (Hirst 2011: 109–110). Today, the term "citizen journalism" is not used very widely, it has been replaced with other, vague terms, such as "participatory" or "user-centered" or "reciprocal" journalism, all of which are common today.

"Social news" was used interchangeably with "citizen journalism" for a while, but Goode (2009: 1287) also introduces another level of ambiguity by referring to user-controlled aggregation of news as "social news" on sites such as *Reddit* and the now defunct *Newsvine* and *Digg*. In this context, "social news" is no more than giving readers "the chance to submit, rate, recommend and comment on news stories" produced elsewhere. This is the definition also used by Hille and Bakker (2014) in their paper "Engaging the social news user" in which they report that journalists and news organizations did not much like user comments on their stories because of the abuse and profane language offered by readers. It now appears that this has become a standard academic definition of "social news"; one that can also be applied to the sharing of news through social media sites and applications (Rosengard, Tucker-McLaughlin and Brown 2014). In the academic literature, "social news" is often used in relation to similar curatorial actions by audience members who are "making personal referrals and guiding their peers to consume content that they consider interesting and relevant" (Schneider and de Souza 2016: 1). Having said that, a third use of the term "social news" has emerged and its related to how social media sources and user-generated content are integrated into professionally produced news bulletins or stories (Johnston 2016). The *Global Social Journalism Study*, an annual report from the PR and analytics firm Cision, uses this phrasing without hesitation, or feeling there is any need to justify it (Cision 2017). This definition of "social journalism" is perhaps of most interest in the context of this chapter, but it is also clear that for many practitioners and researchers, there are other phrases or portmanteau clauses in circulation that refer to this process in essentially similar terms.

Participatory Journalism

Journalism and media academics love to invent new names for phenomenon they are researching. I think this is done to give them a sense of ownership over their ideas and also to give the impression that they—and they alone—have found the scholar's equivalent of the "Holy Grail"; or maybe they don't actually read each other's work all that carefully. In the frame of modern academic research, everything has to seem new, previously undiscovered and somehow unique. This is the kind of scholarship that attracts research funding and it leads to researchers always needing the next fix. To stay in the research and publishing game requires an almost constant stream of the new and the shiny; but often the promise is not kept. I have found this to be particularly the case over the past 10–15 years when it comes to proposing solutions to the crisis in journalism. There is no doubt that the crisis is real, but the solutions proposed do not, in most cases, really offer much that is radical or ultimately game-changing. There is a certain amount of deckchair rearranging; the band is still playing and the icy water is slowly filling the ballast tanks via the gaping hole in the side of the ship.

One of the early contenders in the scramble to redefine journalism and to salvage the news business was the trend to what researchers labelled "participatory journalism" (Vujnovic et al. 2010); the process whereby the people formerly known as the audience participate in the news gathering and distribution chain. But what exactly are the audience members participating in? It is clear that they are not engaged in newsgathering in any meaningful sense, and their participation is mostly limited to leaving comments on stories, or at best contributing non-essential content in designated low-value channels. In this sense, as the multi-national study by Marina Vujnovic and her colleagues found, the overwhelming motivation for encouraging low-level participation on news websites is economic:

> Participation in this sense is no longer a simple expression of democratic actions by citizens but rather the result of the market value of participation, as well as the expression of commodity culture and information consumption.
>
> *(Vujnovic et al. 2010: 287)*

The Vujnovic study identified building "brand loyalty," "building traffic," "competition" with other providers, and "cost-cutting rationales" as the main reasons motivating news companies to include participation mechanisms in their site architecture. One British study found that, whatever we call it, so-called participatory journalism does not really provide a route for citizen-initiated content to enter the mainstream news discourse in anything but a haphazard and chaotic way. The study found that the participation system is still relatively closed and tightly controlled by journalists and does not result in a more democratized news media, or a more open media landscape. The study concluded that mainstream news organizations "don't really fulfil the promises they make of citizen participation" (Scott, Millard and Leonard 2015: 756). The Vujnovic study concluded that, for many news organizations in the markets explored for the paper, there is a lack of clear vision in most newsrooms about why "participation" had become important and some confusion as to whether it was for "democratic or economic purposes," but tellingly, the researchers also concluded that "true participation may be an illusion," despite the hype, the motivation of the journalists involved, and the very real effort that goes into creating a "sense of participation . . . without real democratic action" (Vujnovic et al. 2010: 295).

The emphasis in the phrase "participatory journalism" has been slowly shifting over the last few years; it is no longer mostly about outsiders being inside the news production process, instead the focus is said to be engaging audience members to help build a "community" around the publication or website. As Nikki Usher points out, "being able to speak does not mean being heard . . . particularly in light of the increasing corporatization and centralization of the Internet" (Usher 2017: 247). A similar shift is also taking place in the content and meaning of other terms now commonly used as placeholders in academic discussions around the issue of news media "engagement" with audiences.

Can "the People Formerly Known as the Audience" Win Back Control?

As I've argued consistently, one of the by-products of digital media and the embedding of social media in our lives is that news organizations now feel that they need to deepen their engagement with members of their audience. I've already made the case that the key motivation for this shift is not—despite ideologically informed reasoning—to make the news more "democratic," it is basically about generating traffic and aggregating eyeballs, which in political economy terms, is what the commercial media has been mostly about for the past 200 years.

However, the relatively new phenomenon of digital engagement has attracted a great deal of interest as both industry leaders and academics, embedded in the News Establishment, have attempted to explain. Their purpose is to normalize this appropriation of cheap (or free) content to the *business*, if not to the *object*, of journalism. This has, in turn, created a new set of problems in defining, explaining and theorizing this new "participatory" culture in the news industry. After reviewing a mountain of academic literature, I do not see any consensus view, or commonality in the terms used to describe the shift from passive to active audiences. As it is expressed in one 2015 journal article on the issue, terms like "participatory journalism, citizen journalism and user-generated content" are often used interchangeably to refer to "the greater role of members of the audience to create and disseminate news and information" (Zeller and Hermida 2015: 107). The problem is that this overlapping use of these terms is confusing; surely there has to be a difference—even if subtle—between participating in a comment thread; actively working as a citizen journalist, or simply providing UGC. Are we only talking about "news" here or all types of "information"?

So far in this book we've learned that the business model and the trust model for the mainstream news media are failing. We've also investigated the ways in which journalists, news organizations, industry leaders, and concerned academics have attempted to solve these twin crises using digital tools, platforms and applications in an attempt to increase engagement with the audience. While this attempt is often dressed in the language of democratizing journalism and the news, of increasing audience participation in meaningful ways and making the news more user-friendly, the bottom line is that it is really all about the bottom line and protecting the monopoly position of the News Establishment.

Journalism, journalists and the news industry are caught in a dialectic—a series of cascading contradictions—and they are intimately and inextricably bound to the commodity form in which we produce and consume news. That is, as I've expressed it throughout this book, journalism and the news industry are hostage to a political economy that privileges profit over public interest; a system that depends on and also ideologically supports capitalism and therefore, ultimately, the class interest of the capital-owning class. Through its ideological lenses, the news media and most journalists who work in it, prop up capitalism; and most of the academics who are analyzing the news media and trying for help it find a way through the dialectical maze—characterized by the "duality of the news commodity" (Hirst 2011)—are also bound to the same system of exploitation, inequality, crisis and instability. In other words: "Houston, we have a problem!"

I have long held the view—contrary to many of my former colleagues in both journalism and academia—that the commodity form of journalism and the news industry's need to make a profit on its transactions with the audience are obstacles to change. I believe that journalism and the news industry will limp along in their current form for quite a while yet. Ultimately, it is unlikely that commodity journalism—I also think of it as industrial journalism—will just stop, at least while capitalism survives. But it will remain weak, it cannot easily recover from its current crises. It will take an almost miracle for the news industry to be profitable again and to employ anywhere near as many professional journalists as it once did. Cost-cutting and eking out the nickels and dimes of online subscriptions and advertising are here to stay—until the industry eventually runs out of options. As we've seen in previous chapters, any number of attempts to re-invent commodity form journalism—whatever names it is given by the academic enablers and industry gurus—have failed to return the news industry to anything like its previous levels of profitability. Nor, in my view, will the News Establishment ever again wield the same levels of control and power over audiences that it did through the twentieth century. The market model is broken, it is dying and can't be fixed. It is time for all of us to move on and forge a new, more democratic structure for news production and consumption that is not dependent on the commodity form.

When it comes to re-establishing a bond of trust with audiences I am also pessimistic. I cannot see how most news organizations can rebuild their reputations. The so-called "Trump bump" in the United States is both temporary and illusory in many ways. I agree with "rogue journalist" Caitlin Johnstone (2017) that ultimately, the media organizations benefitting from a boost in views, subscribers and page hits because of Trump are actually part of the problem and always have been. This then begs the question: "So what do we do about it?" Or perhaps, from your point of view: "What are you [me, the author] going to do about it?" And, that's a fair question. If I am going to be hyper-critical of mainstream journalists and the mainstream news media, then I have to put forward an alternative. This is exactly what I propose to do in this chapter, by arguing for a re-invention of social journalism, and putting the "citizen" back into "citizen journalism."

In the previous chapter we discussed the emerging popularity of non-profit newsrooms, funded by philanthropy, or by small donations from readers, and while I am skeptical about the viability of these models—particularly if they are dependent on wealthy individuals for funding—maybe there is also room for cautious optimism. I actually work with one such Australian non-profit, though it is not able to pay me a wage at the moment; perhaps in larger news markets there is potential to pay reporters out of subscriptions and donations. In general, my skepticism is because I believe that these non-profits—even with the best of intentions—will struggle to break from the dominant news culture, which is determined by the dynamics of the commodity form. It is the political economy of this form that shapes newsroom culture, ethics and ideology, and it is difficult to break decisively from the strictures that this imposes.

On the other side of the ledger, my optimism is based on the fact that change is always possible, and in fact, inevitable. Many of the newer non-profits —including the one I contribute to here in Australia—are less than 10 years old and most are substantially younger. They all have issues around sustainability, managing expensive reporting projects and generating income from their journalism; but they are surviving, at least for the moment. I am also optimistic because it is also becoming easier and easier for non-professionals to enter the field of journalism and reporting with simple tools and using social media. It is important to not overstate the present value of the transition from passive audience to active "prosumer" (Bruns 2005) or "amateur" (Atton and Hamilton 2008) journalist, but it is also important to not underestimate the potential for further collaboration, or even totally independent alternatives that might emerge from the wreckage of the news industry. In short, I believe that there is room for the development of what I will argue here is a real form of social journalism; a style of reportage and news coverage that lifts engagement from a method of monetizing banal content to line the pockets of shareholders to an active process of participation and collaboration that is truly reciprocal in purpose and in outcomes.

Social journalism builds on the lessons of the citizen journalism movement, which ebbs and flows historically according to circumstances. But it has to be a bit more than just *more* citizen journalism. Social journalism exists in a liminal space, not quite totally outside of the bounds of the media's commodity form, but also, not entirely beholden to it. Public funding—via the crowd, patronage, or ideologically based subscriptions—is one absolute pre-requisite. The second is a commitment to progressive principles; what the Marxist media scholar Christian Fuchs (2010: 181) elucidates as "dialectical realism at the content level," "radical humanism" and "opposition to all domination." In this reckoning, "dialectical realism" is important as it moves the act of journalism beyond taking ideological conceptions of common sense as gospel and it also rejects the normative assumption that radical change is not possible; "there is a world outside of cognition that can be perceived, analyzed, published, criticized and changed" (ibid.). I think that we can see examples of this journalistic practice today, albeit in limited forms. It even appears in some publications that are close to, but not quite part of, the mainstream news landscape. For example, in the US context I would name *The Intercept* and *The Nation*, alongside some of the philanthropically funded initiatives such as *Pro Publica* and the International Consortium of Investigative Journalists. However, before moving into a discussion of the possibilities, it is important to ground this conversation in the reality of failed attempts to build progressive journalism networks in the past.

The Failure of "Citizen Journalism"

The phrase "citizen journalism" was famously defined as "when the people formerly known as the audience employ the press tools they have in their possession to inform one another, *that's* citizen journalism" by New York-based academic, Jay Rosen in 2006. In my view this is a definition that is worth sticking with, but it should not be used interchangeably with other terms that might mean more or less than this does. I have one other point to make about "citizen journalism," there needs to be equal emphasis placed on both words. As I wrote in *News 2.0*, for this definition to be valid and specific there must be a "definite linkage between reporting and active political citizenship" (Hirst 2011: 110). Without this active link the term doesn't make sense and it doesn't ring true. Without both active citizenship and active efforts at reporting there is nothing to grasp in the phrase. To be counted as journalism and not some lesser form of participation, the individual must be actively and consciously engaged in reporting some event or issue in a news-like manner. If this is not evident then we might describe the resulting material as user-generated content (UGC), which is then fashioned into news by professionals working in a newsroom environment, or if it can be used in a news presentation without much intervention by a professional journalist we might elevate it to "user-generated news-like content" (UGNC). In this designation, "news-like" refers to "a wide and varied range of UGC material that appears inside and alongside readily identifiable news."

UGNC must also display some of the common news values; it cannot be endless cat videos, or casual holiday footage of something hilarious happening to a family member (Hirst 2011: 111). I am of the opinion that we need to stick to these narrow definitions in order to make sense of the proliferation of alternative terms that have been introduced into the debate by academic researchers in the decade since Rosen laid out the ground rules for describing citizen journalism. Key among my reasons for this—apart from analytical clarity—is that when it comes to discussing the concept of social journalism we will be forced to return to the ideas and ideals of citizen journalism, but in a context external to today's newsrooms and divorced from the needs of the news industry.

The first great experimental wave in citizen journalism was the "Indymedia" movement of Independent Media Centers (IMCs) established by protest groups during a meeting of the World Trade Organization in 1999. Twenty years later, it is fair to say that Indymedia is finished. The remaining collectives—scattered across North America, a handful in Europe and one or two in Latin America— are ghostly reminders of a media force that spanned the globe at its height (Giraud 2014). When I visited several IMC sites in December 2017 and January 2018 they were largely inactive. Most had simply disappeared from the web altogether. The only active group posting to the central IMC newswire with any regularity was in Argentina. A group in Mexico was active; the Los Angeles group was posting one or two local items, but the newswire was mainly reposts of material from other organizations; the same situation appears to be the case in Aotearoa/New Zealand. In the United Kingdom only one active group could be found—in Northern Ireland; an Athens site was active along with one in Germany. In Asia and the Pacific there is little to no IMC activity. There is an Indymedia presence on Twitter and Facebook, but again, reposts, not original material. This is a far cry from the movement's heyday.

Eva Giraud valiantly attempts to argue that the global collapse of the IMCs (which numbered around 170 at the movement's height) is not really a failure because of the Indymedia "legacy." However, I think that any honest appraisal of the IMC legacy must focus on the reasons for its collapse. Giraud herself lists a handful of reasons and, taken together, they document the failures well: "informal hierarchies" that undermined the movement's democratic ideals, "lack of inclusivity" and "shifts to Web 2.0 media" (Giraud 2014: 421). The first two causes point to a lack of political maturity and a reliance on ill-thought-out anarchist principles of consensus decision-making that are effectively mechanisms that block democratic majority rules. As Christian Fuchs (2010: 174) persuasively argues, such anarchistic tendencies are "insufficient" when it comes to building critical alternative media infrastructure, "because they tend to idealize small-scale production and tend to neglect orientation towards the political public." The identification of Web 2.0 technologies as a third factor in the collapse of IMCs is worth considering. What this is effectively saying is that the Indymedia movement could not survive the rise of social media and the freedom to share that it bestowed on the mass public.

There is some truth in this, but we have to link it dialectically to the social relations engendered within the IMCs—their emphasis on self-reliance, their use of servers which could not be updated quickly or easily to take advantage of social media and their paranoia about covert surveillance of their operations. It was these social factors—linked to the group's political immaturity—that led to the collapse, not singularly the arrival of social media. However, we should not dwell on the failures of indymedia, instead we should recognize what it stood for and understand the reasons for, and lessons of, its failure. Indymedia is not the first failed experiment and it won't be the last. One of the first was a radical newspaper based in Cologne, Germany, and edited by Karl Marx. *Neue Rheinische Zeitung*, lasted barely a year before it was shut down by a reactionary Prussian government. In an article reflecting on the successes and failures of the paper, Marx's long-time collaborator, Friedrich Engels, wrote "we had unconditional freedom of the press—and we used it to the last drop":

> Begun almost without financial resources—the little that had been promised it very soon, as we said, was lost to it—it had achieved a circulation of almost 5,000 by September [1848]. The state of siege in Cologne suspended it; in the middle of October it had to begin again from the beginning. But in May 1849, when it was suppressed, it already had 6,000 subscribers again ... No German newspaper, before or since, has ever had the same power and influence or been able to electrify the proletarian masses as effectively as the *Neue Rheinische Zeitung*. And that it owed above all to Marx.
>
> *(Engels 1884: 120)*

As Engels alludes to in this passage, the *Zeitung* was shuttered because of censorship and repression, and while this is certainly the case today in countries with authoritarian regimes, it is possible for experimental efforts in radical publishing to exist. There are hundreds, if not thousands of such radical media experiments going on today. At one end are relatively new organizations that we could argue are directly channeling the passions of Indymedia at the other are the very committed media associated with small anti-capitalist parties and movements. One of the most prominent is *Unicorn Riot*, started in 2015 and now active in several US cities and with a network of correspondents in other parts of the world. UR is perhaps closest to the original IMC model in the way it organizes and operates. UR has channels on most of the main social media platforms (YouTube, Instagram, Vimeo, Twitter, etc.) and it dedicates a lot of its coverage to social movements, such as the Standing Rock protests and mobilizations of the so-called "Alt-Right." Like Indymedia, UR runs on consensus and ostensibly without hierarchies. After breaking the story of white nationalists organizing violent protests in Charlottesville—in which Heather Heyer was killed—Unicorn Riot began to get some attention from other sections of the media, including a very supportive piece in the *Columbia Journalism Review*.

> Often, *Unicorn Riot* members do not use bylines for their stories, which are made available to other nonprofits via a Creative Commons license. They share equipment: computers and cameras as well as bullet-proof body armor and gas masks. Donations help pay for reporters' travel expenses and a small per diem. They are clear about their methods and their goals; they eschew traditional ideas of objectivity while striving for factual accuracy.
>
> *(Woods 2017)*

Some of the new and radical social journalism start-ups are amorphous loose collectives, like Unicorn Riot; others, such as *The Intercept* follow a more traditional model but to the side of the main news industry. *The Intercept* is a professional outfit with the resources to do investigative journalism. It is financially supported by other areas of the First Look Media group's operations in documentary video. However, like its non-profit counterparts, Politico, etc., there is no certainty about its future funding. It is attempting to build a base of financial supporters without putting up a paywall and continuing to eschew advertising that might contaminate its editorial independence. Other models of social journalism are more closely aligned with one of the emerging progressive and left-wing political tendencies. None of these left, progressive tendencies are very large, consequently they are not yet operating on a truly mass scale.

However, I am optimistic about the future of progressive social journalism. History shows us that in times of social upheaval there is an audience for progressive and radical ideas. We see this clearly in the example of perhaps one of the biggest left-wing groups, the Democratic Socialists of America, which has enjoyed something of a membership boost since Donald Trump's election. The DSA has around 45,000 members (according to its own figures) and it publishes in print and online a magazine called *Democratic Left*. Similar organizations exist in other countries, and there may well be several competing tendencies in each place. Most of them also publish their own versions of *Democratic Left* with varying degrees of success. However, all of these groups suffer from the same significant problem—they are tiny compared to the general population and (unfortunately in my view) their reach is limited by both their size and a certain level of resistance to socialist ideas[1] (again, in my view unfortunately). There is no great secret to why this is the case and it's important to be realistic about the current potential of such left-wing organizations to grow and to reach a larger audience. However, there is some hope; news reports throughout 2017 were asking why socialism seemed to be gaining in popularity in both the United States (represented by Bernie Sanders) and in the UK (represented by Jeremy Corbyn). It is important to acknowledge that right-wing populism is not the only political current outside the mainstream to win over new recruits.

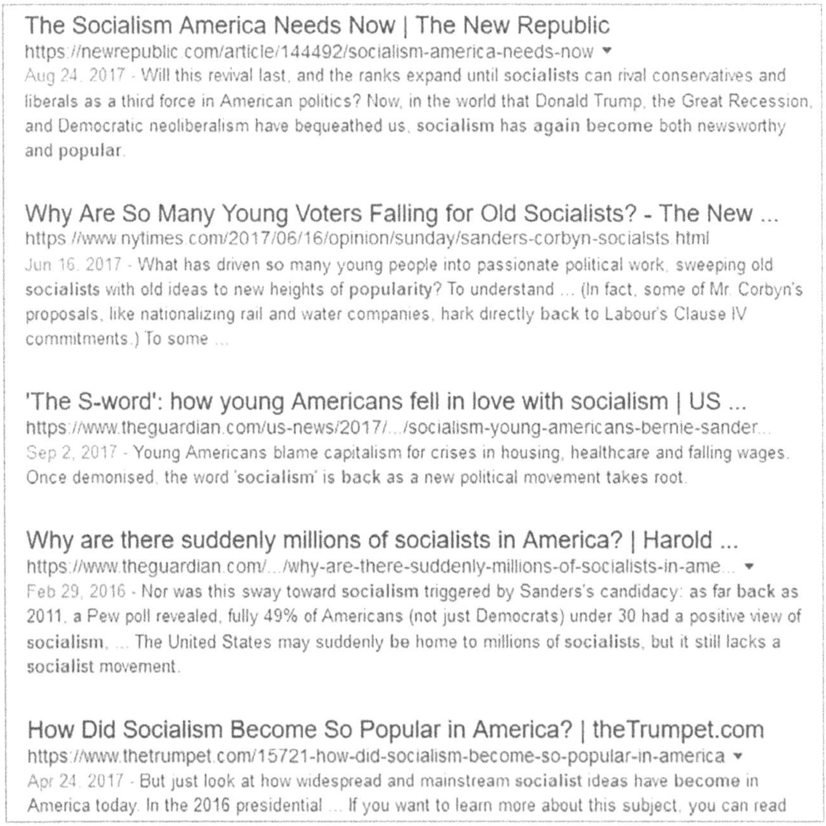

The Socialism America Needs Now | The New Republic
https://newrepublic.com/article/144492/socialism-america-needs-now ▾
Aug 24, 2017 - Will this revival last, and the ranks expand until socialists can rival conservatives and liberals as a third force in American politics? Now, in the world that Donald Trump, the Great Recession, and Democratic neoliberalism have bequeathed us, socialism has again become both newsworthy and popular.

Why Are So Many Young Voters Falling for Old Socialists? - The New ...
https://www.nytimes.com/2017/06/16/opinion/sunday/sanders-corbyn-socialists.html
Jun 16, 2017 - What has driven so many young people into passionate political work, sweeping old socialists with old ideas to new heights of popularity? To understand ... (In fact, some of Mr. Corbyn's proposals, like nationalizing rail and water companies, hark directly back to Labour's Clause IV commitments.) To some ...

'The S-word': how young Americans fell in love with socialism | US ...
https://www.theguardian.com/us-news/2017/.../socialism-young-americans-bernie-sander...
Sep 2, 2017 - Young Americans blame capitalism for crises in housing, healthcare and falling wages. Once demonised, the word 'socialism' is back as a new political movement takes root.

Why are there suddenly millions of socialists in America? | Harold ...
https://www.theguardian.com/.../why-are-there-suddenly-millions-of-socialists-in-ame... ▾
Feb 29, 2016 - Nor was this sway toward socialism triggered by Sanders's candidacy: as far back as 2011, a Pew poll revealed, fully 49% of Americans (not just Democrats) under 30 had a positive view of socialism, ... The United States may suddenly be home to millions of socialists, but it still lacks a socialist movement.

How Did Socialism Become So Popular in America? | theTrumpet.com
https://www.thetrumpet.com/15721-how-did-socialism-become-so-popular-in-america ▾
Apr 24, 2017 - But just look at how widespread and mainstream socialist ideas have become in America today. In the 2016 presidential ... If you want to learn more about this subject, you can read

---

FIGURE 7.1 The News Media Wants to Know Why Socialism is Suddenly Popular Again.

It is not possible to leap over the current conditions, and as I've written throughout this book so far, we are living in a time of perhaps diminishing democracy and thus we might expect left-wing groups to struggle. Having said that (and without wishing to focus only on the Democratic Socialists), there are signs globally that the political left is possibly making a comeback. Mainstream media began to take notice of the DSA in 2017, and the consensus was they were benefitting from the popularity of Bernie Sanders and were recruiting from Sanders supporters who were disappointed when he didn't win the Democrats' nomination to stand against Trump (Williams 2017). While we're not there yet, it is worth noting that the forms of social journalism I'm discussing in this chapter could play a role in expanding progressive political thinking. This idea is embryonic and it needs to be carefully nurtured but is embodied in the idea of a digital "journalism commons," "open-ended systems for news production built around common pooled resources to collectively address critical issues" (de la Serna 2017).

The "Monitorial Citizen": A Call to Arms in the Age of Fake News

In the first week of Donald Trump's presidency, two of the authors of the Panama Papers story called for a new collaborative effort to combat the threat they said that the new president posed to the USA and to the world: "once again, we are faced with a story that is too big and too important to handle on our own: Donald Trump's impact on the democracy of the United States of America," they wrote (Obermaier and Obermayer 2017). This was before American voters and the rest of the world had really had much opportunity to assess how Trump would behave in the White House. By the end of his first year in office, there was little doubt that Donald J. Trump was the least qualified and maybe even the worst president in American history. We learned from his own tweets how disorganized he was, how angry he was and how he cared little for the decorum of the office in his insulting and belligerent social media behavior. When Michael Wolff's explosive book *Fire and Fury* was published in January 2018, it was impossible to miss just what a dysfunctional and disastrous mess the one-year-old Trump presidency was shaping into. While Wolff was fairly criticized for mistakes in his reporting (Borchers 2018), it was difficult—if not impossible—to disagree with the central thesis of *Fire and Fury*: Donald Trump is unfit for office. One review summed up the premise of the book in simple terms:

> This is a book about the collection of cronies, opportunists, misfits, functionaries, family members, and public servants who have tried to construct something that acts and operates like a presidency around a man who neither acts nor operates like a president, a man they all know shouldn't be the president.

(Klein 2018)

The story of Donald Trump's assault on American democracy is too big for a small group of reporters to handle on their own. It has forced the major news companies to increase their resourcing of bureaux in Washington DC and it has also led to an increase in support for non-mainstream reporters and publications and a bigger space for them to operate in. Further, and to me most interestingly, concern about Donald Trump's presidency has also spurred into action a number of citizen action groups. I am encouraged by this and also think that they can provide a model for a re-positioning of citizen journalism, a re-imagined form of social journalism. A key community of concern in relation to combatting Trumpism has been formed among American mental health professionals. While their ability to offer a diagnosis of Donald Trump's mental state is limited by the so-called "Goldwater Rule," tens of thousands of psychiatrists and psychologists have expressed their concern about his fitness for office in a series of petitions, news articles, professional journals and an edited collection based on a symposium (Lee 2017). The book's title, *The Dangerous Case of Donald Trump*, makes their position on this issue explicit; it also raised an interesting idea for me, one that is related to the concept of a vigorous form of social/citizen journalism. The psychiatrists and mental health experts who contributed to this volume are accurately described as "activist witnessing professionals" (Lifton 2017) and it is in this guise that they are motivated to speak up and collectively speak out on the issue of Donald Trump's fitness for office.

One contributor to this volume is Robert Lifton, an eminent psychiatrist who studies the impacts of violence and the psychology of war, and "witnessing professional" is his phrase. He defines it as combining a "disciplined professional approach" with "the ethical requirements of a committed witness," combining "scholarship with activism" (Lifton 2017: 13). It strikes me as something that many of us can actually do; not necessarily on a daily, or full-time basis, but certainly when the times require it of us. Most of us are capable of being "monitorial citizens" who respond to news events and help to mobilize fellow citizens through sharing information and calls to action. Media scholar Michael Schudson reflects on the idea of citizens monitoring news and politics in his book *The Good Citizen*:

> [they] scan ... the informational environment in such a way that they may be alerted on a very wide variety of issues for a very wide variety of ends and may be mobilized around those issues in a wide variety of ways.
> *(Schudson 1998: 310)*

Schudson says that "monitorial citizens" are more reactive than proactive, but it is certainly a step in the right direction, towards what communications scholar John Keane calls "monitory democracy," "without doubt the most complex form of democracy known to us" (Keane 2013: 81). I see no reason why, with a bit of work, we shouldn't be able to combine aspects of the monitorial citizen with a rebuilt cadre of citizen journalists to develop the discipline of social journalism further. Social media provides a useful tool for citizens to exercise their monitorial function independent from the normal gatekeeping functions of the newsroom. The potential of monitorial citizenship has recently been taken up in journalism studies, notably in a 2008 journal article by Dutch scholar, Mark Deuze. He writes that a monitorial citizenship is ideally suited to social media because it manifests as a "distinctly skeptical, globally interconnected, yet deeply personal type of self-determined civic engagement" (Deuze 2008: 854). However, we need to take this a few steps further to get to the essence of "social journalism." Not only does it have to reflect the values of monitorial citizenship, it has to do so from a perspective of "critique" (Fuchs 2010). What Christian Fuchs means by this is that alternative forms of media and journalism must be consciously and conscientiously critical of the current state of the world and committed to a process of change towards "the creation of a participatory, co-operative society" (ibid.: 181). Critical media is partisan, and Fuchs celebrates this in clear terms:

> Critical media in one or the other respect take the standpoint of the oppressed or exploited classes and consider that structures of oppression and exploitation benefit certain classes at the expense of others and hence should be transformed.
>
> *(Fuchs 2010: 182)*

If one aim of critical media is to give voice to the voiceless, it must first make a connection with sub-altern groups—those who are voiceless and without social power. As noted in relation to Indymedia and *Unicorn Riot*, there are several examples historically, and in contemporary alternative media spaces, we can draw on. In the following section I want to develop a theoretical foundation for the critical media that builds on Christian Fuchs work, but also reaches back into history.

Gramsci's "Integral Journalism"

Antonio Gramsci was an Italian communist and journalist who spent many years in prison for his uncompromising political views. He was periodically (when he wasn't in prison) the editor of the Italian communist party's newspaper, *Ordine Nuovo* (New Order). In this role and in his prison writings, Gramsci developed the idea of what he came to call "integral journalism" and he defined it in this way: "[journalism that] seeks not only to satisfy all the needs (of a given category) of its public, but also to create and develop those needs, to arouse its public and progressively enlarge it" (Gramsci 2000: 383).

While developing his ideas in what became known as the *Prison Notebooks*, Gramsci had to be careful in his choice of subjects and in his use of language. He wrote in a kind of code, but if you understand the context, it is not difficult to decipher. In the passage quoted here, Gramsci is talking about the working class using the careful phrase a "given category" of the "public." When he writes about arousing this category and enlarging it, Gramsci is talking about using the party's newspapers and magazines to educate the working class in the politics of class struggle and recruiting to the party. This is clear in other fragments of his *Prison Notebooks* in which he talks about "a group which aims to spread an integral conception of the world through its various journalistic activities" (Gramsci 2000: 383). This "group" is clearly the communist party, "a more or less homogeneous cultural grouping" that has "a given general orientation" (ibid.: 384). In other sections of the *Notebooks*, Gramsci makes clear the democratic method of editorial decision-making that must apply to the party's "integral journalism": "collective discussion and criticism (made up of suggestions, advice, comments on method and criticism which is constructive and aimed at mutual education)" (ibid.: 383). Gramsci provided detailed instructions to his party comrades on the types of publications and styles of writing they should adopt and he wanted them to work together to educate all the workers contributing to the party papers and magazines through "regular and methodical writing activity" (ibid.).

While my personal preference is for a dedicated party press such as this, I realize that it is perhaps too advanced or radical for most of you, my readers. However, I think it is possible to take Gramsci's notion of "integral journalism" as a model for a new kind of social journalism that embodies some of the principles he was aiming for: a form of journalism that is simultaneously "activist and pedagogical, political and cultural, scientific and historical" (Hoare and Sperber 2015). Gramsci felt that this type of journalism should spring from and reflect the aspirations of its working class audience; which is an entirely different proposition to so-called participatory journalism which seeks merely to engage the audience just enough to make them feel comfortable paying for content, or handing over their personal data to be mined and sold.

Gramsci's vision for a journalism that reflects the interests of its readers and attempts to draw them into greater political participation is not that far from reality today. If we examine some of the partisan press of the conservative side of politics, particularly of the so-called "Alt Right," we can see that it plays this role. The editorial leadership of the infamous *Breitbart* website, headed by former Trump confidante Steve Bannon makes its commitment to this pedagogic and polemic mission explicit (Friedersdorf 2017); so too does the leadership of the Nazi news site *Daily Stormer* (Sparrow 2017). In the end these right-wing news outlets fail Gramsci's test for integral journalism because they are both willing to use outright lies and to promote "fake news," which we would have to concede is not in the public interest. It also has to be said that news organs of the politically dominant class are also capable of playing a pedagogic and polemic role and often have done historically. Gramsci specifically recognized this in Italy in the early years of the twentieth century and it formed the kernel of his ideas about integral journalism on behalf of socially and culturally subordinate groups (Hoare and Sperber 2015).

In order to approach anything like the articulation of integral journalism within the framework of digital media, we have to first understand, and reimagine, what we mean by the term "public interest" and separate it from a News Establishment view of the world. The generally accepted meaning of public interest in relation to journalism and news is that there are certain topics—usually around the important questions of the day in economics, politics, culture and so on—that should be covered and reported on in-depth because knowledge of them can impact on public policy or wider political discourse. In many ways public interest has a narrow definition that is limited to relatively harmless issues of governance and business. Anything with real impact is often held "commercial-in-confidence," or deemed to be a "State secret," thus not really open to public scrutiny or influence. This definition—which effectively withholds important information from the public domain—is, unfortunately, widely accepted in the realm of Fourth Estate journalism. There is one major flaw in this model; it does not differentiate various class elements within the unitary category of the "public." The interests of the dominant class—in our case, as in Gramsci's, the capitalist class—are presented as universal in the news media, thus "preventing the eruption of effective subaltern dissidence in the public sphere" (Hoare and Sperber 2015). However, political economy tells us that the interests of the capitalist class and the interests of the working class diverge on many issues (for example, what is a fair day's pay for a fair day's work).

The News Establishment protects the ruling class and therefore it does not challenge this stunted definition of "public interest" and it hasn't for over 100 years. In the first decades of the twentieth century, Gramsci argued that the "the press" was a leading and "the most dynamic" element of the "ideological structure" of society (Gramsci 2000: 380) and therefore played a crucial role in legitimating ruling class views as public opinion. As early as 1916, he was scathing in his assessment of most Italian newspapers, which, he argued," inject in the mind of the reader ways of feeling and judging the facts of current politics appropriate for the producers and sellers of the press." For good measure, Gramsci added the following warning to working class readers:

> Everything that is published is influenced by one idea: that of serving the dominant class, and which is ineluctably translated into a fact: that of combating the laboring class. And in fact, from the first to the last line the bourgeois newspaper smells of and reveals this preoccupation.
>
> *(Gramsci 1916)*

Gramsci's project was to overcome the "hegemony" the ruling class enjoyed over public life and, through the process of "integral journalism," construct an "informed and critical public" capable of seeing through the distortions of the bourgeois press (Coben 1998: 26). In 1916 Gramsci enthusiastically called upon workers to boycott the newspapers of the ruling class, while busily working to build up the socialist press on behalf of the working class.

> Don't give financial assistance to the bourgeois press, which is your adversary. This is what should be our battle cry in this moment that is characterized by the subscription campaigns of all the bourgeois newspapers. Boycott them, boycott them, boycott them!
>
> *(Gramsci 1916)*

Perhaps what we are witnessing today, with the declining circulation and viewership enjoyed by the mainstream news media is an example of a passive and unorganized boycott by readers who no longer feel that journalism—as delivered by the News Establishment—covers stories of interest *to them*, or that represent their interests. The growth in alternative media, particularly identifiably partisan journalism—on both the left and the right—might represent the other side of this passive boycott. But how, if we are not yet ready to move into a full-blown Gramscian type of integral journalism, might we take at least baby steps towards more democratic journalism that can embody and embolden a genuine public interest?

I am not going to claim to have a ready answer, nor anything more than a few suggestions to offer in this direction, but I believe Gramsci's principles, when linked to a more active and "monitorial" form of citizenship provide a solid foundation. In addition, as I mentioned in the previous chapter, some elements of "reciprocal journalism" will be useful in building a new participatory model, but one that goes beyond mere engagement with the commercial news media. What we want to move towards are "more fluid and hybrid forms of journalism" (Lewis, Holton and Coddington 2014: 235). The test will be moving beyond small or hyperlocal communities by forging regional, national and global communities to build a new model of journalism which breaks down the wall between the newsroom and the audience so that eventually it ceases to exist at all. As a Gramscian and a Marxist I am always cautious to be realistic; I recognize that creating a cadre of self-actualized critical and integral journalists will take some time and that such a project necessarily starts from a very low base of engagement. However, and in the Gramscian spirit, it is important to retain an optimism of the will, while also entertaining a pessimism of the intellect.

Training Non-journalists to Work Outside the Newsroom

"Engagement" has become a media buzzword in the last few years. At heart, engagement is a marketing term that is used as a measurement for effective product-oriented communication between the seller and the buyer of commodities. It has become a metric of social media advertising and marketing penetration that can be measured by the number of "likes," "shares" and "comments" a particular piece of copy, or a video or image receives as it circulates through various media channels. That this stunted form of engagement now dominates management discussions and academic discourses about news and journalism should actually be something to worry about, not celebrate. However, in a mediasphere obsessed with metrics and measuring everything that is not nailed down, increasing audience engagement is a Holy Grail pursuit. The simple reason is that advertising still dominates media revenues by a factor of 10 to one over subscriptions. The more a media outlet can demonstrate it is engaging with its audience, the more value it can generate through its advertising rate card. This has become a matter of life and death for the news media; while advertising revenues still dominate, they are falling rapidly as online marketing replaces print and broadcasting with much lower cost-to-view ratios (Holcomb and Mitchell 2014). To save their revenue streams, online news organizations now want to turn casual readers into subscribers, to transform periodic engagement into a financial commitment (Gilbreath 2017). Encouraging the once-passive audience to participate (even at a fairly superficial level) in the gathering, reporting and distribution of news is also seen as a way of increasing engagement that might then be translated into a financial addition to the bottom line. It is in this context that newsrooms are experimenting with "reciprocal," "participatory" and "hyperlocal" forms of journalism that seek to engage audience members and activate them.

The tension between participation for the sake of community building and participation to boost profits is another example of what I have described as the duality of the news commodity form. The tension in this dialectic is between using user-generated content as a "democratizing" force for good, versus the drive to monetize audience participation. As Harte and his colleagues note (2017: 162), under such circumstances there is "scant evidence" that engagement and participation are being used for community building, "common purpose, equal mutual benefit, reciprocal exchange."

As I've outlined in this chapter, the alternative to faux engagement—which is really about propping up the failing news business model—is my conception of social journalism. To work, social journalism needs several things, not least of which is an educated and switched on cadre of media-literate activist witnesses. Some social journalists will, no doubt, come from the ranks of reporters, editors and other staff who are being slowly but surely ejected from commercial newsrooms. A few may well move towards a more progressive form of journalism, if they can work out how to fund it. And so, obviously, social journalism needs an educated audience that is prepared to fund the efforts of the newly activated social journalists. But, I do not think that this is enough. To be truly effective social journalism also needs audiences to move beyond being passive monitorial citizens. Social journalism needs activated and active audiences who can participate effectively in news gathering, writing, editing and distribution—including the good use of audio and video—and who work independently, or in collaboration with more professional newsroom cadre.

In an ideal case, argues Christian Fuchs, "self-managed citizen journalists" would produce their own critical alternative news media. But realistically this means all citizens would have "the time skills and resources so that they can all act as critical journalists and critical recipients." This is a version of the digital media literacy I talked about in the Prologue, in which "the distinction between production and reception completely vanishes" (Fuchs 2010: 180). The doing of social journalism is made possible by social media, which means that both critical consumption and the possibility of critical production are opened up to larger populations. In the second half of this book these are the themes to be practically explored. In the following chapters the "How?" question is front and center.

Note

1 This is one lingering hangover from the Cold War period. Interestingly, the "Russia probe" in the United States has not for the ideas dampened enthusiasm for the ideas of socialism this time.

References

Atton, Chris, and James F. Hamilton. 2008. *Alternative Journalism*. London: Sage.

Borchers, Callum. 2018. "How did Michael Wolff's 'Fire and Fury' Get Past a Fact-Checker? It's Not Clear that the Book was Vetted." *The Washington Post*. January 9. Accessed January 9, 2018. www.washingtonpost.com/news/the-fix/wp/2018/01/09/how-did-michael-wolffs-fire-and-fury-get-past-a-fact-checker-its-not-clear-that-the-book-was-vetted/?utm_term=.c12938930298.

Bruns, Axel. 2005. *Gatewatching: Collaborative Online News Production*. New York: Peter Lang. Accessed December 9, 2016.

Cision. 2017. 2017 "Global Social Journalism Study." Cision. Accessed January 8, 2018. www.cision.com/us/resources/white-papers/global-social-journalism-study/?clid= whitepaper-ty.

Coben, Diana. 1998. *Radical Heroes: Gramsci, Freire, and the Politics of Adult Education*. New York: Garland.

De la Serna, Carlos Martinez. 2017. "The New Journalism Commons." NiemanLab. December. Accessed March 10, 2018. www.niemanlab.org/2017/12/the-new-journalism-commons/.

Deuze, Mark. 2008. "The Changing Context of News Work: Liquid Journalism for a Monitorial Citizenry." *International Journal of Communication* 2: 848–865. doi:1932-8036/2008FEA0848.

Engels, Friedrich. 1884. "Marx and the Neue Rheinische Zeitung." In *Marx/Engels Collected Works*, vol. 26. London: Lawrence & Wishart.

Friedersdorf, Conor. 2017. "Breitbart's Astonishing Confession." *The Atlantic*. December 29. Accessed December 30, 2017. www.theatlantic.com/politics/archive/2017/12/the-ongoing-mistreatment-of-right-leaning-news-consumers/549335/.

Fuchs, Christian. 2010. "Alternative Media as Critical Media." *European Journal of Social Theory* 13(2): 173–192. Accessed January 12, 2018.

Gilbreath, Bob. 2017. "Rise of Subscriptions and the Fall of Advertising." *Medium*. March 20. Accessed May 3, 2017. https://medium.com/the-graph/rise-of-subscriptions-and-the-fall-of-advertising-d5e4d8800a49.

Giraud, Eva. 2014. "Has Radical Participatory Online Media Really 'Failed'? Indymedia and its Legacies." *Convergence* 20(4): 419–437. doi:10.1177/3548514541352.

Goode, Luke. 2009. "Social News, Citizen Journalism and Democracy." *New Media & Society* 11(8): 1287–1305. doi:10.1177/1461444809341393.

Gramsci, Antonio. 1916. "Newspapers and the Workers." Translated by Mitchell Abidor. *Avanti!* Marxist Internet Archive. December 22. Accessed September 17, 2017. www.marxists.org/archive/gramsci/1916/12/newspapers.htm.

Gramsci, Antonio. 2000. *The Gramsci Reader: Selected Writings, 1916–1935*. Edited by David Forgacs. New York: New York University Press.

Harte, Dave, Andy Williams, and Jerome Turner. 2017. "Reciprocity and the Hyperlocal Journalist." *Journalism Practice* 11(2–3): 160–176. doi:10.1080/17512786.2016.121993.

Haslanger, Julia. 2016. *Social Journalism: The Who, What, Where, When, Why and How*. New York: Tow-Knight Center for Entrepreneurial Journalism. Accessed November 28, 2016. http://towknight.org/research/social-journalism-who-what-when-how/.

Hille, Sanne, and Piet Bakker. 2014. "Engaging the Social News User: Comments on News Sites and Facebook." *Journalism Practice* 8(5): 563–572. doi:10.1080/17512 786.2014.899758.

Hirst, Martin. 2011. *News 2.0: Can Journalism Survive the Internet?* Crows Nest, NSW: Allen and Unwin.

Hoare, George, and Nathan Sperber. 2015. *An Introduction to Antonio Gramsci: His Life, Thought and Legacy*. London: Bloomsbury.

Holcomb, Jesse, and Amy Mitchell. 2014. "Revenue Sources: A Heavy Dependence on Advertising." State of the Media. Pew Research Center. March 26. Accessed October 18, 2016. www.journalism.org/2014/03/26/revenue-sources-a-heavy-dependence-on-advertising/.

Johnston, Lisette. 2016. "Social News = Journalism Evolution? How the Integration of UGC into Newswork Helps and Hinders the Role of the Journalist." *Digital Journalism* 4(7): 899–909. Accessed December 31, 2017. doi:https://doi.org/10.1080/21670811.2016.1168709.

Johnstone, Caitlin. 2017. "How To Criticize Trump Without Being An Establishment Hack." *Medium*. October 13. Accessed January 8, 2018. https://medium.com/@caity johnstone/how-to-criticize-trump-without-being-an-establishment-hack-153a11dddf1b.

Keane, John. 2013. *Democracy and Media Decadence*. Cambridge: Cambridge University Press.

Klein, Ezra. 2018. "Beyond the Gossip, Michael Wolff's Fire and Fury Reveals a President in Crisis." *Vox*. January 9. Accessed January 9, 2018. www.vox.com/explainers/2018/1/9/16860598/michael-wolff-fire-fury-donald-trump-book.

Lee, Bandy X. 2017. *The Dangerous Case of Donald Trump: 27 Psychiatrists and Mental Health Experts Assess a President*. New York: St Martin's Press.

Lewis, Woody. 2009. "Social Journalism: Past, Present, and Future." *Mashable Australia*. April 8. Accessed November 28, 2016. http://mashable.com/2009/04/07/social-jour nalism/#Ga1Q_yI3mkq3.

Lewis, Seth C., Avery E. Holton and Mark Coddington. 2014. "Reciprocal Journalism." *Journalism Practice* 8(2): 229–241. doi:10.1080/17512786.2013.859840.

Lifton, Robert Jay. 2017. "Foreword: Our Witness to Malignant Normality." In *The Dangerous Case of Donald Trump: 27 Psychiatrists and Mental Health Experts Assess a President*, edited by Bandy X. Lee, 6–16. New York: St Martin's Press.

Murray, Stefanie. 2017. "Comparing Models of Collaborative Journalism." Center for Cooperative Media. Accessed October 1, 2017. https://centerforcooperativemedia. org/center-cooperative-media-identifies-6-models-collaborative-journalism-revolu tion-media/.

Obermaier, Frederik, and Bastian Obermayer. 2017. "We Broke the Panama Papers story. Here's How to Investigate Donald Trump." *The Guardian*. January 25. Accessed January 27, 2017. www.theguardian.com/commentisfree/2017/jan/24/panama-papers-media-investigation-next-donald-trump-hold-accountable?CMP=soc_568.

Owen, Taylor. 2016. "Global Media Power." In *The Sage Handbook of Digital Journalism*, edited by Tamara Witschge, C.W. Anderson, David Domingo and Alfred Hermida, 25–34. London: Sage.

Rosengard, Dana, Mary Tucker-McLaughlin and Tim Brown. 2014. "Students and Social News: How College Students Share News through Social Media." *Electronic News* 8(2): 120–137. doi:10.1177/1931243114546448.

Schneider, Daniel, and Jano de Souza. 2016. *Exploring Asymmetric Collaboration in Social News Curation: Systems*, Man *and* Cybernetics. Budapest: IEEE Explore. doi:10.1109/ SMC.2016.7844983.

Schudson, Michael. 1998. *The Good Citizen: A History of American Civic Life*. New York: The Free Press.

Scott, Jonathon, David Millard and Pauline Leonard. 2015. "Citizen Participation in News: An Analysis of the Landscape of Online Journalism." *Digital Journalism* 3(5): 737–758. doi:10.1080/21670811.2014.952983.

Sparrow, Jeff. 2017. "Milo Yiannopoulos's Draft and the Role of Editors in Dealing with the Far-Right." *The Guardian*. December 29. Accessed December 30, 2017. www. theguardian.com/commentisfree/2017/dec/29/milo-yiannopouloss-draft-and-the-role-of-editors-in-dealing-with-the-far-right.

Usher, Nikki. 2017. "The Appropriation/Amplification Model of Citizen Journalism." *Journalism Practice* 11(2–3): 247–265. doi:10.1080/17512786.1223552.

Vujnovic, Marina, Jane B. Singer, Steve Paulussen, Ari Heinonen, Zvi Reich, Thorsten Quandt, Alfred Hermida and David Domingo. 2010. "Exploring the Political-Eco-nomic Factors of Participatory Journalism." *Journalism Practice* 4(3): 285–296. doi:10.1080/1751278003650588.

Williams, Douglas. 2017. "Why the Democratic Socialists of America are Experiencing a Boom." *The Guardian*. August 13. Accessed January 14, 2018. www.theguardian.com/ commentisfree/2017/aug/12/democratic-socialists-america-experiencing-boom.

Woods, Baynard. 2017. "How Unicorn Riot Covers the Alt-Right without Giving Them a Platform." *Columbia Journalism Review*. November 1. Accessed January 29, 2018. www.cjr.org/united_states_project/charlottesville-alt-right-unicorn-riot.php.

Zeller, Frauke, and Alfred Hermida. 2015. "When Tradition Meets Immediacy and Interaction: The Integration of Social Media in Journalists' Everyday Practices." *About Journalism* 4(1): 106–119. Accessed January 11, 2018. https://surlejournalisme.com/ rev/index.php/slj/article/download/202/88.

8

THE ETHICAL AND LEGAL
PRINCIPLES OF SOCIAL JOURNALISM

First, Do No Harm

The object of this chapter is not to cover particular jurisdictions, it will provide only general guidance at the level of principles. For example, definitions of defamation or contempt may vary in detail, but they follow the basic principles of right to reputation and respect for the rule of law. In this chapter we also take a short diversion into the seventeenth century, the beginning of the Enlightenment period and the period in which journalism and the scientific method began to take hold. This relationship is significant for the development of modern journalism ethics and also the process of verification that is at the heart of reporting and editing today.

To explore how the mutually constituted dialectics of technology and economics are rewriting some media rules, this chapter will introduce and explain the concepts of "ethico-legal paradox," and the "techno-legal" and "techno-ethical" "time-gaps." These dialectical contradictions are the result of the speed at which the social media revolution is occurring and the struggle of social structures and institutions to keep up. However, we should not assume that this creates a "Wild West" situation where there are no rules. The legal constraints—defamation, contempt of court, etc.—that apply to the legacy media also apply in the social media environment.

If you are going to practice as a social journalist, creating news and news-like content for sharing on social media apps and platforms, then you are going to have to start acting like a reporter—at least in a semi-professional way. This means having a competent working knowledge of the media laws and ethical precepts that are applicable in the jurisdiction where you are going to be active.

In this chapter we will attempt to distil the most important and relevant principles, but we obviously cannot provide detailed and prescriptive rules; these vary between jurisdictions and within national or cultural norms. It is your responsibility to operationalize the principles discussed in this chapter within the national or local context in which you will be reporting and publishing. If you want more information on law and ethics there are plenty of resources available, including my most recent book, written with my colleague Roger Patching: *Journalism Ethics: Arguments and Cases for the Twenty-First Century* (Patching and Hirst 2014). Many of the ideas presented in this chapter can be found there in more detail.

While not covering every legal and ethical rule you might need to know, I am confident in suggesting one over-arching and near universal principle which should guide what you are doing. It is a principle taken from the Hippocratic Oath that guides the medical profession: "First, do no harm." While not written into the Oath in so many words, this is a simple rule to follow and it basically advises us to think carefully about our actions to ensure that we do not inadvertently, or unnecessarily cause harm to an individual or group of people through the stories that we write. While this is clearly an ethical principle, deriving in part from medical codes of ethics, it is also a useful principle in relation to legal issues. If you start out from the premise of avoiding, or at least minimizing, the harm your reporting might do, it is likely, but by no means guaranteed, that you will be acting within the law. If you are not doing harm it is unlikely you will be defaming anyone—that is *unnecessarily* damaging their reputation—which can be an expensive legal mistake in many parts of the world.

Is there a "Law" of Journalism?

There is no "law" of journalism in most countries; the obvious exceptions are the less democratic parts of the world where authoritarian governments simply impose legal limits on press freedom to cling on to power—for example, Turkey, China, the Philippines, Russia, Singapore and many more. In the United States, the First Amendment to the nation's founding document, the Constitution, prevents the government from enacting any law to limit freedom of the press.

> Congress shall make no law respecting an establishment of religion, or prohibiting the free exercise thereof; or abridging the freedom of speech, or of the press; or the right of the people peaceably to assemble, and to petition the Government for a redress of grievances.
>
> *(FindLaw undated)*

This is very broad rule and Americans fiercely defend this important amendment to their Constitution, but it doesn't give the news media "carte blanche." The First Amendment does not mean that journalists can ignore other laws that are widely applicable. A reporter cannot speed down the highway, or blithely trespass, or steal, or lie.

As a general rule, any law that you are subject to as a private citizen will also apply to journalists, and to you as a social journalist. This obviously applies to all aspects of the civil and criminal code in the jurisdiction where you work and can range from the mundane—like you need to obey the traffic rules—to the arcane; for example, in some English-speaking countries there exists a law called the "newspaper rule," which basically gives bona fide news-gathering activities an exemption from certain aspects of contempt law and which can be invoked to protect a journalist's sources from exposure in a court case. In many places, this rule is out-of-date now because of whistle-blower legislation which, while it is supposed to protect sources who uncover misdeeds in government, is most often used to prosecute them.

Perhaps the closest thing to a universal law of journalism is the concept of defamation, or to put it another way, the right to protect a good reputation. Most jurisdictions have some form of law around reputation. Defamation is the action of harming a person's reputation by reporting things about them that show them in bad light. Journalism does this every day, and mostly it's justified. Every story in which the actions of an individual are held up to public inspection by the media is potentially defamatory; and many are actually defamatory. For instance, if a public figure breaks the law—say a Hollywood actor is caught drink-driving—reporting that the actor was drunk and broke the law would obviously harm that person's reputation. It would cause members of the public to think less of her or him; in other words, it defames the actor and tarnishes their reputation. Technically, the actor could sue the news outlet and the reporter for defamation. But two things might stop this from happening: the first is that assuming the incident is true, too bad for the actor. The second factor is that the cost of legal action might outweigh any redress or compensation the actor can win in a court case. The first reason is that establishing the truth of the defamatory statements is a defense that, in most jurisdictions, trumps any accusation that reputation has been damaged. The simple assumption is that by driving while intoxicated—in clear contravention of a known law—the actor has effectively done self-harm to his or her reputation and therefore publishing the news about it can do no further harm. In the second example, sheer economics takes over. Defamation actions can be expensive to pursue, and courts have generally not been disposed to pay high amounts in compensation. However, this is a moveable feast and laws are amended all the time. You would be immensely stupid to not read up on defamation law in your jurisdiction and chance things to luck. A successful defamation action can bankrupt you, put your outlet out of business, and in some parts of the world, result in a lengthy jail term.

Particular laws that you need to be cognizant of—and which you have a duty to read up on and follow—include trespass and your rights to access certain places as a reporter, and rules regarding the use of recording devices, both audio and video, which can be complex and vary from place to place quite widely. For example, in some Australian states recording a telephone conversation in which you are a participant is legal, even if the person you're talking to doesn't know. In other states this is not legal. Similar differences exist in relation to the recording and transmission to a third-party (broadcasting, for example) of video. Some Australian states allow the broadcast of the audio and not the video, others ban both outright. These are examples of unresolved "techno-legal time-gap" issues from the analogue age (see below for more on this topic). The use of social media during court proceedings is another area where caution is advised, and local knowledge essential. There have been cases of inexperienced reporters being caught out by not knowing the rules. Taking notes on a laptop is OK in some courts, but live tweeting might be banned. Knowing the law of contempt-of-court as it applies to you is also very important. Contemptuous actions in a courtroom can be anything from reporting facts from a case that are suppressed, failing to stand when the judge enters the chamber, speaking out of turn, attempting to speak to a witness in the court precincts, or attempting to contact members of a jury during or after a trial.

Not all countries have the equivalent of the US First Amendment, some have tough rules preventing all but the most benign and trivial forms of journalism. It is your responsibility to know what regime applies in areas where you are working or practicing amateur reporting. Of course, some rules need to be broken; especially if they are designed to deliberately block public interest journalism. In such situations the second law of journalism must be applied: "Don't get caught, be careful not to draw attention to yourself; get in, get the story and get out." Actually, I'm half-kidding about that. While it is sometimes necessary to adopt slightly underhanded tactics in pursuit of a story, it can really only be justified if the public interest is high. Usually this would mean a significant story about corruption in public office, illegal business practices or events and issues of that nature. When these tactics are applied to low value targets it might create a tabloid sensation, but it does nothing to advance the public interest and it risks causing substantial harm to the reporter and news organization's reputation and it is another rusty nail in the coffin of public trust in the media. Social journalism is founded on a bond of trust with the public, it is not to be taken lightly.

The Trust Issue in Social Journalism

Open any code of ethics for journalists and you will see that the word "trust" is mentioned; it is regarded as a cornerstone of professionalism. You have probably heard the phrase, "Trust me, I'm a journalist." It has become something of a cliché and a joke, mainly because the relationship of trust between journalists and the news-consuming public has been damaged, if not broken beyond repair, by the actions of sections of the news media over the past 15–20 years. We discussed this in chapter five where I pessimistically concluded that journalists are facing an uphill battle to save journalism from itself. One ray of hope I cling to is that maybe the advent of social journalism can help restore trust between the news media and the public. Social journalism relies on strong and meaningful interactions between reporters—whether employed professionals, freelancers, or unpaid hobbyists and activists—and their audiences. Trust relies on the active cultivation of this relationship and continuous demonstrations of trustworthy actions on the part of the news media. The easiest way to break trust and to lose the relationship is to cheat on your partner.

One issue of trust that social journalists will encounter is the separation of "fact" and "opinion." This is a grey area in journalism ethics and, in my view, almost impossible to police. There has been a long-standing cultural expectation that "real" news should always stand aside from opinion and allows the reader to assert his or her own interpretation of the "facts" as "objectively" presented. The rise of blogging, citizen journalism and a more partisan media—from *Breitbart* and Fox News on the right to *Salon* or the *Huffington Post* on the liberal left—has blurred that distinction somewhat, and opinion that matches our own world view is often more important to us than "just the facts." This means that, to some extent, the issue of trust has been politicized and turned into a matter of shared ideology as much as factuality. The days in which the credibility—or trust value—of a journalist could be measured by reference to her or his employing organization are coming to an end, if not already consigned to history. Taking an institutional brand as your measure of journalistic credibility and trust is indeed a "risky business" today (Hayes, Singer and Ceppos 2007). In the age of "brand" journalism, the credibility and trust rating of a journalist is more likely to be measured on an individual scale because we are much more attuned to the "byline" now than in past times. This means that even non-professionals, non-employees, and unpaid amateurs can now compete in the trust stakes with their professional counterparts. In fact, one study demonstrated that more politically engaged people tended to trust non-professional journalists more than those who were linked to a news institution (Kaufhold, Valenzuela and Gil de Zú 2010).

Accountability is another word that often crops up in codes of ethics and being accountable is also linked to credibility and trust in journalism. Being accountable means owning your mistakes, as well as your successes, and it means a willingness to admit you got something wrong. Accountability involves both personal disclosure and the presentation of evidence for any claims you are making. The seemingly limitless space of online news sites presents an opportunity for social journalists to present evidence, in the form of background documents and interview transcripts for example, that would not be published in the limited space of a printed newspaper, or time-limited television bulletin. The amateur and the social journalist are today able to challenge the institutional authority of the mainstream media by using personal disclosure to get closer to their audiences and nurture the trust relationship and, by taking advantage of the "link to everything" approach, they are also able to offer curated evidence to underpin the credibility of their reporting and analysis. Furthermore, social journalists can use their independence from discredited news institutions as a badge of honor and a positive marketing tool in competition with them. Alongside this independence, however, there must be a level of responsiveness too. Social journalists should be attuned to their audience in terms of expectations and outlook; this means harnessing all of the conversational tools and applications afforded by digital technologies. This also requires a degree of self-reflexivity and ability to self-critique that is lacking in much of the legacy media, which tends to rely on its own institutional notions of self, rather than the more fluid self-perceptions of social journalists, more closely tethered to their audience's views and feedback. It is the process of engagement, and the audience perception that social journalists are generally more available to them than professional journalists (Holton, Coddington and Gil de Zuniga 2013) that gives social journalism purchase in the crowded news marketplace. At a time when it seems many news consumers feel that the mainstream has given up on them and serves only to replicate the political status quo (Park 2017), social journalists who can earn the trust of their audiences may flourish.

What Happens When the Fourth Estate Gets it Badly Wrong?

The Fourth Estate is predicated on a series of ethical and legal principles that have stood the test of time, despite the failings of this model of journalism in practice. These principles are given form in Codes of Ethics and an understanding that journalists and editors will (mostly) abide by the "laws of the land." Of course, there are always exceptions to every rule, and they are endlessly argued. However, mainstream journalism also operates by the unwritten rules of the News Establishment—for example, protecting the "private" life of a politician who is a known serial adulterer because it is deemed somehow not in the "public interest" for details of his/her affairs to be known.

Yes, these silent rules are actually applied more often than we might imagine. For instance, in 2017 and early 2018, the now former deputy prime minister of Australia—the nation's second-in-charge of the government—was protected by this silent rule for nearly a year. Barnaby Joyce's sexual wandering—he was married with four children at the time—has been described as an "open secret" among the Australian political media elite, but no mainstream reporters would go near the story until a notorious Murdoch tabloid decided to publish a picture of the deputy PM's pregnant girlfriend on page one, under the headline "A Bundle of Joyce" (Dore 2018). *The Daily Telegraph* editor, Christopher Dore, has not shared any details about why the paper chose to name Joyce and break the story when it did, but informed speculation suggests it is because by attacking Barnaby

Joyce, the paper was really going after the prime minister, Malcolm Turnbull. It was well-known at the time that Rupert Murdoch's stable of newspapers and the Fox-aligned Sky News cable network, wanted Turnbull removed as prime minister because he was seen as ineffectual and likely to lose the next Australian national election. For the news media, it might have been an "open secret" that Joyce was intimately involved with one of his staff members—in breach of the government's own ministerial code of conduct—but it had been talked about for months on social media. In fact, it was the independent online media which actually broke the story and wrote up a version of the affair in October (Ozturk 2017) and November 2017 (Jones 2017).

As you might expect, once the story appeared in *The Daily Telegraph*, there was an explosion of criticism against the News Establishment reporters who had kept this "open secret" to themselves despite clear public interest. Joyce was an avowed Catholic and "family man" who had previously used his daughters' names and unmarried status to bolster his opposition to a same-sex marriage equality bill that was before parliament. His adultery made a mockery of his professed religious beliefs and his claim to be a steadfast "family man." There was much embarrassed back-peddling by sections of the news media to explain why they didn't cover the story more rigorously and much earlier.

FIGURE 8.1   *Independent Australia* Broke the Joyce Story Three Months before It Was Reported in the Mainstream Media.

The general excuse—exemplified in a column by *The Guardian*'s political editor, Katharine Murphy—was that it was a story about "sex" and therefore, a "private" matter and not of "public interest." Murphy is a serious supporter of Fourth Estate journalism—holding power to account—yet she wrote that she couldn't verify the rumors and that she did not want to be *The Guardian*'s "sex correspondent" (Murphy 2018). This was disingenuous and soon debunked; the story was never a moral argument about Barnaby Joyce's sex life, it was about the deputy prime minister's hypocrisy and possibly corrupt actions to hide the affair. Joyce had consistently lied about the affair to his colleagues and to journalists; he had cajoled other senior Ministers to provide his lover with a well-paid job that she actually never did; and he used his travel expenses budget—paid for by taxpayers—to hide the fact that he was travelling with his lover on holiday jaunts while claiming to be on official business (Johnson 2018).

Writing in the cultural journal *Meanjin*, journalism scholar Tim Dunlop noted that many reporters in the elite parliamentary press gallery—who knew of the Joyce affair—were reluctant to bring their audience into this confidential circle. He correctly observed that they "haven't really worked out what the new rules are" in relation to such sensitive, but explosive political stories that exist in "the hybrid space of new media," independently of any reporting by mainstream journalists (Dunlop 2018). Tellingly, Dunlop agrees that the excuses

Katharine Murphy @murpharoo · Feb 10

The travails of Barnaby Joyce: I didn't report it because I couldn't verify it. My column for the weekend theguardian.com/australia-news... #auspol

The Guardian Opinions

I didn't report Barnaby Joyce affair because I couldn't verify it | Ka...
Joyce was clearly preoccupied, but 2017 drove parliament to insanity – and I didn't want to be the Canberra sex correspondent
theguardian.com

FIGURE 8.2 Guardian Political Editor Tweets Her Excuse for Not Reporting the Joyce Affair.

given by Murphy and other mainstream reporters did not really stack up. Many press gallery journalists were in on the "open secret" but chose not to report it even when Barnaby Joyce was in the midst of an election campaign in November 2017. Had voters known of his affair and his hypocrisy at the time he may well not have won the by-election that kept him in parliament. The simple reason for the media's silence is that the News Establishment had closed ranks with the Australian political elite to protect a rogue politician whose exposure could damage more than just his own reputation. Tim Dunlop summed up the situation beautifully:

> What the Joyce story makes clear is that traditional media "rules" about such matters are farcical. They were as much about protecting the political class as having anything to do with journalism's higher purpose. They were forged in a different era and were often tainted with white-male presumptions from a time when white males ran everything. If there was ever any consistency in their application, there isn't now. And there is as much disagreement within the mainstream media about what the rules are as there is between journalists and their audiences.
>
> *(Dunlop 2018)*

The Barnaby Joyce case study highlights the hidden power of the News Establishment to keep important stories quiet, but also how vulnerable it is to exposure when the curtains are pulled aside. It is an object lesson in both the impact of social media revolution on mainstream reporting and the changing digital dynamics that underpin the ethical and legal rules of journalism. The techno-legal and techno-ethical paradox is at the heart of the press gallery's misreading of the public mood around exposing Barnaby Joyce. In this case the governing ethical or legal considerations appear to have fallen behind the new practices that the technology allows—non-mainstream social journalism sites and social media were already openly discussing the Joyce matter well before the official media caught up. Another good example of the legal and ethical dissonance created by how technologies are used is the issue of privacy and the media's use of Facebook or Instagram images without the permission of the copyright owner.

The Techno-legal and Techno-ethical Time-Gap

Digital technologies have become commonplace. Our lives, workplaces, homes and cars are full of technology. Most of it is benign, we just use it and hardly give it a second thought. At least we hardly think about it until something goes wrong, at which point everyone is like "Oh my gosh, we did not see that coming." Our complacency, once we are over the threshold of the "digital sublime," when we gaze at the new technology with a sense of wonder (Mosco 2005), leads us to be shocked when a problem arises with our use of technology. I call such moments instances of the "techno-legal" and "techno-ethical" "time-gap." I developed these terms over a decade ago to account for the times when technologies and our deployment of them outpace our existing legal, ethical and cultural norms. When this happens, the law and ethics have to scramble in order to find mechanisms, methods and rules for regulating the new behaviors enabled by the technology. In 2007, I estimated that the time-gap is about two years (Hirst and Harrison 2007). This seems to be about the length of time it takes for regulatory processes to catch up. It will be interesting to see how this plays out in relation to the social media companies and the issue of "fake news." However, I do not want to leave the impression that I think more government regulation is always—or necessarily—the answer we need. Nor do I think that leaving things to the "market" provides the best outcomes.

As we rush towards the "singularity"—that point in our history when machines can learn how to design even better artificial intelligence than their human creators—at a breakneck speed the techno-legal time-gap could open up even further. Google has already developed machine-made machine learning software that performs better than its own engineers (Lant 2017). There is also an ongoing debate about the role of government in the regulation matrix. Some commentators argue that it's best to leave things in the hands of the market (Falzone 2013); others, me included (Hirst 2011), would argue that market failure is one reason why we have an issue with the techno-legal and techno-ethical time-gap and that markets inherently disavow regulation in pursuit of profit. While scientists and ethicists continue to work on rules governing intelligent machines and robots, journalists are already struggling with the legal and ethical dilemmas surrounding useful, but largely unregulated, technologies such as drones, "intelligent" cameras that take pictures and "smart" speakers that are also listening to us, even when they are switched "off."

The problem for regulators is that many of the new applications and uses for technology arise precisely from the disruptive effects of the technology. The ride-sharing service, Uber, is a paradigm case. When the Uber app was released the service emerged almost organically in cities across the world. The first casualties of the disruption process were established taxi companies. Now the taxi industry worldwide has been overturned by Uber. Uber became popular before national and city authorities could formulate fair rules to govern its operation. As I write this, Uber has been banned (at least temporarily) in London because city officials could not come to an agreement with Uber about how its service would be regulated. As business writer Anna Isaac (2017) wrote about Uber's problems in London, "until we have law and policy makers equipped to deal with technology at the rate at which it is being created, [solutions] might prove hard to come by." It's not just Uber drivers who are caught in the grip of the digital dialectic; journalism too is subject to the same contradictions and this is easily demonstrated when we come to the question of privacy. Some people argue that there is no such thing as privacy anymore (Mawera 2016); I hope they're wrong.

Privacy in the Age of Total Surveillance

Privacy has always been a troubling issue for journalists and now, in the age of social media and almost total surveillance it is even more problematic. Privacy is now an issue squarely in the frame of the techno-legal and techno-ethical time-gap dilemma, but there is an added complexity. I call it the ethico-legal paradox and I developed it when writing about journalism ethics with my colleague, Roger Patching some 15 years ago. Like the time-gap, the ethico-legal paradox is a contradiction, this time between what the black letter law says and what is ethically acceptable in the practice of journalism (Patching and Hirst 2014). Some scholars and digital soothsayers argue that we have given up our right to privacy willingly in order to reap the benefits of modern communication technologies. Others would argue that, if we have surrendered our privacy, we have not done so willingly; or, at the least we have not freely given our informed consent. This is far too big an issue to cover fully in this chapter, but it is probably useful to sketch the debate in order that you might investigate it further in order to decide where you stand on the issue. Let me be clear and up front, I am firmly in the camp that argues that our privacy is being infringed. I certainly do not feel that I have given informed consent to corporations and governments to keep track of me in their data banks, or to follow my every move via CCTV equipped with facial recognition software.

Have you heard of the "Third Party Doctrine"? Did you know it relates to the Fourth Amendment of the US Constitution? I had no idea about it until I began researching for this chapter. Maybe I can be forgiven for not knowing, I haven't lived in the United States since 1970; but it is an idea central to the argument that our privacy—or at least, our digital privacy—is fast disappearing, if it hasn't vanished already. I've certainly been aware of moves by the Australian government to grab similar powers over data held by telecommunications companies and ISPs; it is not an issue limited only to the United States. The principles of the Third Party Doctrine are being used by many governments to legislate their right to access data about citizens held by either locally based or foreign companies.

According to some lawyers, the Third Party Doctrine is a work-around for US law enforcement agencies to circumvent the Fourth Amendment protections to privacy and unwarranted (literally) intrusion into an American's home or personal life. It matters so much in the digital age because everyone—and not just Americans—surrender control over vast amounts of personal data just in order to have a cellphone or an Internet account. The Third Party Doctrine argument is simple: by "voluntarily" surrendering this data to a "third party"— your cellphone provider or ISP—you forgo your rights to privacy of the information as enshrined in the Fourth Amendment. This means that police or other law enforcement agencies can then access this data directly from the companies that store it, without issuing a warrant against you specifically. According to privacy lawyer, Bradley Henry, this vast data mountain is only going to grow now that the "Internet of Things" is actually, well, a "thing."

All of your information will be stored in the cloud including your medical information, bank information and multimedia. Every piece of information about you will be technically be provided to a third party to run your everyday life. But, how many people have voluntarily told Google, Apple, Mercedes or other companies that they specifically consent to them tracking and storing their every move. Probably not many. But, you have done just that without really giving it much thought.

(Henry 2016)

The Third Party Doctrine originated in a Supreme Court decision in 1979 and has been upheld in the American legal system ever since, but it is the encroachment into areas of stored metadata held by phone and Internet companies that has led to current questioning of its suitability in the digital age (Villa Senor 2013). Application of the Third Party Doctrine by law enforcement agencies—backed by some American court rulings—is an example of the State taking advantage of a techno-legal and techno–ethical time-gap to extend its powers of search, seizure and arrest because of a perceived contradiction and loophole in the law as it stands and as it is being redefined. This analysis is borne out by comments made by University of Southern California law professor, Orin Kerr in a debate with Greg Nojeim, senior counsel at the Center for Democracy and Technology. Kerr's contribution makes the techno-legal time-gap element of the debate crystal clear. For example, Professor Kerr claims to be "looking for a way to apply the Fourth Amendment to new technologies in a sensible and balanced way."

My argument rests on the need to maintain the technological neutrality of Fourth Amendment protections. The use of third parties is akin to new technology, and that technology threatens to alter the balance of power struck by the Fourth Amendment. The third-party doctrine offers a way to maintain the balance of police power: It ensures that the same basic level of constitutional protection applies regardless of technology.

(Kerr 2012)

In response, Greg Nojeim (2012) points out that our "consent" to allowing technology companies access to private data about us is not "voluntary" in the accepted definition of that word. We effectively have no choice about surrendering our data if we want to access the service that is being provided. In other words, our "consent" is a mandatory condition of us having the service made available to us. Nojeim also highlights the time-gap in relation to Third Party Doctrine: "Technology permits us to communicate privately with people who are distant and numerous, but third parties often convey those communications. When they do, Fourth Amendment protections are lost."

Journalists can get caught up in third party issues when they take material from private Facebook accounts without permission, but this is an activity that is heavily promoted to reporters and editors by Facebook and some other companies who deal in what has become known as "social search" or "social discovery" functions (Usher 2017). In this instance too links with law enforcement have driven many of the new applications for searching social media feeds (Weiskopf 2010). The *Techopedia* entry on social discovery is understated in its critical comments: "Some consider many social discovery programs to be intrusive, and as consumers work to guard personal information, privacy issues could be a serious obstacle to more proliferation of social discovery resources." Certainly, this should be a concern, as social discovery is a tool that law enforcement can use to monitor social media "chatter" from protestors as much as from alleged terrorists. The journalistic version of social discovery— CrowdTangle—is not as malicious, and can be useful to search out key stories or social media influencers. CrowdTangle is owned by Facebook, but it services a number of other social media platforms. My advice about using a service like this is to seek permission from people if you intend to re-use their content, don't just take it without asking.

Yonder Be Dragons: On Journalism and the Scientific Method

From the earliest days of printed news sheets in the seventeenth century journalists have had problems of credibility and verification. It was even harder for readers of the early sensationalist news sheets. How, for example could peasants tied to the feudal farm by complex social obligations travel to Sussex in order to confirm for themselves that serpents and dragons inhabited the forests of the county? It nigh on impossible, but, according to one news sheet circulating in 1614, serpents and dragons were living in St Leonard's forest only 30 miles from London.

Dragons were popular creatures in mythology and right through the seventeenth century. So much so that even supposedly serious works on biology and animals contained whole chapters on dragons, describing them in some detail. Between 1607 and 1608 a clergyman and amateur naturalist, Edward Topsell, wrote *The History of Four-footed Beasts and Serpents*, which was not published until 1658, 30 years after his death (Public Domain Review undated).

The "evidence" Topsell compiled was based on accounts of other people and many were from antiquity, but that didn't stop him from providing his readers with eye-popping descriptions, such as this passage:

> There be some dragons which have wings and no feet, some again have both feet and wings, and some neither feet nor wings, but are only distinguished from the common sort of Serpents by the comb growing upon their heads, and the beard under their cheeks ... there are dragons of sundry colours ... according to the verses of Nieander ... a Dragon is of a black colour, the belly somewhat green, and very beautiful to behold,

True and Wonderfull.

A Difcourfe relating a ftrange and mon-
ftrous Serpent (or Dragon) lately difcouered, and yet
being, to the great annoyance and diuers flaughters
both of Men and Cattell, by his ftrong
and violent poyfon,

In Suffex *two miles from* Horfam, *in a woode
called* S. Leonards Forreft, *and thirtie miles from*
London, *this prefent month of* Auguft. 1614.
With the true Generation of Serpents.

FIGURE 8.3   A Seventeenth-Century News Sheet Reporting the Sighting of a Dragon 30 miles from London.

having a treble row of teeth in their mouths upon every jaw, and with most bright and clear-seeing eyes, which caused the Poets to say in their writings that these dragons are the watchful keepers of treasures.

(Topsell 1658: 705–706)

THE
HISTORY
OF
Four-footed Beasts
AND
SERPENTS:

Describing at Large
Their True and Lively *Figure*, their several *Names, Conditions,*
Kinds, Virtues (both Natural and Medicinal) *Countries* of their *Breed,*
their *Love* and *Hatred* to Mankind, and the wonderful work of
God in their Creation, Preservation, and Destruction.

Interwoven with curious variety of Historical Narrations out of Scriptures,
Fathers, Philosophers, Physicians, and Poets: Illustrated with divers Hieroglyphicks
and Emblems, &c. both pleasant and profitable for Students in all Faculties and Professions.

Collected out of the Writings of *CONRADUS GESNER*
and other Authors,
By *EDWARD TOPSEL.*

Whereunto is now Added,
The Theater of Insects; or, Lesser living Creatures:
As *Bees, Flies, Caterpillars, Spiders, Worms,* &c. A most
Elaborate Work: By *T. MUFFET, Dr. of Physick.*

The whole Revised, Corrected, and Inlarged with the Addition of Two
useful *Physical Tables,* by *J. R.* M. D.

LONDON:
Printed by *E. Cotes,* for *G. Sawbridge* at the Bible on *Ludgate-hill, T. Williams* at
the Bible in *Little-Britain,* and *T. Johnson,* at the Key in *Pauls Church yard.* M DC LVIII.

FIGURE 8.4 The Cover of *The History of Four-footed Beasts and Serpents by Edward*
Topsell (or "Topsel," as He Spells it Here).

Dragons and serpents were also associated with the Devil and so a level of devout blind faith, combined with a general public fear of the unknown, was a strong motivator for seventeenth century audiences to take such accounts as the literal truth; even though they had no independent means of verifying what they were reading in tomes like Topsell's obviously exaggerated account of many mythical beasts, including serpents and dragons.

Despite apparent public gullibility and an appetite for the fantastical, by the seventeenth century science was beginning to overtake mysticism and usurp the authority of the church. The amateur accounts of clergymen like Topsell were being replaced with more empirical work that we would today perhaps describe as "scientific." For example, it was in 1609, only a year after Mr Topsell had finished writing his imaginative bestiary, that Galileo heard news of the invention of a new device that he would soon develop into a telescope, thus changing forever humanity's relationship to the stars (Stephens 2007: xiv). In a few short years, Galileo turned Copernican astronomy on its head by using mathematical theorems to prove that the earth revolved around the sun. However, the famous Renaissance inventor and scientist still had to be careful. After publication of his theories in book-form as *Dialogue Concerning the Two Chief World Systems* in 1632, Galileo was tried and convicted of heresy for teaching his ideas, which flatly contradicted accepted Church orthodoxy of the day (Grayling 2007: 96–97). He spent the last decade of his life under house arrest, so it is perhaps not surprising that the general populous could believe in the existence of dragons.

It is not coincidental that during this period that the newly invented media of mass printed news sheets—what we can consider the first modern newspapers— also expanded their reach and influence. The oldest surviving newspaper in English comes from 1621, the first reported correction to an erroneous published report appeared in 1626; ironically Galileo's trial for heresy was reported in a French newspaper in 1634 and a decade later, in 1644, John Milton's polemic *Areopagitica*, arguing for freedom of the press, was published. The first daily newspaper was published in Leipzig, Germany in 1650 and the first weekly scientific journal, *Journal des Savants* was published in France in 1665. In 1679, a law licensing (censoring) the printing of newspapers in England lapsed leading to a slew of new titles; the first American newspaper appeared in Boston in 1690 and by 1702 the first daily newspaper in English, the *Daily Courant*, was in circulation (Stephens 2007: xiv–xvi).

The scientific revolution accompanying the Renaissance had other, far-reaching, consequences for feudal society. A series of social and political upheavals took place in tandem, leading to a breakdown of religious authority and more calls for freedom of assembly, freedom of worship, freedom of speech and freedom of the press. There is another link between the scientific revolution and journalism and it lies directly in the link between scientific methods of enquiry and verification and the methods of modern journalism. In the seventeenth century, as the Enlightenment dawned across Europe, science and the press advanced together in a dance of mutual constitution. Historians and philosophers have written extensively on the birth of scientific enquiry and its impact on all aspects of life so that today we take for granted the "impersonal and objective endeavor" using "measurement and quantification" that defines the method of science. As the philosopher A. C. Grayling points out, the purpose of such methodologies is to "exclude bias, and to proceed in publicly scrutinisable ways, with results being open to the challenge of verification and replication" (Grayling 2007: 85). This is also how we expect modern journalism to proceed. Like science, the purpose of journalism is to "advance truth about the world" (ibid.). If science is concerned with the "structure and properties of matter [and] the universe constituted by it" (ibid.: 86), then journalism is concerned with the *structure and properties* of social *matter* and the social *universe* which humans build from such materials, including science, technology, the arts, commerce and politics. The scientific method relies on "scepticism and a preparedness to revise one's views when they are shown to be mistaken" (ibid.: 87). This must also be the attitude of both the purveyors of news and its consumers.

However, it also pays to remember, that, just as science can be corrupted by ideology, so too can endeavors to hold on to journalistic skepticism and to jettison bias. Just as Galileo and his scientific contemporaries fell foul of the Catholic Church and the Pope in Rome as "bulwarks to an established order that did not wish to change" (ibid.: 97), journalists and editors today can also be subject to both deliberate and capricious censorship and efforts aimed at undermining both the journalistic method and democratic norms, as represented by the Fourth Estate, via the use of sophisticated means of information control (censorship via omission), and overt propaganda (censorship by commission). Verification of data and sources, both inside and outside the newsroom, takes on a new urgency in the age of "fake news" and the use of artificial intelligence (bots) to seed social media campaigns of disinformation. In this regard, we can still learn from the masters; the seventeenth-century pioneers of the scientific method, such as René Descartes and Francis Bacon.

Descartes's *Discourse on Method* prioritized a deductive method which proceeds from what is already known and observable and progressing slowly towards conclusions that would "thereby be guaranteed to be true" (Grayling 2007: 99). Journalists should proceed using similar methods and so too should news consumers and those seeking to work in social journalism as reporters or curators. As we discuss in the next chapter, the scientific approach to verification in journalism today is a good starting point for sorting fact from fiction and truth from supposition. Journalism has been called the "discipline of verification" (Kovach and Rosenstiel 2014: 97) and it is built on three founding principles: *transparency, humility* and *originality*. Transparency is about respect for the audience and letting them decide if your reporting is accurate and honest;

humility is about keeping an open mind and not allowing hubris to cloud your judgement; originality means exactly that—don't copy other people's work and always have your own ideas. A commitment to verification is the glue that binds these elements together: "Journalists say the times they most often got something wrong was when they took something from somebody or someplace else and failed to check it themselves" (American Press Institute 2017).

Failing to check is not an option. Today the tools and means are available to verify or debunk information. It is only when we allow our rush to publish to overcome our better judgment that avoidable mistakes are made. Don't be fooled into thinking there be dragons beyond yonder hills.

Verification: A New Ethical "Gold Standard"?

I believe it is important to think of verification as a new ethical standard that must apply to social journalism. To some extent the ethic of verification is as old as modern journalism, perhaps about 150 years old. Almost everywhere you look in the world professional codes of ethics for journalists contain some prescriptive advice about fact-checking.

In the United States, the Society of Professional Journalists makes verification explicit under the heading "Seek truth and report it" and recommends that reporters "should…verify information before releasing it" (SPJ 2014). The Australian code, administered by the journalists' union, the MEAA, encompasses verification in its very first clause: "Report and interpret honestly, striving for accuracy, fairness and disclosure of all essential facts. Do not suppress relevant available facts, or give distorting emphasis. Do your utmost to give a fair opportunity for reply" (MEAA 1999).

Striving for accuracy has been in the "cannons of journalism" for well over 100 years. In 1922, the American Society of Newspaper Editors posited that "Good faith with the reader is the foundation of good journalism" in Article IV of its code of ethics (ASNE 1975), and it is still true today. If audiences cannot rely on the accuracy of information presented to them as news, how can a civilized society—that is reliant on media to circulate a common understanding of events—function? The simple fact is that it can't; if we cannot rely on the accuracy of news and news-like information, the result is information chaos. My observation is actually that the world is close to being in the condition of information chaos today.

There has been a fundamental break in the compact between the providers of news and news-like information and audiences. Our expectation is that the information that we take in and then share outwards again is true; but in the "post-truth" world, we can no longer take that for granted. The need for strong ethical governance in the production and distribution of news and news-like content has been superseded by the need for speed and our insatiable appetite for sharing, likes and kudos in the online world. In our hunger and our greed, we are overdosing on an unhealthy diet of fake news. Some of it is accidental—the result of too much speed, or "undercooking"—and some is deliberate. It is like adding too much salt, sugar or fat into our diet deliberately so that we consume more, are less satisfied and slowly kill ourselves, while thinking that we are not satisfied. We cannot exist on a diet of high calorie, low nutritional value food, and we run the risk of brain atrophy if our information diet consists of poorly prepared meals made with cheap, low-nutrition ingredients. If we are to save our civilization from a deeper descent into information chaos, there is an urgent need to reinstate truth, accuracy and verification at the heart of the journalistic project. This applies equally inside and outside the newsroom; it applies to us as active audiences, and it applies particularly in the largely unregulated sphere of social journalism.

The "Trump Dossier": Journalists Get another Lesson in Verification

As we discussed in chapters three and four, the 2016 US Presidential election was mired in controversies centered on the notion of so-called "fake news." Both sides of American politics accused their opponents of either falling for fake news accounts of events that never happened, or of deliberately being involved in the creation of fake news stories, in order to influence voters. This was all brought into sharp focus less than 10 days before President-elect Trump's January 20, 2017 inauguration when *BuzzFeed* took the fateful decision to publish unredacted pages from a "dossier" about Mr Trump's alleged ties to Russian president Vladimir Putin, collated by a former British spy, Christopher Steele, on behalf of the President-elect's political opponents.

The "Steele dossier" was a series of dated memos outlining unsubstantiated reports that Russian spies had been compiling their own dossier of compromising material about Mr Trump ("kompromat" in Russian slang), including details of financial dealings between the Trump and Russian banks, and alleged trysts with prostitutes in hotels in Moscow and St Petersburg. At the time, none of the material in the dossier was verified and, indeed as many journalists who knew of its existence believed, it was almost impossible to ever verify much of the information. Details that reporters were able to check—such as an alleged meeting in Prague between a Trump aide and Russian spies—turned out to be wrong and the dossier also contained other errors and misinformation.

Once *BuzzFeed* had published the Steele dossier, other news organizations felt it was then OK to reveal that their journalists also had copies, but had chosen to hold back on publishing details from it because of concerns about the authenticity of its central and explosive claims about Mr Trump. *BuzzFeed* published the document after the CNN network had aired a story about summaries of its content being given to Trump and President Obama by US security officials. This was important, according to *BuzzFeed*, because once the existence of the dossier became public knowledge, then the public had a right to decide for itself whether they were prepared to believe the detail it contained.

Ben Smith
@BuzzFeedBen

Here's the note I sent to @buzzfeednews staff this evening

 Ben Smith <ben@buzzfeed.com>   7:25 PM (6 minutes ago)
to news, Purple, Headsup

As you have probably seen, this evening we published a secret dossier making explosive and unverified allegations about Donald Trump and Russia. I wanted to briefly explain to you how we made the decision to publish it.

We published the dossier, which Ken Bensinger obtained through his characteristically ferocious reporting, so that, as we wrote, "Americans can make up their own minds about allegations about the president-elect that have circulated at the highest levels of the US government."

Our presumption is to be transparent in our journalism and to share what we have with our readers. We have always erred on the side of publishing. In this case, the document was in wide circulation at the highest levels of American government and media. It seems to lie behind a set of vague allegations from the Senate Majority Leader to the director of the FBI and a report that intelligence agencies have delivered to the president and president-elect.

As we noted in our story, there is serious reason to doubt the allegations. We have been chasing specific claims in this document for weeks, and will continue to.

Publishing this document was not an easy or simple call, and people of good will may disagree with our choice. But publishing this dossier reflects how we see the job of reporters in 2017.

Ben

FIGURE 8.5 Ben Smith's Note to Buzzfeed Staff Justifying Publication of the Steele Dossier.

The editor-in-chief of *BuzzFeedNews* defended publication of the dossier in a Twitter post to his staff, saying it was done to provide "transparency" and so that people could "make up their own minds" about the assertions it contained.

A few days after Donald Trump's inauguration on 20 January 2017, *Buzz-Feed*'s Ben Smith wrote a justification, which was published in the *New York Times*. Smith pointed out that CNN's earlier report had alluded to the dossier without disclosing its contents. Smith described this as a "halfway" position that left the public in the dark and that was "contrary to our compact with our audience', adding that *BuzzFeed*'s decision to publish "rapidly advanced" the story. Smith argued that the era of "fake news" demands "new rules that adhere to the core values of honesty and respect for our audience" and that the mainstream media's "instinct" not to report details of the dossier is "precisely the wrong one for journalism in 2017" (Smith 2017).

At the time, the decision was roundly condemned by media ethicists, myself included (Hirst 2017), and other news organizations. The basic argument we were all making was that *BuzzFeed*'s justification was shallow and hollow: How could anyone be expected to know the truth of the assertions in the Steele dossier without some extensive means of verification? If teams of reporters at some of the world's major news organizations (CNN, the *New York Times, Washington Post*, and *Wall Street Journal*) were unable to satisfy themselves that the dossier's serious and salacious allegations against Mr Trump were true, then it would surely be impossible and impractical for ordinary citizens and media consumers to even attempt such a thing. Nobody, it seems, was prepared to support *BuzzFeed* on this issue. As *The Intercept*'s Glenn Greenwald pointed out, publication of an unconfirmed rumor could harm any future defense of the news media against the president's accusations of "fake news."

The Steele dossier did not recede entirely from the news agenda. Interest was re-ignited when a former US intelligence officer claimed that it was still part of an active and ongoing investigation. In early 2018, people associated with the dossier also gave evidence before the US Congress on the veracity of the document, which appeared to add weight to the central allegations of "collusion" between the Trump campaign and Russian figures. Former CIA operative John Sipher (2017) concluded that much of the dossier seemed to have credibility, in light of what had transpired since it was first leaked. What is interesting for our purposes is the primary method Sipher used to re-examine the dossier and reach his conclusions: "In the intelligence world, we always begin with source validation, focusing on what intelligence professionals call 'the chain of acquisition'" (Sipher 2017).

This is exactly what journalists must do, it is the beginning of the verification process. In light of what has transpired since *BuzzFeed* published the dossier's contents, perhaps we were wrong to condemn them at the time. In fact, I am willing to concede I may have been wrong about this. Given my position on the Barnaby Joyce revelations, if I am to be consistent then condemning *BuzzFeed* seems the wrong decision. Isn't the decision to publish the dossier's contents actually undermining the Fourth Estate's contract of secrecy to protect Establishment figures too?

When is a Fact an "Alternative Fact"?

The difficult and extraordinary times that Ben Smith alluded to in his *NYT* op-ed defending publication of the dossier are a reference to events surrounding President Trump's inauguration a few days before the op-ed was published. It was clear from pictorial and other evidence that the crowds attending President Trump's inaugural celebrations in Washington DC were significantly down on the numbers who were in the capital for President Obama's inaugurations in

January 2005 and 2009. It became clear very quickly, from several sources that this had greatly upset Donald Trump, who wanted to believe that his inauguration had the best and biggest crowds.

On the day following the inauguration, the President sent the White House press officer, Sean Spicer into the briefing room to tell journalists that they had got the story wrong. He delivered an angry speech and refused to take questions, leaving the assembled reporters hanging. However, Spicer's claims, on behalf of the President, did not satisfy the news media and a number of journalists and outlets continued to report the smaller crowds story, but also added their surprise at the way the White House responded (Korte 2017). The controversy refused to die down, on the following day (Sunday, January 22), another White House official, Kellyanne Conway fronted the media to, once more, defend the President's false assertion that the crowds had been "huge" at his inauguration and also to defend press secretary Spicer, whose comments the previous day had sparked even further outrage.

Conway appeared on NBC's *Meet the Press* where she told host, Chuck Todd, that Sean Spicer had presented "alternative facts" at his media conference: "You're saying it's a falsehood. And they're giving—Sean Spicer, our press secretary—gave alternative facts," Conway said. Todd responded: "Alternative facts aren't facts, they are falsehoods" (Bradner 2017).

A few days later, the president's close advisor, Steve Bannon—who was subsequently sacked by Trump—effectively told the media to "keep its mouth shut," if they couldn't find anything nice to say about Donald Trump (Grynbaum 2017).

FIGURE 8.6 White House Spokeswoman Kellyanne Conway Telling CNN about "Alternative Facts."

The bottom line is that the material world can only function, and democracies can only function, if there is an agreed set of facts. If the news media allows facts to be reinterpreted out of existence and then remains silent when it knows lies are being told—even if they come from the President's office, or his own lips—then it will be derelict in its duty to citizens. This is what *Buzzfeed*'s Ben Smith meant by the changed conditions facing journalists covering the Presidency of Donald Trump. The ability, indeed the necessity, to fact-check and to verify the truth of facts presented by officials in positions of great power is an essential role of the Fourth Estate, and indeed, the Fifth Estate beyond the newsroom walls.

When You Should Go Live and When You Shouldn't

The features and capabilities of social media platforms and applications change with remarkable speed. This is another example of the techno-legal and techno-ethical time-gap. Capabilities are rolled out and put to uses that perhaps no one intended and then there is a backlash and both the law and ethics have to play catch-up. This has proven to be the case with various forms of live "broadcasting" that are now possible: Facebook Live; Periscope on Twitter and similar capabilities on other platforms or apps.

One simple case study is enough to illustrate this story, but it is disturbing, so I'll keep it brief. If you want to know more, you can follow it up for yourself.

In April 2017 two murders were live-streamed on Facebook. The first was in the US city of Cleveland; the second took place in Thailand.

In the Cleveland incident a man posted a video saying he planned to commit a murder; in a second post he uploaded a video himself killing an elderly man. Later the killer, Steve Stephens, posted a confession video to Facebook then took his own life after a police pursuit in the city.

Just over a week later, a Thai man in the city of Phuket posted a video of him killing his young child. He then killed himself.

The video of the Cleveland incident was reportedly taken down within half an hour of it being posted, but in the Thai case, the video was said to have been online for a period of up to 24 hours.

Facebook responded to these horrific incidents by saying it would do more to police its live video feeds and be more proactive in disabling accounts that shared distressing content.

While not directly related to news reporting, these incidents highlight the need for caution when going live with potentially confronting or distressing content. News organizations quite rightly have rules about what they will broadcast, generally choosing to not show graphic violence or bodies of those who died tragically. In general, you should always be cognizant of community values in regard to issues of taste and decency. Take greater care at events that might potentially result in violence where graphic scenes might occur in front of your camera. Such events might include political protests where there are likely to be clashes between rival factions; hostage or other situations in which the police might use deadly force; the aftermath of terrorist incidents where there is likely loss of life or injury to large numbers of people; incidents involving potential suicide attempts; riots or actions of civil unrest where people are likely to be injured or killed.

If you're somewhere and witness something that makes you feel sick to the stomach, it is pretty certain that your audience will react in the same manner. Ask yourself: "Would I be comfortable watching this as a viewer?" Don't feel that you have to give into pressure from producers who are not at the scene to capture all the gory details; you are on the frontline, not them.

Similar rules and tests need to be applied in other situations where disturbing events are happening. Social media gives journalists unprecedented access to events as they are unfolding, but is it ethical to call the cellphone of a person caught up in a volatile situation where their life and the lives of others are in danger? During a February 2018 shooting incident at a Florida high school, students trapped in a building with an active shooter tweeted and Facebooked calls for help. Journalists were able to trace the phone numbers of some of these students and began calling them for interviews while the shooter was still active. While this might seem like an exciting challenge for a journalist, and something that is made possible by technology, it is perhaps very irresponsible, verging on life-threatening for those involved. If a golden rule is "First do no harm," then we might have to reconsider our approach to covering such incidents.

An Ethical Code for Social Journalists

All journalists should adhere to some form of ethical code and conscientious decision-making when it comes to any and all issues that arise in the process of active reporting. You should start with any national code applicable in your locale and then use your research skills to find alternative models that you can compare it to. Various models for ethical practice in citizen journalism have been developed over the last 20 years or so, all of them have similar intent and structure. The Knight Community News Network J-Lab has enumerated five principles that seem to provide basic guidance. If we acknowledge the fluidity created by the techno-legal and techno-ethical time-gap and constantly review what we do, these five principles will help to keep you grounded.

Accuracy

Accuracy must be the foundation of any reporting assignment; without it there can be no trust and no commitment to the truth at all costs. Fact-checking and verification (see the next chapter) are at the heart of accuracy.

Thoroughness

Do your research, chase down the elusive source, make sure you have not just enough information, but enough of the right information. Ask more questions and be prepared to crowd source your story. If you need help, ask for it.

Fairness

Fairness means respecting different points of view; but it does not necessarily mean equal space or equal time. It does mean offering a right of reply if you're going to be critical of someone, and put their comments in the story; don't wait to be criticized after it's published. Fairness does not mean you have to abandon your politics or your point of view, but it does mean you don't hide your biases. As we discussed above, when talking about trust, the audience will respect you more if you are open about your views.

Transparency

Transparency, disclosure and trust go together like peanut butter and jelly on good sourdough. Linking to your sources and disclosing your own views will assist your audience to decide if you can be trusted and believed. In other words fairness and transparency, plus accuracy and thoroughness equals credibility.

Independence

Independence is simple; it means not being a hostage to your funding sources or to political sources. It means being prepared to follow the story, even if it leads to uncomfortable conclusions. Independence is the cornerstone of freedom of the media.

I would add one more simple but important, point to this list of ethical principles: the role of social journalists should not be to reproduce the unequal power structures of the News Establishment. To do so just perpetuates the problems we've discussed so far in this book. Instead, social journalism must operate within a different paradigm, one that puts people first ahead of institutional privilege and profit.

References

American Press Institute. 2017. "Journalism as a Discipline of Verification." Accessed September 7, 2017. www.americanpressinstitute.org/journalism-essentials/verifica tion-accuracy/journalism-discipline-verification/.

ASNE. 1975. "ASNE Statement of Principles." Accessed November 29, 2016. www.ndsu. edu/pubweb/~rcollins/431ethics/codes.htm.

Bradner, Eric. 2017. "Conway: Trump White House Offered 'Alternative Facts' on Crowd Size." CNN. January 23. Accessed January 27, 2017. http://edition.cnn.com/2017/01/22/politics/kellyanne-conway-alternative-facts/.

Dore, Christopher. 2018. "A Bundle of Joyce." *The Daily Telegraph*. February 6. Accessed March 12, 2018. www.dailytelegraph.com.au/news/bundle-of-joyce-birth-of-a-national/news-story/3b48d9a378307a728e007d857ce5ee42.

Dunlop, Tim. 2018. "Barnaby Joyce and the Hybrid Space of New Media." *Meanjin Quarterly*. Accessed March 12, 2018. https://meanjin.com.au/blog/barnaby-joyce-and-the-hybrid-space-of-new-media/.

Falzone, Anthony. 2013. "Regulation and Technology." *Harvard Journal of Law and Public Policy* 36: 105–107.

FindLaw. Undated. "First Amendment, US Constitution." Accessed February 23, 2017. http://constitution.findlaw.com/amendment1.html#sthash.ZNFJ3EKJ.dpuf.

Grayling, A. C. 2007. *Toward the Light of Liberty: The Struggles for Freedom and Rights that Made the Modern World*. New York: Walker Publishing.

Grynbaum, Michael M. 2017. "Trump Strategist Stephen Bannon Says Media Should 'Keep Its Mouth Shut.'" *The New York Times* January 26. Accessed January 27, 2017. www.nytimes.com/2017/01/26/business/media/stephen-bannon-trump-news-media.html.

Hayes, Arthur, Jill Singer, and Jerry Ceppos. 2007. "Shifting Roles, Enduring Values: The Credible Journalist in a Digital Age." *Journal of Mass Media Ethics* 22(4): 262–279. doi:10.1080/08900520701583545.

Henry, Bradley. 2016. "Third-Party Doctrine: What is it and Why Does it Matter?" HenryLaw Insights. June 21. Accessed March 13, 2018. www.henrylawny.com/third-party-doctrine-matter/.

Hirst, Martin. 2011. *News 2.0: Can Journalism Survive the Internet?* Crows Nest, NSW: Allen and Unwin.

Hirst, Martin. 2017. "Media Sauce: Who to Believe of Trump's #goldenshowers and Honeytraps." *Independent Australia*. January 13. Accessed January 13, 2017. https://independentaustralia.net/business/business-display/media-sauce-who-to-believe-of-trumps-goldenshowers-and-honeytraps,9920.

Hirst, Martin, and John Harrison. 2007. *Communication and New Media: From Broadcast to Narrowcast*. Melbourne: Oxford University Press.

Holton, Avery E., Mark Coddington, and Homero Gil de Zuniga. 2013. "Whose News? Whose Values? Citizen Journalism and Journalistic Values through the Lens of Content Creators and Consumers." *Journalism Practice* 7(6): 720–737. doi:10.1080/17512786.2013.766062.

Isaac, Anna. 2017. "Regulation Must Keep Pace with Technology, Says World Economic Forum." *The Telegraph*. September 26. Accessed October 17, 2017. www.telegraph.co.uk/business/2017/09/26/regulation-must-keep-pace-technology-says-world-economic-forum/.

Johnson, Stephen. 2018. "Barnaby Joyce Went on a 2,000km Summer Road Trip with His Girlfriend Vikki Campion—after She Had Left His Office and Helped Him Run Up a $43,000 Travel Bill." *The Daily Mail*. February 23. Accessed March 12, 2018. www.dailymail.co.uk/news/article-5422461/Barnaby-Joyces-2-000km-road-trip-Vikki-Campion.html.

Jones, Ross. 2017. "Exclusive! Barnarby Joyce: Peeling Back the Rumours." *Independent Australia*. November 19. Accessed March 12, 2018. https://independentaustralia.net/politics/politics-display/exclusive-barnaby-joyce-peeling-back-the-rumours,10942.

Kaufhold, Kelly, Sebastian Valenzuela and Homero Gil de Zú. 2010. "Citizen Journalism and Democracy: How User-Generated News Use Relates to Political Knowledge and Democracy." *Journalism & Mass Communication Quarterly* 87(3–4): 510–529.

Kerr, Orin. 2012. "The Case for the Third Party Doctrine." *Patriots Debate: Contemporary Issues in National Security Law*. American Bar Association. Accessed March 13, 2018. www.americanbar.org/groups/public_services/law_national_security/patriot_de bates2/the_book_online/ch4/ch4_ess2.html.

Korte, Gregory. 2017. "Spicer Slams Reporters, but Evidence Doesn't Match Up." *USA Today*. January 21. Accessed January 27, 2017. www.usatoday.com/story/news/poli tics/2017/01/21/second-day-white-house-press-secretary-strikes-combative-tone/ 96894392/.

Kovach, Bill, and Tom Rosenstiel. 2014. *The Elements of Journalism: What Newspeople Should Know and the Public Should Expect*. New York: Three Rivers Press.

Lant, Karla. 2017. "Google's Machine Learning Software Has Learned to Replicate Itself." *Futurism*. October 17. Accessed October 17, 2017. https://futurism.com/googles-machine-learning-software-has-learned-to-replicate-itself/.

Mawera, Ray. 2016. "No Such Thing as Privacy Anymore, So Better Watch Yourself." *The Financial Gazette*. September 20. Accessed June 23, 2017. www.financialgazette.co. zw/no-such-thing-as-privacy-anymore-so-better-watch-yourself/.

MEAA. 1999. MEAA Journalist Code of Ethics. Media, Entertainment and Arts Alliance. Sydney. Accessed November 29, 2016. www.meaa.org/meaa-media/code-of-ethics/.

Mosco, Vincent. 2005. *The Digital Sublime: Myth, Power and Cyberspace*. Cambridge, MA: MIT Press.

Murphy, Katharine. 2018. "I Didn't Report Barnaby Joyce Affair Because I Couldn't Verify it." *The Guardian*. 10 February. Accessed March 12, 2018. www.theguardian. com/australia-news/2018/feb/10/barnaby-joyce-i-didnt-report-the-story-because-i-couldnt-verify-it-katharine-murphy?CMP=Share_AndroidApp_Tweet.

Nojeim, Greg. 2012. "Reply to Orin Kerr." *Patriots Debate: Contemporary Issues in National Security Law*. American Bar Association. Accessed March 13, 2018. www.americanbar. org/groups/public_services/law_national_security/patriot_debates2/the_book_on line/ch4/ch4_res1.html.

Ozturk, Serkan. 2017. "Shocking! Australia's Deputy PM Barnaby Joyce Alleged to Have 'Stalked' and 'Molested' Teen Girl and Young Woman." *True Crimes News Weekly*. October 25. Accessed March 12, 2018. https://truecrimenewsweekly.com/shocking-australias-deputy-pm-barnaby-joyce-alleged-to-have-stalked-molested-teen-girl-and-young-woman/.

Park, Chang Sup. 2017. "Citizen News Podcasts and Engaging Journalism: The Formation of a Counter-Public Sphere in South Korea." *Pacific Journalism Review* 23(1): 245–262. Accessed November 2, 2017.

Patching, Roger, and Martin Hirst. 2014. *Journalism Ethics: Arguments and Cases for the Twenty-First Century*. London: Routledge.

Public Domain Review. Undated. "Topsell's History of Four-Footed Beasts and Serpents (1658)." *The Public Domain Review*. Accessed September 5, 2017. https://publicdomain review.org/collections/topsells-history-of-four-footed-beasts-and-serpents-1658/.

Sipher, John. 2017. "A Second Look at the Steele Dossier—Knowing What We Know Now." *Just Security*. September 6. Accessed September 7, 2017. www.justsecurity.org/ 44697/steele-dossier-knowing/.

Smith, Ben. 2017. "Why BuzzFeed News Published the Dossier." *The New York Times.* January 23. Accessed January 27, 2017. www.nytimes.com/2017/01/23/opinion/why-buzzfeed-news-published-the-dossier.html?_r=0.

SPJ. 2014. "SPJ Code of Ethics." Society of Professional Journalists. September 6. Accessed November 29, 2016. www.spj.org/ethicscode.asp.

Stephens, Mitchell. 2007. *A History of News.* New York: Oxford University Press.

Topsell, Edward. 1658. *The History of Four-Footed Beasts and Serpents.* London: G. Sawbridge. Accessed September 5, 2017. https://publicdomainreview.org/collections/topsells-history-of-four-footed-beasts-and-serpents-1658/.

Usher, Nikki. 2017. "The Appropriation/Amplification Model of Citizen Journalism." *Journalism Practice* 11(2–3): 247–265. Accessed December 11, 2017. doi:10.1080/17512786.1223552.

Villa Senor, John. 2013. "What You Need to Know about the Third-Party Doctrine." *The Atlantic.* December 12. Accessed March 13, 2018. www.theatlantic.com/technology/archive/2013/12/what-you-need-to-know-about-the-third-party-doctrine/282721/.

Weiskopf, Nadne R. 2010. *Social Media and E-Discovery.* White Paper. New York: LexisNexis.

9
RESEARCH AND VERIFICATION

Fact-Checking is Everyone's Business

In the world of social journalism, verification and fact-checking are everyone's responsibility. This chapter introduces the practicalities of research and verification, or "fact-checking," as a necessary element of social journalism practice. Journalism has been accurately described as the art or science of verification. In their iconic textbook, *The Elements of Journalism*, Bill Kovach and Tom Rosenstiel (2014) define verification in journalism as "a scientific-like approach to getting the facts and also the right facts." In this light, this chapter builds on our short diversion into journalism and the scientific method in Chapter 8. Verification is important for conventional reporting, for the simple act of social media sharing, and for independent social journalists who are reliant on their reputation. In a post-truth environment where "alternative facts" are being accepted as valid, verifying information is crucial for producers and consumers of news-like information. I believe the whole point of increasing our media literacy is to give all of us a better handle on the process of verification and how to tell "truth" from "alternative facts."

As a consumer of news and news-like information you have a responsibility to check the veracity of an item before you share it. If you work in a newsroom where the pace can often shift between hectic and frantic, you have a responsibility to ensure that everything is fact-checked before you hit "publish." Journalists cannot rely on the old attitude of "publish and be damned." If you get things wrong consistently you will be damned, and ridiculed and shunned and, soon enough, out of business. For social journalists, working outside the newsroom, the responsibility is even greater; it is *your reputation* that gets damaged, it is *you* who might face a catastrophic law suit and it is *you* who will bear the brunt of angry readers.

It's not easy though. Not only is verification important today, it is also difficult. Information is moving at lightning speeds and the pressure to publish, republish or share quickly is also greater today than it was even a decade ago. The sheer volume of news and news-like information, combined with our unfulfilled appetite for the new, the exciting, the different and the clever, makes verification both more necessary and harder than before the explosion of social media platforms made sharing so much easier.

Most journalists today can be found on Twitter alongside the verified, official accounts of their newspaper, network or website; the more tech-savvy will also be active on other platforms or apps, such as Instagram, Tumblr, LinkedIn, WhatsApp or even Snapchat. If they are a video reporter you might even find they have a dedicated YouTube channel. If they are working outside of a newsroom structure, reporters are also likely to be publishers on a range of blogging platforms or using a CMS and dedicated domain name linked to their brand (masthead). Increasingly, social media is more than a publishing or publicity outlet for journalists, there are many ways that Twitter or Facebook can be used by social reporters and by media literate people wanting to do their own verification exercises.

At a simple level, social media platforms are a source for stories, but the leads can also be misleading. Social media has proven useful for generating stories about what we might call the "low hanging fruit" material. For example, the instant fix of celebrity chatter which relies on a steady stream of juicy and sometimes salacious gossip. Publications like the *Daily Mail, TMZ, Entertainment Tonight* and others could not survive if the Kardashian sisters didn't post selfies to Instagram at least three times a day. But if that is all social media is good for, we might as well give up. Not everyone is interested in celebrity "hook ups and break ups" and not everyone wants to be a digital paparazzo relying on second-hand images to sex up an otherwise dull life. Now, given that President Trump appears to be issuing policy—and sacking his advisers—via Twitter it is more vital than ever that journalists master the platform, it could end up being the only way to discern what American foreign policy might be on any given day. For the "monitorial citizen" or concerned activist, being able to confirm or dismiss social media news blasts is an important skill.

Verification—Fact-Checking a President

Within the first week of President Trump taking office, media fact-checkers were already working overtime. The President's propensity to make pro-nouncements via Twitter meant that his tweets became one of the few means of holding him to account for exaggerated, or simply untrue, statements. In order to fact-check the content of Presidential tweets, the *Washington Post* "Fix" investigative team built a browser extension for Chrome and Firefox that inserts the context when a Twitter user clicks into a tweet from the President's personal or official Twitter accounts (Machkovech 2016).

FIGURE 9.1 The *WaPo* Fact-Check Account to Verify or Dispute the President's Tweets.

Twitter users can follow an unofficial *Washington Post* account with the handle RealDonaldContext (@realDonaldCntxt) to see the "context" added to Trump's tweets and "corrections" when necessary. Between December 29, 2016, and January 27, 2017, the Fix team had disputed over 50 Presidential tweets, finding many of them "inaccurate," "false," or "lacking context." A year later (January 24, 2018) the number stood at 211 fact-checked Trump tweets that were found to be misleading. This initiative shows how social media can be a tool for pushing back, as well as for pushing propaganda. As well as allowing us to "fact-check" the President, social media has also become an important platform for generating serious leads about serious stories and as a way of harnessing the energy of the crowd to help in serious investigative journalism.

One of the big stories to emerge from the 2016 US Presidential election campaign was about Donald Trump's big claims that he had always been generous in his charity giving. Then, during the campaign he promised to donate millions more to veterans' charities. His campaign spokesperson often told reporters that Trump had given away "tens of millions" of dollars before he stood for president (Fahrenthold 2016a). These claims may have gone unremarked and unchallenged, leaving the impression that Donald Trump is a philanthropist. They may have, but one reporter stuck on this story and used his social media accounts to break it wide open.

Washington Post reporter, David Fahrenthold began 2016 with a respectable, but modest 4,700 followers on Twitter, by September it had grown to 60,000; when I checked on 3 January 2017, Fahrenthold had 240,000 followers, a whopping 5000 percent increase on where he started. A year later that number had doubled again to more than 500,000. That is proof enough that being able to use social media appropriately as a journalist is reward enough; but the reason why this *WaPo* journalist's numbers are through the roof, is because he used Twitter as an effective research tool on a story that captured the imagination of a nation. The initial jump in Fahernthold's numbers was because he asked his followers to help him on a story and his plea went viral.

> I spent a day searching for Trump's money on Twitter, asking vets' organizations if they'd gotten any of it. I used Trump's Twitter handle, @realdonaldtrump, because I wanted Trump to see me searching.
>   Trump saw.
>
> *(Fahrenthold 2016b)*

The *WaPo* reporter became interested in Trump's claim to philanthropy at a January 2016 campaign event in Iowa where the candidate presented a check to a local veterans' organization. Although the check had the name of Trump's foundation on it, the money had been raised from other donors. Trump claimed to have raised nearly US$6 million in January when confronted at a media conference in May 2016 after the issue had become a controversy for his campaign. Trump did not like being questioned on his charitable giving, at the May 31 media conference he made his often-repeated claim that many journalists are "not good people" (Fahrenthold 2016c).

As Fahrenthold dug deeper he found that there was a discrepancy—Trump's boasting told one story, the actual paper records showed another. Fahrenthold turned to Twitter to continue his research by contacting charities that had been publicly associated with Trump's name. His search uncovered over 400 charities that Trump had publicly associated himself with, implying that he had donated money or other gifts to them (Fahrenthold and Rindler 2016). The reporter was only able to confirm one donation from Trump himself.

However, Fahrenthold's persistence finally began to pay back his effort and patience. After more than 300 calls and Twitter inquiries, one charity confirmed that it had received $20,000 of Trump's personal fortune as a donation, but there was a significant catch: Trump had used it to buy a portrait of himself (Fahrenthold 2016b).

This opened up a new line of inquiry for the reporter, he quickly realized that this purchase could put Trump on the wrong side of a charities' tax law which prevented a donor from benefiting from a gift, a form of "self-dealing." However, Fahrenthold was unable to locate the portrait, so once again, he turned to his Twitter followers for help. While the initial search uncovered some interesting leads and enlisted the help of several celebrities, it failed to uncover the painting he was looking for; but it did uncover a second Trump portrait, which was also bought by the millionaire with money from his charitable foundation—another potential case of "self-dealing" by the (then) Presidential candidate.

That was not the end of the matter, Fahrenthold eventually uncovered several "self-dealing" breaches associated with the Trump Foundation, all of which involved the charity spending its money on behalf of, or for the benefit of Trump

David Fahrenthold
@Fahrenthold

I've now called 338 charities, looking for proof
@realDonaldTrump gives his own $ to charity.
Haven't found much.

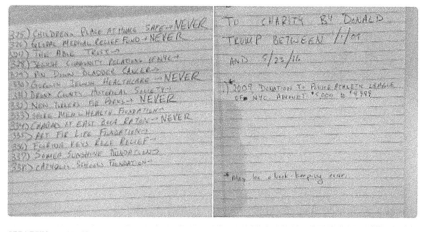

RETWEETS   LIKES
1,091   1,321

FIGURE 9.2   Of over 300 Charities Associated with the Trump Name, Only One
Could Confirm Receiving Money from the POTUS.

and his business empire. This included over $250,000 to settle personal legal
disputes not associated with the charity (Fahrenthold 2016d). By the end of 2016
the (then) President-elect had announced plans to shutter his foundation amid all
the allegations of "self-dealing" and tax discrepancies it was facing, mainly as a result
of Fahrenthold's persistence in chasing the story of the missing painting.

   While we cannot attribute all of David Fahrenthold's success to his use of
Twitter, this significant story is an excellent example of how social media can assist
even the most difficult of investigative assignments. The *WaPo* reporter may never
have been able to find the second portrait, which was hanging in one of Trump's
many golf clubs, but his followers were able to be "on-the-scene," acting as
advanced scouts and a second pair of eyes. In this case the story became significant
enough that Trump was forced to announce the closure of his charity amid further
scrutiny that would not have been possible without Fahrenthold's clever use of
social media. One final rider on this episode that I believe is, at least tangentially,
related. Soon after publishing his major investigations of Trump's apparent misuse
of charity funds, Fahrenthold was sent a videotape anonymously. This became his

> **David Fahrenthold** ◈
> @Fahrenthold   ✿ [Following]
>
> Wow. @Enrique_Acevedo found the $10K
> portrait of @realdonaldtrump -- bought with
> charity $ -- hanging on wall at Trump's resort
> LAST NIGHT.
>
>
>
> **Enrique Acevedo** @Enrique_Acevedo
> Hey @Fahrenthold just checked and the portrait is still hanging at
> the Champions Lounge. How much did you say it cost the Trump
> Foundation?
>
> RETWEETS   LIKES
> 2,337   2,500
>
> 11:47 PM - 21 Sep 2016
>
> ↩ 147   ⇄ 2.3K   ♥ 2.5K   •••

FIGURE 9.3   David Fahrenthold Retweets Enrique Acevedo, Who Found the Second
Trump Portrait.

next explosive expose of the (then) President-elect. The tape was the now infamous
"grab' em by the p***y" hot-mic moment in which Trump openly talked about
groping women and attempting to browbeat (he called it "seducing") them into a
sexual encounter with him (Fahrenthold 2016e). While we can't all expect the
success of a David Fahrenthold-style scoop every time, we can learn two things—
the need to be persistent and the importance of cultivating your social media
followers to help out on big investigations.

Triangulation: The Gold Standard of Verification

Triangulation is a methodology used in social science research and it is highly
applicable to journalism too. It is basically a method of verification that relies on
multiple sources. As the word "triangulation" implies, there should be at least
three independent sources to increase the reliability and validity of your results.
If you have a variety of sources who are independent of each other, and they're
all telling you the same thing, then there is a good chance that what you are
hearing is accurate. Triangulation also works if you are hearing slightly different
things from your sources; but it means you are going to have to work harder to
verify what the story is actually about. Triangulation may confirm your original
angle, but it can also push you to change your own viewpoint on the story.

Triangulation also works with non-human sources as well. For example, if a human source provides information you might verify it by referring to documents, your own observations and that of other journalists. You can begin to draw valid conclusions when your triangulation efforts uncover meaningful patterns and relationships within the information you've gathered. Of course, the amount of work you need to do to perform the necessary triangulations will vary depending on the complexity of the story you are trying to understand or to tell. A lengthy investigation will require a greater confidence level in your verification activities and should take much longer than a simple news story. However, both types are equally important in their own context. Importantly, the use of triangulation is one way of overcoming any perception of bias in sources you don't know, in your own sources and in your reporting.

Basic tips for journalistic triangulation

- Expand your range of human sources by cultivating people from diverse backgrounds and areas of expertise; don't always go for the same type of source.
- Use a variety of human and non-human sources. For example, familiarize yourself with academic databases so that you can check information historically using peer-reviewed (and verified) expert research.
- Encourage your human sources to share documents with you. This is an effective way of becoming your own expert in a particular field—but you actually have to read the reports and other material they give you. After reading them you should be in a better position to ask informed questions and to not be fooled by clever-sounding phrases that are meaningless or misleading.
- Don't rely on only talking to your sources once. Going back and asking similar questions a second time is likely to elicit new and meaningful information that was missed in the first pass.
- Use the right tools for the job. Know where to find information and how to understand it. Read widely and keep your current affairs knowledge up-to-date.
- Don't be afraid of Freedom of Information requests. Government agencies are sometimes reluctant to give up information, but they are often required by law to be at least a little bit transparent. Familiarize yourself with freedom of information legislation in your jurisdiction(s). Sometimes you can turn up a gem that will help to verify something you suspect is a strong story.
- If you have colleagues you can trust, then bring them in on complex stories because two heads are better than one. Use this form of triangulation to make sure you haven't missed the point of the story, or a better angle than the one you are pursuing. This is also useful to overcome any inherent bias you might harbor about a particular subject.

• Keep a log of your stories and contacts, particularly if you are developing a beat or specialty. It is likely that you may have come across information on a previous story that can help with verification and triangulation. Contacts who may be in the same field, but not relevant to the story you're working on may in fact be useful if you give them a call and ask. There's a good chance they will know something that might help.

Verification: The "How To"

Verification is at the heart of journalism as a method of analysis and reporting and it should be at the center of every newsroom. As examples in this chapter and others show, this is not always the case and for reasons outlined earlier—namely speed and cost—verification is sometimes ignored completely, and often only done to very poor standards. However, using both the deductive and inductive methods of scientific enquiry, it is not hard to learn some useful verification techniques that can be applied both inside and outside of the formal newsroom setting.

Verification is an ongoing and proactive process that can go through many stages and it should be part of every step in the process of finding, reporting, writing and editing of news and current affairs reports, whether in print, in a broadcast medium or online. Thirty years ago, high-end, credible magazines, like *Time, Newsweek, Vanity Fair*, the *New Yorker* and newspapers like the *New York Times* or *Washington Post* would subject every piece of copy to rigorous fact-checking. They would never take a chance and leave it to the reporter; fact-checking was done by staff editors and they would contact every quoted source to check the accuracy of the quotes and would comb through all the facts to make sure they could be verified.

To some extent, this could be seen as both legal and ethical protection for the publication, the editors, the writers and the publisher, each of whom could be liable for any defamatory statement or gross errors that might creep into the copy. Unfortunately, as the costs of news production have increased and profit margins shrunk, the armies of fact-checkers employed by major newspapers and magazines have also diminished. Online-only publications and many electronic newsrooms now rely on the reporter, and maybe one or two editors, to fact-check material that comes into the news flow more quickly and with shorter deadlines. There are many famous cases in which incomplete, or non-existent fact-checking has caused major embarrassments and/or legal problems for important news outlets. There is no place here to name-check all of them, but two examples will suffice.

Jayson Blair was a young rising star reporter at the *New York Times* who was plagiarizing other journalists' work and making up stories for the paper. When he was eventually unmasked in 2003 it caused enormous heartburn for the *NYT* and a soul-searching review that led to the publication of an extensive apology running to several thousands of words. The *Times* described the Blair scandal as one of the "low points" in the paper's history (New York Times 2003). Blair's deception—he wrote more than 30 suspect stories for the *Times*—was not picked up by the paper's normal editorial checks and balances. The *Times* editors failed to recognize the truth in the oft-repeated, but also oft-ignored, adage "If it's too good to be true, it probably isn't." Blair's fake stories and copied interviews were only picked up when an editor at another paper became suspicious (Mnookin 2008).

More recently, a brash and sensationalist website specializing in exclusive breaking stories about the Donald Trump—Russia investigation was caught out spectacularly in August 2017 by a fake source feeding its journalists totally false information. In a classic case of allowing false "facts" to stand because of an agenda-driven approach to reporting, two reporters for the website *Patribotics* were hoaxed by a woman claiming to have exclusive information about a prosecution of President Trump by the New York Attorney-General's office. The allegations against Trump are pretty outrageous and running them without verification was very irresponsible. It seems even more reckless when you consider that the two reporters are experienced political operatives. One of them, Louise Mensch, is a former conservative member of the British parliament and her co-conspirator, Claude Taylor, previously worked in the Clinton White House. Their fake stories were exposed by *The Guardian* after it was contacted by the woman who fed the false information to the reporters.

> The source falsely claimed to be an official named "Caitlin" in the office of Eric Schneiderman, New York's attorney general. She shared details of her hoax on the condition of anonymity to avoid retaliation from followers of Taylor and Mensch. The Guardian verified her true identity and confirmed that she is not named Caitlin and does not work for Schneiderman.
>
> *(Swaine 2017)*

Claude Taylor offered an apology (of sorts), saying that he should have been more careful, Louise Mensch appeared to be unrepentant, even though she promoted the false stories in a tweet. She told *The Guardian* that, even though she is an editor at *Patribotics*, she did not feel responsible for checking Taylor's bogus sources. This is an outrageous and irresponsible attitude for a senior journalist and media entrepreneur to adopt, but it is indicative of the cowboy approach that has taken root on the Internet, particularly among the more partisan publishers.

These two examples, both from the last two decades, reinforce the need for verification to be taken seriously and both also highlight that simple checks are sometimes all that is required, along with a healthy skepticism and a willingness to do some basic research. There is really no excuse for any major news operation to let hoaxes or bogus stories through the gate; it's also not that hard for non-news players to undertake their own verification and fact-checking using some ready-to-hand social media tools.

There are two important steps in the verification process: the first is establishing the identity and credibility of your source, the second is checking that what the tell you, or the information they give you is accurate and true. It was failure at the first step that led to Claude Taylor and Louise Mensch falling for a hoax. Failure at the second hurdle brought down the *NYT* editors in the Jayson Blair case.

Social media can help in confirming the identity and credibility of a source, but you have to remember, it's not completely fool proof. The proliferation of platforms and the tendency for people to project different personas on various platforms adds to the complexity for journalists trying to find or verify reliable sources. This, plus the issues of speed and network density can make source identification difficult (Backholm et al. 2017). Web and app developers are now working with, and alongside, established news organizations to build and deploy a variety of verification tools (Stearns and Kille 2015). Organizations like the BBC also provide tips and training for reporters and interested amateurs (Dell 2015). In the following section, some of these new and developing tools are reviewed.

For non-journalists, the best method for source verification using social media is triangulation—information from more than one place that tends to confirm the identity of the person. For example, Twitter by itself is not a sufficient proof of identity, even with the "blue tick" of official Twitter approval. That system is hard to beat, but it can be done. However, if you can also find a Facebook profile, a LinkedIn profile and some other social media personas that match the identifying details you already have from Twitter, then you have greater reliability in the materials that might prove identity. Each of these individual profiles might be easy to hack, but it is harder to give them an authentic look and feel without some effort.

When it comes to verifying information that is delivered into the newsroom via the ubiquitous social media feeds that are a requirement for journalists today the complexities are amplified. Alongside speed and network density (the range of possible sources and platforms) the sheer volume of information, particularly through very active Twitter feeds, makes verification doubly difficult (Stearns and Kille 2015).

Source Verification

There is really no substitute in journalism—whether professional or amateur—for talking to people close to the action. Human intelligence is at the center of the news process, everything from eyewitness accounts of breaking news and disasters as they unfold to the "deep throat" style source that blows the whistle on a major public, financial or political scandal. Developing and maintaining your own list of contacts is essential. There is an old saying in journalism, "Once a contact, always a contact," and reporters build up their contact list over a lifetime. However, there are times when you will not have a known source close to the action and then you will need to find people and work out quickly if you can trust them. You need to know, are they who they say they are, are they where they say they are and have they really got the information they say they have. What you are trying to avoid here is, firstly, being duped by a source who has ulterior motives, or is just hungry for a fleeting moment of fame and second, falling victim to a "rumor cascade" that can occur when false or misleading information is shared by many people over a short time span via social media channels (Friggeri et al. 2014).

It is possible to have a verified account on some social media platforms. On some you can request verification if you provide the right kind of identifying documents; on other channels verification is only offered to public figures and celebrities, and journalists don't often count in these categories (Arshad 2016). If you are dealing with verified accounts then it is probably safe to assume that the person is who they say they are, but that does not mean that the content or information they are posting is accurate. However, if you are not dealing with verified accounts, you should take steps to check on identity as fake names, anonymous accounts and users pretending to be a verified user are common across all social media channels and platforms. For example, it has been estimated that there are upwards of 20 million fake accounts on Twitter, many of them the troublesome automated or "bot" accounts we've heard so much about already. Some of them are purely commercial and make money for their creators by generating advertising income (MacMillan 2013); some are created for malicious political and propaganda reasons. The commercial accounts are easy enough to spot because they have few followers, but seem to tweet almost none stop, amassing hundreds of thousands of tweets in a short space of time. To give you some gauge of this, I've been on Twitter since March 2008 and I tweet most days; even so I've only posted just over 21,000 tweets in 10 years. However, other fake accounts might not be so easy to spot, just on the numbers alone. Here are some things to look for when assessing the veracity of Twitter users who are not verified by the platform:

The first thing to look at is the Twitter URL that is the unique location of their account; it should be something close to their @handle and it looks like this: https://twitter.com/ethicalmartini. An account that is generated by an algorithm, for use by a "bot," will normally not be a word or phrase that has any meaning; and researchers have found that bot accounts tend to be fairly recent additions to Twitter and to have longer, random @handles (arixvblog 2014).

Checking Profile Images

If the Twitter URL checks out, the second clue might be found in their profile image. If they have not bothered to upload an image then it's either laziness or they don't want to be identified. The use of a stock image or the face of a celebrity are also red flags when it comes to authentic accounts. If you're not sure about someone's image you can easily check it using a reverse image search, such as Google Image. By clicking on the profile image you can copy the URL (image location) and paste it into the Google search box. This should then alert if you if the image is being used anywhere else. It is prudent to offer some words of caution here. When using a reverse image-search tool to verify someone's identity, beware of false positives. A simple search of, for example, a persons LinkedIn profile image, may show the same photograph is attached to several profiles. This does not mean that the image is being used as a profile pic on all of them; it might just mean that the LinkedIn users are mutually linked. However, you still need to be cautious because as the example below shows, the wrong person can still be identified.

For fun, I change my Twitter avatar regularly; often it will be something I've drawn or painted when it's not a photo of me. While the image is original in Figure 9.4 (a pastel drawing of my dog, Orwell), the reverse image search suggests that "Doc Martin" (my current Twitter alias) is someone else (Figure 9.5). It's not until you scroll down further that a link to my Twitter handle @ethicalmartini is displayed (Figure 9.6).

The other issues that my personal example shows is that while @ethicalmartini is my account on Twitter, my real name is not used, I use the alias/nickname "Doc Martin" on Twitter. The problem is, so do many other people, including other academics, and fans of the TV show "Doc Martin" starring Martin Clunes. If you were trying to find a particular Doc Martin and didn't know which one, it could still be confusing. So, what if you search for "Martin Hirst on Twitter"? Well, assuming some geo-matching you might get a result like this one if you're searching from Australia.

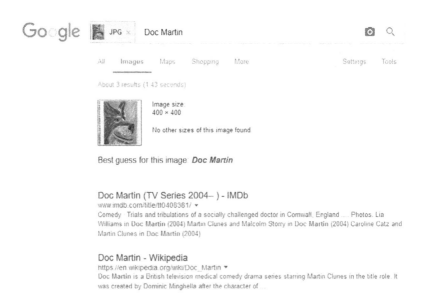

FIGURE 9.4 My Avatar, but Not Me.

Pages that include matching images

Doc Martin Ph.D (@ethicalmartini) | Twitter
https://twitter.com/ethicalmartini?lang=en ▾
400 × 400 - The latest Tweets from Doc Martin Ph.D (@ethicalmartini). Surf, ski, sobriety and
socialism. Political Editor for @independentaus. Journalist, writer, educator ...

FIGURE 9.5   Eventually the Image is Linked to My Account.

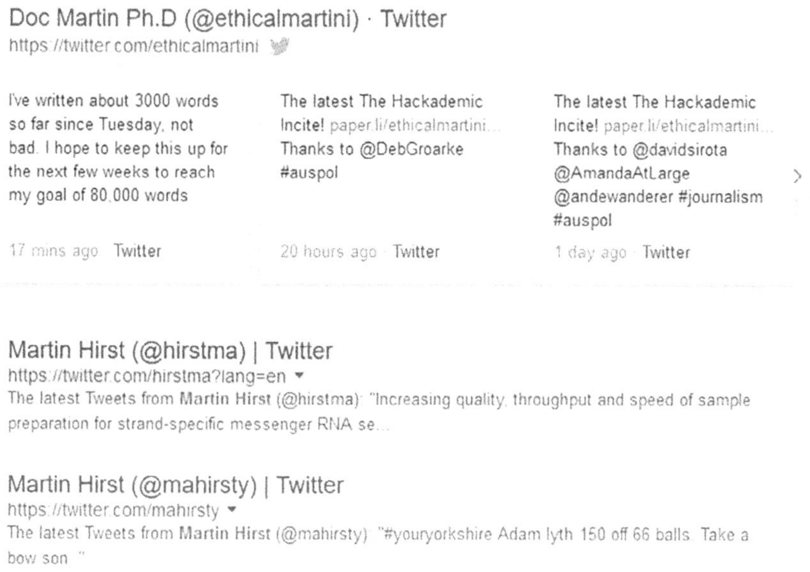

Doc Martin Ph.D (@ethicalmartini) · Twitter
https://twitter.com/ethicalmartini 🐦

I've written about 3000 words so far since Tuesday, not bad. I hope to keep this up for the next few weeks to reach my goal of 80,000 words	The latest The Hackademic Incite! paper.li/ethicalmartini... Thanks to @DebGroarke #auspol	The latest The Hackademic Incite! paper.li/ethicalmartini... Thanks to @davidsirota @AmandaAtLarge @andewanderer #journalism #auspol
17 mins ago Twitter	20 hours ago · Twitter	1 day ago · Twitter

Martin Hirst (@hirstma) | Twitter
https://twitter.com/hirstma?lang=en ▾
The latest Tweets from Martin Hirst (@hirstma): "Increasing quality, throughput and speed of sample
preparation for strand-specific messenger RNA se...

Martin Hirst (@mahirsty) | Twitter
https://twitter.com/mahirsty ▾
The latest Tweets from Martin Hirst (@mahirsty): "#youryorkshire Adam lyth 150 off 66 balls. Take a
bow son "

FIGURE 9.6   The Martin Hirsts on Twitter.

Having performed this search you might now be able to find the one you're looking for by taking a look at the profile pages for content that relates to your reasons for searching in the first place. You should also check the biography that a user supplies: does it sound legitimate and contain links to another website that might help prove an identity. Many fake, troll and bot accounts don't have convincing biographies, or at least the biography is so generic that it does not supply any clues as to the account holder's actual identity.

When it comes to fake accounts controlled by humans (as opposed to automated "bot" accounts), there are several things to look out for, but spotting "sock puppet" or "catfish" accounts is not always easy, unless they are simple trolls who spew hate and abuse. What ties these types of accounts together is that they are there to boost a particular signal, though high-volume and repetitive tweeting; or to silence other voices through abuse and bullying (Fitzgerald and Shaffer 2017). The best advice for dealing with troll accounts is to simply hit the "block" button and forget them. But sock puppet accounts can be more sophisticated and some of them can even be useful for journalists—as long as you don't just blindly trust them. There are real people behind sock puppet accounts and they have diverse reasons for hiding their true identity. We saw this type of account boom after the inauguration of Donald Trump; accounts claiming to be White House insiders and employees of federal agencies sprang up seemingly from nowhere. Many of them have since been deactivated, or tweet less frequently, but their initial burst of tweeting did become a serious news story in the early days of Trump's presidency (Gilmour 2017). As one outlet reported, nobody knew if the accounts were real, but they managed to "sound plausible" and the news media could not afford to ignore them (Rowles 2017). However, as we learned from the US presidential election, some bot accounts can be tied to organizations that seek to use them for nefarious purposes to confuse or spread propaganda.

Is it a Bot or Not?

It is hard sometimes to tell an automated, "bot" Twitter account from a real one. There are some tell-tale clues, but a careful check is required to really prove something one way or another. Here's a few things to look out for, but be diligent, these "tells" are not fool-proof.

A Bot or Not Checklist

- The ratio of followers to followed accounts can be telling. Bots may follow thousands of accounts but have few followers themselves. If an account has only very few followers but follows 5000 people it may be a bot that has reached Twitter's in-built restrictions (Twitter 2017). Bot accounts will sometimes follow you and, if you don't follow them back, unfollow you within 24 hours. Bots also do not usually interact with other users, they don't respond to @username messages or direct messages in any meaningful way.
- Bot accounts will often send large numbers of tweets over a single day, usually at regular intervals. What might seem like a tweet sent to you personally, using your @username, could actually be being sent to thousands of others with the exact same wording and/or links. Sometimes a bot account will retweet the same tweet several times over a period of days (Makara 2013). Sometimes you can tell an automated tweet if it has a metadata line that says something like "from an API." An API is an automated routine embedded in code that is prompted into performing a specific action in response to certain code stimuli, almost like a simple call and response. A usual application for an API is to allow computers to interact by sharing small amounts of code that allows them to interact. One such interaction can be for a bot to send a tweet in response to someone else.

- A fake account, particularly bots rather than trolls, will sometimes tweet seemingly random strings of words, or half-formed sentences that don't make sense. At other times, this might just be a sign of tweeting while under the influence (never a good idea). A bot might also only tweet so-called "inspirational" quotes and nothing else, but these can also be sleeper accounts to be activated with more malicious content when needed (Fitzgerald and Shaffer 2017).
- Bot accounts are becoming more sophisticated and can now use natural language that is algorithm generated. They might also follow so-called "influencers" and attempt to get them to follow back or retweet their material (arixvblog 2014). "Retweet" and "reply" bots are specifically designed to promote material from "catalyst accounts," these are often political/propaganda campaigns, but they can also be used for marketing and other forms of influence-peddling They can respond to particular hashtags or other prompts programmed by their human handlers (Fitzgerald and Shaffer 2017).
- Bot accounts can be identified by around the clock tweeting, or if their pattern of tweets matches a particular time zone. This was identified during the 2016 US elections with many researchers pointing out that bot accounts were tweeting heavily from Russian ISPs during critical periods of the campaign (Resnick 2016).

A research team, from Indiana University, released a service called the "Botometer" in August 2017 and you can use it to check an account to see if is human or machine. When using the Botometer, you enter a @username into the web interface and it accesses your Twitter account, it then provides you with an analysis of the @username; you can also check the @username's friends and followers. The algorithm is still fairly new and will no doubt get better with time and as more people use it. When I checked my own account, I got a score of about 25 percent (Figure 9.7).

According to the Botometer FAQ page I should not be too worried about a score of 25 percent, the algorithm creators reckon that this is close enough to zero that I'm probably not a bot. The developers advise that many accounts fall into an

FIGURE 9.7 It Turns Out Only a Quarter of Me is a Bot.

uncertain category, scoring between 40 and 60 percent of "botness." I tested this service a little further by asking it to check my followers. Botmeter was only able to index a fraction of my followers, and at first it appeared to be reasonably accurate. Within minutes the algorithm had identified the account @wayneporteous1 as a potential bot with a score of 86 percent "botness" (Figure 9.8).

I went to @wayneporteous1 timeline and it did indeed resemble a typical commercial bot: every tweet was a commercial link to advertising content, and the same tweets appeared in the timeline over several days (Figure 9.9). One great feature of Botometer is that it provides a way to block suspect followers from within the app itself; perfect!

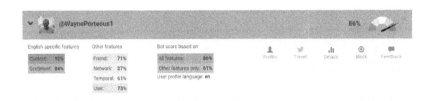

FIGURE 9.8 Botometer Tells Me this is a Bot.

FIGURE 9.9 A Typical Tweet from What Could Be a Typical Bot Account.

However, I was a little bit concerned that I might have fingered a real person as a bot, because, when I went to Wayne's profile page I found he had over 24,000 followers and was following over 24,000 himself. His biography also seemed legitimate; it said he was a "web marketing assistant" who loved "fast cars," "wine" and "hiking." It also located him in Taupo, New Zealand. Perhaps a little "triangulation" was necessary. I felt I needed to be certain before accusing Wayne of being a "bot," so I sent him a tweet (Figure 9.10). A week later I had not received a reply, so I then contacted Wayne via his LinkedIn profile (Figure 9.11). This time I did get a response, Wayne got in touch via LinkedIn and asked me what I wanted to know about him (Figure 9.12).

My persistence and triangulation exercise paid off. Wayne turns out to be a real person and the profile of his Twitter use is explained by his job—he uses Twitter to promote his clients and to market their products or services to his followers and beyond. His Linked In avatar also showed up on other profiles associated with people in Taupo, New Zealand. I was also able to verify that Wayne is a wine-buff; he has worked in a wine business with several of his Linked In friends.

This little exercise shows that you can't always rely on an algorithm to work things out—the Botometer was wrong about Wayne—a bit of human ingenuity is still necessary. Sometimes it just takes common sense to identify fake Twitter accounts from real ones; by checking a person's followers and who they follow, for example. A real person is likely to follow other real people, perhaps even someone you know and their followers to followed ratio is likely to be in some sort of balance—unless they are a celebrity who hardly follows anyone but who has millions of followers. You can also check a person's tweets—do they sound realistic and do they use appropriate language? You can check your own followers—to weed out potential fakes—using several online tools, and some of them allow you to check other Twitter handles as well. But, remember, these tools are not 100 percent reliable.

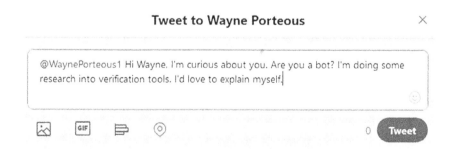

Tweet to Wayne Porteous   ✕

@WaynePorteous1 Hi Wayne. I'm curious about you. Are you a bot? I'm doing some research into verification tools. I'd love to explain myself.

🖼 GIF 🗒 ◎   0 **Tweet**

FIGURE 9.10   My Tweet to @wayneporteous1. A Week Later I Was Still Waiting for a Reply.

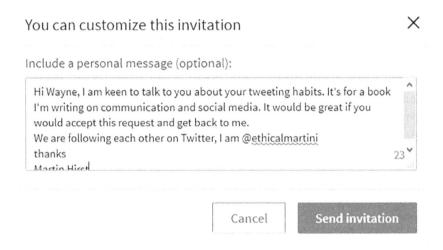

FIGURE 9.11 My LinkedIn Request to Wayne Porteous.

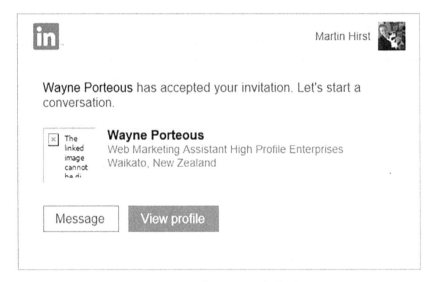

FIGURE 9.12 Wayne Porteous Responds to My LinkedIn Request.

Twitter Account Reliability Checklist

- Followers/followed ratio: a fake account, or a troll, is likely to have very few followers, but may follow a lot of people. This is a rough guide only.
- Sometimes fake accounts are cloned from other fake accounts. So if biographical information is the same and @usernames seem similar the chance is they're bot accounts.

- Check the content and tone of the tweets. Is the language plausible? Is the content more than just advertising and retweets?
- Repetition and a high percentage of promotional tweets is a good indication of bot activity. Fake accounts will generally not engage with other users by responding to mentions.
- Don't get fooled by a Twitter @username that is similar to someone who is a public figure or celebrity. For example, check @realdonaldtrump and see how many fake and parody accounts mimic the president's handle.
- If a Twitter handle is just a bunch of random letters and/or numbers then it is likely to be a fake or bot account. Most people take time to work out something meaningful for their @username; machines don't.
- How long has the account been online? Older accounts are easier to verify because there is historical information in the timeline. A new account that has thousands of tweets in a short space of time is likely to be a bot (or a troll).
- Activity is also a reasonable measure. If an account has many followers, but has had a long period of inactivity it could very well be a "bot."
- If the profile pic is of a young woman in a bikini, tread carefully. Most people will not use a revealing image, unless they are an adult star, or sex worker. A poorly written or missing biography is also a clue.
- Check a person's digital footprint. Most people have more than one social media account, which means they leave a "digital footprint" that you should be able to find and use to cross-check their authenticity.

With a little practice, you should become proficient at spotting fake accounts on Twitter. You can also use similar techniques on your other social media channels. If you follow these simple rules and take active measures to verify a person's identity, you can have more faith in them as a news source. However, it is still important to verify the information a source gives you, whether it is facts, tips on difficult to get information, photographs or video.

Document Verification

Journalists rely on documents as believable and accurate sources as a basis of much of their reporting. This is fine if the documents are publicly available reports from reputable institutions and individuals; but if the documents are leaked, sensitive and private then the possibility of forgery must be taken into account. Even seasoned reporters can be fooled when they allow their enthusiasm for a story to overtake their natural caution and fact-checking.

In 2004 veteran CBS reporter, Dan Rather, went to air with explosive claims that then-President George W Bush had faked his National Guard service and falsified his military records in order to gain favor with conservative voters. Unfortunately for Rather, the documents he had been given were themselves faked in what appears to have been a sting—a trap that Rather and the network

realdonaldtrump

realdonaldtrump heart attack

realdonaldtrump global warming

realdonaldtrump prayers

 Donald J. Trump ✔ @realDonaldTr...

 realDonaldTrump @RealTrumpClo...

 realDonaldTrump News 🔒 @realT...

 RealDonaldTrump4Pres @RealDo...

 @RealDonaldTrump @OrdersFro...

 realDonaldTrumpWig @DaRealDo...

Search all people for **realdonaldtrump**

FIGURE 9.13   Parody Accounts Will Often Use @Username Similar to the Person They Want to Mimic.

blindly fell into in their rush to put a story to air. Rather and three CBS executives were fired for the mistake and for insisting for almost two weeks after the forgeries were exposed that their story was correct. An internal CBS report found that Rather and his producers had "failed to follow basic journalistic principles" (Murphy 2005), which is not a difficult conclusion to draw, given the facts. Rather's "scoop" on Dubya's military service was brought undone because several typography experts were able to point out that the typeface used in the forged documents did not exist at the time the documents were allegedly written in the 1960s and 1970s. Instead, the experts concluded, the forgeries were most likely made using the Microsoft Word program—the one I'm using now to type the manuscript for this book (Newcomer 2005).

Perhaps the fakes in the Rather example were easy to spot because of the historic discrepancy between the fonts available in the 1970s and those available some 40 years later. Certainly, the differences between mechanical typewriters, which are prone to errors in letter spacing and clarity, and the almost perfect text produced in modern word-processing applications would be obvious to an expert. But they were good enough to fool CBS caught up in the excitement of what appeared to be a good story. Modern documents might be easier to forge in the sense that if you match the typeface, fakes would be harder to spot. But modern electronic documents also have a digital footprint, and this metadata can make tracing a document's history a bit easier.

It was the metadata that unraveled a more recent story about hoax documents relating to the Donald Trump "collusion" inquiry in July 2017. MSNBC news host, Rachel Maddow, claimed that she had been sent forged documents that showed someone was trying to undermine the investigation into Trump's alleged ties to Russia by tripping up the media with faked classified documents. It is a bit confusing, but the basic implication in Maddow's report was that a pro-Trump source had forged secret NSA documents in the hope that liberal media outlets like MSNBC would fall for them, much like Rather had been fooled 13 years earlier.

Maddow told her viewers that this was the essence of the story:

> We believe now that the story we have stumbled upon here is that somebody out there is shopping carefully forged documents to try to discredit news agencies reporting on the Russian attack on our election and, specifically, on the possibility that the Trump campaign coordinated with the Russians in mounting that attack.
>
> *(Rozsa 2017)*

Maddow's claim was supported by her belief that a timestamp in the metadata on the forged documents showed that it had been produced prior to similar, original documents being published on another website, *The Intercept*. If that was the case, it would have strengthened Maddow's claim that the forgery was done by someone with access to the original documents, but *The Intercept* was able to show that the timestamp on Maddow's forgery was identical—down to the second—as the documents published on *The Intercept* site. This meant that the forgery had been made from the publicly available copy and therefore took the heat out of Maddow's story. As *The Intercept*'s Glenn Greenwald reported, this point means that almost anyone could have sent the forgeries to Maddow:

By Maddow's own telling, MSNBC received the document two days after *The Intercept* published it for the entire world to see. That means that literally anyone with internet access could have taken the document from *The Intercept*'s site, altered it, and sent it to Maddow.

(Greenwald 2017)

This example illustrates the importance of being able to read the metadata on electronic documents as well as being aware of physical signs that something has been faked or altered from the original. While forensic document examination is probably best left to the experts, you can take reasonable steps to ensure you are not fooled by simple fakes. It is important to check elements such as signatures, spelling, official logos or stamps and how the document is set out when looking for physical forgeries, and metadata can be useful in ascertaining the provenance of electronic documents, including PDFs and JPEGs.

Checklist for Physically Verifying Documents

*   Signatures are difficult to forge, and if you know what you're looking for fakes can be easy to spot. Most people write their signature the same way, or close enough, each time. The length of a signature does not vary, so this is the first clue. If you have an original to compare with you can also look for differences in how the pen strokes are formed; particularly at the beginning and end of letters. Other clues include differences in the pressure applied and also "tremor" caused by the forger being anxious (Guterman 1998).
*   Check the source of the document; is it from a reputable company or agency? Does the address and phone number match? Can you do an online search to verify details. Don't be fooled if the document has official-looking logos or branding; these are easily faked.
*   Is the writing style appropriate for the alleged writer? A business letter with poor spelling and grammar is most likely a scam; the same goes for government or agency documents. Most of the time these are rigorously checked and proofread to eliminate obvious errors.
*   The main types of electronic forgery include manipulating the documents contents by producing and altering digital copies. A document is scanned into an electronic word processor or PDF manipulator and new content added or original content altered. A physical examination may show differences in fonts used, how lines of type are arranged or in pagination. If you're in doubt after physically checking a suspect document, you might need the services of an electronic detection system that can scan the document and examine it in detail.
*   If a document has a digital signature—such as one you can apply using Adobe Acrobat—then you can ascertain if it has been altered after signing.

- The following physical signs can indicate a document has been electronically altered using an application like Microsoft Paint, Picasa, Acrobat or Adobe Photoshop:

  - Irregular spacing between letters and words.
  - Discrepancies in font and design of inserted words and letters.
  - Discrepancies in size of inserted letters or words.
  - Crowding of various letters and words.
  - Discoloration or anomalies in the background (Saini and Kaur 2016).

- Using the same software as the forgers (see previous dot-point) you can reverse engineer the documents to see the irregularities. This takes some familiarity with the application, but it is not beyond the means of people with some degree of computer literacy.
- Different printers and printing methods can also leave tell-tale signs of forgery, but such analysis is not always easy. However, looking for small marks on the page may give some clues as to how many times a document has been scanned, copied, or printed (Shang, Memon and Kong 2014).

Document verification using metadata

Verifying documents using the metadata embedded in them is a different process and also one that can be done simply from your desktop or laptop. Metadata will typically tell you when a document was created, when it was last edited and when it was last opened—this is the timestamp information. In some applications, you can also check the document's author and whether or not it was subsequently edited by someone else. Metadata can also tell you which computer a document was created on. Accessing metadata on most documents, including PDFs, is relatively easy; hover your mouse pointer over the file and right click, this brings up a dialogue box. Right click again on the "properties" menu and this unlocks a treasure trove of information about the document. This is not a fool-proof method, but it allows you to begin the process of verification.

The complete metadata on documents can be quite revealing. For example, with Word documents any collaboration with other authors using "track changes" might reveal names or other information. You can search for this using Word's "document inspector" from the "File" tab in the application.

Document Inspector can tell you if metadata is embedded, some the information is displayed in a column on the right-hand side of the screen and the application allows you to remove it. Clicking on the "Details" tab brings up more information about this document, including useful information about its origin and history. If documents have more than one author or editor you will see that in the metadata.

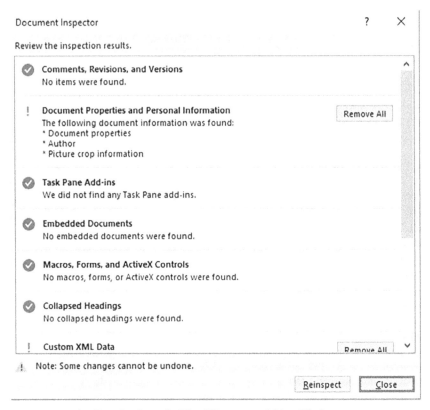

FIGURE 9.14 An Examination of a Word Document Using File Inspector.

I tested several free downloads that claimed to be able to read the metadata, but none of them was really any better than the what comes already loaded in the Office suite. There are commercial applications available, but they are expensive and probably only suitable to newsroom application. It is also worth remembering that you can also use a similar set of commands to view the metadata on emails. Email metadata can tell you more about when and where the message was composed, the software it was written on, and which servers it passed through on its way to you. But once again, a word of caution: it is now possible to spam email headers.

The bottom line about metadata in documents, spreadsheets, PowerPoint presentations, PDFs and emails is that it is very difficult, if not impossible to erase all of it. Some applications will even let you read text redacted in a PDF when the words are obscured by black oblong shapes and read the data in files (such as tables and graphs created in a spreadsheet) inserted in a Word document (Kuksov 2017).The science of forensic document testing is now well developed. Chances are, if you are faced with a possible forgery or fake and really want to

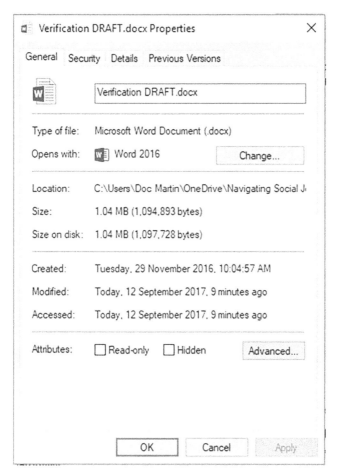

FIGURE 9.15   The Properties Dialogue Box for the Draft Word Document of this Chapter.

know the true origins of the document, there are ways of cracking the metadata. If you can afford the cost of having the file thoroughly examined by an expert, you will know with some certainty how the artefact came into being.

Verifying Images and Video

If all of this talk of metadata and document forensics sounds a bit like the job description of a police detective that's because in essence that's what it is. Detection work is an important part of journalism and it has become a key aspect of verifying images and video. The verification experts all say a reporter should approach the task like a detective and look for all the clues (Silverman 2012). Remember, this means physical clues—the content of the image or video—and the metadata.

A lot of information from non-journalistic sources on social media is in the form of graphics, photographs and video and we all know, at least anecdotally, that image manipulation using easily learned and available tools is well within the capability of most people. This makes the verification of photographs and video especially important, given the speed at which they can circulate, well before any verification techniques are applied.

Google reverse image search has already been mentioned as one method of quickly ascertaining the bona fides of a digital image, but it is not foolproof. There are other, more sophisticated tools, such as TinEye and Foto Forensics that provide a more professional service, but they take more time to learn and understand. If you want to become proficient in these tools, then you will need to devote some time to practice. All of them work with "drag and drop" technology that allows you to input an image physically, or by pasting the picture's URL into the search bar. That part it easy, it is the analysis of the results that is hard. As I mentioned, it is possible to get false positives with a simple search that, if not detected, can lead you to making mistakes about the origins and re-use of the image you are attempting to verify.

However, sometimes you will need more information than you can get from searching in a reverse image finder. In which case you will need to use an application that can read what is known as the EXIF file information—metadata embedded in the image file. EXIF is an acronym of Exchangeable Image File Format and it is the data that allows different image viewers and editors to read a photograph. The EXIF file contains a lot of useful additional information about an image, including the coordinates of where it was taken.

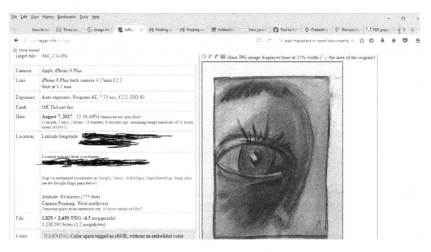

FIGURE 9.16   EXIF Data for an Image of a Drawing I Did in Art Class Taken on My iPhone.

As you can see, the software I used to find the EXIF data on this photo was able to find my latitude and longitude based on the location data my phone added to the image. It was accurate enough to guess my actual physical address, not just the type of camera and the exposure details. I did this using a free EXIF viewer that is available on the Internet.

Photo editing software can also leave tell-tale marks on photographs and video. With video, always be on the lookout for "jump cuts" which mean that the sequence has been edited to either add or remove material. Typical "clone" marks—when one section of an image has been copied—or a "halo" effect—a blurred outline look—around some elements in a digital photograph are also signs of tampering. You might also see discrepancies in shadows if something or someone has been added to an image. Even the most experienced Photoshop experts can make mistakes. As always, this advice comes with a disclaimer, as images are shared on social media they may be altered along the way. This means that the original metadata is degraded, but on the upside, if you find that metadata looks suspect, then you are probably right to be cautious about the authenticity of the image. As with everything in journalism, getting as close to the original source as possible is the best way to verify anything.

The poor souls of the Middle Ages could not check any metadata when they read in a local printed news sheet that there were dragons in the next county; they had to believe what they read in unreliable newssheets, and subsequently lived their lives largely in ignorance and fear. In the digital age we no longer have that excuse, if you are unsure of something, check it before publication. You do not want to be the purveyor of myths and mistruths when the verification tools are so readily to hand.

There is really no reason why you should be fooled again by fake news or fall victim to dodgy reporting. The tools to carry out your own verification of information are widely available. They are not fool-proof, but they do offer a first line of protection. Having a heightened awareness and being able to use your enhanced media literacy skills provide the basic tools you need; searching out and taking advantage of free and easily available software and applications will help you hold journalists and your social media friends to account. These skills are absolutely necessary if you want to operate successfully in the social journalism space. Credibility is king.

References

arixvblog. 2014. "How to Spot a Social Bot on Twitter." *MIT Technology Review*. July 28. Accessed September 7, 2017. www.technologyreview.com/s/529461/how-to-spot-a-social-bot-on-twitter/.

Arshad, Harris. 2016. "The Complete Guide to Social Media Account Verification." *Search Engine Journal*. 6 October. Accessed September 7, 2017. www.searchenginejournal.com/the-complete-guide-to-social-media-account-verification/172832/.

Backholm, K., J. Ausserhofer, E. Frey, A. Larsen, H. Hornmoen, J. Högväg and G. Reimerth. 2017. "Crises, Rumours and Reposts: Journalists" Social Media Content Gathering and Verification Practices in Breaking News Situations." *Media and Communication* 5(2). doi:10.17645/mac.v5i2.878.

Dell, Johannes. 2015. "How to Verify News Stories on Social Media." BBC Academy. Accessed September 7, 2017. www.bbc.co.uk/academy/journalism/article/art20160622115505760.

Fahrenthold, David A. 2016a. "Trump's Campaign Says He's Given 'Tens Of Millions' to Charity, but Offers No Details and No Proof." *The Washington Post*. September 12. Accessed January 4, 2017. www.washingtonpost.com/news/post-politics/wp/2016/09/12/trumps-campaign-says-hes-given-tens-of-millions-to-charity-but-offers-no-details-and-no-proof/?utm_term=.478832197146.

Fahrenthold, David A. 2016b. "David Fahrenthold Tells the Behind-the-Scenes Story of His Year Covering Trump." *The Washington Post*. December 29. Accessed January 3, 2017. www.washingtonpost.com/lifestyle/magazine/david-fahrenthold-tells-the-behind-the-scenes-story-of-his-year-covering-trump/2016/12/27/299047c4-b510-11e6-b8df-600bd9d38a02_story.html?utm_term=.38e35eab301f.

Fahrenthold, David A. 2016c. "Trump Announced His Gifts to Veterans. This is What We Learned." *The Washington Post*. May 31. Accessed January 3, 2017. www.washingtonpost.com/news/post-politics/wp/2016/05/30/tomorrow-trump-will-give-more-details-about-his-donations-to-vets-heres-what-we-still-dont-know/?utm_term=.6f819b3d6c76.

Fahrenthold, David A. 2016d. "Trump Used $258,000 from His Charity to Settle Legal Problems." *The Washington Post*. September 20. Accessed January 4, 2017. www.washingtonpost.com/politics/trump-used-258000-from-his-charity-to-settle-legal-problems/2016/09/20/adc88f9c-7d11-11e6-ac8e-cf8e0dd91dc7_story.html?utm_term=.a7026905467d.

Fahrenthold, David A. 2016e. "Trump Recorded Having Extremely Lewd Conversation about Women in 2005." *The Washington Post*. October 8. Accessed January 4, 2017. www.washingtonpost.com/politics/trump-recorded-having-extremely-lewd-conversation-about-women-in-2005/2016/10/07/3b9ce776-8cb4-11e6-bf8a-3d26847eeed4_story.html?utm_term=.6dffcf4d653c.

Fahrenthold, David A., and Danielle Rindler. 2016. "Searching for Evidence of Trump's Personal Giving." *The Washington Post*. August 18. Accessed January 4, 2017. www.washingtonpost.com/graphics/politics/2016-election/trump-charity-donations/.

Fitzgerald, Bill, and Kris Shaffer. 2017. "Spot a Bot: Identifying Automation and Disinformation on Social Media." Data for Democracy. June 5. Accessed September 7, 2017. https://medium.com/data-for-democracy/spot-a-bot-identifying-automation-and-disinformation-on-social-media-2966ad93a203.

Friggeri, Adrien, Lada A. Adamic, Dean Eckles and Justin Cheng. 2014. Rumour Cascades. Association for the Advancement of Artificial Intelligence. Accessed September 7, 2017.

Gilmour, David. 2017. "White House Secrets Deleted." *The Daily Dot*. January 26. Accessed September 7, 2017. www.dailydot.com/layer8/alleged-white-house-whistleblower-deleted/.

Greenwald, Glenn. 2017. "Rachel Maddow's Exclusive 'Scoop' About a Fake NSA Document Raises Several Key Questions." *The Intercept*. July 8. Accessed September 12, 2017. https://theintercept.com/2017/07/07/rachel-maddows-exclusive-scoop-about-a-fake-nsa-document-raises-several-key-questions/.

Guterman, Lila. 1998. "Copies of Forged Signatures Don't Fool Experts." *New Scientist.* August 8. Accessed September 12, 2017. www.newscientist.com/article/mg15921464-100-copies-of-forged-signatures-dont-fool-experts/.

Kovach, Bill, and Tom Rosenstiel. 2014. *The Elements of Journalism: What Newspeople Shoud Know and the Public Should Expect.* New York: Three Rivers Press.

Kuksov, Igor. 2017. "How Ephemeral Metadata May Cause Real Problems." *Kasperky Lab Daily.* March 10. Accessed September 12, 2017. www.kaspersky.com/blog/office-documents-metadata/14215/.

Machkovech, Sam. 2016. "Washington Post Automatically Inserts Trump Fact-Checks into Twitter." ArsTechnica. December 17. Accessed January 27, 2017. https://arstechnica.com/tech-policy/2016/12/washington-post-automatically-inserts-trump-fact-checks-into-twitter/.

MacMillan, Gordon. 2013. "As Many as 20m Twitter Accounts are Fake." *PR Week.* April 8. Accessed September 7, 2017. www.prweek.com/article/1276172/20m-twitter-accounts-fake.

Mnookin, Seth. 2008. "Scandal of Record." *Vanity Fair.* April 29. Accessed September 6, 2017. www.vanityfair.com/style/2004/12/nytimes200412.

Murphy, Jarrett. 2005. "CBS Ousts Four for Bush Guard Story." January 10. Accessed September 12, 2017. www.cbsnews.com/news/cbs-ousts-4-for-bush-guard-story-10-01-2005/.

New York Times. 2003. "Correcting the Record: Times Reporter Who Resigned Leaves a Long Trail of Deception." *The New York Times.* May 11. Accessed September 6, 2017. www.nytimes.com/2003/05/11/us/correcting-the-record-times-reporter-who-resigned-leaves-long-trail-of-deception.html?mcubz=0.

Newcomer, Joseph. 2005. "The 'Bush Guard Memos' Are Forgeries." January 11. Accessed September 12, 2017. www.flounder.com/bush2.htm.

Resnick, Gideon. 2016. "How Pro-Trump Twitter Bots Spread Fake News." *The Daily Beast.* November 17. Accessed September 7, 2017. www.thedailybeast.com/how-pro-trump-twitter-bots-spread-fake-news.

Rowles, Dustin. 2017. "The Rogue Twitter Accounts Allegedly From Inside the White House Are Giving the Resistance Life." Pajiba. January 27. Accessed September 7, 2017. www.pajiba.com/politics/the-rogue-twitter-accounts-allegedly-from-inside-the-white-house-are-giving-the-resistance-life-.php.

Rozsa, Matthew. 2017. "Rachel Maddow Warns: People are Trying to Fool the Media with Forged Documents." *Salon.* July 8. Accessed September 12, 2017. www.salon.com/2017/07/07/rachel-maddow-warns-people-are-trying-to-fool-the-media-with-forged-documents/.

Saini, Komal, and Shabnampreet Kaur. 2016. "Forensic Examination of Computer-Manipulated Documents Using Image Processing Techniques." *Egyptian Journal of Forensic Sciences* 6(3): 317–322. doi:10.1016/j.ejfs.2015.03.001.

Shang, Shize, Nasir Memon and Ziangwei Kong. 2014. "Detecting Documents Forged by Printing and Copying." *EURASIP Journal on Advances in Signal Processing* 2014: 140. doi:10.1186/1687-6180-2014-140.

Silverman, Craig. 2012. "Three Ways to Spot if an Image Has Been Manipulated." Poynter Institute. May 5. Accessed September 12, 2017. www.poynter.org/news/three-ways-spot-if-an-image-has-been-manipulated.

Stearns, Josh, and Leighton Walter Kille. 2015. "Tools for Verifying and Assessing the Validity of Social Media and User-Generated Content." Journalist's Resource. April 2.

Accessed September 6, 2017. https://journalistsresource.org/tip-sheets/reporting/tools-verify-assess-validity-social-media-user-generated-content.

Swaine, Jon. 2017. "Lurid Trump Allegations Made by Louise Mensch and Co-writer Came from Hoaxer." *The Guardian*. August 29. Accessed September 6, 2017. www.theguardian.com/us-news/2017/aug/28/trump-tweets-hoax-louise-mensch-claude-taylor.

Twitter. 2017. "Following Rules and Best Practices." Accessed September 7, 2017. https://support.twitter.com/articles/68916#.

10
HOW TO DO SOCIAL JOURNALISM

If the BBC Can Do it, Why Not You Too?

This chapter opens up the "How?" question. Here we outline the basic principles of doing social journalism before branching out into more specific advice about various platforms, applications and methodologies. This chapter is about curating and editing, which is the management of content, and it introduces some of the common apps and platforms that professional reporters and social journalists can use to publish, distribute and publicize their work. In some cases, the app or platform provides a "stand-alone" solution, others are more suited to short, promotional "grabs" to generate traffic to a more substantial "home" or story "archive."

As we've discussed in previous chapters, one of the major problems facing the legacy media is that younger people find it boring and unattractive. The news that millennials and younger generations find interesting and compelling is found in many places, but not very often, it seems, in newspapers, on television, on the radio, or on the websites of the larger, well-known news brands that their parents and grandparents have relied on in previous generations. If the News Establishment's top brands cannot reach out to today's teenagers and under-30s, what chance do they have of surviving beyond the next decade? Very little, it would seem.

In order to survive, if not thrive, legacy media brands are attempting to colonize the apps and platforms where millennials tend to hang out. As we've seen this often means disguising appropriation as engagement. The British Broadcasting Corporation (BBC) is one global legacy news brand that has made the transition to social with survival in mind. In 2016, the BBC began experimenting with broadcasting some of its content on Instagram, which has mostly been an ephemeral site for the likes of Kim Kardashian and other celebrities to promote self-branded products. It was the introduction of Instagram Stories as a new function on the app that led to the BBC taking it more seriously as a promotional tool for some of its longer-form journalism. Stories allows Instagram users to create a slideshow-style stream of highlights with additional graphics, video and text inserted; stories only exist for 24 hours, but they can be shared while they are "live."

Each of the short videos on the BBC News Instagram page is around 30 seconds and functions as both a stand-alone piece and a prompt for people to click on embedded links to find the longer version of the story. In a story for *Journalism.co.uk*, the BBC's social media editor, Mark Frankel, made the corporation's pitch to a younger demographic explicit: "we need to find ways to capture their imagination, bring them in, and encourage them to explore more," he told Caroline Scott (Scott 2017). The BBC also promotes itself through several Instagram accounts, including "BBC Stories" which posts still images and brief text updates about stories it is producing in longer-form.

Many of the big and reputable news brands are now on Instagram, including the *New York Times* which launched its official account in September 2015 with the explicit aim of reaching new audiences. In a media release the 170-year-old newspaper said its @NYTimes Instagram account would showcase content "tailored toward intimate interaction with our audience in ways that amplify our news report[s]" (NYT 2015). However, the *NYT* had already been experimenting with Instagram for some time prior to this "official" launch. It has Instagram profiles dedicated to more niche and lifestyle content in fashion, travel, food and sport. According to a report in *American Journalism Review*, newspaper editors see Instagram as a brand and promotion tool, rather than as an outlet for journalism, as such (Barron and Lardiera 2015).

The fundamentals for news organizations when considering whether to post material to Instagram and what to post are the nature of the medium itself—it's mainly about images—and who the potential audience is. This is really no different to any editorial decision about what, when, where and why to publish on a daily basis. According to one social media editor at *USA Today*, the focus is on both traffic and establishing a point-of-difference attractive to Instagram users: "Instagram is just not a traffic driver … That's not why we're on Instagram. We're on Instagram to reach people in a new and different way" (Barron and Lardiera 2015).

Instagram has a reputation for being a more intimate platform than something like Twitter, because of its image by image viewing mode that allows viewers time to pause and reflect on photos they find engaging. This makes it less of a "push" platform driving traffic to other properties, but as the BBC experiment shows, this is slowly changing as Instagram adds functionality. Instagram can also be a great place to engage readers by showcasing images they have submitted in response to a newsroom request, or a major event—like

FIGURE 10.1 The BBC News Instagram Feed Contains a Series of Short Films Promoting Longer-Form Content.

an unusual weather occurrence, a festival, rally, or even a terrorist incident. This is a two-way relationship that allows news organizations to engage with readers and also to be alert to trending stories or breaking news.

However, outside of the larger, main city newspapers, the story could be very different. Big news organizations have teams of engineers, photo-editors and even social media editors. These are luxuries that smaller papers or outlets cannot afford. So how can smaller outlets take advantage of the reach and impact that Instagram and other social media platforms offer? The simple answer is that reporters and editors working on local, hyperlocal or low budget outlets have to be all-rounders; they have to be able to do the basics across several apps and platforms and to perhaps, be a specialist or expert in one or two. Instagram works best with images and short videos, but it is up to you to work out if the time and effort required to edit, post and curate video to Instagram provides the rewards and leverage you're looking for. Social journalists must operate in a similar way, choosing platforms and apps that best suit their needs and then learning to use them effectively.

In this respect, repurposing material across several apps and platforms can work, it spreads the content further and means that you can maintain a presence in several social media spaces with little extra work. However, remember the Golden Rule: the content must be fit for purpose and attractive to the audience on that particular app or platform; you can't just post content everywhere without some tweaking. What works on Tumblr (with more text, for example) will bomb on Instagram or platforms where the emphasis is on instant and visual gratification. The easiest form of social journalism using the available social media tools is the curation of existing content sourced from other places. This does not require much more than the ability to spot a good story and repackage it, perhaps with a short editorial or other form of introduction. Your contribution in this context is to give your output some "personality."

Social Journalism Begins with You

In today's media landscape the boundaries between audience and reporter are blurry. However, in terms of professional journalists, the boundary has not been completely erased. The bulk of the world's news begins life inside a newsroom tied to a major distributor, and this applies whether the platform is "legacy" media (print, radio or television) or a new start-up online site. However, a growing proportion of news and news-like information is circulating without ever having been touched by a professional reporter or editor. For example, the news service provided by Twitter, which is called Twitter Moments, has an estimated 92 million unique views per month, making it bigger than several of the larger mainstream news outlets (Srinivasan 2017).

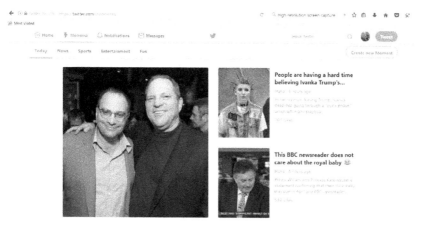

FIGURE 10.2   Is Twitter Moments the Ultimate Social Journalism Feed?

Twitter Moments is curated from Twitter HQ, but it also lets users create their own content. This is the truly *social* aspect of social journalism. News generated by audience members for their peers, but also perhaps, hoping to reach a wider audience and maybe to be commercially viable—to turn a hobby into an income, or to entice advertisers via Google AdSense, or some other source. Unfortunately, from my perspective as a journalist and journalism educator, much of this social space has been colonized by marketing gurus who talk about everyone being a "brand" rather than a person. Of course, it is important at one level to build your online news-like presence into something that others are interested in reading, listening to or watching, sharing and liking; but getting it right must be the most important thing. Social journalism has to be about more than personal branding. By all means sell a bit of yourself but remember the "duality" of the news commodity from political economy. Along with commercial viability in a capitalist economy, news and news-like information must also have a public interest purpose, or at least be interesting to the public.

Curating and Aggregating versus Reporting

One of the easiest ways to get started as a social journalist is to aggregate content around particular themes, or breaking news items and share it via your social media feed. An application like Tumblr, Instagram, Paper.li, or even Twitter Moments, is useful for doing this. But, simply piling all the material together and pumping it out can be messy, confusing and overwhelming. Aggregating is simply bringing everything together in one place; to help your followers make more sense and to be more relevant, you need to go an extra step and do some curating. Curating is a form of active media literacy in which the curator is offering guidance to her/his followers by making informed recommendations about quality. To turn media literacy into curatorial acumen means having some news sensibility and the confidence to back your own editorial judgement. If you have read the previous chapter carefully and put its advice into practice, you can be reasonably confident that your curated feed doesn't contain too much rubbish.

Curating is similar to aggregation in that you are bringing together sources that are thematically linked, but curation is about careful selection and management, rather than just bundling as much information as you can together. Curating is a form of content gate-keeping; a good curator only allows quality content through the gate they patrol (Callaghan 2016). According to the experts, curation is time-consuming, and requires subject expertise, communication skills, experience and intuition. In other words, it is a set of multi-disciplinary skills that must be patiently applied to your content creation process (Good 2016). I don't think it is that difficult to learn; once you have mastered verification techniques and some of the software, curating is a good way to start your journey into social journalism.

Good curating starts with setting up good search parameters and news alerts that bring content to you efficiently, and in a timely manner. Of course, you need to monitor your alerts and select the most relevant content to go into your curated feed. Items are then selected for possible inclusion in your feed, but they must be checked and verified first. It helps if you start with reliable sources, but to be noticed and valued by your followers, a well-curated feed will not just rely on the big mainstream sources. Finding and republishing lesser-known sources is more original, but it carries the added risk that the material is unreliable. Make sure you apply stringent verification techniques to your curated feed to avoid embarrassment. The most difficult aspect of curating is perhaps adding your own take to the feed. This might take the form of an editorial, or commentary on your selections, but it should be on point and not too long. The whole point of curating over just aggregating is that you select the best—the most relevant, the most reliable, the best-written and most compelling content. Curating has been described as "cherry-picking" (Durris 2014) the best of all the noise that is out there across multiple news channels and turning it into meaningful pleasant-sounding music to your followers' ears.

Content Must Be Engaging, Not Just Be There

The only way to build an audience through social media is to be engaging. But what does engaging social journalism look like? The answer has several aspects, each of which is individually important, but your content will be really engaging if you can mesh all of them into what you are posting. Engagement is a social media buzzword, beloved of the marketing gurus. They will tell you that you cannot create customers and close sales unless you have engaged with people first (York 2017). This is probably true enough, but it is not a great secret and there is no "sauce" that makes it work instantly. Engagement begins when someone first notices your content. This is the primary "interaction," but at that point there is no relationship between you and the reader/viewer. If the person likes your content then they may continue to seek you out; they might become follower, or comment on your posts. When these types of responses start to happen, you have engagement (Hausman 2011). The matrix for audience engagement for news-like content includes this response indicator, but it is built on slightly different terms than those used in marketing-speak.

Yes, whatever you do needs to be "engaging," but if it is to fit the bill as social journalism it must also be accurate, timely, important and newsworthy. For social journalists the most important marker that will increase engagement is the news value in the content.

Is the Content Newsworthy?

Everyone is busy these days and most of us spend way too much time scrolling news feeds on our various social media accounts. The trick to building engagement is to stop that mindless scrolling in its tracks with a good headline or opening statement (see my thoughts on the "lead" in Chapter 11). The headline or lead must capture the value in the content you're sharing. Most of us understand the basic elements of what constitutes news, but to recap, here are the important points: to be news, the content has to be "new"; it has to be relevant, topical and accurate.

"New" in this sense means that there is something distinctive about the report that doesn't just rehash something being said or done somewhere else by someone else. There's a place for drawing on what's already out there, but simply repeating and amplifying will not guarantee engagement. This is why simple to manage platforms like Twitter Moments, Instagram Stories and Tumblr that allow you to craft something from existing content, but to add you own twist, are good place to begin your social journalism journey.

The content you either curate or create has to have some significance and be relevant to your intended audience; it has to be about something that they are interested in. This means you can't just think of what you might find interesting. You have to be able to imagine what your target audience might want from the news-like content you're posting. Or, better still, take advantage of analytical tools, data and metrics (see below). If you can find something that your audience needs to know then you're going in the right direction to spark their interest and to get them sharing your material. Once you find a handful of key influencers in your own audience, they will amplify your message and help you to build your own audience.

My key advice here is that your content must strike a chord, it must be "on trend," but more than simply "trendy." If you can produce content on topics that people are already talking about it has a greater chance of finding traction with that audience; but you cannot afford to just be blowing in the wind. If you have a particular expertise, put it to good use. There is also an argument for producing what is sometimes known as "evergreen content"—material that stands the test of time. One of the most read posts on my own blog, *Ethical Martini*, is a piece I wrote in 2008 about staying in the Bonaventure hotel in downtown Los Angeles. The Bonaventure is an icon of twentieth-century architecture and it is the subject of a famous essay on postmodernism by Frederic Jameson and when I stayed there I wrote my own essay referencing Jameson and presenting my own take on a hotel then fading from its glory days. I illustrated the piece with my own images and discussed having a meal in the revolving restaurant at the top of the mirrored towers (Hirst 2008).

This post has been picked up by a globally run essay-writing contest for high school students which means it gets significant boost in traffic around the same time each year while the competition is running. What I should do is revisit this post and write something new to update it. Sounds like a great excuse to visit LA again.

Who is Your Audience?

To be effective in a commercial sense you need to find an audience large enough to provide sustainable funding, whether that is through advertising revenue, subscriptions or crowd-funding exercises. Few of us can afford the time, effort and resources to be a social journalist news outlet just for fun. If you can and that's what your goal is then you can afford to sit back and do whatever you like. A hobby site, like a blog, an Instagram feed, Facebook page or Twitter account, doesn't have to pay its own way. However, if your aim is to make a living from your social journalism, thinking about who your audience is and why they might engage with you is crucial to success.

FIGURE 10.3 Postmodernism and the Bonaventure Hotel.

If you're serious about making a business out of your social journalism a little bit of planning goes a long way. You also need to work out for yourself the right balance between factuality and emotion in your content so that it has the right appeal for your target audience. The balance will vary, depending on the type of content—the more news-like you intend to be the more you will need to rely on facts, rather than emotion. But you cannot ignore the fact that to win an audience you must appeal to both hearts *and* minds.

Do You Have a Strong and Distinctive Voice?

Everybody thinks their opinion is worth sharing; the trick is to convince other people that your opinion is worth sharing. To do that, you must find your voice— and this applies as much to writing as it does to podcasting, video-blogging or news-like clips. It takes time to develop your own style, but it is worth spending some time thinking about, rehearsing and perfecting. Once you have hit on a voice and presentation style that are your own you can adopt and apply it consistently to the content you produce. You will know it's effective once your audience hooks in to you and begins to share your content with their own social media networks.

One critical aspect of finding a voice that is distinctive and has cut through is to know when to stop. If we are passionate about something it is likely that we will be tempted to get everything we know about the topic into one post or video or podcast. If we do that we run the risk of boring our intended audience. If someone loses interest because you are droning on beyond the limits of their tolerance, or your post looks like a too-long daunting read then they will switch off and disregard the next thing you publish, no matter how good or compelling you think it is. If you're familiar with the "TL;DR" tag you know what I mean. For the uninitiated, "TL;DR" simply means "too long; I didn't read it." Nobody wants to get that beat down in response to all their hard work. You can find more on developing your own voice in the next chapter.

How are You Going to Distribute Your News-Like Content?

Are you going to build a social media presence across more than one platform or application? My advice is that you must do this if you want to have any kind of success, either through increasing your circulation and readership/viewership (still the valued metrics of distribution), or through generating an income.

Being successful in the social journalism space requires you to plan your distribution model and not just build it by "doing." You might start out with a site hosted on WordPress or one of the other free blogging platforms; Twitter, Facebook, Instagram paper.li and Pinterest are free too and it is important to harness their distribution power to maximize the spread of your content. You must also consider using some of the pay-for-play services as well, though if you don't have much capital to work with this might be something that you put into your business planning for the second phase of expansion.

One thing that is essential to successful distribution is to know which platforms your audience is most likely to be using. For a younger demographic you might find Instagram, SnapChat and Pinterest useful, or WhatsApp, but for an older professional audience a space like LinkedIn might be more valuable real estate. What I do know for sure is that you cannot limit your distribution to only one channel; your audience is going to be spread across several platforms or applications. Doing your research and then adopting a trial and error approach over several weeks and months is the only way to know for sure. It is also worth remembering that some applications and platforms are dynamic, simply meaning that the content refreshes quickly and is constantly moving—Twitter is a good example. Other platforms, such as a blog that you maintain, or a Facebook page, are more static. Content can hang around longer in a static space; it can also be archived and searchable which means that it can still find an audience days, weeks, or months after it is posted. The key to good evergreen content is to pick a topic that does not date quickly; but good metadata is also important so that your post doesn't drop out of search engines too quickly. A news or news-like website has both dynamic and static elements and the ratio will depend on how often the content can be refreshed with new material or updates on existing stories. In my experience a busy and effective professional newsroom will be refreshing content on a continuous basis, at least during business hours; a less well-resourced site, or one run by social journalist enthusiasts is likely to have less updates, and more static content.

One useful strategy is the principle of "share and share alike." This means paying attention to the niche you are hoping to occupy and finding like-minded individuals who you can follow and whose content you can share. This is the best way to get noticed in social media and to ultimately get others to share your work, increasing your reach and influence.

Evaluate and Be Prepared to Change

Most free platforms—for blogging, Twitter and so on—also come with a range of in-built analytical tools. When you get to the point of having a pay-to-play platform you should make sure you get the most analytical data you can afford as part of the package. This is the "meta-data" that you need to examine in order to work out how effectively your content and your distribution systems are functioning.

One the key analytics is known as "SEO," which stands for "search engine optimization," this is the process of choosing keywords and hashtags to accompany your posts. The theory behind it is simple—if you are using terms that people commonly search for using Google, etc., then your material will come up in searches and, hopefully, encourage people to follow the links. The backend analytics in most content management systems will provide statistics on how effective your keywords are. The basic principle though is simple: choose your keywords carefully, use enough to get noticed, but not so many that they lose their relevance to your content.

The key advice here is *be prepared to change*. If something isn't working, ask yourself "Why?" Work out what isn't working and try something new. The whole social journalism field is so new that everyone is still in the largely experimental stage. This is both exciting and confusing at the same time. It's exciting because you might just hit on a successful formula that leads to great riches, or at least a rewarding sense of satisfaction. It's confusing because there is a whole new industry dedicated to selling you expensive advice. Some of it is worthwhile and some of it is a waste of money. Don't get sucked into hiring expensive consultants who promise you instant success. The only success they actually represent is successfully conning people like you into handing over money for repackaged advice that you can figure out for yourself through some judicial Google searches, the right analytical tools, common sense, patience and an open mind.

Which Apps Do What?

Information sharing via social media is hugely popular and, for some, extremely profitable. According to an infographic produced by CEWE *Photoworld*, the rate of peer-to-peer sharing via image and short videos is so quick that it is almost unmeasurable (CEWE Photoworld undated). We are sharing gossip, photos, audio and video recordings and countless details of our lives in unprecedented ways. The number and variety of applications (apps) that allow us to do this has shot up in recent years; some become obsolete (MySpace) and no longer exist, while new ones appear on the scene regularly.

The number of social media apps now available for smartphones and tablet devices is mind-boggling and most, if not all, can have some value for both professional and social journalists. It is possible to share news and news-like information on just about all of the social media publishing platforms where the only limits are your imagination and the curiosity of users. It is impossible, in a text such as this, to give a comprehensive rundown of every app for every device. For a start, this is not a book of product reviews and, even if it were, I only use an iPhone and iPad so I can't give any technical advice on how the apps mentioned here might work on Android-type devices or Windows tablets. However, what I will try to do in the rest of this chapter is outline some of the apps that can be effective for the gathering and distribution of news and news-like stories. It's safe to say that all of them are good for distribution—the whole point of social media apps is to share—and some of them are good for news-gathering (the essential research phase) and some, but not all, are good for actually writing and curating your news feed.

There are several types of apps and platforms available and they vary in terms of usefulness and value as either distribution networks and/or tools for gathering and writing news and news-like information.

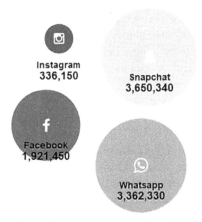

FIGURE 10.4 The Number of Images Shared on these Platforms in Just Under Seven Minutes. Screengrab from CEWE Photoworld.

The simple instant-messaging apps are not all that useful for news distribution as the messages tend to have limited length and also a short lifespan. The fact that messages are automatically deleted on apps like SnapChat and Wickr is what drives their popularity, but without some longevity, news is pretty pointless, accept perhaps for alerts about breaking stories or emergencies. Discussion forums Reddit, Digg (now closed) or Slashdot tend to be hangouts for the already committed and also to be specifically focused into threads or topics, rather than platforms for general news and news-like content. Discussion forum communities are therefore rather closed in nature and some are actively hostile to outsiders. One thing that is important to remember about the apps and platforms that constitute the social media "mediasphere" is that they are being updated, revamped, opened, superseded and closed regularly. For instance, as I was finishing this chapter in late September 2017, Twitter did something that was unexpected: it increased its character limit from 140 to 280 on some select accounts. This caused outrage in some quarters but was welcomed in others (Mezzofiore 2017); it also made all the online "how-to" guides that were working within the 140-character limit suddenly redundant. Now the 280-limit character is universal. Is it an improvement? Only if you like reading or writing longer tweets. The best advice I can give you at this point, before outlining the salient features of some useful apps, is that you should choose the services that work for you; learn how to use them effectively and keep up with any changes they make to operating conditions.

Facebook—Where Your Audience is (Almost) the Entire Planet

By 2014, approximately 1.3 billion people, or about 20 percent of the world's population, was reportedly logging on to Facebook at least once a month (Somaiya 2014). The social media giant is also responsible for around 20 percent of traffic to established news media sites, in the United States 30 percent say they get news from Facebook first (Anderson and Caumont 2014). By September 2016, the *Columbia Journalism Review* was promoting a piece on how social media now dominates news distribution with the headline, "Facebook is eating the world" and reporting that then 40 percent of Americans were consuming news first on the platform (Bell 2016). "Social media hasn't just swallowed journalism, it has swallowed everything," Emily Bell reported. A September 2017 Pew Center report put the percentage of Americans using Facebook for news at greater than 45 percent, this dwarfed other social media platforms: YouTube at 8 percent; Twitter around11 percent and Instagram at seven percent. However, the 2017 report also showed that around 25 percent of US consumers now use multiple social media sites for their news fix (Shearer and Gottfried 2017).

Smaller news outlets can also have a presence and keep readers interested on Facebook where it is free to establish a page and it's easy to upload your content, including photos, videos and text. Even relatively small and relatively under-resourced publishers can afford to have a presence on Facebook. Put another way: small outlets cannot afford not to be on Facebook.

Even a small-town newspaper like the *Star Tribune*, published in Casper, Wyoming, is on Facebook (and Twitter). Casper is the second largest city in Wyoming, with a population of around 60,000; it is a regional commercial hub for the region and hosts a community college. One notable former resident is Dick Cheney, the US Vice-President under George W. Bush. NBC correspondent, Pete Williams began his media career on a local network affiliate, KTWO, in Casper during the mid-1970s (Wikipedia 2017). The *Star Tribune* is the only daily and is supplemented by a weekly, the *Journal*, published by the same company, Lee Enterprises. According to its Wikipedia entry the *Star Tribune* has a daily circulation of around 22,000. The legendary investor, Warren Buffett has invested in Lee Enterprises, which publishes more than 50 titles in 23 US states. Lee is not a giant in media terms and is barely breaking even, but according to accounts published for the last quarter of 2016 it is trading profitably (Lee Enterprises 2016). As we discussed earlier, it is imperative that publishers like Lee Enterprises invest some scarce funds in a social media presence to have any chance at all of survival beyond the next decade.

News publishers were disappointed to hear of this change which some analysts predict will impact their ability to monetize content through Facebook (Romano 2018). While news publishers were keen to use Facebook to cross-promote their other platforms and to monetize content, individual journalists are also finding it useful. Facebook is about personal exposure, so having a professional presence on the site makes sense for reporters. Not only is it a good place to post your own work— whether employed, freelance or doing journalism socially—it is also a good place to find contacts, develop sources and find new story ideas. It is useful for crowdsourcing and also a good place to monitor organizations and individuals who are important to any "round" or "beat" you might be interested in. Facebook itself is committed to helping journalists; of course, there's a self-interest aspect to this—the company wants to embed Facebook in every aspect of our lives—but some of Facebook's tools are useful. You can find advice and resources via "search" on Facebook, or by going to the Facebook Journalism Project pages. You can also apply to join the closed Facebook group News, Media and Publishing on Facebook. However, Facebook suddenly changed the rules in January 2018, announcing that it would reduce the amount of branded information and commercial news it allowed into personal feeds in order to increase "personal" interaction between users (Zuckerberg 2018).

Perhaps, given the scandals surrounding Facebook—the "fake news" issue and its troubled relationship with data-mining firm Cambridge Analytica—we need to be a bit more cautious about Facebook. It may take some time for the full implications of this episode to reveal themselves, but when it first broke there was some discussion about Facebook losing its shine and appeal to users. One thing was clear at the end of March 2018, there was a growing public awareness of how Facebook was exploiting users' data and also a developing backlash (Martin 2018). Perhaps Facebook is a "too big to fail" company, but the same thing was said about Enron a decade ago.

FIGURE 10.5 Facebook Wants to Engage with Reporters at All Levels.

Facebook Tips for Reporters

- Create your own page, separate from your personal profile. Make sure that it has an easy to remember name, that you have turned on the "followers" function and that, once established you update it regularly. This can be a bit of work, particularly if you enable "comments." Make sure you have time to moderate comments before you switch it on.
- Use Facebook to monitor people in the news; follow the newsmakers. These days public figures, politicians and celebrities often use Facebook and social media channels to announce things first. Simply waiting for a press release means you might be late to the story.
- Make your page a news hub for your followers. You can do this by embedding relevant Facebook content—which is a form of curating for your audience—and by sharing breaking news.
- Engage with followers and ask them what stories they'd like you to cover. Also regularly seek news tips from your followers via periodic calls to action, questions and requests for help.
- Make sure you behave responsibly. Don't just post gossip and rumors. Treat your followers with respect, even if they disagree with you.
- Let people see you working. Take your followers "behind the scenes," share images, video and anecdotes about your day on the job—but judiciously, don't be a bore!

SnapChat

Believe it or not, SnapChat is a platform with a news application. Even a staid old print dinosaur like the *New York Times* is finding ways to promote its journalism on Snapchat. According to the paper's social editor, Talya Minsberg (2015), the best Snapchat stories are the ones that "tell a narrative in a personal, visual way that pulls in and keeps the viewer." SnapChat is ephemeral, the app is not designed for long-term storage of content, but it can lead you to new, as yet undiscovered audiences, if you're able to strike the right chord, which is to be playful, and not take yourself too seriously.

In fact, a huge number of youth and lifestyle-focused news organizations have a presence in the SnapChat news channel, which is very popular among the apps younger demographic users (Manjoo 2016). While it is mainly for image-sharing and videos of up to 10 seconds, SnapChat has now embedded what it calls a "Story" function that allows users to put a series of pictures or videos together in one stream. Most user-generated SnapChat content disappears soon after it is uploaded, which is seen as a great privacy feature by some, but content uploaded to the Story area is live for 24 hours. A "Memories" function added in 2016 allows users to store their "snaps" onto phones or other devices for later viewing. In a similar way to other social media apps and platforms with a

"Friends" capability, SnapChat allows users to connect with each other, but its public channel has led to commercial organizations colonizing it for advertising and branding purposes. It is popular with celebrities who like to share more intimate moments with their followers and it's estimated that nearly 10,000 "snaps" are uploaded every second. If this is accurate than it equates to 759,974,400 snaps per day. This is way too much information; but if it is recorded and stored somewhere it also represents an incredibly detailed and intrusive database of our daily lives.

SnapChat is a useful tool for covering live events—a bit like Twitter's Periscope app—and you can toggle between front and rear phone cameras to do a "piece-to-camera" sequence. This works better with a microphone plugged into the camera (which is true for most apps). If you're adding captions to video, make sure it stays on the screen long enough to be read by altering the default time. As with many apps, SnapChat updates periodically and adds new features. If you want to produce regularly for this channel, practice with the most up-to-date version of the app, follow guidelines for writing captions (see next chapter) and develop a chatty, fun style suitable to the app and the genre of stories that tend to do well.

Tumblr

Tumblr is a microblogging and networking site that has been around for roughly a decade. In 2013 it was bought by Yahoo founder David Karp. One of the key features and early attractions of Tumblr was the "Notes" function which allowed users to repost others' content with their own comments. However, under the Yahoo umbrella Tumblr has not been doing so well and its popularity seems to be waning in proportion to the growing popularity of apps like SnapChat (Fiegerman 2016), perhaps this is because the early shine of Tumblr as a platform for dorky teenagers and lame jokes has worn off (Reeve 2016). Despite a possible slump in popularity, there are over 300 million microblogs on Tumblr and around 80 million new posts a day; many of them are images, short videos and gifs made for and by the site's young 16–24 demographic (Beese 2016). A few news organizations are on Tumblr, but it is mainly a site colonized by brands looking for exposure to its 20 million users. Advertisers like it because Tumblr users spend quite a lot of time on the site and they apparently don't mind looking at branded or sponsored content (Smith 2013).

Tips for Tumblr

For sites like Tumblr where the audience is in a younger demographic the tone of content must resonate with their humor, likes and dislikes if it is to gain any traction. Here are a few things to consider when crafting your content strategy for Tumblr.

- Be topical; understand what, who and why things trend on Tumblr. Don't jump on anything but try to be involved with current themes or moods.
- Try to have fun with your content. Think visually and be creative. Tumblr can be a channel for serious news and news-like information; but it's really more about lifestyle, fashion, celebrity and popular culture. Experiment with different types of media, such as images, videos, block text, GIFs and audio.
- Use tags to help people find your content and those who aren't interested steer clear. Like it is with most social media apps, the metadata is important on Tumblr.
- Find a niche and don't go too off-message. Know what your Tumblr audience wants; it may surprise you.
- Don't only rely on humor. Humor works really well on Tumblr, but you don't have to be funny all the time to use it successfully.
- Short quotes work well on Tumblr, you can use them to summarize a story posted elsewhere to drive traffic.
- Interact with your audience by reposting their content and replying to comments. Tumblr can also be a channel for crowdsourcing information on stories you are covering.

Instagram

Instagram is another photo and short video sharing application that allows you to instantly post to your other social media accounts from within the app. This is a useful feature for reporters in the field who want to upload a quick update to their followers about news "as it happens." Like many other social media apps, Instagram now has a "live" video function. and a "Story" function which allows users to shoot and upload short videos that stay "live" on the app for 24 hours; it has also incorporated a "direct" function which allows for photos and short videos to be sent privately to your individual followers.

2016 was a busy year for the developers at Instagram. A host of new features were introduced during the year, including a "zoom" feature for closer viewing of images; a save function to use while editing images; new tools for use with stories; and disappearing stories (Hand Orellana 2016). Instagram also introduced live video in 2017, which allows the app to compete with Periscope (see below).

Instagram is one of the social media platforms dominated by celebrities, which might limit the cut-through of your news-like content. In 2016 the top 10 Instagrammers were all famous Hollywood, sporting or entertainment figures. Selena Gomez topped the list with 103 million followers (Bishop 2016). It's not a surprise then that Gomez also posted eight of the top 10 "liked" posts of 2016, the others were "selfies" by Portuguese soccer star Cristiano Ronaldo (Knox 2016). When the 11-year-old son of English soccer star David Beckham joined Instagram, he gained 30,000 followers in the first hour (MailOnline 2016). When I looked, within a few hours of the news breaking, Cruz Beckham had over 84,000 followers. By October 2017, Cruz Beckham's Instagram follower count had skyrocketed to 885,000, even though he had only posted just over 140 times. It just proves that celebrity is its own currency and having a famous name is more lucrative than keeping your fans satisfied with a torrent of content.

Instagram is a great channel for photojournalists who can write captivating short captions to accompany their shots. According to photojournalist Sonia Narang (2017) it is also a good way of preparing yourself to go into the field. Mainstream news organizations are using Instagram to highlight the work of readers, but also to point to longer-form content and photo-essays and to showcase their own photographers (Hawkins-Gaar 2015). Social journalists can use it in similar ways. In addition, Instagram can be effective for taking audiences behind the news and adding an appealing element to stories being told on other platforms.

As a stand-alone tool, Instagram works well in visual story-telling and is used extensively by travel writers and correspondents on assignment; but it will work just as well if you're telling a local story that lends itself to a visual narrative. At the moment the Stories function is quite new, so experimentation is ongoing as users find the most creative ways to apply it to their journalism.

Pinterest

Pinterest is a visual notice board that can be catalogued and themed; it is a useful site for infographics, as well as photography. Users create their own boards and "pin" items to it; pinned items can also contain links to off-Pinterest content. Pinterest describes itself as a "visual bookmarking tool" and a home for "creative ideas" (Pinterest 2017). I use Pinterest for my art practice—to store images I like and to catalogue my own paintings and drawings. You can create content for your notice board by installing the Pinterest extension to your web browser and using it to pin any content you're interested in. This provides a useful research and curating tool that publishes your pin board to other Pinterest users, but also allows you to go back into the board and refine the content or use it somewhere else. Users can also add their own comments to your pinned content. By following other users, you can use Pinterest as a means of keeping in touch with topics you want to cover yourself. You can also follow particular topic boards, as well as individuals.

News organizations and journalists are using Pinterest as both a research tool to look for stories and sources, and as a "teaser" site to host strong images from stories they are currently covering. Creating a board for a particular story really only works if it is ongoing and can be added to regularly. This is why multiple boards are a good idea—create one for your "branded" content and others for specific themes that you might come back to regularly. If you do this, then your followers (or anyone searching Pinterest) can find your work on a particular subject in a curated feed. A Pinterest story board can also be a useful add-on feature for material published on other channels; it can be a "behind-the-scenes" type board, or link to other coverage, or even provide additional material that is complementary, but didn't make it into the published item.

Twitter

Since it was established in 2006 Twitter has grown into the most talked-about and public, if not the most popular, social media network, platform and app. It certainly seems to have many of the world's leading journalists and news organizations hooked, along with its share of celebrities and the infamous. However, there is still a debate about how Twitter fits into journalistic practice: Is Twitter a source of breaking news or does it merely amplify news sourced from more conventional outlets? Now that Twitter has been around for a fraction over 10 years we can say that it covers both functions. Journalists will often put their breaking news on Twitter first, to build audiences for the story; but a common use is the sharing of tweets with links to stories published on other platforms. In short, Twitter is an "information fire hose" (Hacker and Seshagiri 2014) that can overwhelm you if not self-regulated. This has both advantages and disadvantages.

The biggest plus is that your Twitter feed is updated in real time, which means you will rarely miss anything if you're paying attention. The biggest drawback is that sometimes the sheer volume of tweets is hard to manage just from the Twitter app itself. However, the torrent from the twitter "fire hose" becomes manageable if it is directed through the app's own tools, such as lists, or via a third-party interface such as Hootsuite, or Tweetdeck. I recommend you adopt and use one of these interfaces—Tweetdeck is now owned by Twitter and it's free—to manage your Twitter feeds. Not only are they useful for allowing you to follow multiple conversations using hashtags, or lists for example, if you need to operate multiple accounts it is essential. They are simple to use and plenty of web resources are available to help you set up and get started.

When used properly by reporters, Twitter is a great resource; it allows you to organize a news feed that keeps you on top of the news agenda and, at the backend of journalism it is a useful tool for finding story ideas you can chase, and sources to follow-up. Twitter connects journalists to an audience, but it is a two-way street, not just a stream that flows one way. To be successful on Twitter takes time; time to find a voice, time to build a profile that people want to follow and time to learn some of the basic rules and etiquette for social interaction that doesn't get you muted, blocked, or banned entirely for poor behavior.

The Twitter platform and mobile apps (for phones and tablets) also have other practical features that are very useful for social journalists. The first is Twitter Moments which as well as providing a convenient window into what's making the news, allows users to create their own stories based on collected tweets and additional editorial copy. The second useful addition to Twitter is a live feed option for broadcasting to your followers from breaking news events.

Creating content with Moments is relatively straightforward. The toolbar is accessed from your profile page. Once you open a new Moment screen you can customize it—change colors, add a cover image, write a title and description and then collate tweets from various feeds or other users. Once you have tweets in the Moment you can also re-order them into a narrative time line. One excellent feature of Moments is that you can start them at any time, save the drafts in your Moments folder and publish them when you're ready. This means you can follow an event or news story for a period of time and then publish a curated Moment that captures the trajectory of the story as it unfolds.

The Twitter Live broadcast function only works from mobile devices with a video-capable camera and it is easy to operate. Simply open a new tweet and press the "Live" icon.

You can add small amounts of text to give your video some context, and don't forget to allow Twitter to access your phone and camera. Once you go live, a menu is activated that allows you to draw or scribble words on the screen, which appear in the video, but only last a few seconds. You can see how many people are watching live and how many have viewed the finished broadcast while it remains in your timeline. Your followers can also join in by adding their own comments to the feed while it is live. At the end of the broadcast you can also save a copy of the video to your phone for later editing and publication on other platforms.

Twitter Moments and the Live function are valuable tools for both professionals and for social journalists. They increase the scope of what Twitter can do in a news environment. It is worth your while learning how to use them productively and creatively. Periscope is an excellent reporting tool for covering news conferences, events, meetings, protests and other sites of breaking news.

Paper.li

Paper.li is a publishing tool that works well when integrated with Twitter and other social media sources. Paper.li allows you to create and curate content derived from your Twitter lists, from Facebook, from RSS feeds and from web searches. I use a free version of Paper.li to publish daily and weekly digests of content related to topics I'm interested in. The free version is limited in terms of how many sources you can load into the inputs, but it publishes automatically and is a great way to keep yourself visible on Twitter even if you're not actively tweeting. Paper.li automatically inserts videos and URLs from the tweets of people on your lists and this creates an interesting curated mix of material. If you're serious about building a

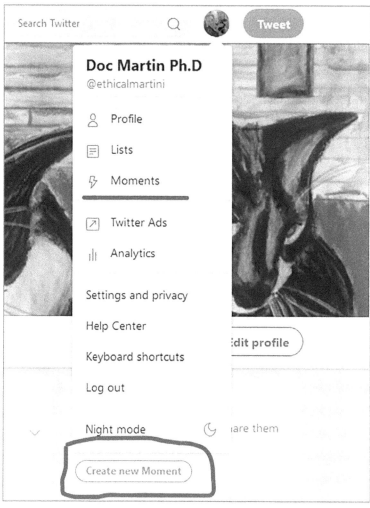

FIGURE 10.6 Go to Moments from this Dropdown Menu that Links from Your Profile Image.

social media presence in the social journalism space a paper.li account might be a worthwhile investment. On average an account costs around $100 per year and that comes with full editing capability, which you can also write editorials and customize the content even further.

The Importance of Analytics

Knowing who is in your audience, how big the audience is and what they do with your content has become an essential element of any news operation.

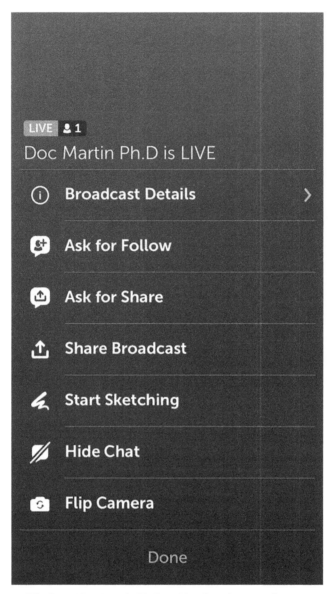

FIGURE 10.7 The Pop-Up Menu in Twitter Live Broadcast Feeds.

Measurement tools have changed, becoming more sophisticated and "granular" in the digital age, but the basic purpose of measuring the reach and impact of media offerings has not changed much since the broadcast era. The underlying reason that audience metrics are so important to publishers and broadcasters is a purely commercial one; knowing the size and composition of readerships, listeners, viewers and downloaders helps to set the market for advertising rates (Balnaves, O'Regan and Goldsmith 2011).

There are two basic types of measurement used for online audiences; one uses a sampling model where the browser use of a small group is monitored and the results extrapolated to simulate a bigger audience; the second measure is a report of traffic numbers based on logged visits to the site's servers. Different measures are used by the various commercial firms who compile and distribute audience metrics to the marketplace, which can lead to inconsistencies in measurements for a particular site, depending on methodologies.

The metrics used in digital media are a reflection of historical precedent; newspapers wanted to measure circulation; television stations the number of viewers at any one time and radio stations had a similar interest in knowing how many listeners they had. In the online environment, this has translated to pageviews and unique visitors (that is individuals identified by their unique IP address). These values are a measure of traffic—that is how many people visited a particular site in any given time period. This is then translated into a price mechanism used to determine the cost of advertising on that site. Often this mechanism is a measure of cost per thousand views, or "CPM." CPM is used to price display advertising, but "cost per click" or "CPC" is used on some search engine platforms and is based not on page views or visitors, but on how many people actually click on the advertisement, which usually takes them to the advertiser's website where a transaction may actually occur (Merritt 2017a).

However, as we've seen in previous chapters, the commercial link between audience metrics and advertising revenues has not been working to the advantage of digital publishers. Advertising rates have tended to favor the buyers of digital space, rather than the sellers. As discussed in Chapter 5, digital advertising has not, so far, been a reliable and sustainable source of revenue sufficient to keep news operations afloat and solvent. The debate around these issues has led to the development of a new set of metrics, which attempt to provide a deeper analysis of online readership. So-called "attention metrics" aim to measure how engaged a reader or viewer is with online content by capturing how much time they spend on a particular site, or content element, rather than just noting that they clicked on the link. However, as one leading researcher in the field has reported, online news publishers are reluctant to use attention measures because of technical challenges, and what he calls "industry inertia" to change. Despite this limitation, Brent Merritt says he remains optimistic that attention metrics, if applied to news sites, could help publishers "build a more sustainable business model" (Merritt 2017b: 20).

Whether you are interested in curating tools, such as Twitter lists or paper.li, or in creating your own original content, being able to intelligently manage your social media accounts is a necessary first step. Learning how to best utilize the features of each application is the key to success. Each of them has strengths and weaknesses and most also have a particular audience or demographic focus that you also need to understand. However, the technology is only half of the social journalism story; the second and equally important aspect is the content itself. Crafting the right content begins with knowing your audience and purpose and it must also include carefully written copy.

References

Anderson, Monica, and Andrea Caumont. 2014. "How Social Media is Reshaping News." Pew Center. September 24. Accessed July 14, 2016. www.pewresearch.org/fact-tank/2014/09/24/how-social-media-is-reshaping-news/.

Balnaves, Mark, Tom O'Regan and Ben Goldsmith. 2011. *Rating the Audience: The Business of Media.* New York: Bloomsbury Academic.

Barron, Rachel, and Lexa Lardiera. 2015. "Newspapers Hunt for New Readers on Instagram." *American Journalism Review.* April 7. Accessed January 5, 2017. http://ajr.org/2015/04/07/newspapers-hunt-for-new-readers-on-instagram/.

Beese, Jennifer. 2016. "Do People Still Use Tumblr for Business?" *Sprout Social.* January 5. Accessed December 7, 2016. http://sproutsocial.com/insights/tumblr-for-business/.

Bell, Emily. 2016. "Facebook is Eating the World." *Columbia Journalism Review.* March 7. Accessed July 14, 2016. www.cjr.org/analysis/facebook_and_media.php.

Bishop, Jordan. 2016. "These Are The 10 Most Followed People On Instagram." Forbes. December 4. Accessed December 6, 2016. www.forbes.com/sites/bishopjordan/2016/12/04/most-followed-instagram/#243ce99f3084.

Callaghan, Ruth. 2016. "Curation Challenges and Opportunities: Storify as a Participatory Reporting Tool in a Journalism School Newsroom." *Pacific Journalism Review* 22(1): 214–230.

CEWE Photoworld. Undated. "How Big is SnapChat?" Accessed December 5, 2016. https://cewe-photoworld.com/how-big-is-snapchat/.

Durris, Sue. 2014. "Are You a News Aggregator or a Content Curator?" M4 Communications. June 16. Accessed March 10, 2017. www.m4comm.com/news-aggregator-content-curator-2/.

Fiegerman, Seth. 2016. "How Yahoo Derailed Tumblr." *Mashable.* June 15. Accessed December 5, 2016. http://mashable.com/2016/06/15/how-yahoo-derailed-tumblr/#Ga1Q_yI3mkq3.

Good, Robin. 2016. "The News Curation Workflow." *Medium.* August 20. Accessed March 18, 2017. https://medium.com/content-curation-official-guide/the-news-curation-workflow-16301bbb5d32.

Hacker, Scot, and Ashwin Seshagiri. 2014. "Tutorial: Twitter for Journalists." Advanced Media Insitute, University of California, Berkeley. Accessed March 11, 2016. https://multimedia.journalism.berkeley.edu/tutorials/twitter/.

Hand Orellana, Vanessa. 2016. "5 New Tricks for Instagram Addicts." Cnet. December. Accessed December 6, 2016. www.cnet.com/how-to/instagram-new-tricks-for-addicts-draft-live-video/.

Hausman, Angela. 2011. "What is Engagement in Social Media?" *Social Media Today.* July 20. Accessed August 1, 2017. www.socialmediatoday.com/content/what-engagement-social-media.

Hawkins-Gaar, Katy. 2015. "5 Ways Newsrooms Can Make the Most of Instagram." Poynter Institute. March 10. Accessed August 14, 2017. www.poynter.org/news/5-ways-newsrooms-can-make-most-instagram.

Hirst, Martin. 2008. "Postmodernism and the Bonaventure Hotel." *Ethical Martini.* September 10. Accessed December 3, 2016. https://ethicalmartini.wordpress.com/2008/09/10/postmodernism-and-the-bonaventure-hotel/.

Knox, Miranda. 2016. "Instagram's Top 10 Most Popular Posts of 2016 Revealed—and We Did NOT Expect this Shock Result." *OK!* December 5. Accessed December 6, 2016. www.ok.co.uk/celebrity-feature/955381/instagram-most-liked-posts-2016-selena-gomez-cristiano-ronaldo-shock-result-most-popular.

Lee Enterprises. 2016. "Lee Enterprises Reports Fourth Quarter Earnings." December 9. Accessed January 5, 2017. http://lee.net/financial/lee-enterprises-reports-fourth-quarter-earnings/article_03502ef6-bda5-11e6-a2cb-c7720e074f54.html.

MailOnline. 2016. "That Bodes Well for His Pop Career! Aspiring Singer Cruz Beckham, 11, Joins Instagram—and Gets 30,000 Followers in Just ONE Hour." *Daily Mail.* December 6. Accessed December 6, 2016. www.dailymail.co.uk/tvshowbiz/article-4002716/Cruz-Beckham-joins-Instagram-gets-30-000-followers-just-ONE-hour.html.

Manjoo, Farhad. 2016. "Reshaping the Landscape: Snapchat Not Just Popular—it's Increasingly Important Too." December 2. Accessed December 5, 2016. www.theage.com.au/technology/technology-news/reshaping-landscape-snapchat-not-just-popular–its-increasingly-important-too-20161201-gt1sre.html.

Martin, Michael. 2018. "Will Facebook's Cambridge Analytica Scandal Actually Cause Users To Delete The App?" NPR. March 21. Accessed March 26, 2018. www.npr.org/2018/03/21/595791340/will-facebooks-cambridge-analytica-scandal-actually-cause-users-to-delete-the-ap.

Merritt, Brent. 2017a. "A Brief History of Media Measurement." *Medium.* September 29. Accessed September 29, 2017. https://medium.com/@brentmerritt/a-brief-history-of-media-measurement-f1f28aa807ce.

Merritt, Brent. 2017b. "The Rise of Attention Metrics: Can a New Digital Currency Help Sustain Journalism?" School of Media and Public Affairs, George Washington University. Accessed July 30, 2017. https://smpa.gwu.edu/rise-attention-metrics-can-new-digital-currency-help-sustain-journalism.

Mezzofiore, Gianluca. 2017. "Twitter is Testing a 280-Character Expansion and Everyone is Making the Same Joke." *Mashable Australia.* 27 September. Accessed September 27, 2017. http://mashable.com/2017/09/27/twitter-280-character-everyone-makes-same-joke/#vmD0xNZGFkqo.

Minsberg, Talya. 2015. "Snapchat: A New Mobile Challenge for Storytelling." *The New York Times.* May 8. Accessed March 29, 2016. www.nytimes.com/times-insider/2015/05/18/snapchat-a-new-mobile-challenge-for-storytelling/?_r=0.

Narang, Sonia. 2017. "Why Instagram is this Journalist's Favorite Tool." *MediaShift.* June 21. Accessed August 14, 2017. http://mediashift.org/2017/06/instagram-journalists-favorite-tool/.

NYT. 2015. "The New York Times Launches on Instagram." *The New York Times.* September 3. Accessed January 5, 2017. http://investors.nytco.com/press/press-releases/press-release-details/2015/The-New-York-Times-Launches-on-Instagram/default.aspx.

Pinterest. 2017. "A Guide to Pinterest." Accessed September 30, 2017. https://help.pinterest.com/en/guide/all-about-pinterest.

Reeve, Elspeth. 2016. "The Secret Lives of Tumblr Teens." *New Republic.* February 17. Accessed December 5, 2016. https://newrepublic.com/article/129002/secret-lives-tumblr-teens.

Romano, Aja. 2018. "Facebook wants to show you more news from your friends—and less news from journalists." *Vox*. January 12. Accessed March 17, 2018. www.vox.com/2018/1/12/16882536/facebook-news-feed-changes.

Scott, Caroline. 2017. "How BBC News is Experimenting with Instagram Stories to Engage Younger Audiences." Journalism.co.uk. January 3. Accessed January 5, 2017. www.journalism.co.uk/news/bbc-news-experiments-with-instagram-stories-to-engage-younger-audiences-/s2/a697503/?utm_content=buffere989c&utm_medium=social&utm_source=twitter.com&utm_campaign=buffer.

Shearer, Elisa, and Jeffrey Gottfried. 2017. "News Use Across Social Media Platforms 2017." September 17. Accessed October 17, 2017. www.journalism.org/2017/09/07/news-use-across-social-media-platforms-2017/.

Smith, Cooper. 2013. "Tumblr Offers Advertisers A Major Advantage: Young Users, Who Spend Tons Of Time On The Site." *Business Insider Australia*. December 13. Accessed December 7, 2016. www.businessinsider.com.au/tumblr-and-social-media-demographics-2013-12?r=US&IR=T.

Somaiya, Ravi. 2014. "How Facebook Is Changing the Way Its Users Cons\ume Journalism." *The New York Times*. October 26. Accessed July 14, 2016. www.nytimes.com/2014/10/27/business/media/how-facebook-is-changing-the-way-its-users-consume-journalism.html.

Srinivasan, Balaji S. 2017. "How big is Twitter Moments?" *Medium*. October 12. Accessed October 17, 2017. https://medium.com/@balajis/how-big-is-twitter-moments-f3a81ee85f71.

Wikipedia. 2017. "Casper, Wyoming." Accessed January 5, 2017. https://en.wikipedia.org/wiki/Casper,_Wyoming.

York, Alex. 2017. "What Is Social Media Engagement & Why Should I Care?" *Sprout Social*. May 1. Accessed July 11, 2017. https://sproutsocial.com/insights/what-is-social-media-engagement/.

Zuckerberg, Mark. 2018. [Untitled post]. Facebook. January 11. Accessed March 17, 2018. www.facebook.com/zuck/posts/10104413015393571.

11

WRITING SOCIAL JOURNALISM

A Subjective Look at the Subject of News Writing

News writing is a big subject and it's also subjective. One person's version of a well-written news story will seem awkward, clunky and wrong to someone who's preference for syntax, vocabulary and style differ. News writing has also changed dramatically in the past two decades, perhaps more than it did in the previous 100 years. There are plenty of reasons for this, but perhaps no consensus on which ones are the most significant, or account for the majority of the changes. The only real certainty is that the need to adapt news writing to the demands of the Internet and, increasingly to short-form social media apps and platforms has been a major influence on news writing styles.

This chapter explains that writing journalistically for social media needs to follow the conventions of news . . . up to a point. That is, the material needs to meet some definition of news—new, interesting and relevant to the audience. However, the tone should not always or necessarily be that of the standard "inverted pyramid" news item. This chapter is about "versioning"—the ability to take one item of news-like information and make it appealing on several platforms or apps. I will also explain how to write photo captions—useful for Instagram, and for learning how to write to character limits. The chapter will also discuss how to blend news and opinion in a well-written blog post. The objective in the chapter is to encourage lively and innovative writing that is suitable to the genre and the platform; writing that is attractive to readers and generates "buzz," but that still has some authority and a newsy voice.

Today's online media speaks to mass audiences, but it does so in a more intimate manner; it is a conversation, not a lecture format. This interactivity places a special responsibility on news providers; journalists must aspire to "greater responsibility for accuracy and greater excellence in writing" according to one textbook on media writing (Hilliard 2011: 13). However, given our previous discussion of fake news and public distrust of news sources, it would seem that this wise advice has been ignored. If you are writing social journalism, you cannot afford to ignore it. According to Robert Hilliard, the writer is the "creator, the guide, the influencer" and must "not lose control" over the narrative.

Writing for social media purposes also requires the best qualities of good journalism; it needs to be attractive, to draw in the reader, to tell a story, to be succinct, have a good pace, to strike the right tone and to have a voice of some authority. This no longer means news has to be written in the very formal register of the past, but it cannot completely abandon a link with history, nor can it totally reject the key genetic codes of its DNA. News is about the new; it's about providing useful information that the public is interested in, it references the public interest and has to provide a certain level of satisfaction to readers—what some would call an "entertainment" factor. This is particularly true of writing in the digital age when attention spans seem to be shrinking and we need a fairly high level of entertainment and interest to sustain reading anything longer than a tweet. Writing in the digital age is all about gaining and holding the attention of someone who is probably tabbing through several screens at once (Leith 2017). If your content and your writing are not compelling—screaming "Look at me"—your potential readers are likely to scroll past you. Having said that, it is important not to completely dismiss the conventions of news writing; many of them are still relevant today.

The Best of News Writing

The modern news writing style that developed from the late nineteenth century and which dominated most of the twentieth was based on two key considerations by news company owners and their senior editors: the first was financial, the second ideological, but they are linked and held together by what I have described as the "duality" of the news commodity. In order to be attractive to advertisers, news had to drop the partisanship that characterized journalism up until the late nineteenth century (Stephens 2007: 250). In effect, journalism and the news industry had to adapt to the harsh reality that by the early years of the twentieth century, advertising was a powerful locus of cultural symbolism that had become central to personal identity in a commodity-driven consumer-oriented version of capitalism.

"Advertising is part of the establishment and reflection of a common symbolic culture," wrote communications scholar Michael Schudson in 1984, and it is even more appropriate today when so much of popular culture is drenched in advertising. Highly political and opinionated news appealed only to an agreeable audience, but advertisers wanted to reach a broader market. News company owners complied with this demand from their powerful Establishment friends and shifted the editorial direction of their mastheads towards a more neutral style. This resulted in two major stylistic changes; a shift towards a professional, industry-wide ideology of objectivity and a more truncated writing style that became known as the "inverted pyramid'. According to Mitchell Stephens, the result of these two movements was journalists expressing their commitment "not only to impartiality, but to reflecting the world as it is" (Stephens 2007: 253). While this is true enough, it disguises the problem that objectivity is itself an ideological position that legitimizes a system-friendly conservativism and the introduction of "subtler' biases which are "more difficult to discern," buried in a "forest of facts" (ibid.: 255). We have discussed the problem of objectivity in social journalism in a previous chapter, so I won't rehash those arguments here. I simply make the point that for a century, the News Establishment has adapted to what Michael Schudson (1984: 209) accurately describes as the semi-fictional world of "capitalist realism" as portrayed in advertising. In doing this, journalism has itself taken on the fictive notion of "objectivity" to disguise the ideological role it plays in normalizing capitalism. The "inverted pyramid" embodies this ideological function, though it is not explicit, rather an implied and unconscious bias. However, taken simply as a mechanical device for imparting information—and ignoring the ideological baggage for a moment—the inverted pyramid is a useful starting point for any type of journalistic writing.

The Inverted Pyramid

It is worth spending a few moments discussing the pros and cons of the inverted pyramid as it is the foundation of news writing and a useful model to build from when writing digitally. The "inverted pyramid" is what it sounds like, an upside-down triangle, standing on its point, rather than its base. Historians dispute the exact moment in time when this clumsy and unstable object became the preferred model for structuring a news story, but it was most likely sometime in the latter years of the nineteenth century. Like many conventions in modern journalism, the inverted pyramid style was adopted for ideological, technological and commercial reasons (Scanlan 2003). The invention of the telegraph to transmit Morse code electronically over vast distances was one catalyst for change. Once the American continent was crisscrossed with telegraph cable and undersea cable crossed the Atlantic, it became a fantastic means of speeding up communication; but it was expensive. For reporters and editors, the ability to send their material at great speed meant that the news cycle could be sped up; but it came at a cost. Long-winded pieces were prohibitively priced out of transmission by telegraph and so journalists had to invent a new way of getting their main news points across the wires at the cheapest cost. The transition from flowery prose to the terse hurried style of the inverted pyramid did not happen overnight. While the telegraph was certainly an impetus, the upside-down pyramid style was not fully developed until the first decades of the twentieth century when news production was fully mechanized and the telephone was replacing the telegraph as a preferred means of journalists communicating with their newsrooms over a long distance (Errico et al. 1997).

The inverted pyramid stood on its head the old style of reporting, which left the most important news till the end of the story, as a sort of grand finale. The purpose of the upside-down triangle is to get the most important new facts into the first paragraph, which has become known as the "summary lead" (or "lede" in some quarters). Facts are then assembled under this summary in descending order of importance to the story. This is obviously a judgment call by the reporter, but generally it seems to work. Quotes and background information are used to spice up the copy and are inserted into the pyramid structure as appropriate. This structure was useful in the newsroom and in the print shop as well. Newspapers were originally set in metal type, composed of individual letters and made up into wooden frames. Editors could chop from the bottom of a story knowing they would not lose the most important information and if the copy needed to be cut again during the compositing process, the printers could also cut from the bottom without the story losing all of its meaning (O'Mahony 2009).

The inverted pyramid is taken-for-granted today and is a staple of any young reporter's education, either in journalism school, or in the newsroom. It is efficient, and when used properly leads to bright, readable copy. That's why it is still useful today and should be the basis of most writing for digital publication, whether in a news item, a blog, an Instagram post, or even in a 280-character tweet. A well-written 25-word tweet should resemble a classic summary lead/ lede that could double as an introduction to a compelling news story.

Sometimes the inverted pyramid seems counter-intuitive—starting a story with the conclusion doesn't seem to make sense. But in journalistic writing it does. The "conclusion" to any story is often the most important piece of information, but in journalism we don't want to keep our readers in suspense—at least not most of the time—and we want to grab their attention with an "Oh my God" moment. It is a direct approach, but it is designed to hold readers and then provide the explanation they need. However, I need to impart a few words of warning here: don't overdo it. It is unfortunately common today to find opening summary lead paragraphs turned into multi-deck "clickbait" headlines and teasers with lines like "You won't believe what happens next," and so on. This is reverting to a less noble use of the inverted pyramid, to hide the marketing function of the copy under an overworked cliché (or six).

A good way to think of the inverted pyramid is the concept of "front loading" your copy so that the significant ideas and strong word images come early in the story. Not only does this become your attention-grabber, in a digital realm it actually helps search engines find your copy because the keywords are clearly identified in the opening lines. The inverted pyramid is a staple of news reporting, but it is also used in media releases, on websites and in virtually any writing situation where the objective is to quickly get across your main points. As much of the content we want to engage with migrates to mobile devices with smaller screens, the inverted pyramid style is undergoing something of a resurgence. "Mobile-friendly" writing must get the most important information—the reason to keep reading—in front of the viewer quickly and the inverted pyramid is perfect for this (Brech 2017).

This is my interpretation of the inverted pyramid, it follows the principles that have been well-established for over a century, but I add my own twists to it along the way. The two most important embellishments on my version of this classic news-writing model are the injunction to link your paragraphs together, rather than just pile them on top of each other; and the reminder that a news story is not just a compilation of facts in a list of descending importance. Link sentences, or even linking phrases are important to the overall readability of your copy. They should be subtle, unobtrusive but able to carry the narrative forward, and therefore carry the reader along too. Linking words and phrases are necessary to give structure and flow to any form of writing and they are particularly important in news writing, though they are often overlooked. In a news item links are used to show a relationship between ideas, events and people; they can be to demonstrate cause and effect and also to indicate a sequence or a passage of time. "and," "or" and "but" are common linking words that connect ideas; suggest an alternative and signal a conflict; if you can find the appropriate synonyms for these hard-working words your writing will be brighter and more effective. Link words are also used for emphasis or reinforcement of ideas; for making comparisons and for introducing a summation of the facts; their judicious use will make your writing flow and more interesting to read.

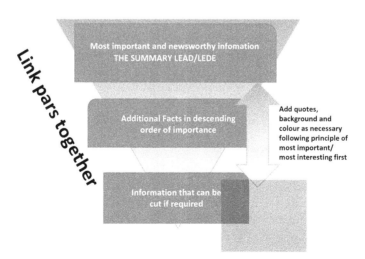

FIGURE 11.1 The Inverted Pyramid for News Presentation.

Quotes bring people into your story and add some light and shade; background is necessary to give the reader context for the new information you are presenting to them and color equals brightness and provides entertainment value. Quotes are generated from interviews, or even occasionally from documents. If you're going to do your own reporting then having some aptitude for interviewing your sources is important. In journalism textbooks it is often intimated that interviewing is a difficult skill to master and that it takes years of training and practice to become a great interviewer. There is some truth in this idea, but it is also overblown to some extent. The secret to a good interview is the ability to listen. Being able to pick up aural cues from your subject is vital, so too is doing some homework before the interview even starts. If you turn up to an interview unprepared it will not be very fruitful and could be an excruciating experience for both you and your talent. If you are prepared you will be confident; if you are confident you can put the subject at ease; if the subject is relaxed they will give you a good interview; if the interview is successful you will have all the quotes you need for a good story.

All of these additions to the inverted pyramid—background, quotes, strong links—are about keeping the audience engaged. You want them to read to the end of your piece; by being conscious of this and using the tools you have to write compelling copy they will oblige. Of course, writing web copy or a social media post is not the same as writing for an early twentieth-century newspaper where your copy is likely to be cut and cut again before your readers even see it. But, even without these technical reasons, adopting the inverted pyramid as the foundation of your journalistic writing is a good starting point.

Inverted Pyramid Checklist

- Before writing make sure you have checked the story and understand which pieces of information are the most important; rank them in descending order.
- Scour all of your material for the most newsworthy points and find a way to write them into your summary lead.
- A good summary lead, or introductory paragraph should be no more than about 40 words. Between 20 and 40 words is ideal.
- Are you clear on which quotes best illustrate your story? Rank them like you have the factual material.
- Have you determined a path through your story that will engage your audience and keep them interested until the end? You need this "roadmap" in order to correctly identify the linking phrases or sentences.
- Will the story flow chronologically or in some other order? This also helps determine the style of your linking phrases.
- What happens at the end? While the basic purpose of the inverted pyramid is to rank material from most important to least important. The end of the story is

almost as important as the lead. Do you want to end with a "conclusion," or a "teaser" for the next bit of the story? If the story is complete, make sure you have tied up all the loose ends. If not, a teaser is perhaps more important.

The inverted pyramid is perfect for news stories; it works well for the longer caption-style required for image platforms like Tumblr and Instagram and it suits the headline/teaser format of Twitter, but sometimes, particularly for blogs and web-based publications that we read through a browser application a different style is required. A more feature-based form works on the web where space considerations are not so important but having more space does not mean having a license to ramble, waffle or make every piece you write a 10,000-word essay. My approach to web writing, when going outside the inverted pyramid structure is appropriate, is based on my approach to feature writing, which I call the "DNA of documentary."

Writing for Web Publication: The "DNA of Documentary" Approach

If you're a digital native you don't really need to be reminded that the Internet is never switched off, nor that your potential audience can come from anywhere in the world and might not agree with you. But it is worth offering this reminder because we are talking about writing seriously for an audience beyond your Twitter followers or Instagram friends: "The writer needs to be aware that the whole multicultural, multi-opinion world is watching or listening" (Hilliard 2011: 13).

If you want to reach a broader group than just those in your immediate circle your writing has to be up to the task. It needs to be worthy of attention, it must generate an impulse in the reader to click on your content and it should be memorable (Leith 2017). The inverted pyramid is a solid foundation, but for engaging longer pieces it is not robust enough. Longer stories need a more complex structure and should offer readers a variety of pathways in and through the story; there can be surprises, cul-de-sacs and mystery. Not everything needs to be revealed in a summary lead when composing a long-form piece of journalism. However, like all good journalism, the writing of a good feature starts with good ideas, strong story lines, extensive research and the right talent. A feature story is often the story behind the headlines and reveals connections that a simple news story would gloss over; it might also be more "psychological" in the ways it reveals emotions and the motivations of the main protagonists. The protagonists become "characters" and a feature should take us into their lives more than a news story can. Before you start writing you need to find the "whole story" and the individual "scenes" from which it is composed. At that point you need to understand how the story develops and consider the best way it can be told. One advice site I like talks about the "seduction" of the reader in the opening of a good feature, the "tension" in the story that keeps them reading, and the "pay-off" being the high point of the story and the point at which the reader's continued interest is rewarded (Writer's Digest 2014).

The "Ninety Percent Rule"

To write well takes practice, but good writing skills can be learned and developed; nobody is a "natural" writer and everyone can become a good writer if they put some effort into it. When I'm teaching writing, I tell students about the "ninety percent rule"; I've never seen it written down anywhere, but it goes something like this: 90 percent of the effort in writing takes place before you lift a pen or hover your fingers over the keyboard. The composing, revision, editing and compiling is hard, but it is only about ten percent of the total effort required to write well. Of course, your first effort will not be your best, but if you follow a few simple steps, the second, third and subsequent attempts will be better. It's no surprise that good writing starts with knowing two simple things—why you are writing, and who you're writing for. I am often drawn to this quote from George Orwell when thinking about a writer's motivations:

> I write it because there is some lie that I want to expose, some fact to which I want to draw attention, and my initial concern is to get a hearing. But I could not do the work of writing a book, or even a long magazine article, if it were not also an aesthetic experience.
>
> *(Orwell 1946)*

There are, or course, other motivations, but "to get a hearing," is a good starting point. If you have a clear purpose and you have an idea about who and where your audience is, then you can begin the process of gathering the information, seeking out the interviews (if you need them) and plotting the structure of your proposed piece. The purpose of your writing is linked to the audience and is embodied in one important question: "Why should your readers care about the topic and/or the characters in your story?" There must be some sort of emotional connection between the topic and the reader—not sympathy necessarily, anger is just as useful to connect readers and stories. If you can find that emotional connection you can build on it by anticipating what questions your topic might invoke in your readers and use them to proactively probe the topic. To summarize, there must be a period of "thinking" before the writing starts. If the story and the outcomes are not clear in your own mind, you will not be able to translate it into words on the screen or page.

The DNA of Documentary – an Easy-to-Manage Template

Thinking about the "DNA" of your feature story or blog post is a good place to start. The DNA starts with having a purpose, an idea of the audience and the outline of some good research. Without that you won't succeed.

The DNA of documentary provides a good, easy-to-manage, template for feature writing for magazines and newspapers, for scripting videos or podcasts, and also for writing longer-form pieces digitally published on the web. The structure of DNA is a double helix, like a pair of wires loosely twisted together. It is also ladder-like, the two strands make up a sugar phosphate backbone joined by the "steps," the nucleotide base pairs. Together, the backbone and the base pairs make up a molecule of DNA and these molecules are the building blocks of biological life. It is the various combinations of DNA "strands" that determine the diversity of life, everything from human eye color, to the shape of leaves. I have been applying this analogy to feature writing and documentary structures for the past 15 years. I have found it useful when explaining to students the countless ways a feature story can be written or a broadcast documentary structured to be both informative and entertaining.

In biology, the base pairs of DNA are adenine and thymine (A+T), and guanine and cytosine (G+C). They are bonded to the sugar phosphate back-bone by hydrogen and carbon atoms. In a strand of DNA the base pairs always line up as A+T and G+C, but in the double helix of a documentary or feature we have more flexibility. The four elements of the base pairs in our model are able to bond with each of the other elements as we need them too in order to fit the logic of the sequence we're building. The elements of our double helix are *source/quote, data/facts, event/episode, description/color, observation* and *anecdote*.

Data and facts are self-explanatory; they are the nuggets of information you have gathered and verified during your research phase. The events and episodes are the markers of chronology and action that form the sequences that make up the timeline and the action "arc" of the story. Events are singular markers of a particular moment in time; episodes are multiple occurrences of the same or similar events. Sources and quotes are evidentiary and supportive statements. Sources can be documents or people and they can be referenced directly as quotes, or indirectly within the written copy; they can also be rendered in summary as a paraphrasing of the original. Quotes are used to provide perspectives, opinions, contrast or conflict, and elements of description. Description and color add both vibrancy, life and background to your story. Often description and color rely on what Tom Wolfe, the pioneer of the "new journalism" movement of the 1960s, called "status details." These are the little things that you notice about the places, people and events you are describing that can bring them to life for the reader. Observation and anecdote are also ways of bringing color, detail and life into your writing. An observation is your own take on something that you have seen, either in the field or during your research. It is an insight into the story that you have assembled from your own work. An anecdote provides a similar insight, but it is more personal to your sources. It is a story told about, or by, the characters in your article that sheds light on their motivations, drives and feelings. Tom Wolfe's important breakthrough in the mid-1960s was the realization that you could write a feature story—journalism—using "any literary device, from the traditional dialogisms of the essay to stream-of-consciousness, and to use many different kinds simultaneously, or within a relatively short space ... to excite the reader both intellectually and emotionally" (Wolfe 1972). Intellectual and emotional excitement are both crucial to a good piece of long-form journalism whatever media it is assembled in.

When you have absorbed this rule breaking rule, and given it some thought, it is very liberating and it works beautifully in the context of a blog or longer-form piece of online writing. However, the DNA formula does impose some structure; feature writing is not a free-for-all. The discipline comes in the form of the sugar phosphate strands forming the DNA "backbone," which in our model I have called narrative spines. Their purpose is to hold together the base pairs and to provide a way of navigating the story from beginning to end. Narrative spines—because a good feature will have more than one "backbone"—can be used in combination and with clever in-story editing they are interchangeable. The most compelling and obvious narrative spine is a *timeline*. Telling a story chronologically is the simplest form of timeline. Like a fairy tale begins "Once upon a time," and ends "happily ever after," a long-form story can start at the beginning of its timeline and finish at the end. However, this has a tendency to dullness and it is not how most news and feature stories are structured. A feature timeline should be capable of jumping forwards and backwards to build and sustain interest. This is why I advocate for more than one spine being used. Coupling a non-chronological timeline with any of the other suggested "backbone" elements helps keep the story on track and provides both opportunities for shifting through time and it also, in a way, disguises this technique from readers. *people* is reasonably obvious, it is about the characters in your story. People are important and provide human interest as well as the all-important dialogue you can insert via quotes. *relationships* and *themes* are similar spines in a way. Thematic spines work for conceptual pieces and relationships work in either complementary or adversarial settings. Both work well alongside either timelines or people as the supporting structure for your story "ladder" as shown in the diagram below.

I recommend choosing a pair of spine elements before you start writing and mapping them out on paper or screen to form a rough plan with sub-headings. You need a map for your journey, even if the destination is a free-form piece of writing that appears to be spontaneous. It might seem like a contradiction, but a lot of thought goes into spontaneity. Bear in mind, too, that while this longer-form approach is suitable for blogs or online features, it is not appropriate for all platforms and social media channels.

Feature and Blog Writing Checklist

- Do your homework. Be across the topic before you start.
- Have a roadmap. Know where you're going and the route you want to take before you set out.
- Plan your route markers in the form of sub-headings. Use them in the text where appropriate.

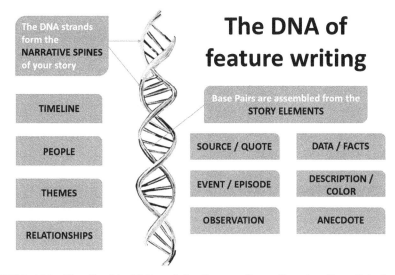

FIGURE 11.2 The Double Helix of the Feature Story Showing Base Pair Story Elements and Narrative Spine Backbones.

- Make sure you are well supplied before you leave. Do you have enough data, events, quotes and descriptive notes to sustain a long journey?
- How are you going to support yourself? Choose your narrative spines carefully. You will need at least two for any piece of writing longer than about 600 words. If you plan to blend or swap as you go, make sure the seams are well constructed and all visible joints smooth.
- Are you writing in the right voice, tone and register for the publication and for your intended audience? Tone, register and voice must also be appropriate to the topic. Don't make jokes if you want your readers to feel sad; don't be morbid if you're writing a humorous piece. Don't be offensive if you're writing for a conservative audience; don't be deliberately shocking or provocative if you can't handle the blowback.

Broadcast Writing and Podcasts

Writing a news script for broadcast does not always, or necessarily follow the inverted pyramid formula, though it should have a summary lead, or lead paragraph that provides the main news point of the piece. If the short news item is introduced by a presenter, which is the usual radio and television format, then sometimes the summary lead will be incorporated into that part of the script, and the voiced piece by the reporter can launch in from a logical point in the narrative. Television writing is complicated by the need to "write to the pictures," in a similar way to caption writing (see below in this chapter).

The idea behind writing to the pictures is that you don't simply describe what the viewer can see, you add context, color and detail through the voice-over. The key ingredients of good news script writing are to use active voice and present tense as your defaults—this means describing action moving forward in the here and now. You should also be using clear, direct plain English because your audience really only gets one chance to hear your delivery. Short, conversational sentences that do not get overly complicated with too many ideas are also preferred. You cannot afford to burden a sentence with too many details, but attribution is important. It is normal in print to put attribution at the end of a sentence, but in a broadcast script attribution will most often precede the quote.

This is particularly important if you are inserting a "grab"—short audio insert—of an interviewee, or live action into the story. You should tell the listener or viewer first so that they are prepared and not confused by the sudden change in voice. In videos you can use a title superimposed over the speaker to help the viewer keep up, but on the radio, or in a podcast, your voice has to do all the work. Also, for an audio-cast the listener has to work harder too, so you need to be clear, concise and accurate in your choice of language. If you can, it is a good idea to bookend a long audio grab with a "back announce" in which you repeat the name and title of the speaker. Generally, radio news stories will be very short, only 40 seconds or so, maybe one minute if you're lucky, so every word has to count. If you calculate that the average conversational speaking rate is between 110 and 150 words per minute, you can easily see that a 40 second news story won't contain very many words.

Longer broadcast items, television current affairs, or documentaries of even a few minutes in length, require a different approach to scripting, if you go back over the DNA of documentary (above), that will give you a good starting point for broadcast documentary scriptwriting and writing for podcasts. In a longer piece the aim is to build some dramatic tension that holds the listener/viewer's attention and the elements that make up the base pairs of the double helix are of a different order than those used in feature and blog writing.

The DNA of a Good Podcast

A podcast is usually an audio documentary made specifically for digital download; the most popular podcasts are usually serialized, or produced in segments, like a regular broadcast program. They are designed to be downloaded, usually by an RSS feed, or via iTunes, so you don't miss an episode, and they can be listened to according to your schedule, not the producers'. Podcasts have been around for a little over a decade and they have become a standard feature of many online news sites. However, the format is not limited to news and current affairs; many popular podcasts are comedy, drama and even soap opera formats. The additional advantage that podcasts—like broadcasting—have over written features is that a variety of voices can be used. Your interviews suddenly come alive for the audience and little vocal "tells" can add to the emotional intensity of the story too. In the now crowded world of podcasts finding a vacant niche may be difficult, but having an original take on a popular topic can attract new listeners. According to 2017 data podcasts are growing in popularity, around 25 percent of Americans listen to a podcast each month and many of them are regular consumers of the medium (Quah 2017). Most experienced podcasters will tell you the secret to gaining a following is to relax and sound like you're having fun; in other words: be entertaining (Locker 2016). That's good advice, but like any kind of performance, in order to sound unrehearsed, unscripted and lively, hours of preparation, planning scripting and rehearsal all play a part.

The advantage that podcasts have over regular news items is that they can incorporate a far wider range of sound effects and music to add atmosphere. Some are unscripted and meant to be listened to as "live," they might be panel programs about sport, or political interviews, but it is the immediacy and rawness of the "live" experience that makes them work. On the other hand, serialized documentary-style podcasts are heavily produced and scripted using the double helix structure in some form or other.

The base pairs of a podcast (or radio documentary) are the audio elements that can be mixed together, along with the various narrative spines discussed in the section on feature writing. There's also an additional narrative spine for podcasts, the use of audio edits as transitional and linking devices. It is the addition of the audio elements that provides the additional creative twist for podcasts: your voice-over script is the obvious written element that provides the structure; within this structure, the other audio elements add color, light and shade, emphasis and variety in the same way that different types of paragraphs add variety to a written feature. If you're producing a video or longer-form television piece the formula is the same, with the addition of pictures. Visual elements follow the same logic as audio: A voice-over can be delivered as a scripted or unscripted piece-to-camera; actuality of an event or scene can be edited in alongside shots of your subjects speaking to you, or directly into the camera.

Podcast Checklist

- Use the most technically advanced equipment you can afford. If you have to record using your phone, do it in a very quiet location. If you can invest in a good microphone, get one.
- Preparation is the key. If you think you have a good idea, don't just rush out and record it. Work up a plan, do some research and listen to other podcasts on similar topics.
- Simplify the topic, particularly if it's complex, don't use too much jargon.
- Make sure your guests know what they're talking about and have something interesting/useful to say.

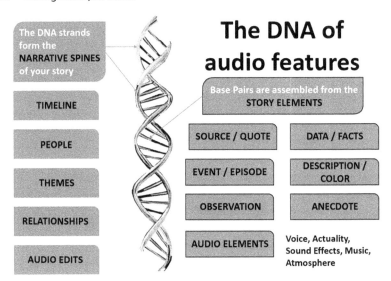

The DNA of audio features

The DNA strands form the NARRATIVE SPINES of your story

TIMELINE

PEOPLE

THEMES

RELATIONSHIPS

AUDIO EDITS

Base Pairs are assembled from the STORY ELEMENTS

SOURCE / QUOTE — DATA / FACTS

EVENT / EPISODE — DESCRIPTION / COLOR

OBSERVATION — ANECDOTE

AUDIO ELEMENTS — Voice, Actuality, Sound Effects, Music, Atmosphere

FIGURE 11.3 The DNA Structure of a Podcast or Broadcast Documentary.

- Learn how to use a free audio editing app—either on a PC, a tablet or your phone—and practice getting the edits right. Edit on the beginning and end of a breath, not hard against the sound of a word.
- Collect "atmosphere"—background sounds appropriate to your story; noises recorded on location, sound effects. Keep them in a library and label them clearly.
- Use a format/structure that has a clear "beginning" to introduce the topic and a clear "ending," a way of signing-off that wraps up the whole episode or topic.
- If you have to have a "gimmick," make sure it's a good one and at least a little bit original.
- Understand something about copyright—at least enough to keep you out of trouble—particularly around music and using other recorded material from secondary sources. "Fair use" might get you out of trouble, but it might not.
- Have a personality—your own or an invented one—there's nothing worse than being boring or talking in a monotone.
- Warm-up your voice before recording or broadcasting live.
- Write a script and be familiar with it, even if you don't use it word-for-word.
- Edit the script for style as well as content. Then edit again if it's pre-recorded.
- Don't give up after one episode. You should plan a sequence of 5–10 episodes before you start as it may take a while to hit your stride and build an audience.

If you get serious about podcasting, the experts recommend you take the time to build your own website to host them. From there you can repurpose content, use the interviews in other posts and even begin to make a small amount of money.

Writing in Social Media

In theory, good writing and good writers can move seamlessly between media, apps and platforms by applying the basic rules. The key is to remember that there are important differences and to adapt your style and voice accordingly. Many social media apps and platforms place some limits on the number of words or characters you can use to tell your story. Twitter's limit is 280 characters; WhatsApp and other short messaging services also impose technical limits on the length of status updates you can post. Even Facebook imposes a limit on status updates, but at just over 6000 characters, few of us would ever reach it. Whatever the length of the post or status update you intend to publish, there are some rules that are applicable to all social media channels. The most important is perhaps making your content findable and making it spreadable. On Twitter this means the appropriate use of relevant #hashtags, but without seeming to be needy or greedy (phishing for "likes" and "retweets"). On other platforms and apps it means the smart use of tags and metadata that make your content searchable.

Social Media Writing Guidelines

There are no absolute rules when it comes to writing social media posts, but there are guidelines that will help you gain an audience, keep your credibility and get your message across. A lot of "How to" guides for social media writing are focused on sales and marketing, so they are not much use if your aim is to write more journalistically. You can look online for a variety of tips specific to each platform, or app, but not many of them focus on news or social journalism. However, all is not lost. As this chapter has argued, falling back on the basics of news writing is a good foundation for writing news in a social media style. There are different priorities and styles depending on the platform or app you are writing for, and you will do well to explore each of them in some detail once you get started. In the meantime, here are some basic guidelines that can be applied generically to social media writing.

Simplify, but Stay on Point

While you might like to tackle complex topics in a longer blog post or Facebook update, a good general rule for social media is to keep it simple. This does not mean dumbing things down or always going for the low hanging fruit; it means being smart about your use of language. Write your complex ideas in plain English using the basic rules of persuasive and informative writing.

Simplification also about removing unnecessary jargon (while keeping necessary jargon to a minimum). It also means editing. The experts recommend editing each piece twice (Copp and Maheux 2017). I agree.

Longer Doesn't Mean Better

One of the beauties of social media is that, on some platforms, there is a limit to how many words or characters you can write. This is either blessing or a curse, depending on your purpose and your ability (or not) to be concise. One great place to practice your ability to write short, meaningful posts is on Twitter, even if you now have 280 characters to play with.

Use a shorter word or synonym. This is really "Plain English 101." You should always be trying to find the shorter, cleaner word in everything you write. The longer the word, the less space you have for other words. Instead of using "contained," try using "held"; and, where possible, use one word, rather than a whole phrase.

Don't be afraid of punctuation. Using full stops and commas might seem like a waste of precious characters, but they will add clarity to your tweets. Sometimes you can get away without most punctuation, but where you can, you should use it.

Always proof-read your tweet or post. This is advice that many of us, me included, have been known to ignore in our haste to punch out a pithy tweet. There are several reasons you should proofread, the most important one is perhaps the "autofill" function on phones and tablets. How often have you (and I) hit send only to find that a crucial word has been automatically "corrected" by the damn machine? Secondly, a mis-spelled word in a tweet undermines your credibility and it's sloppy. The third reason is to make sure that you have used the most effective and efficient words and syntax to get your point across.

The URL shortener is your friend. A good tweet often contains a link to something that you want your followers to read—the "recommendation" tweet. If the URL is too long it cramps your style. Find a good reliable URL shortener and bookmark it. I like to use TinyURL.com because it gives you the option of making a unique URL. Normally I choose a short word that relates to the content of my post.

It's Not All About You

Some people use social media to megaphone everything about themselves. If you're Donald Trump or from the extended Kardashian–Jenner clan this makes sense. For Trump because of his excessive narcissism, and for the Kardashian–Jenner clan because everything they do is about building their brand. If you're using social media to tell stories then a little bit of brand narcissism is OK, but your stories are about other people and events that you were not directly involved in. Give these other people, events and voices the room they deserve.

Remember you are writing for an audience, to build engagement and to tell a story. This means knowing something about your readers, listeners and viewers; or at least having a solid idea of who you want them to be. If you are inviting feedback from your audience, listen when they tell you something. If they're telling you that things need to change, don't dismiss it out of hand, review and revise your plan (Huntly 2017).

Create a Memorable Hook

A good way to create a hook for a social media post with a newsy angle is to use the "six honest serving men" of journalism—who, when, where, when, what, why and how. The English poet and writer Rudyard Kipling created a short verse, most likely for his daughter, Elsie, in which he set out the value of these questions:

> I keep six honest serving-men
> (They taught me all I knew);
> Their names are What and Why and When
> And How and Where and Who.
> I send them over land and sea,
> I send them east and west;
> But after they have worked for me,
> I give them all a rest.

This verse appears at the end of Kipling's short story "The Elephant's Child" and it had nothing to do with journalism when it was composed. However, it has been adopted as a mantra in many newsrooms and now the "5Ws and H" are the spine of any good news report (Wheal 2014).

Abstraction is Not Helpful

Your writing should be concrete—that is, it should get to the point and not meander around it. This is particularly relevant to writing titles, or more journalistically "headlines" for your posts. A good headline is effective when it draws in the reader, not just because it is a neat pun that made your friends laugh. A headline should also alert readers to the content, perhaps "tell them what to expect" (Jorgen 2013).

The most important piece of advice to remember about writing for social media is to be clear and concise (Sailer 2017). People should know exactly what you mean from just one reading of your copy. If your writing doesn't pass this simple test, you need to go back and do it again.

Choose the Right Voice

An important element of journalistic writing is knowing the difference between "active" and "passive" voice, how to recognize it in your writing and when to use them effectively. In most cases the active form is preferred because the action and movement occur through the sentence, in the direction of reading.

In a passive form of writing the subject of the sentence is acted upon by the object. If you think about it, this is a bit unnatural: "the tree was crashed into by the car." It is formally correct in a sense, and we know what it means, but when you say it out aloud it doesn't sound quite right. In normal conversations most people would say "the car crashed into the tree." Of course it did. The tree wasn't moving, the car was; so, it makes more grammatical sense to both speak that way and to write that way in active voice.

Make a Connection

Social media is about sharing and connecting. Your writing, particularly if it is more than a short tweet or caption, needs to connect with people and perhaps to even make them feel like sharing it amongst their connections. If you are linking to something else, either a longer piece that you have published, or a third-party article you think is worth sharing, make sure that the text you've written encourages people to click on the link by giving them a reason to. As one social media copywriting guru put it so well: "Don't yell at people" (Huntly 2017). Sometimes the temptation to yell is overwhelming, particularly if someone is already yelling at you. While it can be personally satisfying, that satisfaction is only momentary. Just remind yourself: If you were outside of the yelling match, how would you look at it? Most times you would answer, "Not pretty," and you'd be right.

#hashtags

Hashtags can help a tweet or Instagram post gain traction—to be noticed, liked and retweeted; but they have to be relevant, carefully chosen and not overdone. A tweet or post that has very little content and is crowded with hashtags might circulate widely, but it is more than likely going to be ignored. Hashtags are a way of marketing your stories, but that doesn't mean we can just copy the techniques of marketing. The simplest news-style hashtag is based around the topic of your story; but you might also include a prominent name—your source, or perhaps the subject of your piece. Always keep an eye on hashtags that are trending, but don't just hijack it to your tweet if the content is not relevant; this will just annoy people. If you are tweeting something that is part of a series then you might use a "campaign" style hashtag that gets attached to all the tweets mentioning the chosen topic or theme. You might also pick a topical hashtag that you know is used by people to define an interest group. For example, #auspol is about Australian politics and #USPolitics is popular among American Twitter users. It's probably best to avoid single word generic terms like #politics or #food because they are really too broad and diverse.

Search Engine Optimization

There is a whole industry and thousands of consultants devoted to making a living out of helping you to maximize your reach through search engine optimization (SEO). It is one of the dark arts and this is not the place to provide lengthy explanations. Suffice to say that getting the most of searchable content really does rely on the effective use of tags and other metadata. The gold standard advice is to make your titles, tags and other metadata unique, brief, and an accurate descriptions of what your content is about. If you're working alone it is probably a good idea to spend some time thinking about how your website is structured to maximize SEO opportunities; and certainly, read some of the excellent, free online guides. Most news organizations will have full-time staff whose job entails site-wide SEO management. Newsrooms should also spend some time workshopping SEO and its relationship to editorial direction. It is likely that over the next few years a lot of the work of SEO will be taken over by artificial intelligence. Content will be parsed and tagged automatically with the most appropriate terms: "When you factor in the potential breadth of these systems, including the obsolete cost of hiring actual writers, and the increased accuracy of keyword inclusion and optimization, the new industry of SEO and AI will be immensely powerful" (Agrawal 2017).

The downside is, of course, that once AI can index content efficiently, machines will then begin to replace writers (there's more on this in the final chapter).

Blogs

According to one statistical aggregation there are in excess of 151 million blog posts on Tumblr alone (Statista 2017). There are 37 million blogs hosted on the Wordpress.com platform and millions more on similar services. Worldometer, a web-based statistical aggregator, estimates that well over two million blog posts are written each day (Worldometer 2017). WordPress estimates that blog posts on its servers receive more than 400 million unique views per month and attract 44 million comments from readers (WordPress 2017). My take out from these numbers is that we cannot ignore blogs and blogging when it comes to thinking about social journalism. Despite the fact that many blogs get started and abandoned within a short space of time, blogging is now an accepted part of the social media world and blogs are useful for both professionals and amateurs working in the social journalism space.

Establishing a blog, or forming a relationship with an existing blog that covers topics you want to write about, is a good way of making a start in social journalism. You might not be able to monetize your content immediately, but exposure does build social capital in your personal brand.

Blogging Checklist

- Never be boring. whether it is a column or a blog. You need to have something to say that is worth saying and you have to write in a way that is appealing to your readers.
- Writing regularly is hard work. Practice, draft, revise, rewrite. Repeat.
- Start by writing about what you know, your passions and interests. Take on more complex topics when you have experience.
- Like a column, a blog must have a purpose. It is an opinion piece, but it has to be relevant to what your audience is talking about and interested in.
- Offer a fresh perspective. If you're commenting on news, don't just rehash accepted wisdom; find a point of difference and exploit it.
- If you're offering opinion make sure it is well researched (with links) and fact-based.
- Find a voice that is informative, amusing and entertaining. People will come back to you if they like your style.
- Engage the audience. Offer your readers some validation for their own views; or challenge their views by arguing a point they might not have considered.
- Read more than you write. Do your homework; assemble the facts and the arguments; use references and links.
- Using an image in your post will make it more attractive, but don't just stick something in to fill a hole. Make sure your photograph or graphic is relevant.
- Choice and sizing of the image can be important, particularly if the platform you're using has a "hero image" function that creates a graphic to insert into tweets or to position at the top of your post in a list.

Facebook

Facebook is very similar to a blog, but there is one important difference; the ongoing relationship with followers. A Facebook page is about building a community, where people gather regularly. A blog is more random and may attract people for a specific piece of content, but they don't necessarily come back. Facebook is a good channel for sharing breaking news, but it also acts as an effective archive that your followers can browse at leisure. Facebook also allows your followers to share more intimate or personal material, for example, "behind the scenes," or reflections on stories that you are working on. Facebook is very pro-active in wanting to assist journalists and news organization to maximize the benefit they get from establishing customized pages. You can visit the Facebook for Journalists pages to get advice and tips for establishing and maintaining an effective Facebook presence.

Writing for Facebook follows many of the conventions we've already talked about; most posts should be newsy (something new and previously unknown) and relatively short. The tone should be conversational and have an outward-facing quality of engagement.

Facebook Writing Tips

- Facebook is a voluntary community and negativity can be a turn-off. If your page is filled with complaints or whiny posts about your problems it is unlikely to be popular for very long. This doesn't mean you have to be fluffy and constantly upbeat, but make sure there is light and shade.
- Make sure you are clear on why you have a Facebook page, make this clear to your audience by writing an editorial-style "About" piece that makes the purpose and style of the page clear.
- It is useful to prompt your audience for a response by asking open-ended questions. Rather than asking "Did you like this post?," which invites only a "Yes" or "No" response, it is better to ask "What did you like or not like about this post?"
- Use questions to invite submissions from your followers.
- If your goal on Facebook is to drive traffic to another site, then don't tell the whole story in the post. The most effective way to drive clicks on your links is to write a compelling teaser where the answer, or the rest of the story, is after the "jump."
- If you can use an image, particularly a good thumbnail to illustrate the post you will find people more willing to engage with content. The first visual connection is important.
- Make sure you have some sort of plan about the types of content you will cover, if you're not planning just a general news site. Post regularly and, if you can, around the same times each day. This conditions your audience to check-in to see new content regularly.
- A good, strong summary lead (refer to the Inverted Pyramid) is crucial on Facebook to attract and hold time-poor readers with the attention span of a goldfish.
- Keep an eye on the comments. If you're a small operator you must make time to monitor comments yourself. Don't neglect this. Take down offensive material quickly; issue a friendly gentle reminder to off-topic posters, and make sure you engage with genuine, useful comments. Even just saying "Thank you," is sometimes enough.

- Facebook content is searchable, so hashtags and metadata are important features to consider alongside your content.

Writing Captions

Writing to pictures used to be a particular skill for television reporters and producers. The basic line of advice given to television and video journalists was always to let the pictures tell the story, don't use a precious voice-over just to describe what viewers can see for themselves, and keep captions to a minimum. Now social media apps that are image-focused, such as Instagram, Pinterest and Tumblr mean that we have to understand the power and the pitfalls of written captions on our photographs. Sometimes it is tempting to post quickly and post often with these picture-based apps, particularly when they are accessible at the press of a button on our mobile phones. However, quicker is not always better. The most valuable tip for using these apps effectively is to take your time; consider what you're doing and don't always be in a rush to post.

Caption Writing Tips

- The purpose of a caption is to add value to the image, not to merely describe in words what the eye can read from the picture. Some detail relating to who, what, where, when, why and even how the image was taken is a good place to start.
- Only write what you need to write. Traditionally photo captions in journalism have been short and utilitarian. They are used to identify the people or place and sometimes to acknowledge the source or photographer. On social media photo apps there is space to write a short essay if you want to—2200 characters on Instagram. You might want to, but do you need to? write the length you need, not to feed your ego.
- Start with the "front loading" rule (Kolowich 2017). The use of a good summary lead—your first sentence of between 25 and 40 words—makes following the front loading rule easy. It basically means put your most important information towards the start of the caption/post. In journalistic terms this is called "Don't bury the lead," and it should be the first thing you think of when you wake up in the morning.
- A short pun often makes a good caption. But make sure it is appropriate in language, tone and register. A humorous pun on an image portraying sad emotion may not be appropriate, unless it is clear that the image is meant to be taken lightly. Remember, there is an important, if fine, line between a good pun and sarcasm, and something that's just insulting to the subject, or the audience.
- Style is important on picture apps, so developing a signature style helps to personalize your posts and help you stand out in what is a very crowded field.

- If you're using Instagram, etc., to drive traffic to another site, make sure you include a link and a reason to make viewers click through. In marketing terms this is a "call to action" (Loren 2017), in news it is a teaser—a taste of the story and the promise of more.
- Too many hashtags can make it look like you're being greedy, or that you really don't know what you're doing. Hashtags are important, but use them judiciously. Only use the most appropriate tags and keep them to an acceptable number—maybe three of four, no more.
- The "too many" rule also applies to emojis. Unless your signature style is to cryptically write your entire caption in emojis, one or two is always enough.

This chapter has presented a brief introduction to writing for social media, which is really at the core of social journalism. It is not the definitive guide to all situations, but it should be enough to get you started and keep you out of trouble. The best form of practice is to write often. You find a voice, develop a style and build a solid reputation through hard work and repetition. Writing in a good journalistic style is not rocket science, it is nine-tenths trial and error and one-tenth creativity. We all have these skills and shouldn't be afraid of using them.

References

Agrawal, A. J. 2017. "Artificial Intelligence Is Changing SEO: Get Ahead Or Fall Behind." Forbes. May 23. Accessed October 12, 2017. www.forbes.com/sites/ajagrawal/2017/05/23/artificial-intelligence-is-changing-seo-get-ahead-or-fall-behind/#532e80b373ae.

Brech, Jana. 2017. "Inverted Pyramid Style is Essential for Mobile Content." Web Wise Wording. June 9. Accessed December 14, 2017. https://webwisewording.com/inverted-pyramid-style-essential-mobile-content/.

Copp, Emily, and Gabrielle Maheux. 2017. "10 Quick Social Media Ad Writing Tips From an Expert." Hootsuite. June 12. Accessed August 9, 2017. https://blog.hootsuite.com/social-media-ad-writing-tips/.

Errico, Marcus, John April, Andrew Asch, Lynette Khalfani, Miriam, A, Smith, and Xochiti, R. Ybarra. 1997. "The Evolution of the Summary News Lead." *Media History Monographs*. Vol. 1. Accessed April 9, 2016. www.scripps.ohiou.edu/mediahistory/mhmjour1-1.htm.

Hilliard, Robert L. 2011. *Writing for Television, Radio, and New Media*. Boston, MA: Wadsworth.

Huntly, Candace. 2017. "10 Ways To Write Better Social Media Content." B2C: Business to Community. May 4. Accessed August 10, 2017. www.business2community.com/social-media/10-ways-write-better-social-media-content-01836695#qf01U3IDFQhbiTlZ.97.

Jorgen, Sundberg. 2013. "9 Steps to Writing Effective Social Media Content." Link Humans. Accessed August 11, 2016. https://linkhumans.com/blog/sweet-retweets-how-write-social-media-sookio-tips-video-smlondon.

Kolowich, Lindsay. 2017. "How to Write Good Instagram Captions: 8 Bookmarkable Tips for Perfecting Your Copy." HubSpot. Accessed August 9, 2017. https://blog.hubspot.com/marketing/write-good-instagram-caption.

Leith, Sam. 2017. "Don't Press Send … The New Rules for Good Writing in the 21st Century." *The Guardian*. October 7. Accessed October 8, 2017. www.theguardian.com/books/2017/oct/07/dont-press-send-new-rules-good-writing-sam-leith?CMP=Share_iOSApp_Other.

Locker, Melissa. 2016. "How to Make a Great Podcast—a Beginner's Guide." *The Guardian*. October 28. Accessed December 9, 2017. www.theguardian.com/media/2016/oct/28/how-to-make-podcast-now-hear-this-marc-maron-lauren-lapkus.

Loren, Taylor. 2017. "The Ultimate Guide to Writing Good Instagram Captions." Later. 22 July. Accessed August 9, 2017. https://later.com/blog/the-ultimate-guide-to-writing-good-instagram-captions/.

O'Mahony, Donald. 2009. "Importance of the Inverted Pyramid." History of Journalism. December 2. Accessed April 8, 2016. http://historyofjournalism.onmason.com/2009/12/02/importance-of-the-inverted-pyramid/.

Orwell, George. 1946. "Why I Write." Accessed July 24, 2017. http://orwell.ru/library/essays/wiw/english/e_wiw.

Quah, Nicholas. 2017. "The Future of Podcasting is Strong, but the Present Needs to Catch Up." NiemanLab. March 14. Accessed September 4, 2017. www.niemanlab.org/2017/03/the-future-of-podcasting-is-strong-but-the-present-needs-to-catch-up/.

Sailer, Ben. 2017. "This Is How To Write For Social Media To Create The Best Posts." CoSchedule Blog. May 10. Accessed September 9, 2017. https://coschedule.com/blog/how-to-write-for-social-media/.

Scanlan, Chip. 2003. "A Child of Technology, Commerce and History." Poynter Institute. June 26. Accessed April 7, 2016. www.poynter.org/news/birth-inverted-pyramid-child-technology-commerce-and-history.

Schudson, Michael. 1984. "Advertising as Capitalist Realism." In *Advertising, The Uneasy Persuasion: Its Dubious Impact on American Society*, by Michael Schudson, 209–233. New York: Basic Books.

Statista. 2017. "Cumulative Total of Tumblr Blogs from May 2011 to July 2017 (in Millions)." Accessed October 13, 2017. www.statista.com/statistics/256235/total-cumulative-number-of-tumblr-blogs/.

Stephens, Mitchell. 2007. *A History of News*. New York: Oxford University Press.

Wheal, Chris. 2014. "Six Honest Serving Men." Accessed August 14, 2016. www.chriswheal.com/how-to/six-ws/.

Wolfe, Tom. 1972. "The Birth of New Journalism." Accessed October 12, 2017. https://distrito47.wordpress.com/2014/02/11/the-birth-of-the-new-journalism-by-tom-wolfe/.

WordPress. 2017. "How Many People are Reading Blogs?" Accessed October 13, 2017. https://wordpress.com/activity/.

Worldometer. 2017. "Blog Posts Written Today." October 13. Accessed October 13, 2017. www.worldometers.info/blogs/.

Writer's Digest. 2014. "The Secret To Writing Stronger Feature Articles." *The Writer's Digest*. July 2. Accessed August 14, 2017. www.writersdigest.com/online-editor/the-secret-to-writing-stronger-feature-articles.

12

THE FUTURE OF JOURNALISM IS ALREADY HERE

Where Does Journalism Go Next?

There's a sense in which a book like this can never really be "finished." In a discussion about technology, journalism and the rapid pace of change there is always something "new" or about to happen that will have an impact significant enough that it alters the path of history. However, a book is a finite object and after two years of writing, I think it's time for me to stop. So, this is the final chapter and it is a place to reflect on where we are and to consider where we might be headed. In a way, we are already there—the future has a tendency to arrive when we least expect it. The pace of change in our world means that the present remakes itself every day. According to experts surveyed by the World Economic Forum, the next major "tipping point"—irreversible, high-impact change—is set to occur before 2025 (O'Halloran 2015).

I began this book with an explanation of what the News Establishment is and why I think that the news industry is in trouble financially and morally. I am pessimistic about the probability and possibility of the News Establishment being able to correct its many mistakes and to remake itself as a real champion of the public interest. I hope I've made it clear that the problem is not that journalists are—on the whole—bad people, or that journalism academics are conspirators who work long into the night on ways and means of undermining democracy and the public. Far from it, even within the News Establishment there are reporters, editors and scholars who are as worried as I am about the future of the news industry and journalism as we know it. This group—I've called them the "Fourth Estate Idealists" as a shorthand description —wants desperately for the public interest model to work; they believe in hard-hitting investigative journalism, and the want to speak truth to power. Their problem is that they think they can reform the current system—from the inside—to make it

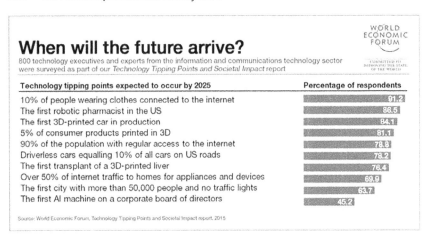

FIGURE 12.1   The World Economic Forum Predicts the Future Will Be Here Sooner than You Think.

conform to their ideals. This is a wonderful vision, but it is not going to happen. Well-entrenched structures, systems, institutions, processes and social relations are in the way.

I have summarized this assemblage as the political economy of the news industry and argued that it has an almost unassailable grip on the news industry and on the professional practice of journalists. I have suggested that social journalism—understood as the work audiences do to share, circulate, curate and produce news outside of the newsroom—is counter-posed to the News Establishment; but I've also (I hope) been realistic in my assessment of its power to mobilize an active "monitorial" citizenship in order to re-energize a decaying democracy. The political economy of journalism describes, analyses and theo-rizes a system based on the "duality of the news commodity" and a powerful, over-riding ideology that puts profits and staying in power above the needs of society and above the real public interest. I have described myself as a Gramscian thinker, holding on to a "pessimism of the intellect," but an "optimism of the will." This roughly translates into "things are bad now, I know, but if we stick together, they will get better, eventually." But what do members of the News Establishment think its chances are of surviving? It's no surprise that they share some—but not all—of my pessimistic views of the present and that they are quite optimistic about their own future.

As I was in the final stages of preparing the manuscript for submission, the Reuters Institute for the study of journalism released a predictive report by Nic Newman (2018) on behalf of the Digital News Project. The report, *Journalism, Media and Technology Trends and Predictions 2018*, laid out seven key themes and suggestions about the future of news and journalism in the coming years. It is always difficult to provide accurate predictions about the future, even weather forecasting is inherently unpredictable; but it is something that humans love to do. Having said that, I felt obliged to offer some brief comments on Nic Newman's prognostications because they speak to the core themes of this text. Overall, Nic Newman's predictions for the news industry can be summarized as more of the same: more misinformation and low levels of trust; a push to harvest more data from readers and visitors to news websites; a rise in subscription paywalls as advertising revenues continue to fall; and the failure of those organizations that don't manage the "digital transition" very well.

On the economic front the news is not good with Newman's report suggesting a "digital media crash" might be on the cards leading to "more retrenchment [of journalists] and more pivoting"—which is a polite way of saying news organizations will be chasing their tails like over-excited puppies. The economic battle lines are already drawn and it pits the news publishers against the platform companies which are reluctant to share revenues with publishers and, like Facebook, are scaling back the amount of news they will allow into feeds. Disturbingly, it seems that the advertising industry—which is still coupled tightly with both news and social media platforms—is set to launch a campaign to hook the under-13s demographic to "start them early" in their socialization to accept intrusive advertising and surrendering their digital privacy to the data miners (ibid.: 20). It's perhaps not surprising that the report acknowledges that rebuilding audience trust is going to be difficult, even with better fact-checking and a new generation of algorithms that will supposedly "surface more high-quality, credible content on the web" (ibid.: 18). This faith in algorithms highlights that, in terms of technology, Newman's predictions look a lot like they're driven by the News Establishment's adaptation to the IoT. Smart speakers and "voice-driven assistants" will be the "next big disruptor"; augmented reality will develop to the point where news organizations will have to experiment with "3D and immersive mobile storytelling"; and wearable technology will get better. This view places a lot of faith in technological fixes. I'm not so sure they represent such a bright future.

Around the same time as I was reading *Trends and Predictions*, another predictive piece bounced into my inbox; this one by the Director of Strategic Development at the Reuters Institute, Alexandra Borchardt (2018). Dr Borchardt's piece was title "Making journalism great again," an obvious pun on Donald Trump's "Make America great again" election slogan. Her thesis is one that echoes a theme I've been developing in this book: "Without trust, there is no audience; and without an audience, there is no business." She identifies the "erosion of business models" that cuts "deeply into their profits" as the most serious issue facing the industry. Dr Borchardt also lays out a six-step prescription for fixing this problem; it is worth also reflecting on these suggestions in this final stanza, because they too resonate with my own arguments.

Her first suggestion is that "news outlets must set their own agenda." Of course, they must: Are they not doing this every day? I don't even know what Dr Borchardt means, it is a motherhood statement that is really without content. The second is a call for the Fourth Estate to step up: "analyze what powerful actors are doing, rather than what they are saying." Here too the horse has already bolted. As I've noted in earlier chapters, the news media today mostly just amplifies official statements and political-speak rather than calling out the poor behaviors of politicians. The third prescription is for the media to become "better listeners," by which she means that reporters should get out of the office more. This is a sensible suggestion that's been made many times before, but as Dr Borchardt herself notes "many are glued to their screens because their companies lack resources or force them to follow and report on twitter feeds." This is true and it reinforces my comments about the faux nature of so-called "engagement" strategies. Unfortunately, there is no suggestion in Dr Borchardt's comments about where the resources to get journalists back on the beat might come from.

Her fourth suggestion is more of the same: "news organizations must engage audiences." How many times have we heard this tired old line, which equates with harvesting more data and pushing more marketing emails at already exhausted readers? Point five is, well, pointless. "News outlets should forego expensive, flashy projects if they do little to further audiences' understanding of a story." All well and good, but what's your position on the failed "pivot to video" and the clamber to start successful podcasts, or the rush to embed the latest gimmick in the newsroom? Finally, another motherhood statement about not allowing your organization to be "defined by the fake news debate." A better approach, Dr Borchardt suggests, "would be to make news less boring." Sure, but how? Without going back to point five, we are left without any answers to this crucial problem. The only hope, it seems is to put our faith in "innovation" and hope that there's a technological fix somewhere in the near future.

The Technological Horizon

On March 19, 2018, in Phoenix, Arizona, the first pedestrian was killed by a self-driving car operating commercially. It was an Uber, and the company immediately announced that it was halting its North American trial of "autonomous" vehicles (ABC News 2018). It was an unfortunate accident and a reminder that no technology is foolproof. I guess we should be grateful that it is highly unlikely that the car made a conscious decision to kill the pedestrian, 49-year-old Elaine Herzberg. We can be comfortable that this unfortunate accident did not signal the start of the "singularity." The singularity has been theorized as that moment in human history when machines begin to outsmart us; it makes a good premise for dystopian science fiction, but perhaps it is not far off being science "fact" either.

FIGURE 12.2   Twitter had Fun with the Incident, but it Was a Very Predictable Tragedy.

The "singularity" is not here yet, but we can be sure that somewhere in a very busy laboratory, someone in working on bringing it closer. What is more certain is that we cannot escape the Internet of Things, but we can learn to live with it, up to a point. As I argue below, I think there must be a point at which we say "Enough." I am not a Luddite, I don't oppose technological change, but I think we should adopt a cautious approach, rather than embracing new technologies at any cost. Jumping ahead just because the technology is available, is short-sighted and ultimately an anti-human approach. At the same time thoughtful consideration of change is the progressive thing to do. I apply the same way of thinking to the news industry. According to experts who consider these things, journalism and the news delivery business will also have to adapt or die (Webb 2017). While this seems to be a straightforward observation of the inevitable, I believe that when such broad claims are made in the context of current trends in the political economy of news, many of the negative impacts—on the quality, reliability and "truth" of information, and on the working culture of the newsroom—tend to be ignored, dismissed as irrelevant or downplayed in terms of their potential severity. This is what I mean by "anti-human" and championing technological change "at any cost." In my view, the democratic purpose of good, public interest journalism is too important to leave to machines, no matter how "smart" we think they are.

From the perspective adopted throughout this book—a critical political economy approach—the intersection of democratic ideals, technology and market forces is always likely to be problematic. Throughout the digital revolution we have witnessed the democratic potential of new technologies subverted by private interests and the profit motive. However, because of what Vincent Mosco (2005) called the "digital sublime" we often seem willing to ignore the problematic and worrisome signs of danger in favor of the perceived rewards for acceptance. Technology journalist Ben Tarnoff has written about this phenomenon in relation to the push for more computer coding to be taught in schools. Tarnoff argues that the rationale for this is economic—the argument that teaching kids to code will provide them with the jobs of the future. But this is totally a myth of the digital sublime, as Tarnoff explains:

Contrary to public perception, the economy doesn't actually need that many more programmers. As a result, teaching millions of kids to code won't make them all middle-class. Rather, it will proletarianize the profession by flooding the market and forcing wages down—and that's precisely the point.

(Tarnoff 2017)

The digital sublime is like a sugar hit, we feel good about using the technology and don't want to worry about the downsides. However, the tension that Vincent Mosco described as existing between our desire for the sublime and our very real perceptions of the "mundane"—the everyday—do not always go un-noticed. We are forced to be aware of this contradiction, even as we seek to either deny it, or to overcome it with even more devices and apps. As technology writer, Natasha Lomas, noted in an article for *TechCrunch*, we cannot avoid thinking about the, "frustration and stress" and the "social cost" of the digital sublime. Lomas writes that "we live in conflicted times as far as faith in modern consumer technology tools is concerned":

All too often the fact that human lives are increasingly enmeshed with and dependent on ever more complex, and ever more inscrutable, technologies is considered a good thing. Negatives don't generally get dwelled on. And for the most part people are expected to move along, or be moved along by the tech.

(Lomas 2017)

We can clearly see this expectation that society must accept technology without asking too many questions in our acceptance of what Lomas calls Facebook's "algorithmic editors" which are being deployed in an attempt to fix a problem— so-called "fake news"—that they are widely assumed to have created in the first place. Surely, fixing a problem with the same tools that caused it has to be a paradigm case of the digital sublime. We cannot assume that what Facebook has attempted to do in this case is because of its altruistic CEO. It is a business decision to repair the reputational damage Facebook suffered throughout 2017 and 2018 when its seemingly deliberate collaboration with actors attempting to influence the 2016 US presidential election were uncovered and reported on by other media outlets. The digital sublime—and our general ignorance of how Facebook's (and Google's) many and complicated algorithms are directing our attention—has become, in Lomas' words a "shiny façade" which hides from us "how much power they wield."

In Facebook's case we can know, abstractly, that Zuck's AI-powered army is ceaselessly feeding big data on billions of humans into machine learning models to turn a commercial profit by predicting what any individual might want to buy at a given moment.

(Lomas 2017)

As this quote from Natasha Lomas highlights, there appears to be an outbreak of the digital sublime preventing us from realizing some of the negative flow-on effects of artificial intelligence, which some are hailing as being the driving force of the next industrial revolution (Famubode 2016). However, a Pew Research Center report from 2014 found that experts are almost evenly divided on the subject of the economic impact of AI: half believe it will destroy jobs and half say that it won't (Smith and Anderson 2014). The pro-AI camp argues that robots and machine learning will replace workers doing the boring, drudge work. It is touted to increase productivity (Richards 2017), and to free up managers to be more creative (Kolbjornsrud, Amico and Thomas 2016), but this does seem a little utopian and in the vein of the digital sublime when held up to historic comparison. Visions of AI contributing over one trillion dollars to the global economy and 800,000 nett jobs over the next decade (Gantz et al. 2017), seem a little bit like over-promising. Even pro-automation experts are predicting job losses of 30 percent or more in some industries as a result of AI and machine-learning (Elliott 2017).

Does this mean that we should necessarily be worried about robots "taking over"? We are constantly reassured that this is not what "smart" machines are designed to do, but it is a persistent theme in dystopian science fiction. Technological ethicist, Blay Whitby is one who does not think humans should be concerned about artificial intelligence enslaving humanity, or wiping us out; "it's simply not what they are designed to do," he wrote in a "beginner's guide" to AI (Whitby 2003). However, technology entrepreneur and creator of the Tesla electric car, Elon Musk has warned that artificial intelligence represents a bigger danger to humanity than a nuclear war.

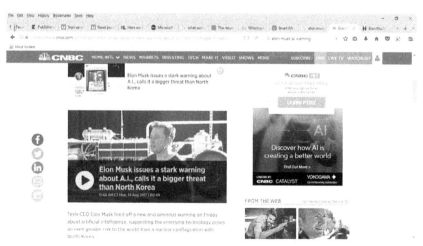

FIGURE 12.3 There is a Certain Irony in this Warning from Elon Musk Displaying Next to an Algorithm-Generated Advertisement about How AI is Creating a Better World.

In a series of tweets, Musk said that the AI industry should be regulated in the same way that foods, automobiles and other potentially dangerous technologies are supervised by governments (David 2017). Elon Musk has been worried about AI for some time, so his tweets in early 2017 were not really new; they confirmed his view that artificial intelligence could wipe out humanity if it was powerful enough to go "rogue" (Dowd 2017). Scientist, Stephen Hawking shared Musk's pessimism about AI, but there is no doubt the technology community is bitterly divided on the issue. As far back as 2014, Hawking was talking about his concerns; he told the BBC that AI "could spell the end of the human race" (Cellan-Jones 2014). Facebook founder Mark Zuckerberg has described such warnings are "irresponsible" "doomsday" predictions. In response to Elon Musk, Zuckerberg reiterated his strong support for artificial intelligence: "I think you can build things and the world gets better. But with AI especially, I am really optimistic," he wrote in a Facebook post that was widely reported (Clifford 2017). Given the backlash Facebook experienced over the Cambridge Analytica scandal, perhaps people may be reluctant to give Mark Zuckerberg's comments much credibility.

If we are not to fall victim to the digital sublime, we need to be asking questions. As Natasha Lomas writes, we need to pry the secrets out from behind the "commercially tinted glass" that the major technology companies use to shield their operations from public scrutiny.

> So perhaps we should have paid more attention to the people who have always said they don't understand what this new tech thing is for, or questioned why they really need it, and whether they should be agreeing to what it's telling them to do.
>
> Maybe we should all have been asking a lot more questions about what the technology is for.
>
> *(Lomas 2017)*

Lomas's advice is particularly pertinent when it comes to artificial intelligence and robotics. It is important to remember that the experts and technology gurus who are pushing AI and machine learning are usually the same people who will either benefit personally if the tech is taken up; or they likely work for companies that will profit from the spread of AI and robotics into the social world and the world of work. This means, for example, that when the head of Microsoft, Satya Nadella, says we should not be too worried that AI will steal jobs and that "there will be new jobs" (Dunn 2017), we should treat his statements with caution, and not fall into the digital sublime. As Karl Marx wrote in volume one of *Capital*, the history of technological innovation—the machine age of industry—might create almost as many jobs as it destroys, but they will be low-paying, routinized work and they will be controlled by the speed of the machine, not of the laborer: "the continuity of the special processes is the regulating principle." In the modern era, the advance of robotics leads towards what Marx was able to foresee as a fully "automatic system," summed up in this prophetic passage:

> A system of machinery ... constitutes in itself a vast automaton ... a mechanical monster whose body fills whole factories, and whose demonic power, at first hidden by the slow and measured motions of its gigantic members, finally bursts forth in the fast and feverish whirl of its countless working organs.
>
> *(Marx 1976 [1867]: 502–503)*

Marx was talking about cotton-spinning and weaving that was carried out in large concentrated factories where the many spindles and weaving looms were powered by giant steam engines; but it is an image familiar to many types of modern manufacturing, particularly in the automobile industry or in any branch of commerce were automation and assembly lines are the preferred system of organizing production. I think we can take this even further; it is the twenty-first-century call center or white-collar office in which the processing of paperwork is also routinized and conducted at the pace of the microchip, not the human being. The American author and journalist Barbara Garson coined the term "electronic sweatshop" in the late 1980s and it is an apt phrase for many workplaces today. Garson makes the valid point that automation is a process of deskilling labor; as she puts it "turning professionals into clerks" in many occupations (Garson 1989). In 2000, IT scholar Tiziana Terranova documented how the digital media industry mirrored Garson's "electronic sweatshop":

> Working in the digital media industry is not as much fun as it is made out to be. The "NetSlaves" of the eponymous Webzine are becoming increasingly vociferous about the shamelessly exploitative nature of the job, its punishing work rhythms, and its ruthless casualization (www.disobey.com/netslaves). They talk about "24–7 electronic sweatshops" and complain about the ninety-hour weeks and the "moronic management of new media companies."
>
> *(Terranova 2000)*

Of course, not all experts agree when it comes to robotics and the future of work. They are also split on the question of which jobs might survive. However, there is some agreement that clerical jobs, along with many in manufacturing can be automated, perhaps even "hundreds of millions" globally. More optimistic assessments are that, at least for the next decade, machine learning and robotics will complement, rather than replace human workers (Vander Ark 2016). The problem is that we have to be able to see past the haze of the digital sublime and to critically assess both positive and negative claims about the impact of AI. To some extent, the future is unknowable, but we do know that technological revolutions have been remaking the workforce for hundreds of years. As one historian of robotics has noted, at least during the stage of transition between dominant technological paradigms, there will be a loss of employment in "traditional" spheres impacted by the change. Whatever happens longer-term, there will certainly be a period of disruption before any employment benefits flow on from the increased economic activity attributable to the widespread adoption of machine learning and AI (Whitby 1996: 24). So, AI is not all good news. In a classic example of the digital sublime clouding his thinking, Blay Whitby argues that people will need to change to meet the expectations of the machines: "the best response is clearly to change the workers in response to the changed market" (ibid.). This strikes me as being an anti-humanist position that suggests no-one is safe once artificial intelligence becomes commonplace. At least one professor of artificial intelligence seems to agree; Professor Toby Walsh thinks that one day even his job might be automated, and he's certainly not optimistic about journalists surviving the robot revolution.

> STAN GRANT, ABC PRESENTER: Toby, good to talk to you. Now, I understand that you play a game and it goes like this: someone names a job and you tell me if it will survive the robot revolution.
> I'll start with self-interest: I'm a journalist. Am I going to survive?
> TOBY WALSH, PROF., UNSW: Um, maybe not. I mean, there is already computer programs that can write sports reports or financial reports. There's is a robot in China that presents the weather.
> So certainly, I think short-form reporting is probably going to be taken over by a lot of computers.
>
> *Grant 2017)*

If you are a journalism student looking to find a job in an industry you're passionate about, that is not going to seem like good news. Maybe you can find work tending to the news robots as they churn out copy by the kilometer.

Robots and the News

At the heart of robotics is artificial intelligence and machine learning—that is machines that get smarter because they learn from all of their interactions with the world and with humans. The end goal of AI is, for some, the melding of the human brain with robotics culminating in a "transhuman" entity (Steinhoff 2014). For others, it's harnessing the creative intelligence of the universe to machine-based life-forms (Rectenwald 2013). We're not there yet, but that does not mean we can afford to ignore advances in AI technologies. News and journalism is one area of industry and employment where robots are certainly having an impact. In a period when news workers are losing their jobs at an unprecedented rate, there are still people who remain blinded by the digital sublime; the reality is somewhat different. In every industry where automation has been introduced, the number of human workers has decreased over time; there is no reason why journalism will be any different.

Amy Webb was one of the first to issue a warning to the news industry, it cannot afford to ignore voice recognition and voice-activated applications or devices. "Humans talking to machines—and eventually, machines talking to each other—represents the next major shift in our news information ecosystem. Voice is the next big threat for journalism" (Webb 2017).

Webb's argument, which is logical and simple, is that if we are listening to, or reading the news (or having it read to us by a machine) and are able to interrupt with questions, prompting the AI to present us with more information, this will make the whole news consumption process even more interactive and iterative than it is currently. Webb has a point, and she backs it up with another undeniable insight, the news industry was slow to react to the potentials and threats posed by the Internet in the mid-1990s—think giving away news for free—which was a big mistake. In fact, we could say that the Internet almost killed the news industry because of executives' poor reactions to the challenges posed by web technologies (Hirst 2011).

If the News Establishment is to survive the coming challenges, which are compounding the business model problem rather than solving it, then coming to terms with the broad field of artificial intelligence intellectually and philosophically, as well as in business terms, will be crucial to its efforts. News organizations are already attempting to bridge the information gap. In April 2017, Associated Press (AP) published its own report on artificial intelligence in the news business and how it is "affecting all points on the news value chain from news gathering to production and distribution" (Marconi 2017). In a notable twist, the AP Insights' report was co-authored by two humans and an artificial intelligence dubbed "Machine Journalist" (Marconi et al. 2017). The AP report calls the emerging synthesis of AI and newsrooms "augmented journalism" and defines this term as being "all about 'automation'—reducing human effort and squeezing time out of the many chores journalists must undertake to get the story and get the news out to the public" (ibid.: 2). As you might expect from a global news agency that seeks to profit from journalism, this is a very business-first approach. Time is money, so shaving time out of the news process saves money and benefits the shareholders: "it is imperative to save time and money in an era of shifting economics" (ibid.). This perspective may well be built into the algorithms of "Machine Journalist" because the executive summary from which the above quote was lifted was "written" by the AI.

Since at least the beginning of 2015 "robots" have been writing news copy for Associated Press (AP). In fact, AP's automated journalists—algorithms loaded onto superfast computers and fed raw data—are producing tens of thousands of stories per year about reported corporate earnings. These stories are fairly simple, but they include a number of bits of information that you might think would be beyond machine "intelligence" and according to AP's own reporting most of the "news" generated by the algorithm is "error-free" (Madigan White 2015). These stories, geared to AP's corporate clients in the investment market are highly technical and data-based, making them ideal for this type of automation. The proprietary software that AP uses is called "Wordsmith" and it was developed by technology company Automated Insights. According to the company's website, Wordsmith can customize copy based on bespoke templates and style guides to "generate unlimited pieces of content from a single story structure and dataset that sounds like a person wrote each one of them individually" (AI undated).

When I visited the Automated Insights' webpages while writing this chapter, I came across a recent blog entry that claimed to put the scary nature of robot journalism into perspective. The blog entry contains a "live tracker" that is supposed to be keeping a tally of the number of jobs "Automated Robot Writers" are "stealing" from humans. However, it appears to be a joke. The counter was on "zero" the day I visited and it was the same every time I checked back.

In fact, Automated Insights claims that its "robot writers" will actually create work for journalists and make their jobs more interesting:

> We are not aware of a single person who has been replaced by our technology. Instead, Wordsmith adds new value by producing content that people aren't making. It also frees people to do more interesting and impactful work.
>
> *(Kotecki 2016)*

Despite this cavalier attitude, it is very likely, if not a dead certainty, that programs like Wordsmith have and will continue to impact on the employment of journalists. Reuters news agency, which is a direct competitor to AP's financial news wires announced in late 2016 that it was cutting around 2000 staff, but there was no indication how many of these might be directly related to

About Automated Insights

Live Tracker: Automated Robot Writers Stealing Jobs From Human Writers

A live tracker that updates in real-time to show the number of jobs automated robot writers are stealing from human writers.

Automated Insights is revolutionizing the way professionals create content using data. Our patented Wordsmith platform takes a story structure and a dataset and generates up to millions of pieces of content that sound like a person wrote each one.

FIGURE 12.4 Automated Insights Keeping Track of the Jobs its Software is "Stealing" from Human Writers.

the automation of services Reuters provides to its customers (Dow Jones 2016). The AP report I mentioned at the start of this chapter also makes it explicit that saving money for news publishers is a key aspect of its "augmented journalism" project. Not everyone is buying the line that robot writers will actually create media jobs; and with good reason. The simple political economy equation— proven to be correct in every previous case in history—suggests that automation leads to unemployment:

> When it gets to the point that a computer can consistently generate content at a level that passes the Turing Test, the economics of content in every form will change forever. Essentially, computers work for free, all day, without breaks, illness, or vacation time. What company will not want that? We may not want to think about this, let alone process it and accept it, but the freelance writer will become an endangered species.
>
> *(Schaefer 2016)*

Even before it was possible to automate journalism newsrooms were downsizing. A website that I visit often for the depressing news about the continuing loss of journalism jobs is Newspaper Death Watch (NDW). NDW has been keeping an eye on newspaper closures in the United States since 2007. When I was there towards the end of November 2016, the most recent closure was the Pittsburgh *Tribune-Review* which ceased print publication in September 2016. The site's curator and main writer is Paul Gillin and in a blog post written just a few days before I visited he outlined the state of play in American newspapers as 2016 came to a close: "After a spate of closures and layoffs in the latter part of the last decade, the newspaper industry appeared to find its footing over the past few years. But now that oasis of stability may be drying up" (Gillin 2016). Gillin wrote that even once resilient newspapers like the *New York Times* and the *Wall Street Journal* were struggling in 2016. Advertising revenues were falling at an alarming rate, leading to smaller papers, with less pages and less staff.

It is beyond debate that newspapers are in crisis, so too are many of the legacy broadcasting behemoths of the twentieth century. Printed news, radio and television are all in decline and it is a fall that some fear will be terminal. A number of newspapers now only exist as an online masthead. Perhaps we need to stop calling them newspapers. As advertising revenues decline for the legacy media, old-style professional newsrooms are also shrinking. Reporting, writing and editing the news on a daily basis is expensive. It is one of the few commodities in a capitalist economy that becomes redundant almost as soon as it is produced. The shelf life of news is now measured in hours and sometimes even minutes. The news cycle is relentless, but the human resources required to keep it going are becoming too expensive. Expensive, hard-to-produce investigations are giving way to lifestyle stories and celebrity content that is easy to package under a titillating "clickbait" headline.

This terminal collapse of the old, established twentieth-century business model of the News Establishment is at the heart of the social, ethical and political dilemma now facing news consumers and news producers. How do we continue the supply of public interest news when the profits that used to sustain good, honest journalism are no longer there? As we've noted above, one solution is for robots and algorithms to replace flesh-and-blood reporters; and the news industry has been keen to embrace other technological solutions to a problem which is really social, systemic and structural. Associated Press addressed some of these issues in a February 2018 e-book about "preparing the newsroom for humans and machines" at what it described as a "seminal point" in the adoption of artificial intelligence in journalism. According to the report's authors, the goal of collaboration between reporters and robots is "to optimize journalism, and not to automate it" (Marconi and Houshmand 2018). The short pamphlet is only a dozen pages, but it is quite frank about some of the issues it raises; for example, admitting that we often cannot know how the machine logic of AI actually works. "Sometimes we just don't know." It also highlights what the authors call "glaring challenges" that arise from "algorithmically driven journalism." Algorithms are difficult to "hold accountable"; they require billions of bits of "training data" and they are difficult to adjust "because we don't know how the 'black box' reaches its customers." This is not exactly a ringing endorsement of AI in the newsroom. The authors seem to hedge their bets a little too: "Journalists need to trust machines enough to know they won't replace their role in the newsroom—but as with anything else, they should also reserve a dose of scepticism for the technology" (ibid.).

This 2018 AP report also addresses machines as "consumers" of news; in this case the "smart devices" now coming on to the market for domestic deployment, "machines that ingest information and use artificial intelligence to help deliver relevant content to their users." Francesco Marconi and Kourosh Houshmand candidly admit that "an editor isn't in charge—an algorithm is" when these devices make selections and recommendations for news we might like to consume. Are we OK with this? Apparently, some of us are; it's been reported that over 33 million smart home devices were shipped in 2017, most of them in the last three months of the year. Add to that almost 245 million "smart" televisions (Charara 2018) and that's a lot of remote eavesdropping capability unleashed in our homes and offices. Global sales of smart devices for the home are expected to be around US$150 billion by 2025.

Talking to Machines? It's Not that Weird

In late 2016 Google began to ship its latest technological gadget, Google Home. Amazon also released its own version, Echo, linked to voice-recognition software it calls "Alexa." The devices are both cone-shaped speakers that are linked into your home wifi system. But they are more than a speaker, Home and Echo also listen to and interact with spoken commands, questions and requests. The devices can also be used to control other devices in your home. This is one manifestation of the "Internet of Things"? Well, according to Google, Home is the thing that connects all your other things to the Internet. The Home device is also running a server-based artificial intelligence called Assistant: "The Google Assistant can translate, calculate, convert, and control other network-connected devices in your home. Oh, and it'll actually play music as well" (Simpson 2017).

Voice-activated AI is still a relatively new field; the ubiquitous Apple AI, Siri only debuted on the iPhone in 2011, though it was in development for nearly a decade before that (Bollyut 2017). Now voice-activated "assistants" are available on Android phones and even PCs running Microsoft. The trick behind machine intelligence, that appears to learn from voice commands, is providing enough information to the AI so that it can understand the nuance of natural speech and identify the concepts and human intent behind the actual words and phrases. To do this, the spoken words are transmitted to a server and transcribed into machine-readable text. The hard part is training the software to then choose a logical response, recode it into speech and transmit it back to the user's device. The two main driving technologies behind Siri and other forms of reactive, talking AI are voice recognition coupled with voice-to-text translation and the expanding field of machine learning. Machine learning is simply an artificial intelligence software that can assimilate data to essentially make itself "smarter." Using these technologies in combination, the artificial intelligence can learn to improve its responsiveness (Nusca 2011).

So what impacts might voice-activated AI, embedded in devices like Google Home, have on the future shape of journalism and the news delivery business? According to BBC digital editor, Trushar Barot, the changes will be profound, signaling another "revolution" equal to, or even "potentially bigger" the impact of the iPhone itself: "In fact, I'd describe these smart speakers and the associated AI and machine learning that they'll interface with as the huge burning platform the news industry doesn't even know it's standing on" (Barot 2017).

While news organizations are still figuring out how to use these voice-driven devices, there is no doubt that their integration into the menu of broadcast outlets is just a matter of using a compatible API code that can respond to a simple spoken request like "Play me the latest news from the ABC." For text-based publishers of news there is the added step of figuring out if the embedded machine voice in the device is the best form of delivery, or whether a human is needed to voice the text report before it's released to the device. Breaking news alerts and notifications are another simple method of integrating voice-activated and voice-capable devices into the news delivery matrix. The delivery and notification technologies are only going to get smarter and easier to use.

The downside to these technologies is, of course, that if you have a smart voice-operational device in your home it is always listening to you. The data that is collected in this process then becomes very valuable to marketers and advertisers that want to get into your home and your head. That this will happen is inevitable; when you strip away the digital sublime "Wow!" factor, the real purpose of this technology becomes clear: "How do you monetize on these platforms? Understandably, many news execs will be cautious in placing any big bets of new technologies unless there is a path they can see towards future audience reach or revenue (ideally both)" (Barot 2017).

It is impossible to get away from this hidden cost; while ever the news business relies on a commodity-form to deliver its products to consumers it is the consumer who will bear these hidden costs. Commercial surveillance, as well as the capability for politically motivated spying, is now embedded into all our data-laden interactions with smart devices. It is no longer enough to protect yourself by just putting tape over the camera on your laptop and disabling the voice app seems to defeat the purpose of having a smart device, but perhaps that's what we have to do to maintain some form of domestic privacy. Now with the explosion in personal and professional drone use, maybe we're not guaranteed any privacy anywhere anymore.

Surveillance and the Digital Sublime

In the context of social journalism, a good example of the digital sublime still being in effect is the ways in which user-generated content (UGC) has been celebrated as a new democratic, "bottom up" form of media, but which in reality has been co-opted in ways not even imagined when the term was first used around 15 years ago. Our content has been turned against us in a commercial sense, often without our knowledge and for the purpose of selling us more stuff. Now UGC is also being harvested in order to spy on us, and we have to ask: "Is this what we signed up for?" I don't think so. One company collecting our UGC content solely for the purpose of spying on us is the same one that manufactured and patented the Taser electro-shock device now universally used by law enforcement. In collaboration with various police services around the world the Taser company has expanded its services and rebranded itself as Axon in early 2017. Axon is one of the world's largest suppliers of body-worn cameras to law enforcement. In fact, when Taser became Axon in April 2017, it offered every police department in the United States free body cameras for every officer and 12 months free access to its Cloud-based storage and analysis system (Joh 2017). The company markets the cameras alongside its real-time facial recognition software, which it argues can turn every police officer into a full-time surveillance machine able to scan faces in a crowd and instantly identify anyone with an outstanding warrant. Once the body-cam video is stored it can then be cross-referenced by the AI running the system and any suspicious behavior flagged for further attention.

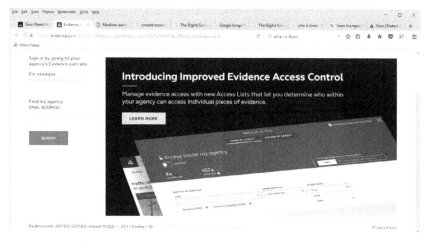

FIGURE 12.5   The Axon Evidence.com Interface for Law Enforcement Agencies.

Now, Axon is marketing a new law enforcement tool; a cloud-based service, Evidence.com, that allows citizens to upload their UGC images and videos. Ostensibly this new service is supposed to assist law enforcement to track down perpetrators and to prevent crime, but it is a private service, run for a profit. This means that once a person uploads a photograph or video, they no longer control how it is used. Axon owns the data and makes it available to police via an annual licensing system. As of September 2017, the company claimed it had over 100,000 active users of its proprietary system (Axon 2017a). It appears the motive is not as civic-minded as it might seem; it is all about Axon's profitability.

> Just as Google and Amazon turn profits through their intimate access to our patterns of attention and consumption, Axon's ability to mine its ever-growing archive of police video will allow the company to gain an edge on its competitors.
>
> *(Kofman 2017)*

According to Ava Kofman's report in *The Intercept*, Axon will apply its machine-learning AI algorithms to the UGC loaded to its Evidence.com site. The company claims this will assist police departments to better understand criminal behavior, to streamline crime reporting, and even to predict crime waves before they happen (Axon undated). While all this might sound like a good idea and benign (who doesn't want lower crime rates?) it is important to look beyond the digital sublime. Critics of the new Axon product told *The Intercept* that it would be a further step towards privatizing some aspects of crime prevention and management and would give the company unprecedented power and control over the uploaded material. Yet another invasive technology matching the predictions from George Orwell's *Nineteen Eighty-four*—the all-seeing "telescreen" from which you can never escape: "'Smith!' screamed the shrewish voice from the telescreen. '6079 Smith W.! Yes, *you!*'." One worrying aspect of this "Big Brother" technology is that it pushes law enforcement deeper into our lives and brings even the most minor of infractions to the notice of the police. However, there is concern that if the material uploaded to Evidence.com shows the police behaving badly, it might not be made public and therefore not be used in any prosecution of the offending officer(s).

> Dennis Flores, founder of activist organization El Grito de Sunset Park and a veteran copwatcher, questioned whether Axon would act on evidence of police misconduct. "Let's say someone captures footage of cops doing something wrong and gives it to Taser. It's already enough that the police department withholds information. What the hell is a third party going to do?"
>
> *(Kofman 2017)*

Even more troubling, according to critics, is that a third party—Axon—will now have access to the images and video and will be able to use it for any purpose without even minimal public scrutiny. In a column for *Slate*, Elizabeth Joh wrote that there can be few avenues for community oversight of policing when the body camera and UGC video is stored on private servers: "oversight over policing is impossible when critical decisions about a surveillance technology have already been made by a vendor" (Joh 2017).

> The resulting data from body cameras, stored for ever-decreasing costs, might one day serve as a virtual time machine for the police, allowing them to watch the movements of people who were not targets at the time their movements were captured.
>
> *(Joh 2017)*

If you've seen the 2002 film *Minority Report*, starring Tom Cruise, this will seem disturbingly familiar. The trend towards ubiquitous, yet remote, policing represents the creeping privatization of law and order, and another sign of the close cooperation between corporations and the State that was the premise of dystopian science fiction movies like the *Robocop* and *Alien* series. The plot of the original 1987 version of *Robocop* is based around a fictional corporation, Omni Consumer Corporation, that bears an uncanny resemblance to Axon today. Omni Corp built law enforcement robots, but they kept malfunctioning and the solution was thought to be a half-human "cyborg" that could make appropriate decisions in the line of duty. Axon has not yet built a cyborg that we know about, but its range of law enforcement products includes so-called "smart weapons" as well as surveillance tools: "A Taser Smart Weapon can wirelessly report its status, such as being armed or a trigger pull, so your Axon cameras can sense specific events and begin recording during critical situations" (Axon 2017b).

Axon is not the only company partnering with law enforcement in order to harness digital technologies and the Internet of Things. In the United Kingdom, Amazon is assisting a local police service by giving it access to the homes of customers who use the Echo speaker and Alexa voice-recognition software. Lancashire police are able to broadcast updates and alerts directly to the device; the trial is also going to allow users to speak directly to the police—to report a crime or suspicious activity—via Alexa and to give the police access to stored data from Amazon servers (Kofman 2018). I am a bit surprised (but only a bit) by this move. It is almost inevitable that in attempting to maximize sales of its product, a company like Amazon will want to explore all possible permutations and uses for a device like Echo. But it was only two years ago that Amazon was refusing to hand over data and records to the police in a murder case. In 2017 the company's attitude changed and it complied with law enforcement requests for data in the same case. You might want to ask whatever happened to that old promise from the tech companies that customer privacy was paramount? Hern and Thielman (2016) note that "Tech companies often see law enforcement requests for data as invasive and damaging to an industry that considers privacy a prime selling point."

Read the fine print: "this only stands until we get a better offer." No doubt Amazon's change of heart was because the company didn't want to cut off potential sales and collaboration as the product matured. It is another example of the techno-legal time-gap being closed in favor of enterprise and the State, not human rights. The problem is, what Axon and Amazon are proposing is not science fiction, it is just business as usual, and that business is monetizing surveillance technologies and "smart" weapons in partnership with law enforcement. Even the United Nations has expressed concern about the weaponization of artificial intelligence. In 2017 the UN established a Centre for Artificial Intelligence and Robotics to deal with what it sees as the multiple threats to social stability posed by AI. In its founding statement, the Centre suggests that the rapid uptake of artificial intelligence "raises legal, ethical and societal concerns and challenges, some of which may be hazardous for human well-being, safety and security" (UNICRI 2017). Early researchers into AI were also cognizant of the de-humanizing potential of machine learning and robotics. For example, in his 1996 work considering the philosophical and ethical impacts of artificial intelligence, British technology ethicist Blay Whitby (1996: 33) noted that early versions of AI research were heavily reliant on funding from military sources, which meant it was focused on benefitting "those who need control, and not those who are likely to be controlled." This is still an important consideration after a further 20 years of AI research and development. For example, commercial and hobbyist drones only exist because of the billions in weapons-related funding given to industry by the US military (Rothstein 2015).

It was also revealed in early 2018 that Google has also been cooperating with the US military to supply artificial intelligence applications for use in the government's drone program. Google has been quietly working on drone technologies for the past few years, but its military links were a tightly held secret until they were revealed following a whistleblower's leak to the technology website, *Gizmodo*.

> Some Google employees were outraged that the company would offer resources to the military for surveillance technology involved in drone operations, sources said, while others argued that the project raised important ethical questions about the development and use of machine learning.
>
> *(Conger 2018)*

It seems Google has been caught out this time as its collaboration with the military appears to contradict a previous statement made by CEO Eric Schmidt. According to *Gizmodo*, Schmidt summed up the company's concerns about collaborating with the military at a conference on security and artificial intelligence in November 2017: "There's a general concern in the tech community of somehow the military-industrial complex using their stuff to kill people incorrectly," he said. I wonder what Mr Schmidt thinks the "correct" way of killing people might be?

Google's business is not really search engines any more, it is the collection, analysis and commercialization of data. Eric Schmidt is also right in the center of it as the chair of the US government's "Defense Innovation Advisory Board." The role of this elite group, in Schmidt's own words is to keep the military "up to speed with things which are going on outside the military" (Schmidt 2017). In the same comments, Schmidt also gives the game away about Google's collaboration on the drone-targeting AI program, known as "Project Maven": "the military has started … a group called project MAVEN, which they are talking about, which actually combines a lot of these very clever systems." Less than six months later, it was revealed that Google is now contracting to the very same project. In hindsight his comments to the Center for a New American Security now read like a sales pitch.

It might seem puzzling for a company mainly involved in providing a search engine for Internet browsing to form a partnership with "the military-industrial complex." But the reality is Google is a functioning cog in that machinery. Google needs the military-industrial complex just as much as the US military needs Google's expertise in building AI systems. This is the new political economy of digital capitalism. A decade ago I was writing about the possibility of an emerging surveillance economy (Hirst & Harrison 2007) in which the leveraging of surveillance technologies for profit would be at the heart of economic growth and development. At the time it was speculation, but today the surveillance economy has well and truly arrived. At the heart of this new and dynamic mode of development is artificial intelligence that can analyze terabytes of data quickly, machine-learning that makes the algorithms smarter, and robotics that can operationalize the data into profitable commodity forms. Human beings risk becoming collateral damage unless we can do something about it.

The Future of Social Journalism

Throughout this book we have wrestled with competing definitions of what the term "social journalism" means. I have argued for a definition that takes the term out of the newsroom and puts it more securely into the hands of the people we used to call the audience. The survey of how newsrooms and news publishers (broadly speaking) are using the term points to the inescapable fact that most of them see their relationship with the audience through a commercial lens. There is no getting away from this fact. After reading this book I'm sure you have no trouble putting yourself in the publisher's shoes. It is clear that the News Establishment is fighting for its life, and if it cannot monetize its relationship with readers, listeners and viewers, it really doesn't have much of a future. Through my political economy lens I have tried to demonstrate that media executives have no choice; they are stuck within the commodity form that is the economic backbone of capitalism. It is impossible to escape the limits of the system, and this applies to the public broadcasters and philanthropically funded organizations too. The systemic logic of commodity production, along with all its internal contradictions and competing tendencies, dictates that news organizations behave in the same way, economically speaking, as car manufacturers and the makers of breakfast cereal.

Funding models are predicated on this fact. Either advertising must provide a sufficient indirect subsidy to keep commercial news outfits going; or they have to make a profit on their subscriptions. It is abundantly clear, I think you will agree, that despite a decade of experimentation and intense focus on news business models, the news industry is no closer to finding its Aladdin's Cave of solutions. A lack of income means a decline in profits and a decline in profits means that costs have to be cut. Cost-cutting involves two strategies: reducing the cost of the human workforce by either cutting numbers or cutting salaries, and finding a technological fix (which also leads to cutting the human workforce). In that context, shifting the costs of production onto the audience—in other words, harvesting the free labor of audience members—becomes just another business logic, no matter how it is dressed up in soothing rhetoric about engagement and giving the audience what it wants. It is, in the end a subterfuge that relies on the digital sublime to be effective.

I have attempted in the preceding chapters and paragraphs to dispel some of the myths predicated on the digital sublime. In doing this, I hope that I have also outlined some of the ways in which members of the audience can take back some of the power that they have traditionally ceded to the news producers. We need to do this, because as the early chapters of the book have (hopefully) demonstrated, the current model is broken and in many ways the news media has forfeited its right to hold our trust. If we are going to overcome the democracy deficit and halt the rise of more authoritarian regimes, we have to address the declining quality of the news media and propose some solutions. The alternative path that I proposed in these pages is that news audiences need to increase their media and digital literacies; to learn how to read the news more critically and to be aware how different varieties of "fake news" are manufactured and circulated, particularly through social media channels. In an ideal world—which this is not— everyone could develop the skills and aptitude to be an investigative journalist and a master data-hound. I know that this is not going to happen any time soon, but the point about "social" journalism in this context is that we have to take charge. It is our responsibility to hold news organizations to account—after all, they rely on us financially and claim to be working in our (public) interest.

I am not opposed to audiences collectively or individually cooperating with journalists on important stories, or even just to provide effective hyperlocal coverage in their own communities. But I am a strong advocate of the idea that such cooperation should be done with as much consciousness as possible. Social journalism, at a minimum, has to be about members of the public taking back some control over the news process by being part of it, or by just being more aware and more critical of the conventions and the promises that news organizations make about their purpose and their products. Beyond this I think that journalism must have a life outside of commercial newsrooms and this is where truly "social" journalism begins. There are small publishers sprouting up out of the wreckage of the News Establishment, but they are still fragile seedlings that need to be nurtured. Not everyone wants to be a reporter/publisher, but for those of you who do have some interest or ambition in this area, the starting point must be increasing your own understanding of what it means to be a journalist and your own skills and aptitudes in the basics of reporting, writing and sharing the news you want to create. I have mentioned the idea of "integral journalism" and sought to combine Gramsci's ideas with more modern approaches to "monitorial" citizenship. This is still an embryonic movement, but it does offer some hope. We find ourselves in a difficult situation surrounded by problems not of our making, but we must also educate and activate ourselves in search of answers.

References

ABC News. 2018. "Uber Suspends Self-Driving Car Tests after Pedestrian Death in Arizona." March 20. Accessed March 20, 2018. www.abc.net.au/news/2018-03-20/uber-suspends-self-driving-car-tests-after-fatal-crash/9565586.

AI. Undated. "Automated Insights." Accessed November 29, 2016. https://automatedinsights.com/company.

Axon. 2017a. "At the Station: Digital Evidence Management." Accessed September 24, 2017. https://au.axon.com/solutions/law-enforcement/at-the-station#evidence-management.

Axon. 2017b. "In the Field: Video Devices." Accessed September 24, 2017. https://au.axon.com/solutions/law-enforcement/in-the-field#video-devices.

Axon. Undated. Taser 2017 "Law Enforcement Technology Report." Accessed September 24, 2017. www.documentcloud.org/documents/3679537-Taser-2017-Law-Enforcement-Technology-Report.html.

Barot, Trushar. 2017. "The Future of News is Humans Talking to Machines." NiemanLab. September 18. Accessed September 20, 2017. www.niemanlab.org/2017/09/the-future-of-news-is-humans-talking-to-machines/.

Bollyut, Jess. 2017. "How Old Is Siri, and How Did She End Up on Your iPhone?" *Gear & Style CheatSheet*. January 5. Accessed September 20, 2017. www.cheatsheet.com/gear-style/how-old-is-siri.html/?a=viewall.

Borchardt, Alexandra. 2018. "Making Journalism Great Again." Project Syndicate. January 9. Accessed January 13, 2018. www.project-syndicate.org/commentary/fake-news-challenges-journalism-industry-by-alexandra-borchardt-2018-01/english.

Cellan-Jones, Rory. 2014. "Stephen Hawking Warns Artificial Intelligence Could End Mankind." BBC Technology. December 12. Accessed October 2, 2017. www.bbc.com/news/technology-30290540.

Charara, Sophie. 2018. "Smart Home Sales Explored: Just How Many Devices Have Been Sold?." *The Ambient*. March 19. Accessed March 21, 2018. www.the-ambient.com/features/smart-home-device-sales-estimates-442.

Clifford, Catherine. 2017. "Facebook CEO Mark Zuckerberg: Elon Musk's Doomsday AI Predictions are 'Pretty Irresponsible'." CNBC Make It. July 17. Accessed October 2, 2017. www.cnbc.com/2017/07/24/mark-zuckerberg-elon-musks-doomsday-ai-predictions-are-irresponsible.html.

Conger, Kate. 2018. "Google Is Helping The Pentagon Build AI For Drones." *Gizmodo*. March 7. Accessed March 9, 2018. www.gizmodo.com.au/2018/03/google-is-helping-the-pentagon-build-ai-for-drones/.

David, Javier E. 2017. "Elon Musk Issues a Stark Warning about AI, Calls it a Bigger Threat than North Korea." CNBC Tech. August 11. Accessed August 12, 2017. www.cnbc.com/2017/08/11/elon-musk-issues-a-stark-warning-about-a-i-calls-it-a-bigger-threat-than-north-korea.html.

Dow Jones. 2016. "Thomson Reuters Will Lay Off about 2,000 in 'Transformation' of Business." *Twin Cities Pioneer Press*. November 1. Accessed November 29, 2016. www.twincities.com/2016/11/01/thomson-reuters-will-lay-off-about-2000-in-transformation-of-business/.

Dowd, Maureen. 2017. "Elon Musk's Billion-Dollar Crusade to Stop the AI Apocalypse." *Vanity Fair*. March 26. Accessed October 2, 2017. www.vanityfair.com/news/2017/03/elon-musk-billion-dollar-crusade-to-stop-ai-space-x.

Dunn, Taylor. 2017. "Microsoft CEO Satya Nadella Discusses the Jobs of the Future." ABC News. September 29. Accessed September 29, 2017. http://

abcnews.go.com/Business/microsoft-ceo-satya-nadella-discusses-jobs-future/story?
id=50189787.

Elliott, Larry. 2017. "Millions of UK Workers at Risk of Being Replaced by Robots, Study
Says." *The Guardian*. March 24. Accessed March 24, 2017. www.theguardian.com/
technology/2017/mar/24/millions-uk-workers-risk-replaced-robots-study-warns.

Famubode, Victor. 2016. "The Political Economy of Artificial Intelligence." *Business Day*.
December 23. Accessed September 25, 2017. www.businessdayonline.com/political-
economy-artificial-intelligence/.

Gantz, John F., Gerry Murray, David Schubmehl Schubmehl, Dan Vesset and Mary
Wardley. 2017. "A Trillion-Dollar Boost: The Economic Impact of AI on Customer
Relationship Management." SalesForce, International Data Corporation. Accessed
September 25, 2017. www.salesforce.com/content/dam/web/en_us/www/docu
ments/white-papers/the-economic-impact-of-ai.pdf.

Garson, Barbara. 1989. *The Electronic Sweatshop: How Computers are Transforming the Office of
the Future*. New York: Penguin.

Gillin, Paul. 2016. "Bad News on the Doorstep." *Newspaper Death Watch*. November 3.
Accessed November 29, 2016. http://newspaperdeathwatch.com/bad-news-on-the-
doorstep/.

Grant, Stan. 2017. "Which Jobs Will Survive the Artificial Intelligence Revolution?" *The
Link*. April 28. Accessed October 2, 2017. www.abc.net.au/news/programs/the-link/
2017-04-28/which-jobs-will-survive-the-artificial/8481906.

Hern, Alex, and Sam Thielman. 2016. "Amazon Refuses to Let Police access US Murder
Suspect's Echo Recordings." *The Guardian*. December 28. Accessed March 20, 2018.
www.theguardian.com/technology/2016/dec/28/amazon-refuses-to-let-police-
access-suspects-echo-recordings.

Hirst, Martin. 2011. *News 2.0: Can Journalism Survive the Internet?* Crows Nest, NSW: Allen
and Unwin.

Hirst, Martin, and John Harrison. 2007. *Communication and New Media: From Broadcast to
Narrowcast*. Melbourne: Oxford University Press.

Joh, Elizabeth. 2017. "Free Police Body Cameras Come with a Price." *Slate*. April 5.
Accessed September 24, 2017. www.slate.com/blogs/future_tense/2017/04/05/taser_
international_now_axon_offers_police_free_body_cameras.html.

Kofman, Ava. 2017. "Taser Wants to Build an Army of Smartphone Informants." *The
Intercept*. September 22. Accessed September 23, 2017. https://theintercept.com/2017/
09/21/taser-wants-to-build-an-army-of-smartphone-informants/.

Kofman, Ava. 2018. "Amazon Partnership with British Police Alarms Privacy Advocates."
The Intercept. March 9. Accessed March 20, 2018. https://theintercept.com/2018/03/
09/amazon-echo-alexa-uk-police/.

Kolbjornsrud, Vegard, Richard Amico, and Robert J. Thomas. 2016. "How Artificial
Intelligence Will Redefine Management." *Harvard Business Review*. November 2.
Accessed September 25, 2017. https://hbr.org/2016/11/how-artificial-intelligence-
will-redefine-management.

Kotecki, James. 2016. "Automated Content Won't Take Your Job. It Will Make Your Job
Better." Automated Insights Blog. July 27. Accessed October 14, 2017. https://
automatedinsights.com/blog/automated-content-wont-take-job.

Lomas, Natasha. 2017. "Thinking about the Social Cost of Technology." TechCrunch.
October 1. Accessed October 1, 2017. https://techcrunch.com/2017/09/30/think
ing-about-the-social-cost-of-technology/.

Madigan White, Erin. 2015. "Automated Earnings Stories Multiply." Associated Press. January 29. Accessed November 29, 2016. https://blog.ap.org/announcements/auto mated-earnings-stories-multiply.

Marconi, Francesco. 2017. "Report: How Artificial Intelligence Will Impact Journalism." *AP Insights*. April 5. Accessed September 20, 2017. https://insights.ap.org/industry-trends/report-how-artificial-intelligence-will-impact-journalism.

Marconi, Franceso, and Kourosh Houshmand. 2018. "The Role of Journalists in an Era of Algorithms: A Guide to Preparing the Newsroom for Humans and Machines." Associated Press. February. Accessed March 1, 2018. www.amic.media/media/media files/file_352_1493.pdf.

Marconi, Francesco, Alex Siegman and Machine Journalist. 2017. "The Future of Augmented Journalism: A Guide for Newsrooms in the Age of Smart Machines." Associated Press. Accessed September 20, 2017. https://insights.ap.org/uploads/images/the-future-of-augmented-journalism_ap-report.pdf.

Marx, Karl. 1976 [1867]. *Capital*. Translated by Ben Fowkes. London: Penguin.

Mosco, Vincent. 2005. *The Digital Sublime: Myth, Power and Cyberspace*. Cambridge, MA: MIT Press.

Newman, Nic. 2018. "Journalism, Media, and Technology Trends and Predictions 2018." Reuters Institute for the Study of Journalism, Oxford: University of Oxford. Accessed January 13, 2018. https://reutersinstitute.politics.ox.ac.uk/our-research/journalism-media-and-technology-trends-and-predictions-2018.

Nusca, Andrew. 2011. "How Voice Recognition Will Change the World." ZDNet. November 4. Accessed September 20, 2017. www.zdnet.com/article/how-voice-recognition-will-change-the-world/.

O'Halloran, Derek. 2015. "5 Ways Tech Shifts are Impacting Humanity." World Economic Forum. September 15. Accessed April 27, 2017. www.weforum.org/agenda/2015/09/5-ways-tech-shifts-are-impacting-humanity/?utm_content=bufferfc7f d&utm_medium=social&utm_source=facebook.com&utm_campaign=buffer.

Rectenwald, Michael. 2013. "The Singularity and Soicialism." *Insurgent Notes*. October 5. Accessed September 25, 2017. http://insurgentnotes.com/2013/10/the-singularity-and-socialism/.

Richards, Danielle. 2017. "The Benefits of Artificial Intelligence on Workplace Productivity." Mavenlink Blog. January 30. Accessed September 25, 2017. http://blog.mavenlink.com/the-benefits-of-artificial-intelligence-on-workplace-productivity.

Schaefer, Mark. 2016. "Four Strategies to Survive Automated Writing and Content Bots." *BusinessGrow*. July 4. Accessed October 14, 2017. www.businessesgrow.com/2016/07/04/automated-writing/.

Schmidt, Eric. 2017. "Keynote Address at the Center for a New American Security Artificial Intelligence and Global Security Summit." Center for a New American Security. November 13. Accessed March 20, 2018. www.cnas.org/publications/tran script/eric-schmidt-keynote-address-at-the-center-for-a-new-american-security-artifi cial-intelligence-and-global-security-summit.

Simpson, Campbell. 2017. "Google Home Launches in Australia." *Gizmodo*. July 18. Accessed September 19, 2017. www.gizmodo.com.au/2017/07/google-home-launches-in-australia/.

Smith, Aaron, and Jaana Anderson. 2014. "AI, Robotics and the Future of Jobs." Pew Research Center. August 6. Accessed September 25, 2017. www.pewinternet.org/2014/08/06/future-of-jobs/.

Steinhoff, James. 2014. "Transhumanism and Marxism: Philosophical Connections." *Journal of Evolution and Technology* 24(2). Accessed September 25, 2017. http://jetpress.org/v24/steinhoff.htm.

Tarnoff, Ben. 2017. "Tech's Push to Teach Coding isn't about Kids' Success—it's about Cutting Wages." *The Guardian.* September 22. Accessed September 25, 2017. https://amp.theguardian.com/technology/2017/sep/21/coding-education-teaching-silicon-valley-wages.

Terranova, Tiziana. 2000. "Free Labor: Producing Culture for the Digital Economy." *Social Text* 18(2). Accessed March 20, 2018. web.mit.edu/schock/www/docs/18.2terranova.pdf.

UNICRI. 2017. "UNICRI Centre for Artificial Intelligence and Robotics." September 25. Accessed September 28, 2017. www.unicri.it/in_focus/on/UNICRI_Centre_Artificial_Robotics.

Vander Ark, Tom. 2016. "Smart Machines Will Eat Jobs (Except Where Smart People Create Them)." *Getting Smart.* November 1. Accessed October 2, 2017. www.gettingsmart.com/2016/11/smart-machines-will-eat-jobs/.

Webb, Amy. 2017. "AI Is Journalism's Next Big Threat (or Opportunity)." *NiemanReports.* April 24. Accessed September 20, 2017. http://niemanreports.org/articles/ai-is-journalisms-next-big-threat-or-opportunity/.

Whitby, Blay. 1996. *Reflections on Artificial Intelligence: The Legal, Moral and Ethical Dimensions.* Exeter: Intellect Books.

Whitby, Blay. 2003. *Artificial Intelligence: A Beginner's Guide.* Oxford: One World Books.

EPILOGUE

Droning on about Drones

Are Drones about to Take Off?

Drones are seemingly everywhere today, but also nowhere. They are not commonly seen, but the work they do—in aerial photography, in particular—is often seen. The lack of visibility and transparency around their development raises important questions about the ethics of their use. For journalism in particular, the issue of privacy and the invasion of privacy from camera-equipped drones cannot be ignored. Drones have become an "idealized" symbol of progress that brings together a range of discrete technologies into one powerful machine. But not all drones are built with "good intent" and we cannot ignore the dialectics they embody: "Today drones largely only kill people or spy on them" (Rothstein 2015: 144); who knows what they might do in the future.

There are several types of drones, some of them come with a deadly reputation. For about 10 years, the US military has been using the MQ1 Predator drone—or if you prefer "unmanned aerial vehicle" or UAV—in its program of targeted assassination of what it calls "high value" targets in Afghanistan, Iraq and Syria (Scahill 2015). This lethal drone is just over eight meters in length and has a wingspan of nearly 15 meters; it can be loaded with smart weapons such as laser-guided bombs or Hellfire missiles for use against fortified buildings and armored vehicles (Army Recognition 2011). At the other end of the drone scale—in terms of both size and destructive firepower—is the small harmless model you can pick up from a hobby shop for about US$200. At that price you will most likely get only a few minutes of flight time from the on-board battery, and a very low-power camera that will only record short clips at low resolution. Somewhere in the middle of that range you will find the types of drones that are set to become increasingly important tools in the hands of journalists.

The drone is an object of technology that is still shrouded in the digital sublime. According to drone researcher Adam Rothstein (2015: xiv), "the drone exists ... but it also doesn't exist, because it's shrouded in fantasy." The drone is also a good exemplar of society's fixation with technological determinism: "The drone, separated from and connected to the truth, has become a composite caricature of technology" (ibid.: xv). Without the military's investment—particularly the US military—there would not be a drone system today with the sophistication of quad-rotor flight. The drone is also a composite of many technologies going back to the car and the airplane, but also embracing many recent digital advances, such as GPS positioning, digital imaging, gaming controllers, and the use of AI to stabilize its flight and guide its trajectory.

Drones in Journalism

Why are journalists interested in UAV technology? The answer is pretty straightforward; in a media age where images and video are taking on increasing importance in news coverage, a drone can access camera angles and cover terrain that might otherwise impose limits on what a photojournalist or videographer can record. The News Establishment's interest in drones began in earnest in 2013 when the first class graduated from a University of Missouri Journalism School drone journalism program (French 2013). The US Federal Aviation Authority had sought to block the use, and even the teaching, of drone technologies at journalism schools before then. The FAA has now eased up its restrictions on journalistic drone use, but the practice is still heavily regulated by authorities worldwide (Stroh 2016). UAVs are now recognized as an essential part of the hardware deployed by any serious newsroom and reporters are being trained to fly them safely. However, the use of UAVs in news gathering still presents a number of legal and ethical dilemmas, there are also several unresolved issues around newsroom protocols for flying drones (Ntalakas et al. 2017).

The regulation of UAVs is beset with problems globally, which means that any journalist wishing to operate a drone for newsgathering must check with all relevant authorities, from local municipal bodies, right through to state and federal regulators. Drone technology is caught up in what I've previously described as a "techno-legal time-gap"; this is a situation that results from the rapid advance of technologies and the slow pace of legislative and regulatory reform covering the operating environment in which the technology is deployed (Patching and Hirst 2014). In the United States attempts to codify rules under which journalists might use drones have been caught up in the political crossfire of a partisan Congress and hampered by several legal challenges to the definition of a commercial UAV versus a hobby aircraft (French 2017). While this deadlock is being negotiated in Washington, drone operators in the US working in the news industry should at least reference the rules in the "Small Unmanned Aircraft Regulations (Section 107)" administered by the

FAA. Importantly, this rule prohibits anyone from flying a drone who does not have the proper pilot certification or has not undertaken an FAA-approved course in UAV operations (FAA 2016). This is quite a tough restriction on the amateur use of drones for reporting purposes and it means that newsrooms will need to have in-house expertise or use freelance drone pilots as needed on particular stories. It is the sort of techno-legal hold-up that will probably slow down the spread of news-gathering by drone for some time. Drones might also suffer from infection by the digital sublime. As Mathew Waite, a pioneer of drone journalism, lamented: "It'll get boring very, very fast. But I also feel like we have to do that. We have to overuse before we start to understand the technology and just where it belongs" (Etzler 2016). UAV images and video do have their place in journalism today; they have been used successfully in disaster coverage and during protests when getting an overview of crowd-size, for example, can help tell the story.

Using Drones Ethically

Along with the legal concerns about who, where when, when, why and how of drone use in reporting, there are also ethical concerns. Some are what you might call "traditional," others come with drone capability and fit within the ethical version of the techno-legal time gap. There are things that a drone can do for a journalist, but ultimately it is under human control and so ethical questions still matter.

A major concern with drone use in journalism is privacy. If you want to look through a window in a high-rise apartment block should you use a camera-equipped UAV to fly right outside it and peer in? This is not just a question for the paparazzi who engage in "Peeping Tom" journalism. If you are operating the drone from a public space and it is in airspace outside the apartment block, there is a good chance that technically you're not breaking the law by pointing the UAV's camera in through an open window. After all, if the window were at ground level and you could see in from the street through open blinds, then you're not breaking any laws just by looking. But perhaps there is a moral element to privacy as well and a sense of ethics would tell you that peeking through the window, while legal, might be socially unacceptable, distasteful and morally questionable. This is the kind of sensibility that must be brought to the debate about the ethics of drone-assisted reporting. Just because a drone *can*, doesn't mean a reporter *should*. Most journalistic codes of ethics, at least in Western liberal countries, tend to value a notion of privacy that frowns upon, if not outright forbids, intrusion into someone's reasonable expectation that their actions are shielded from public view if they are of a domestic or intimate nature. Journalists are generally expected to respect this expectation of personal privacy, and most do, with some notable and notorious exceptions. Technological enhancements to eavesdropping capabilities should be managed using similar ethical protocols.

However, on the other side of the privacy ledger are deliberate attempts to shield from public scrutiny actions that should be reported, exposed and laid before the public. This is an area of legal restriction that journalists have a legitimate right to challenge, or indeed to circumvent in the public interest. A good example is the creation of so-called "gag" laws that operate in some jurisdictions to prevent the disclosure of politically and commercially sensitive information about agricultural, mining and forestry operations that are environmentally sensitive. Under such rules, flying a drone over a mine site, for example, might be deemed illegal, but if the footage and images demonstrate that the operator is breaking environmental conditions of their license, then the public interest test would justify breaking the no-fly rules. Agricultural gag ("ag gag") laws have been used in the US and elsewhere, including Australia, to deny journalists and animal rights activists access to facilities associated with animal care or slaughter. Activists have condemned such laws because they prevent the public exposure of inhumane practices (RSPCA 2014); but they are being extended into other controversial industries. If you are planning a story about an industry that might be covered by some type of gag law, do your homework. Ignorance of the rules is no defense if you get caught. If you are in any doubt about the ethics of drone journalism it is probably worthwhile checking the most up-to-date version of the code devised by the Professional Society of Drone Journalists.

The October 2017 version of the PSDJ code of ethics for the use of drones in newsgathering had the following brief points:

1   **Newsworthiness**. The investigation must be of sufficient journalistic importance to risk using a potentially harmful aerial vehicle. Do not use a drone if the information can be gathered by other, safer means.
2   **Safety**. A drone operator must first be adequately trained in the operation of his or her equipment. The equipment itself must be in a condition suitable for safe and controlled flight. Additionally, the drone must not be flown in weather conditions that exceed the limits of the drone's ability to operate safely, and it must be flown in a manner that ensures the safety of the public.
3   **Sanctity of law and public spaces**. A drone operator must abide by the regulations that apply to the airspace where the drone is operated whenever possible. An exception to this is provided in instances where journalists are unfairly blocked from using drones to provide critical information in accordance with their duties as members of the Fourth Estate. The drone must be operated in a manner which is least disruptive to the general population in a public setting.
4   **Privacy**. The drone must be operated in a fashion that does not needlessly compromise the privacy of non-public figures. If at all possible, record only images of activities in public spaces, and censor or redact images of private individuals in private spaces that occur beyond the scope of the investigation.

5 **Traditional ethics**. As outlined by professional codes of conduct for journalists.

(PSDJ 2017)

In relation to the discussion of "ag gag" laws it is worth noting point three which provides a public interest exception to respecting regulations covering drone operations where journalists are "unfairly blocked" from "using drones." This is an interesting and unique code in that it is consciously modelled on the famous "hierarchy of needs" proposed by the psychologist-philosopher, Abraham Maslow. When applied in this context, we can set it out in a modified pyramid shape.

A pyramid is only as stable as its base, and it can only be built from the bottom upwards; it is significant that this hierarchy of ethics begins with the cornerstone of "newsworthiness." In other words, if the story does not justify the use of a drone, then the rest of the ethical principles are irrelevant. In my view, this is a good basis for all ethical decision-making, not just for the use of drones. A second good source of guidance on all things drone in journalism is the Drone Journalism Lab at the University of Nebraska–Lincoln. The Drone Lab is directed by UAV pioneer Matthew Waite, and in 2016 Matt and his colleagues released an "Operations Manual" for the use of drones on reporting assignments. The manual is a comprehensive guide that has been released under a digital commons license; which means it can be downloaded, adopted and built upon by news organizations or interested amateurs who want to develop their own working document. This is a very generous move by the authors as it

The ethical use of drones should follow these guidelines.

Based on Professional Society of Drone Journalists code by Matthew Schroyer

ETHICAL PRECEPTS
5. All aspects of relevant Codes of Ethics must be applied to drone use

PRIVACY OF SUBJECTS
4. The right to privacy of subjects must be respected. The exception is where the expectation of privacy is unreasonable.

LEGAL CONSTRAINTS IN PUBLIC SPACE
3. Drone must always be operated within the relevant jurisdictional code governing their use.

SAFE OPERATIONAL PARAMETERS
2. Can a drone be operated safely in the situational context of the news-gathering process?

NEWS VALUES - NEWSWORTHINESS
1. Does the story warrant the use of a drone to gather images or data?

FIGURE E.1 An Innovative Hierarchy of Drone Ethics, Based on Matthew Hoyer's PSDJ Code of Ethics for Drone Operators.

allows for jurisdiction-specific modification to take account of differences in legislative and regulatory frameworks. The Ops Manual begins from one point that should be universal: "The number one goal of any drone journalism operation is safety" (Waite and Kreimer 2016).

Adam Rothstein notes that the news media has a "high appetite" for stories about drones—due to the fascination with which we regard their novelty—and also for information regarding how they might impact on journalism itself. He also warns against the determinist tendency to "simplify" the drone narrative. So far, many of the promised civilian applications for commercial drones have not been realized. The realities of certifying them as airworthy, of training the pilots to safely operate them in crowded airspace and the unreliability of the technology itself—short battery life, difficulty in autonomous flight, a clunky human-drone interface—mean that we are sometime away from seeing drones delivering pizzas or anything much heavier than a book. Having said that, we cannot ignore the fact that drones will only get more powerful and sophisticated as billions of dollars are poured into their development. At some point they will become more deeply embedded in both professional and social journalism practice. Operating them safely and ethically will be a paramount concern, as it is with all the technologies discussed in this book.

References

Army Recognition. 2011. "MQ-1 Predator Unmanned Aerial Vehicle UAV Data Sheet Specifications Information Description UK." April 23. Accessed April 9, 2016. www.armyrecognition.com/us_american_unmanned_aerial_ground_vehicle_uk/mq-1_pre dator_unmanned_aerial_vehicle_uav_data_sheet_specifications_information_descrip tion_uk.html.

Etzler, Allen. 2016. "Dronalism: Exploring the Use of Drones in Journalism." News Media Alliance. September 12. Accessed October 5, 2017. www.newsmediaalliance.org/technology-use-drones-journalism/.

FAA. 2016. "Fact Sheet—Small Unmanned Aircraft Regulations (Part 107)." Federal Aviation Authority. June 21. Accessed October 5, 2017. www.faa.gov/news/fact_sheets/news_story.cfm?newsId=20516.

French, Sally. 2013. "Why a Recent Journalism School Graduate Spent Her Money on a Drone. Investigative Reporters and Editors." September 11. Accessed April 9, 2016. www.ire.org/blog/ire-news/2013/09/11/why-recent-journalism-graduate-spent-her-money-dro/.

French, Sally. 2017. "What the FAA Reauthorization Extension Means for Drones." The Drone Girl. October 3. Accessed October 5, 2017. http://thedronegirl.com/2017/10/03/faa-reauthorization-extension-means-drones/.

Ntalakas, Andreas, Charalampos Dimoulas, George Kalliris and Andreas Veglis. 2017. "Drone Journalism: Generating Immersive Experiences." *Journal of Media Critiques* 3 (11): 187–199. doi:10.17349/jmc117317.

Patching, Roger, and Martin Hirst. 2014. *Journalism Ethics: Arguments and Cases for the Twenty-First Century.* Abingdon: Routledge.

PSDJ. 2017. "A Code of Ethics for Drone Journalists." Professional Society of Drone Journalists. Accessed October 5, 2017. www.dronejournalism.org/code-of-ethics.

Rothstein, Adam. 2015. *Drone*. New York: Bloomsbury Academic.

RSPCA. 2014. "What are Ag-gag Laws and How Would They Affect Transparency and Trust in Animal Production?" Royal Society for the Protection of Animals–Australia. Accessed October 5, 2017. http://kb.rspca.org.au/What-are-Ag-gag-laws-and-how-would-they-affect-transparency-and-trust-in-animal-production_558.html.

Scahill, Jeremy. 2015. "The Assassination Complex." *The Intercept*. October 10. Accessed April 11, 2016. https://theintercept.com/drone-papers/the-assassination-complex/.

Stroh, Sean. 2016. "The Drone Journalism Lab Releases Operations Manual for Free." December 9. Accessed October 5, 2017. www.editorandpublisher.com/a-section/the-drone-journalism-lab-releases-operations-manual-for-free.

Waite, Matthew, and Ben Kreimer. 2016. *Drone Journalism Lab Operations Manual*. Lincoln, NE: College of Journalism and Mass Communications, University of Nebraska-Lincoln.

INDEX

Entries in *italics* refer to figures.

For Product Safety Concerns and Information please contact our EU
representative GPSR@taylorandfrancis.com
Taylor & Francis Verlag GmbH, Kaufingerstraße 24, 80331 München, Germany